A NORMAL TOTALITARIAN SOCIETY

Non indignari, non admirari, sed intelligeri
— Benedict Spinosa

A NORMAL TOTALITARIAN SOCIETY

How the Soviet Union Functioned
and How It Collapsed

VLADIMIR SHLAPENTOKH

M.E.Sharpe
Armonk, New York
London, England

Library of Congress Cataloging-in-Publication Data

Shlapentokh, Vladimir.
    A normal totalitarian society : how the Soviet Union functioned and how it collapsed /
by Vladimir Shlapentokh.
        p. cm.
ISBN 1-56324-471-3 (cloth : alk. paper) ISBN 1-56324-472-1 (pbk. : alk paper)
Includes bibliographical references and index.
    1. Communism—Soviet Union. 2. Soviet Union—Politics and government.
    3. Totalitarianism. I. Title.

HX311.5 .S53 2001   2001032247
947.084—dc21   CIP

Printed in the United States of America

The paper used in this publication meets the minimum requirements of
American National Standard for Information Sciences
Permanence of Paper for Printed Library Materials,
ANSI Z 39.48-1984.

∞

BM (c)   10   9   8   7   6   5   4   3   2   1
BM (c)   10   9   8   7   6   5   4   3   2   1

To my father, Khaim (Emmanuil) Samoilovich Shlapentokh.
As the son of bourgeois parents,
he suffered greatly under the Soviet regime.
To his dying day, he never regarded the society as normal.

Contents

Acknowledgments

I would like to extend a special thanks to Joshua Woods for his high intellectual contribution to this book. As my editor, he not only improved my English immensely, but offered numerous critical comments and suggestions that significantly enhanced the quality of the manuscript. Answering Joshua's perspicacious and often merciless questions, I was forced to rethink the logic of the narration, look for new arguments, and find more data to meet his concerns as my first and most demanding reader.

Thanks also to Emil Golin, Aron Katsenelinboigen, Vladimir Kontorovich, Mikhail Loiberg, and Dmitry Shlapentokh, who shared their deep knowledge of Soviet society and gave me excellent advice. Of course, none of them shared *all* of my views on the Soviet past. I would like to thank Jeffrey Brooks for reading and commenting on this manuscript prior to publication. I deeply appreciated Patricia Kolb's intellectual support of the project. My special gratitude goes to Rebecca Ritke for her exceptional and useful work as a copyeditor. I would also like to thank Vera Bondartsova for her help in preparing the manuscript.

Introduction

When Harry Greene's book *Snakes: The Evolution of Mystery in Nature* hit the stands in 1997, nobody suspected him of emotional bias in his study of the history of snakes. As a herpetologist, Greene predictably discussed snake evolution, locomotion, adaptation, nomenclature, mimicry and habits. Circumventing emotional sympathies, he delved into the anatomy and physiology of his subject with scientific rigor. I hope my efforts in this text will be accepted as those of the herpetologist who views his subject without preconceived sympathies.

I admit that my attitude toward the Soviet state, in which I lived for roughly fifty years, was anything but affectionate. I spent much of my adult life loathing the Soviet system. In the late 1940s, I and my late friend and confidant Isaak Kantorovich realized that the totalitarian essence of Soviet society was no different from that of Hitler's regime. The deep anti-Semitism of the Soviet political elite deepened our hatred of the system. As students at Kiev University, however, we kept our conclusions about the system strictly to ourselves. In these years, we dreamed of leaving the Soviet Union, a fantasy that seemed as feasible as a voyage to Mars. We even invented a code name for this enterprise: the Dzungarian Gate (a mountain passage from Soviet Central Asia to China's Xinjiang Province).

I maintained my hatred for the system even after 1953, when mass terror disappeared. I never became a member of the Communist Party. In 1979, I emigrated from the Soviet Union with great joy. With a clear understanding of this emotional past, I have nonetheless attempted to examine Soviet society dispassionately.

Today, the analysis of twentieth-century Russian history is fraught with strong and conflicting opinions. It polarizes all branches of the social sciences, from history and economics to sociology. The concept of consensus is alien to this field; European, American, and even Chinese and Indian history look quite homogeneous in comparison. The lack of consensus can be attributed to the heavy influence of moral assessments in the analysis of Russian society. No other country in the world has been the object of such ideologically and politically opposed passions. The birth, life and death of Soviet society were unprecedented in world history. Those who study this society come from vastly diverse ideologies and positions, leaving even the simplest questions unsettled.

Scholars, historians, economists and sociologists who study Soviet society should take a lesson from the herpetologist and conduct their analysis without placing moral judgments on the subject. As scientists, they should drop the terms "good" and "bad" from their professional lexicon. They should also resist measuring the subject by preestablished criteria (i.e., "true" Marxist socialism, civilized capitalism, or ideal Russian society based on national traditions). Both Soviet and post-Soviet society should be approached as social animals (reptiles, for that matter). Our goal as scientists is to understand the anatomy and physiology of the subject, not to anchor our understanding in the endless circle of moral comparison. We should take this path even if it looks naive to the postmodern relativists, who reject "historical reality" in the same way the admirers of the "class approach" denounced "bourgeois objectivity" as a political sin in Soviet times.[1] A different view on the role of morals in the study of Soviet society has been advanced by patriarchs of Sovietology such as Richard Pipes and Robert Conquest, who think that moral judgments should play an important role (Pipes 1993a, p. 512; Conquest 1994, p. 3).

If our aim is the objective analysis of the Soviet past, we must purge our feelings and delete the concepts of "higher" and "lower." We should abandon the example of various Sovietologists of the past who expressed moral indignation toward Soviet society or who used a "revisionist" blueprint of Soviet society for a moral censure of the West. The time has come to retire the cold war paradigm that tainted the debates on the Soviet Union with pious ideologies of left and right.

In Russia and other former Communist countries, despite the struggle between Communists and their adversaries, we see the trend of a more dispassionate view of the Soviet past than only a few years ago.[2] This more detached approach is also becoming quite visible among historians of the British empire. In his book *The rise and fall of the British empire*, Lawrence James wrote: "I have been as careful as possible to sidestep the quagmire of post-imperial guilt, that peculiar angst which has troubled the British and American intelligentsia for the past 30 or so years. . . . Wherever possible, I have avoided battles over the rights and wrongs of empires" (James 1994).

Another British historian, Andrew Porter, who reviewed James's book, contended that the author was less original in his approach than he thought because this approach "is now wide spread in universities where the subject is discussed . . . neither in simplified terms of 'right' or 'wrong' nor according to the partisan post-imperial presumptions" (Porter 1996).

In this book, I focus primarily on the elements that secured the function and reproduction of the Soviet Union as "a normal social system." I also pay special attention to the developments that led to the collapse of the USSR. I hope that my combination of the historical and sociological approaches will give the reader a comprehensive and detached look at Soviet society—how it was born, how it functioned, and how it collapsed. I have also drawn on a number of non-Soviet examples for comparison, finding many commonalities between the Soviet Union and other nondemocratic societies in history.[3]

The book comprises four parts. The first develops the main theoretical premises; the second examines Soviet ideology as well as the political and economic systems; the third analyzes the chronic "diseases" of the USSR; and the fourth looks at the reforms that brought the society to its knees in 1991.

Throughout this book, I explore the character of the Soviet system as would a coroner. I scrutinize the cadaver so as to better understand the life and death of the fallen state. In his book *Les Tibaults*, Roger Martin Du Gard wrote that one can only fully understand a person after his death. When finally the human being is "isolated, only then is it possible to look at him from all sides, see his insides and make a general judgment" (Martin Du Gard 1993, p. 153). The same is true of societies.

List of Abbreviations

ANT	Aircraft Scientific Technological Association
Cheka	Emergency Committee
GPU	The Main Political Directorate
GRU	The Main Directorate of Intelligence
KGB	The Committee of State Security
Komsomol	The Union of Communist Youth
MOPR	The International Organization for the Aid of Revolutionary Fighters
MVD	Ministry of Internal Affairs
NEP	New Economic Policy
NKVD	The People's Commissariat of Internal Affairs
Osoaviakhim	The Society for Aiding Defense, and the Aircraft and Chemical Industries
SALT	Strategic Arms Limitation Talks
SRs	Socialist Revolutionaries
VTsIOM	The Russian Center for Public Opinion Research

A NORMAL
TOTALITARIAN
SOCIETY

1

Theoretical Concepts

As the relatively brief existence of the Soviet Union fades into the annals of history, Soviet society continues to be a subject of rich debate. The prodigious interest in the USSR stems not only from its key role in world politics throughout much of the twentieth century but also from the understanding that its rise and fall were deeply intertwined with crucial issues such as social equality, the role of the state, the maintenance of order, militarization, and the coexistence of different ethnic groups.

Seven Premises

This book approaches the postmortem analysis of Soviet society from seven central premises. The first is that Soviet society was *totalitarian*, as it has been described by various authors in the United States and abroad (see Arendt 1951; Friedrich and Brzezinski 1956; Fainsod 1963, p. 87; Tucker 1963, 1987, 1990; Daniels 1987a, 1987b; Inkeles and Bauer 1968; Pipes 1992a, 1992b, pp. 3–4, 1993, pp. 497, 500; Malia 1994). Second, the USSR, despite the horrors of its past, was a "normal" society in that it functioned and reproduced itself over many years. Third, the society had a consistent structure, and its main institutions remained largely intact after its emergence in 1918–1920. This premise acknowledges significant differences among the various periods in Soviet history but assumes that the system as a whole functioned as a classic totalitarian state from beginning to end. My fourth premise is that it is necessary to distinguish between the Soviet regime and the empire. Though these two entities certainly interacted, the function of each was quite distinct. Whereas the regime dealt with the Russians and represented the metropolis, the empire controlled non-Russians, in particular non-Slavs. The fifth premise supposes that the USSR's policies and socialist ideology were dictated by the desire to catch up with and surpass the West. This overwhelming yearning dates back to Russia's emergence as a nation-state in the fifteenth century. The sixth premise suggests that the official ideology and the declarations of Soviet politicians should never be taken at face value. The views of Soviet officials apropos of the official ideology were complex constructions adapted to the regime and empire. Seventh, I assume that a comparison between the Soviet and post-Soviet periods helps us understand the nature of the USSR as a "normal totalitarian society."

Historical science rarely changes its vision of past epochs because historians unearth new facts (or artifacts) about the past.[1] In most cases, historical science revises its global ideas about past civilizations and key events because new human experiences push us to see the past from new perspectives and to reinterpret familiar facts. Thus far, the post-Soviet experience has been rich with unexpected developments. Scholars who lived in Soviet society or studied it from outside can now look back from a completely new perspective and see more clearly how well this repressive society worked. All the major aspects of Soviet history (the efficiency of the economy and bureaucracy, the impact of ideology, the people's views, the standard of living, social order, morals, crime, corruption, and national relations) look much different to experts of post-Soviet society.

The Functionalist (or Civilizational) and Hierarchical Approaches

The terms *normal* and *abnormal* when applied in the study of society have two distinct aspects: normative or hierarchical and functionalist.[2] Using the first sense, one might describe societies as "natural," "superior," or "at the apex of progress." The second, functional definition implies nothing more than the ability of a social system to survive and reproduce itself over a significant period of time. The hierarchical approach assumes that societies are good and bad, normal and abnormal. In the contemporary world, the criteria of "normalcy" might include the well-being of the majority, personal freedom, economic efficiency (in liberal ideology), social equality (in socialist ideology), or popular devotion to religion (in various religious ideologies).

Former President Ronald Reagan's famous description of the Soviet Union as an "evil empire" is an example of hierarchical judgment. All the major empires in history (including the empires of Alexander the Great, Genghis Khan, Tamerlane, and Napoleon) have been judged in a similar fashion. Many who subscribe to the hierarchical concept of "normalcy" suppose that "abnormal" societies cannot function and are doomed to a quick demise. The hierarchical idea of normalcy is closely related to the concepts of universalism and nationalism in its application to society. Those who define a given society as "normal" might apply a universal standard (for instance, considering Communism or liberal capitalism the standard for the entire world) or a culture-specific standard (for instance, considering liberal capitalism an appropriate standard only for the West). The concept of "normalcy" is often used to justify assessments of the "superiority" or "inferiority" of one society with respect to another.

The hierarchical mind-set of societies and civilizations dates back to ancient times, when Greek and Roman historians defined the inhabitants of the world outside their respective empires as barbarians. The ancient Chinese made a similar judgment about outsiders. Between the seventeenth and twentieth centuries, the ethnocentric ideology of European, Atlantic, and American exceptionalism prevailed in Europe and North America. This ideology held that the institutions (political, economic, and cultural) in these lands were superior to those of all other societies. Such a belief was deeply embedded in the mentality of many people. In fact, the idea of the "normalcy," or the "ultimate superiority," of Western society over the rest of the world was a dominant fixture in all Western countries during this time period and continues to prevail.[3] This idea reached its peak in Francis Fukuyama's theory of the absolute victory of the Western model (Fukuyama 1992). The admirers of liberal capitalism accepted "the end of history" as the unavoidable future of mankind.

At the same time, intellectuals have also tended to express dissatisfaction with their own societies. They promoted other societies, present and past, or invented the image of an ideal society. In France, for instance, François Rabelais in the sixteenth century, and Charles-Louis Montesquieu in the eighteenth century, analyzed their contemporary society by comparing it either with societies that existed only in their imaginations or with oriental societies (such as Turkey and Persia). European romanticism (a powerful movement in literature and social science) described contemporary society as "abnormal," depraved and corrupt. It praised the society of the "noble savage" as well as life in the Middle Ages, or Antiquity. At the same time, utopianism, another intellectual trend in the West, beginning with Plato's *Republic* in the fourth century B.C., advancing with Thomas More's *Utopia* in the sixteenth century, and continuing in the twentieth century with Burrhus Skinner's *Walden Two*, used various ideal models of society as the bases for critiquing contemporary society. Developing these utopian ideas further, Marxists in the second half of the nineteenth century and the beginning of the twentieth century offered their vision of an ideal society. Marxism was a critique of contemporary capitalist society, which, since the publication of the *Communist Manifesto*, had been depicted as abnormal and depraved and ripe for replacement by a new, classless Communist society. In the second half of the twentieth century, the two prevailing, hierarchical ideologies (socialist and liberal capitalist) clashed with respect to the true definition of normalcy. Proponents of each ideology accused the opposite society of being "abnormal" and predicted either radical changes or collapse.

The arguments offered in this text, in contrast, gravitate toward the functionalist (or "civilizational") approach, which suggests that a system should be evaluated by its ability to function and reproduce itself. In other words, the civilizational approach focuses on the ability of a system to satisfy the major requirements for its survival. Like a biological system, a "normal" social system is able to reproduce and sustain itself through a number of reproductive cycles (see Smelser 1988, p. 109; Alexander 1985; Elster 1979).[4] Rapid and drastic reforms are dangerous for a system because they may introduce incompatible elements that cause the system to self-destruct. The collapse of the Soviet Union was a direct result of Gorbachev's reforms, which turned a "normal" Soviet system into an abnormal "hybrid" that could not withstand even the slightest test. Essentially, the civilizational approach underlies the mode of thinking typical of many who have studied civilizations in past decades, including Oswald Spengler (1962), Arnold Toynbee, Fernand Braudel and Samuel Huntington. These and other scholars reject the hierarchical approach, though it remains widely accepted among Sovietologists.

The civilizational approach does not claim that all social systems are the same from the humanistic point of view. Looking at the Soviet society from this perspective would lead one quickly to the monstrosities of its past. Indeed, the Soviet system was one of the cruelest regimes in history. From the humanistic position, I consider the liberal capitalist society the superior system. As a matter of fact, I personally prefer living in Western civilization. But it is not my goal in this book to provide yet another normative critique of Soviet society. At the same time, I have not forsworn humanistic criteria, which are in fact invaluable to the study of any society insofar as that society's humanistic dimensions influence its ability to function and reproduce itself.

Cyclical Trends in Soviet Society

Normative critics of the Soviet regime argue that the society was doomed from the start and that its imminent decline began shortly after its birth and invariably persisted throughout its life span.[5] In this way, they might equate the abnormality of the society to the abnormal life of a baby with a terminal, degenerative disease. The advocates of "Soviet abnormality" refer to the decline of Marxist ideology, its ever-lessening impact on the people, the people's dwindling support for the regime, and the decline of the economy. If all of the society's major trends were indeed negative, it would certainly be feasible to call it abnormal. However, these and similar arguments remain highly controversial. One may rightly claim that the convictions of the people with respect to the Communist future and the precepts of the official ideology (social equality and the dominance of the working class) weakened during the 1970s. However, in general, the evolution (or devolution) of the ideology, like that of many other important factors in Soviet society, was in no way uniform. After its erosion during the New Economic Policy (NEP), Communist ideology in the 1930s gained new momentum. The introduction of nationalist elements underwrote the ideology's vitality until 1987, when it was exposed to the ideological attack inspired by Mikhail Gorbachev through the official media. In the first half of the 1980s, most Russians believed—as demanded by propaganda—in the superiority of Russian culture, the preeminence of the planning system and the virtue of public property.

The people's attitudes toward the regime fluctuated. The number who supported the regime evidently increased between the late 1920s and the late 1930s. High levels of emigration (mostly of those who were deeply hostile toward the Soviet system), the numberless deaths during the mass terror, and the success of propaganda increased the proportion of those devoted to the system. Support for the system clearly increased again during the war with Germany, then slowly declined in the next decades.

The quality of cadres also was not in constant decline. On one hand, the nomenklatura's devotion to the system declined almost uniformly after the civil war. But on the other hand, the level of their education and managerial skills rose consistently until the termination of the system.

The decline of the Soviet economy is a complicated issue. Taking into account only the rate of growth, the decline was seemingly evident. However, this limited assessment provides an inadequate explanation, since few countries after World War II sustained a high rate of growth. Comparing the Soviet economic situation in the 1950s–1970s to that in the 1930s–1940s shows dramatic economic progress and a much stronger and more efficient economy in the latter decades. The Soviet economy competed with Western economies in arms production. Excluding the United States, the country had no rivals in the production of many military products.

Like those in any Western economy, trends in the Soviet economy were cyclical rather than uniformly in decline. The standard of living endured peaks and valleys, which are typical for any regime, regardless of its political foundation. There was growth during the NEP and decline in the late 1920s and the first half of the 1930s, followed by a rise in the late 1930s, a wartime decline, and a recovery subsequent to the war, particularly evident in the late 1950s. This up-and-down pattern continued, with a decline in the early 1960s, significant growth in the late 1960s and early 1970s, and then a new decline in the second half of the 1970s.

Normalcy and Time

One may assume that a normal system functions with a relatively long life expectancy, while an abnormal system does not function properly and has a short life expectancy. By itself, however, the age of a system is not a proper indicator of a system's normality or abnormality. Turning to history, social systems derived from conquests or rebellions were often unable to reproduce themselves with new generations. The empires of Alexander the Great, Charlemagne and Napoleon were unable to reproduce and thus might also be considered "temporary," abnormal formations. In contrast, the command of the Soviet system was transferred, devoid of turmoil, from one leader to the next (though not without some tensions, particularly in 1953 after Stalin's death, and in 1964 after Khrushchev's dismissal). Before the empire met its end, power changed hands from Lenin to Stalin, Stalin to Khrushchev, Khrushchev to Brezhnev, Brezhnev to Andropov, Andropov to Chernenko, and Chernenko to Gorbachev.

The death of Soviet society as an argument for its abnormality emerged only after 1991. Scholars who employed this argument had failed to predict the collapse of the Soviet Union. The regime fell so unexpectedly that the leading Sovietologists on both sides of the Atlantic were astonished. However, after the downfall, many began to assert that the collapse had been unavoidable; they reasoned that no "normal society" could founder so quickly, and thus, that the short life span of Soviet society proved its abnormal character. The Soviet Union was doomed from the start. This view—now shared by various politicians—should be rejected. As will be carefully elaborated in the chapters to come, the Soviet Union, secure behind its "nuclear shield," and absent any serious internal opposition, could have propelled itself several years into the future. The sudden death of the empire cannot be used as a final argument for the abnormality of the system; ultimately, all regimes come to an end. The ease with which the USSR collapsed also is not unique in history. The abrupt fall of the Russian empire in February 1917, after 300 years of existence, was no less surprising for contemporaries than the fall of the Soviet empire in August 1991.[6] The demise of the Austro-Hungarian Empire, after nearly 1,000 years of history, also occurred quite swiftly.

All social organisms (civilizations, societies, regimes, empires and classes) have limited life spans and inevitably decay under the pressure of various "objective" trends. However, the time and character of a social organism's demise is dependent not only on long-term material factors but also on the conduct of individual actors and the occurrence of individual events, which cannot, in most cases, be fully explained by "objective" processes. As is true of all social organisms, the Soviet regime could not live forever; but its collapse in 1991 was in no way preordained. In fact, there were several vulnerable periods in which the collapse may have occurred prior to 1991: in 1933, amidst mass starvation; in 1941–1942, during the war against Germany, when the Red Army suffered one defeat after another; in the aftermath of Stalin's death in 1953; or in October 1964, when Khrushchev was demoted. However, the regime did, in fact, survive these trying times, and thus demonstrated its ability to protect itself. We cannot exclude the possibility that the Soviet Union could have endured the crisis of 1990–1991. World history would have changed dramatically, had the Soviet Union collapsed prior to 1991 or persisted until the end of the century.[7]

The Views of Different Actors

The "normal-abnormal" criterion can be successfully applied when designing a typology of politicians' and scholars' views of Soviet society throughout its history. There were four major groups. The first group described the society not only as normal but as superior to all other societies, present and past. The most consistent advocates of this view were official Soviet ideologues, as well as the allies of the Soviet Union among Western left radicals and liberal intellectuals. This view was espoused mostly in the 1920s and 1930s.

The second group depicted the society as normal and similar to Western society. Most representatives of this group were official Soviet ideologues with liberal leanings and Sovietologists with liberal and left orientations in the United States and other West European countries. This view was most prevalent in the 1970s and early 1980s. Later, in post-Communist Russia, a significant number of Russians joined this position. Sergei Kara-Murza, a well-known publicist in post-Soviet Russia, was among the theorists who defended the Soviet society as a good system. He believed that post-Stalin Soviet society was closer to the ideal than any other society in Russian history (Kara-Murza 1994a; 1996a; 1996b; 1997a; 1997b).

Third, there were scholars and politicians who appraised the society negatively, as "abnormal." They treated the Soviet regime as a temporary evil, as a "perverse" and "deviant modernity," or as a "gross aberration." This group predominantly comprised anti-Communists who advocated the totalitarian model; it also included many who believed in the ideal of "true socialism" (i.e., Trotskyists and advocates of "Communism with a human face").

The fourth and smallest group consisted of those who took a negative view of Soviet society but categorized it as "normal." They suggested that Soviet society may have been "bad" or negative by Western standards, but that after the period of Stalin's terror, this despotic, military-oriented society functioned as an effective social organism. The society solved many of its major goals and achieved and maintained a lofty geopolitical position. Most Soviets were well-adjusted to their system and supported it.[8] I am a member of this group of scholars.

The Two Approaches in Sovietology: Dominance of the Hierarchical Approach

The hierarchical approach and the normal/abnormal criterion were entrenched not only in the bedrock of Soviet studies but in the general perspective of politicians and experts in both the Soviet Union and the United States. Soviet ideology demanded that social scientists submit their analyses to the "class approach," which meant crediting the USSR as the superior system in all respects. In many ways, the Western anti-Communist ideology—in its vulgar versions—was no less absurd. This ideology led to several unfounded models of the Soviet regime. The opposing ideologies were nearly symmetrical with respect to their proponents' lack of objectivity (see Brovkin 1998).

The hierarchical approach was firmly cemented in the two major schools of American Sovietology: the totalitarianists and the revisionists. Neither the former nor the latter referred to Soviet society as a normal totalitarian society. The first school advocated the totalitarian model for describing the Soviet Union, and considered the society deeply abnormal. The revisionists rejected the totalitarian model, and most of them contended that Soviet society was either essentially the same as or better than Western society. The totalitarianists who described the USSR in the 1970s–1980s from outside the Soviet Union (Pipes, Conquest, and Laqueur), as well as the insiders (Andrei Sakharov, Alexander Solzhenitsyn, and other dissidents) who viewed Soviet society as totalitarian, were closer to the real picture than the revisionists.[9]

Revisionists in the 1970s and 1980s conducted some useful studies, focusing on the functioning elements of the society; but they almost completely rejected the concept of "totalitarianism," which made it almost impossible for them to understand the character of the Soviet system (Gleason 1995a, p. 3; Hough 1980, pp. 3–4; Lewin 1988; Bialer 1980, pp. 70–73). Many of them were so sure of the existence of political pluralism and conflicts raging inside Soviet society that even seemingly stark totalitarianists like Zbigniew Brzezinski, at the outset of his career as a Sovietologist, also began searching for these structures.[10] Soviet insiders could only shake their heads when they became casually familiar with these new ideas coming from the other side of the Atlantic.[11]

Meanwhile, the acceptance of the totalitarian model of Soviet society in no way implies that this society was not complex; in fact, it was run by a very sophisticated mechanism of totalitarian control, a mechanism that in some form served as the basis for many institutions in the West, from corporations to the army.[12] Demonstrating the complexity of the Soviet totalitarian machine and each of its elements (political structure, ideology, the empire, and economy) was one of my major objectives in writing this book.

While Soviet society was strongly centralized, it was not necessarily efficient. There were always attempts by low-level officials to ignore the directives from the center, cheat the rulers, and in rare cases sabotage the orders. This was true at all stages of Soviet history, including Stalin's times. The totalitarian model certainly does not suppose that the state was able to control each individual's public and private life. In fact, the degree of the state's control over the individual varied from one period to another: from the harsh control of the nomenklatura's and intelligentsia's private life combined with mild control of the population in Stalin's times, to the significant relaxation of this control after Stalin, to the near indifference toward the people's private life in the 1970s–1980s. Coercion and repression were not the only methods used to secure the people's cooperation in the totalitarian society. Acceptable behavior was generated by the people's belief in the legitimacy of the system and even its superiority over prerevolutionary Russia and the capitalist West.

In fairness to both schools, it should be pointed out that the revisionists were closer to understanding the objective developments in post-Communist Russia than the "totalitarianists." In 1991–1995, scholars of the totalitarianist school believed that the collapse of the Communist Party and of Marxist ideology, coinciding with the restoration of private property, would provoke the almost immediate creation of a capitalist, democratic society in Russia. They abandoned their derisive attitude toward Russia with the coming of the first post-Soviet regime. Revisionists, on the other hand, were evidently irritated by the demise of the system, which they had respected. Contrary to the totalitarianists, they quickly took up a critical stance toward Yeltsin's regime, pointing out many more problems with the new system than the totalitarianists. For instance, articles by Richard Pipes were highly optimistic, even euphoric, compared to the more critical analysis by Stephen Cohen (see Pipes 1992c, 1993b, 1995; and Cohen 1992, 1994, 1996).

Homogeneity of Soviet History: Totalitarianism from Beginning to End

Over the years, scholars have offered evidence for the periodicity of the Soviet past. The various periods identified include: the civil war and War Communism versions of the totalitarian regime headed by Lenin (1917–1920); the softening of this totalitarian regime during the NEP (1921–1926); the reconstruction of the totalitarian regime under Stalin (1927–1929); the harsh totalitarian regime headed by Stalin (1929–1953); the soft regime led by Khrushchev (1954–1964); the hardened totalitarian regime of Brezhnev and his two heirs (1964–1984); and the erosion of the regime under Gorbachev (1985–1991).

Comparisons of the Lenin and Stalin periods as well as of the Stalin and post-Stalin periods are especially important (combined, these periods embrace 80 percent of the Soviet past). There are great variations between the different stages of Soviet history, particularly with respect to the ordinary citizen and the level of repression. But while the differences between the periods are certainly important, they do not undermine the unity of Soviet history. All the major political, social and economic institutions, and most importantly the totalitarian rule of the leader, remained the same during these periods.[13] From the beginning, the totalitarian state and socialist ideas were consistently used for the modernization of the country in order to catch up with the West, maintain the empire and expand Russian influence throughout the world. The major institutions of society also remained essentially the same after their creation by the leadership: the absolute dominance of the supreme leader in the decision-making process; the political monopoly of one party; the political police as the most powerful instrument of the regime; the militarization of society; aggressive imperial policy; the totalitarian ideological indoctrination of the population; the ban on religion; the complete monopoly on media, education, science and culture; the dominance of the central administration over the provinces; the absence of democracy; the official morale based on the class approach; the centralized control of the economy; public property as the means of production; and the rejection of private economic activity.[14]

Core and Periphery

One of the main methodological precepts of this discourse holds that the USSR was a direct continuation of the Russian empire, with a multiethnic formation dominated by a central ethnic group. Two separate entities should be distinguished when describing the Soviet Union: the core of the empire with Russians as the dominant ethnic group, and the provinces with several non-Russian ethnic groups.[15] The non-Russian, Slavic republics (Ukraine and Belorussia) held a sort of intermediate position between the core and the provinces of the empire. The status of Ukrainians and Belorussians was nearly equal to that of Russians with respect to the selection of bureaucrats. However, like the non-Slavic republics, Ukraine and Belorussia were subject to Moscow's absolute intolerance for any moves toward autonomy or separatism.

As in most empires in history, there were many significant differences between the core and the periphery in the Soviet empire. Economic differences were generated by the military industry, the backbone of the Russian economy, which was located almost completely in Slavic republics. At the same time, most of the industrial workers in non-Slavic republics were Slavic (primarily Russian). There were also ideological variations between the core and the periphery. In general, socialist ideals were advanced more in the periphery than in the core, while Russian nationalism was extended more in the core than periphery. The different peoples maintained divergent attitudes about the Soviet system, its ideology and politics. Support for the regime was stronger in the core than in the provinces. During the war, several ethnic groups were less hostile toward the Germans than their Russian counterparts—a circumstance that aroused Stalin's ire. This subject will be discussed in detail in later chapters.

Conclusion

Employing the functionalist approach and treating the USSR as "a normal totalitarian society" allows us to avoid the two extremes of Sovietology and to understand better the nature of the country itself. In the following chapters, the benefits of this approach will become clear in the analysis of the society, its ideology, political order, economy, and national relations. This approach will also prove useful for determining the cause of the Soviet collapse.

2

Two Components of Soviet Ideology
Socialism and Russian Nationalism

The Bolsheviks came to power with Marxist convictions, but soon thereafter they adjusted their beliefs to the new reality. The Bolshevik ideology quickly became a crossbreed of two major trends in twentieth-century Russia: socialism and Russian nationalism. These parallel trends combined in an ideology that dominated society and legitimized the system in the eyes of many Russians from the moment the Bolsheviks took power until the collapse of the Soviet Union. Although these two components closely interacted, they played different roles in the ideology. The socialist and Marxist elements of the ideology prompted the leaders to establish a planned, centralized economy based on state property. In this way, socialism functioned as a major ideological pillar of the totalitarian society. The nationalist components of the ideology were introduced gradually and remained almost invisible to most rank-and-file Bolsheviks in the first years of the new regime. Nevertheless, in the minds of the ruling elite, Russian nationalism began to encroach on the ideology almost immediately after the October Revolution.

By the late 1920s, the ruling elite recognized socialist ideology mostly as an instrument for achieving nationalist goals. During the war with Germany, Stalin clearly claimed the superiority of nationalist values over socialists ones. Despite some fluctuation in the public ideology after Stalin's rule, nationalist values would guide the country toward its central goals—modernization, technological parity with the West, and the protection of the empire, its borders and geopolitical interests—until its collapse in 1991.

Soviet Russia was not the only country to use the ideological blend of socialism and nationalism. Nazi Germany also used it, although the Nazis advanced different perceptions of socialism, being strongly hostile toward Marxism, the class struggle and internationalism. They focused instead on the unity of all Germans, whatever their social status, and sought to diminish inequality through the cooperation of the different classes under the total control of the supreme leader. The marriage of socialism and nationalism, in one or another variant, was also very popular in almost all underdeveloped countries of the twentieth century (China and India among others).[1]

The two components of Soviet ideology were utilized in the public domain in different forms. In general, the Soviet leaders, from Lenin to Gorbachev, almost always advanced the socialist component in the mass ideology over the nationalist one. For this reason, the outside world tended to overestimate the importance of the socialist components and underestimate the nationalist elements of the ideology. The interaction between these two ideological trends represents a remarkable episode in world history. The purpose of this chapter is to deconstruct the Soviet period in order to explain how these two ideological components functioned in society.

The Importance of Socialist Ideas Before and After 1917

Socialist ideas have played a prominent role in world history since the end of the nineteenth century.[2] The Bolsheviks were not members of some secret utopian sect. They were part of a worldwide movement. In the twentieth century, the ideas of socialism, its parties and organizations, influenced the political, social and cultural life of nearly every country in the world.[3] Intellectuals from around the globe perceived socialist society, with its removal of class antagonism, as economically, morally and culturally superior to capitalist society.[4]

In Russia, socialist ideas were not only popular among radical intellectuals but also with the entire intelligentsia. As Nikolai Berdiaev observed, revolution was religion for the thinking class in Russia (1948, 1937). Sergei Frank wrote about "the idol of revolution" as the sign of the times in the beginning of the twentieth century (Berdiaev 1967). Even in the Russian salons of high society, socialist ideas and the prospects of revolution were frequent topics of discourse.[5]

The concept of socialism remained important to intellectuals and politicians in many different countries following WWI, the October Revolution and the emergence of Soviet society. Many intellectuals in France, England, and the United States were influenced by socialist ideas in the 1930s, including the concept of a positive role for the interventionist state in production and distribution.[6] The socialist doctrine survived WWII, the horrors of Stalin's regime, and the Chinese Cultural Revolution. Socialist thinking outlived the demise of the USSR, taking new forms, such as the "third road," "humanistic capitalism," and "humanistic socialism" found in Russia and West European countries (Judt 1998; Giddens 1998).

Was Soviet Society Socialist?

The character of Soviet socialism has been the subject of hot debate inside and outside Russia since the early days of the regime. The participants in this debate can be divided into three groups: those who categorically denied any connection between "true" socialism and Soviet society, those who considered the Soviet brand of socialism "abnormal," and those who deemed it "normal." All of the participants based their verdict on their definition of socialism.

The members of the first group focused on the political dimension and the totalitarian character of the system. They rejected the idea that the USSR was a socialist entity. This group was predominantly made up of Russian and Western social democrats. Many Russian socialists who remained outside Lenin's party (right Mensheviks and socialist revolutionaries) also rejected the socialist nature of the Bolshevik regime. Western social democrats, starting with Karl Kautsky, followed the same line of thinking. This view was shared by major socialist leaders in the West until 1991. In the 1960s, many so-called Old Bolsheviks (those who had joined the Bolshevik party before the revolution or during the civil war, and who were sent to the Gulag by Stalin) also refused to recognize the socialist nature of Soviet society.[7]

Those who characterized Soviet socialism as "abnormal" focused on the socialist character of the economy, which was based on public property, central planning and the absence of a capitalist class. At the same time, they recognized the high level of social differentiation and the lack of democracy. Among the members of this group were left Mensheviks, Trotskyists (both inside and outside Russia), and some Western socialists. Many Soviet intellectuals (the so-called neo-Leninists) belonged to this group during Stalin's time and in the 1960s.[8] From the late 1960s to 1985, the most prominent advocate of socialist abnormality was Andrei Sakharov.[9] This concept was also popular among youth who took Marxist ideals very seriously and could not reconcile them with the Soviet reality.[10] As a rule, those who saw the country as an abnormal socialist society in the 1960s and 1970s were confident that it could be radically improved and turned into "socialism with a human face," with the right reforms.

The members of the third group, which recognized the Soviet brand of socialism as "normal," can be divided into two subgroups. One consisted of official Soviet ideologues and intellectuals, who declared that the society was "truly" socialist, notwithstanding some flaws. The second subgroup comprised mostly conservatives from the West and a few liberal Russian intellectuals (in the 1960s–1980s), who assumed that any society built on socialist ideas would look like the Soviet one. The major advocates of this view were Vasilii Grossman, Alexander Solzhenitsyn and Alexander Zinoviev. I too belong to the second subgroup, because I assume that the Soviet brand of socialism is the only type of socialism that can exist, assuming that state property (as the means of production) and the planning system are, by definition, the generic features of socialist society. The totalitarian political structure of the USSR was an unavoidable derivation of its economic structure. Historical experience corroborates this thesis completely. While societies based on private ownership have existed under different types of political order, it remains impossible to cite a single society throughout world history in which state economic control was not combined with nondemocratic (i.e., totalitarian or authoritarian) political order (Dahl 1972).

The Bolsheviks built a completely new type of society. They implemented several Marxist ideas and based the society on public property and central planning. The Bolsheviks managed to construct a relatively egalitarian society (especially when compared to post-Communist Russia), in which the average citizen maintained negative attitudes toward private property, individualism and religion, while supporting the centralized economy and collectivism. Soviet propaganda also inculcated socialist ideas among non-Russians in the empire and many foreign intellectuals and leftist politicians.

The Goal of Soviet Ideology: To Overcome Russian Backwardness

The ultimate goal of Soviet ideology (as it found its shape in the late 1920s) was not so much to construct a socialist society as to overcome Russian backwardness and "catch up with the West" in order to protect the empire from foreign invasion and to advance its geopolitical interests.[11] The ideological blend of socialism and nationalism served as the means for achieving this goal.

Before the October Revolution, the Bolsheviks, most Western socialists and many Russian socialists disagreed about how to develop society.[12] This disagreement stemmed primarily from their different attitudes toward Russia's role in establishing the future, socialist society. Western socialists as well as some Russian Mensheviks, who criticized Lenin's maximalism, saw the country's low level of productivity and predominantly uneducated population as major obstacles to the implementation of socialism. For the Bolsheviks, however, reversing Russian backwardness was, in fact, the major reason for revolutionary radicalism and "the creative use of Marxism." It justified their rejection of the democratic evolution of Russian society and their praise for violent revolution, terror against their enemies, and the dictatorship of the proletariat. Indeed, "overcoming backwardness" was a determining factor in the policymaking of Soviet leaders throughout the history of the USSR.

The Bolsheviks' dream of catching up with the West had been handed down from their predecessors (namely, the majority of Russian politicians since the seventeenth century). This fixation fueled Peter the Great's interest in the West in the early eighteenth century, Catherine the Great's flirtation with the ideas of the Enlightenment, the liberal reforms of Alexander the First and Alexander the Second, the first Russian Revolution (1905–1907), the second revolution (February 1917), and the socialist project initiated by the October Revolution in 1917. All these developments were inspired by the elite's desire to eliminate the West's superiority over Russia.[13] The same was true for the last two major developments in Russia in the twentieth century: Mikhail Gorbachev's perestroika in 1985–1991, and the anti-Communist revolution in 1991, with the subsequent attempt to build a liberal capitalist society. As the Russian philosopher Valentina Fedotova noted, "Bolshevik leaders were second to none in their emphasis on the necessity for Russia to become part of Europe (Lenin), to catch up to Europe (Trotsky and Stalin), and to catch up and surpass America (Khrushchev)" (Fedotova 2001, p. 8).

Bolshevik writings before 1917 criticized the exploitation of the working class (industrial workers and poor peasants) and social inequality. At the same time, they lamented the gap between Russia and advanced capitalist countries. They spoke vehemently about the economic, political and cultural backwardness of tsarist Russia.[14] They insisted that capitalism, the Russian bourgeoisie, and their political parties (Kadets or Octobrists) were unable to solve the historical task of modernization. The Bolsheviks claimed that a classless socialist society would complete this historical mission and transform the country into a modern society. The leadership envisioned a society that would utilize the energy of the liberated masses to build an effective socialist economy and overcome the many centuries of backwardness.[15] In fact, all factions of the Russian socialist movement (Bolsheviks and Mensheviks; left and right Bolsheviks before and after the revolution; Stalinists and Trotskyists) agreed that rapid modernization was the country's most important goal.

After the revolution, the country's technological and cultural retardation remained an idée fixe in Soviet ideology. Complaints about "the general backwardness of the country" permeated the minutes of the party congresses in the 1920s and 1930s (*Kommunisticheskaia partiia Sovetskogo Soiuza v rezoliutsiiakh I resheniiakh s"ezdov, konferentsii i plenumov TsK*, Vol. 2, 1954, pp. 299, 308, 378, 472, 526, 645). However, the leadership's ideological goals did not include overcoming the country's political backwardness. In the words of Anatolii Vishnevsky, the Bolsheviks' project of "conservative modernization" excluded the creation of truly democratic institutions and focused on the elimination of illiteracy, the creation of a skilled labor force, the eradication of infectious disease, and the construction of modern industry and infrastructure (Vishnevsky 1998, pp. 31–36).[16]

While modernization underpinned the ideology until 1991, the growing importance of the nationalist component changed how the leadership talked about this issue in public. Over time, the advancement of nationalist ideological elements in society made it impossible to acknowledge any form of economic or social retardation in the country. Fueled by nationalist fervor, the leaders even began boasting about the technological and scientific superiority of the USSR over the West. After the war, Stalin abandoned the class approach and launched the anti-cosmopolitan campaign, which proclaimed that not only Soviet science but even pre-revolutionary Russian science was far ahead of the West in all areas.[17] After Stalin's death, his successors downgraded his rhetoric, but they continued to talk about Soviet superiority in some areas, such as the space industry (which was in fact quite strong). The specific information about the country's technological retardation was strictly relegated to secret internal documents and used for the purpose of spying and stealing Western technology. Only during the transition from one leader to the next was the technological inferiority of the USSR revealed to the public.[18]

The Fear of Foreign Aggression

The people's fear of foreign aggression fueled the nationalist component of Soviet ideology. The "foreign factor" in the ideology gave the leaders a strong argument for modernizing the country. "Backwardness" was treated as a direct threat to Russia's sovereignty and geopolitical interests. In his 1931 speech, Stalin argued with those who wanted to slow the rate of industrial growth. He said: "To diminish the rate of growth means to lag behind. But those who lag behind are beaten (by their enemies). . . . The history of old Russia shows that it was incessantly beaten for its backwardness." Stalin went on in his speech to enumerate all the country's enemies, past and present. This kind of public warning was a leading theme in many of Stalin's speeches (Stalin 1952b, p. 361).

The foreign threat benefited both components of the ideology. The socialist elements of the ideology supposed and propagated the idea that capitalist countries were a threat to the people's socialist achievements. From the nationalist perspective, the threat from abroad meant a threat to the mother-land. The people's concern about foreign aggressors legitimized the regime from both the nationalist and the socialist standpoints. For this reason, So-viet leaders maintained the concept of "the besieged fortress," or later, "threats to the socialist world."

The leadership's focus on foreign dangers was a continuation of the policy of the Russian ruling elite, which had propagated this fear since the begin-ning of Russian statehood. However, their propaganda was supported by real historical facts.[19] The invasion of the Mongols in the thirteenth century, the Polish aggression in the early seventeenth century (the Time of Troubles), and Napoleon's invasion in the beginning of the nineteenth century were all central elements in the ideology of the pre-revolutionary monarchy. These events were also deeply rooted in Russian folklore, literature and art. The period following the war with Napoleon in the nineteenth and early twenti-eth centuries, when Russia was aggressively expanding its empire, did not change the dominant view about Russia as a primary target of foreign en-emies. The defeats in the process of expansion (i.e., the Crimean war in 1854–1856, the Russian-Japanese war in 1904–1905, and the war with Ger-many in 1914–1918) only heightened the people's historically embedded fear of foreign aggression.

The Threat of War: Real or Imaginary?

Did Soviet propaganda reflect a real danger of war? Was the prospect of war inflated in order to legitimize and justify the cost of industrialization, mass repression and militarization? Was it reasonable for the leaders (thinking long-term) to assume that a weak Russia would be attacked by its neighbors or by its leading rivals in the West? Was the fear of war generated mostly by the aggressiveness of the Kremlin itself?

In order to answer these questions it is important to examine four periods in Soviet history: the civil war; the period from the end of the civil war until the rise of Nazism in Germany in 1933; from 1933 to the end of WWII in 1945; and from 1945 to the beginning of perestroika in 1985. During the civil war, several foreign countries sided with the enemies of the Bolsheviks. This danger was taken quite seriously by Lenin, who feared intervention by a coalition of fourteen foreign countries. From the end of the civil war until the early 1930s, the danger of war was minimal, though the Kremlin artifi-cially enhanced the threat for domestic purposes. The Kremlin identified France and England as the country's two major enemies. These countries had no clear intention of attacking the USSR in the 1920s or 1930s (Haslam 1983). Overall this was a rather calm period, though there were a few exceptions. The peak of danger in these times came in 1927 when Moscow jeopardized Soviet-British relations with its intervention in British labor conflicts and its meddling in India.[20] Another event that caused substantial fear was the Japanese seizure of Manchuria in 1931, which exacerbated the conflict between Japan and the USSR and led to armed conflicts in the Lake Khanka area in 1938, and in Mongolia, near the Khalkyn river, in 1939.

One of the leadership's "real" (nonpropagandistic) fears, which was deeply embedded in the ideology, was a possible anti-Soviet insurrection inside the country, abetted by foreign intervention. The leaders were very suspicious of Russian emigrants and emigrant organizations in the West. They believed that some of these organizations could foment insurrection in the country and coordinate aid from the Western powers. The political police therefore targeted emigrant leaders and monitored their organizations. In 1923, an emigrant organization murdered Vatzlav Vorovsky, a Soviet diplomat. This and similar events increased Soviet leaders' anxiety about internal rebellion and foreign intervention.

The danger of war was evidently more intense after 1933. As subsequent events would demonstrate, the propaganda during this period hardly exaggerated its claims. After 1933, the threat of Nazi Germany became an objective fact. The propaganda reflected this danger quite realistically, with the exception of the period between August 1939 and June 1941 (during the Soviet-German pact), when the media downplayed the real danger of war.

After 1945, the threat of war subsided, returning to the prewar level. Before the war, when the Soviet Union was the only socialist country in the world, the underpinning fears were generated by the propagandized "capitalist encirclement." After the war and the glorious victory over Germany, the USSR's survival was no longer in question. Several other socialist countries had emerged, and Soviet ideology accordingly adopted new terms for the foreign threat: the "defense of the socialist camp," and the protection of "national interests."

With Moscow's initiation of the cold war, a new situation took shape. A nuclear catastrophe could now be triggered by both superpowers. Anatolii Dobrynin, the Soviet ambassador in Washington during the cold war, wrote: "The possibility of a nuclear war with the United States was considered seriously indeed by Khrushchev, Brezhnev, Andropov, and Konstantin Chernenko. All these leaders and their associates proceeded from the assumption that the United States was a real military threat to the country's security" (Dobrynin 1995, p. 522). Sergei Khrushchev added weight to this thesis, showing on the basis of his observations of his father's everyday activities how seriously the Soviet premier took the possibility of the United States initiating nuclear war (S. Khrushchev 2000, pp. 223–568). Outstanding scholars, such as Andrei Sakharov and Yulii Khariton, also accepted the ideology on this issue and believed that a nuclear catastrophe could in fact occur. They saw the establishment of a Soviet nuclear arsenal as a necessary deterrent against a nuclear war triggered by American generals.[21] Soviet spies in the United States understood their bosses' fear of an attack and sometimes fed them false information about American intentions in order to aggrandize their own importance (see, for instance, Andrew and Mitrokhin 1999). The leadership's fears were amplified in the mass propaganda, keeping the country in permanent military hysteria. The level of fear was highest in the cold war period before 1953, but also during certain episodes after 1953, such as Andropov's war scare in 1983 (V. Shlapentokh 1984b).

During the cold war, the Soviet Union and the United States vied for geopolitical dominance using almost identical strategies: to expand influence whenever possible, oust or murder undesirable leaders, invade foreign countries, recruit spies from the opposing political and cultural establishments, collect information, and fund hostile propaganda. For instance, the Soviet Union helped stage coups against the regimes in Czechoslovakia in 1948 and in Afghanistan in 1979; the United States did the same in Iran in 1953 and in Chile in 1973. Both superpowers secretly financed foreign oppositional movements and periodicals that supported their positions.

The USSR was more aggressive than the United States with its policy of extending its influence in the world.[22] The decline of international tension after Stalin's death in 1953, and further under Gorbachev after 1985, proved that the probability of war was determined first of all by Moscow.

The fear of war was deeply embedded in the Soviet mentality, regardless of whether the threat was "real," invented by propaganda, or inspired by aggressive foreign policy. For this reason, Russians not only accepted the official thesis about the gravity of foreign threats but mostly supported the Kremlin's foreign policy. During the civil war, many of those who were against the Bolsheviks reluctantly supported them rather than the foreign powers. Despite their anti-Communist tendencies, these people saw the Bolsheviks as the leaders of Russia, "their homeland." Later, the absolute majority of the population continued to believe that the Kremlin represented their country's interests even when it pursued its geopolitical games. Any threat to the regime was perceived by most Russians as a threat to their own survival. The people saw the state as a reliable guard against outside aggression. Their feelings of national security were shattered by the first two disastrous years of the war with Nazi Germany; but after the war and the glorious victory over the enemy, the state restored its prestige as the protector of peace in the eyes of the masses.

The Restoration and Expansion of the Empire

The nationalist ideology that set the goals for the leadership contained not only the defensive ingredient but also an aggressive element that demanded the preservation of empire (an important task for the Bolsheviks during the civil war), followed by its expansion and the increase of Soviet influence in the world. This element of the nationalist ideology, along with the real practices of the leadership during the civil war, were supported by many tsarist generals who joined the Red Army in 1918. Other supporters included several Russian monarchists in the 1920s, such as Vasilii Shulgin; the advocates of National Bolshevism; and the champions of Eurasianism, such as Nikolai Ustrialov. In the mid-1930s, Stalin began highlighting the continuity between the USSR and the pre-revolutionary Russian empire (the Bolsheviks previously had refused to recognize this continuity, labeling the Russian empire "the prison of the nations").[23] After Stalin's death, this continuity was vehemently denied by his successors (see Khrushchev 1970; Brezhnev 1972, 1976, 1981).[24] In post-Communist Russia, it was recognized as an indisputable fact by almost all Russian liberals, though they did not agree about whether it was a positive or negative sign for the country.[25] Russian nationalists and even some Communists accepted this fact and saw it in a positive light.[26] Western scholars were split on the issue.[27] The leadership's dream of expanding the empire to the West (which was practically absent in the 1920s and 1930s) reemerged in 1939–1940 with the annexation of several territories (West Ukraine, West Belorussia, and several others), and particularly after the victory of WWII, when Stalin transformed a number of East European countries into Russian satellites.

The post-Stalin leadership continued the policy of expansion. The Kremlin used all of its ideological, political and military instruments to transform weaker countries into Soviet satellites. It created military bases whenever feasible, and planted its agents in the ruling circles and media of the countries it considered enemies of the USSR.

The Strong State: A Servant of Socialism and Russian Nationalism

Before the October Revolution, the Bolsheviks' attitudes toward the state were very ambivalent. In August of 1917, when Lenin was writing *State and revolution*, the chances for him to acquire power looked slim at best. At this point, he regarded the state as an institution that must be destroyed (after a short transitional period) with the victory of a socialist revolution. Unlike the anarchists, he followed the line of Marxist thought that held that the revolutionary state would be needed for only a brief period of time, during the transition to a Communist society. A few months before he became the head of the Russian revolutionary state, Lenin explicitly said: "After Marx, the proletariat needs only a withering state" (Lenin 1947–1951, Vol. 25, p. 374). By Lenin's calculations, the final result would be an absolutely new type of state. The majority of the population would maintain direct control of the state machine, thereby obliterating the border between the classical state and civil society. As Lenin said, referring (along with Marx) to the experience of the Paris Commune (1871): "Since the majority of the people *itself* suppresses its exploiters *there will be no need* for a 'special entity'" (Lenin's italics; see his 1947–1951, Vol. 25, p. 374).

If Lenin and his comrades-in-arms approached October 1917 with a belief in the necessity of violent revolution (a beloved term in Lenin's vocabulary[28]), they meant this violence to be directed at a minority of individuals inside the country, along with foreign enemies. However, after the Bolsheviks took control, they completely reversed their attitudes toward the state. They soon began restoring the state machine with its bureaucracy and recruiting tsarist officials as well as the political police and the army so as to impose their will on the population. Under the guise of "the dictatorship of the proletariat," the cult of the totalitarian state began to develop almost immediately after the seizure of power in 1917. The leadership quickly abandoned all democratic elements of the socialist idea, such as the active role of the masses in governing society, and political freedoms (elements regarded as vitally important by Western Marxists).[29] The inclusion of the nationalist component in the ideology only magnified the cult of state in society. In fact, the cult of state united Russian Marxists and nationalists because they both needed the totalitarian state to achieve their goals. In the first two decades of the regime, the leadership avoided public discussions about the prominence of the cult of state. In the mid-1930s, however, Stalin broke with this tradition and openly praised the state as the most important Soviet institution.[30] The high stature of the cult of state played a pivotal role in the ideology until 1987–1989.

The leadership used the totalitarian state as the primary means for maintaining order in society, fighting crime and social parasitism and implementing socialist principles (in the first place, the abolishment of private property). The official ideology supposed that only with state violence was it possible to expropriate private businesses in the cities and implement collectivization in the countryside. The powerful state was the necessary condition for establishing a planned economy and for preventing the resurrection of private business. The state apparatus suppressed public discontent and imposed the official ideology on the masses.

The powerful state was also important for implementing the goals set by Russian nationalism. Without a strong army and political police, the leaders could not have restored, maintained and expanded the empire. Only with the totalitarian state could Russia, with its relatively weak economy, protect its sovereignty, particularly during the war with Nazi Germany, and achieve military parity with the United States after 1945. The "State," as a central value in Soviet ideology, advanced the political police, the army, the military industrial complex and the ideological machine as the country's priorities. The official ideology's focus on the state was supported by the masses, who saw the strong state as a guarantor of order inside the country and a protector against foreign enemies.

The cult of state in the ideology was in consonance with the zeitgeist that dominated the world in the first two thirds of the twentieth century. The idea of the interventionist state as the instrument for reaching national goals such as victory in war, modernization of society, or economic recovery, earned great popularity in the warring countries during WWI. After the war, its reputation only improved; in most countries, its popularity increased during the 1920s–1940s (McCleland 1996). Even apart from Soviet Russia (an obvious champion of the state), the economic theories of John Maynard Keynes, Roosevelt's New Deal, and the Fascist and Nazi regimes exemplified the prominence of the interventionist state. During this period, the glorification of state (with reference to such famous philosophers as Plato, Hobbes, and Hegel) was a key component of the dominant ideologies in almost all countries of the world (Bushnell, Shlapentokh, Vanderpool, and Subdram 1991, pp. 6–7).[31] The Soviet leaders, particularly since the early 1930s, advanced the cult of state by praising pre-revolutionary Russian traditions. Stalin promoted the cult of the cruelest tsars in Russian history, such as Ivan the Terrible, Peter the Great and even Nicholas the First (who ordered the execution of the Decembrists).

The Ideology and Practices of Militarized Society

National defense and high geopolitical status were the primary goals of the ideology. The ideology called for the almost total militarization of society and the mobilization of most state resources for foreign policy.[32] Indeed, after 1918, the USSR was one of the most militarized societies in the world.[33] In the last decades of its history, direct military expenditures were enormous, absorbing between 30 and 40 percent of the GNP (see Birman 1991; Ellman and Kontorovich 1998, p. 65; Yasin 1999). Military production constituted 60 percent of the machine-building industry (Shlykov 1991). The Soviet Union in 1985 had an army of 5 million and an extensive network of military colleges, research institutes and other military institutions.

The civil economy was designed to serve military needs, directly or indirectly, whenever necessary. Many plants and factories were built not to satisfy the civil needs of society but to ensure a high potential for the production of military goods. The automotive and electronic industries were the most conspicuous examples of this economic organization.[34] The best argument a manager could make in favor of any industrial project was to suggest that "it would contribute to defense." Each plant had an official mobilization plan for the immediate transformation of production for military purposes.

Industry was not the only part of the Soviet military machine. Science was oriented toward the satisfaction of military needs as well. Most projects in civil research institutes, including those which were part of the Academy of Sciences, served the military. The best minds in the country were always involved in national defense projects. The military dimension of health services was also evident. Each hospital had its own mobilization plan. Women were less likely than men to enter medical colleges, largely due to military considerations. The militarization of education at all levels was another important feature of Soviet life. Each school had a military teacher. Most colleges had a military department responsible for preparing students, usually males, to become junior officers before graduation.

Cultural institutions were deeply involved in military activities. Organizations of writers, musicians, movie makers and painters—the so-called creative unions—had special military units which successfully encouraged their members, through their novels, poems, films, songs and pictures, to contribute to defense. Many Soviet military songs and movies praising the army in peaceful times were of high artistic quality and extremely popular.[35] The state and party apparatus, the army, the KGB, media, scientific institutions, and various youth organizations served the objectives related to the USSR's confrontation with the external world.

The young Russian reformers in the early 1990s evidently underestimated the depth of the militarization of the economy. They believed the introduction of the market with free prices and the key role of mass consumers would lead within a few years to the conversion of the military industry into a civil one. As they found out, the military industry was quite inflexible. They could not begin to produce new civil products without sacking millions of workers. The economic difficulties of the late 1990s were inherited directly from the Soviet empire with its colossal military industry. "Shock market therapy" simply could not work in Russia.

Conclusion

Socialism and Russian nationalism were the two major forces behind Soviet ideology throughout the history of the regime. Together, these principles dominated society, legitimized the system in the eyes of the people, and commanded the changing perceptions of the leadership. Over the years, the ideology fluctuated as Russian nationalism became more important to the regime. Chapter three provides a more specific analysis of the ideological shifts with respect to the leadership's treatment of the masses, proletarian democracy, egalitarianism, and collectivism.

3

Adjusting the Revolutionary
Ideology to Totalitarian Goals

After the Bolsheviks came to power, they not only reconfigured the major
precepts of the ideology (socialism and Russian nationalism) but also adjusted all their underlying ideological perceptions to the new reality. They
changed their attitudes toward the masses (workers, peasants, and the members of the party rank and file), proletarian democracy, egalitarianism, collectivism and the World Revolution. In this chapter, four of these ideological
changes will be discussed. The World Revolution will be treated exclusively
in the next chapter.

The Masses in the Bolsheviks' Pre-revolutionary Ideology

Lenin and other Bolsheviks were not idealists who blindly adored the masses.
In fact, from the beginning they harbored suspicions about the sagacity of
the masses and the proletariat. The Bolsheviks shared the views of Karl
Kautsky, who believed that socialism should be conveyed to the proletarian
movement "from above." This was an important part of the ideology formulated by Lenin in 1902, in his book *What is to be done?* According to this
text, without the acumen of a revolutionary party equipped with the knowledge of historical laws, the masses could not extricate themselves from bourgeois society.

However, the Bolsheviks' attitudes toward the masses were, in some ways,
contradictory. Bolsheviks as true Marxist disciples considered the proletariat

the most progressive class in society. They believed in several virtues of the masses, particularly of the working class and poor peasants, who made up the majority of the population.[1] The Bolsheviks were influenced not only by Marx and his most astute essays, such as *The Civil War in France* and *18 Brumaire of Louis Bonaparte*, but also by populist writers and other Russian writers like Leo Tolstoy (Lenin 1947–1951, Vol. 10, pp. 121, 157; Tsipko 1989b, pp. 215–216).

The Bolsheviks envisioned a clash of two minorities: a revolutionary minority (the vanguard of the proletariat, headed by the Marxist party), and a small group of landlords and exploiters (the bourgeoisie). They believed that the majority of the masses would indeed support the revolutionary minority. With the support of the people, the Bolsheviks would introduce a new form of democracy (far superior to the false, bourgeois democracy) based on the dictatorship of the proletariat.[2] The first Russian revolution, in 1905, was congruent with the Bolsheviks' image of the masses. The mass workers' strikes and riots, the workers' insurrection in Moscow's Presnia district, and the burning of landed estates in the countryside reinforced their confidence in the people's solidarity. They were certain that in the next revolution, the masses—headed by the vanguard of the working class—would join forces with the Bolshevik movement.

At the same time, the brutal impact of anarchistic tendencies and the overall destructive milieu of 1905 were not overlooked by Bolshevik leaders. There were numberless incidents of pogroms, looting, destruction of property, wild violence in the countryside, and ethnic carnage in the Caucasus. The looting of liquor and wine shops was the goal of several riots, many of which were incited by the army and navy. In many cities, police forces collapsed and the mob controlled the streets. This was indeed a time of very serious social disarray.[3] However, the Bolsheviks and the radical liberal intelligentsia ascribed most pogroms to the police.[4] They said that the anarchic developments were by-products of the revolutionary elan opposing the current social system; they refused to consider these developments antisocial, or against social order per se. They wanted to protect the image of the masses and therefore avoided discussions on the specific social composition of the participants and the brutal nature of their actions.

Pre-revolutionary Russian liberals (primarily the Constitutional Democrats [Kadets]) who dreamed of establishing Western-style democracy in the country, reacted much differently to the mass disturbances than the Bolsheviks. Unlike the Bolsheviks, they were appalled by the masses. Fear of the masses was the overall theme of the famous collection of articles entitled *Landmarks* (Berdiaev et al. 1967). The liberal authors of this collection were horrified by what they saw during the revolution, especially the disturbing conduct of the people. They called upon the intelligentsia's support for the tsarist government as the protector of order. The radical intelligentsia responded with disgust. Lenin and other radicals were inflamed by these authors and their views of the masses.

The Competence of the Masses

The Bolsheviks were certain not only that they could rely on the masses in the next revolution but also that the masses themselves, according to the tenets of Marxism, would actively participate in the governance of society, creating the highest form of democracy—proletarian democracy. Having witnessed the revolution of 1905 and the events which occurred shortly after, the Bolsheviks became more and more confident in the ability of the masses to run society. All across the country, workers created various organizations to defend their interests. Moreover, in the spring of 1905, workers and professionals began to establish trade unions in defiance of the law (Ascher 1988, pp. 141–142). Of special importance were the soviets, which emerged almost spontaneously and enjoyed prestige in a few cities (e.g., Ivanovo-Voznesensk, and Petersburg, where Trotsky played the leading role). These self-governmental bodies represented workers as well as other groups of the population, and tried to create order in the cities. The Bolsheviks saw the development of the soviets as a sort of continuation of the historical precedent set by the Paris Commune (1871), in which the people took control of society. The rapid growth of soviets following the February 1917 revolution served as further evidence of the masses' ability to run society. After the Petrograd Soviet formed on February 27, 1917, 600 democratically elected soviets emerged in the next month. By October, 1,429 soviets functioned in the country. While this could rightly be considered progress for the Bolsheviks, they soon realized that the soviets were much more complicated than they had assumed (see Anweiler 1974).

The Bolsheviks also encouraged the expansion of the Red Guards (by October 1917, there were 200,000 Red Guards across the country). The Red Guards consisted of elected officers and ordinary people who mixed their professional work with military exercises. The Bolsheviks believed that the Red Guards would replace the conventional armed forces, just as the working militia would replace the professional police force.[5]

The Road to Realism

Following the February Revolution, the Bolsheviks watched the gradual disintegration of the state and society with sadistic pleasure. They contributed to this process with defeatist propaganda directed at the army. Adopting slogans such as "Worse is better," they used the collapse of Russia as an opportunity to legitimize their claim as the only party in the country that could prevent disaster.[6] Indeed, Russia in 1917–1918 was described unequivocally as a society in the grips of anarchy and chaos, where drunkenness played a leading role.[7] But the Bolsheviks treated the mass protests and riots as "normal" manifestations of the people's dissatisfaction with the conditions of life. On March 1, 1917, they welcomed the initiative of soldiers from the Petrograd Soviet, who issued the famous Order No. 1, which annulled the military hierarchy in the army, introduced the election of commanders, and directed the military to obey only the orders of the Soviet and not those of the Provisional Government.[8]

The anarchy continued after the October appearance of the Bolsheviks in the Smolny. Many Russians, especially in the capital, saw the Bolshevik Revolution as yet another sign of their ever increasing "freedom"—that is, they believed their behavior would now go unchecked by social constraints. Following the seizure of the Winter Palace, a gigantic drunken bacchanalia took place in Petrograd (William 1967, p. 181; Beatty 1918, pp. 330–332; Buchanan 1918, p. 215). The actions of the Baltic sailors were particularly characteristic of this anarchic behavior (among other things, they murdered two ministers of the Provisional Government in a hospital).[9] Every possible form of social disorder flourished in the provinces.

In the first months after the October Revolution, the Bolsheviks continued to conduct themselves in accordance with their initial views of the masses. Soon after, however, their attitudes toward the masses changed radically. Once in power, they saw the country with new eyes (see Rosenberg 1997, pp. 632–644). They no longer had a use for the tumultuous social environment. All the problems (food riots, widespread drunkenness, rampant criminality, mass pilfering and thefts, labor absenteeism, "labor desertion," strikes, the disappearance of civility, the pawning of factory equipment by workers, widespread speculation and petty trade) were now theirs to solve.[10] These new issues and problems eclipsed the goal of building a socialist society. Curbing the antisocial comportment of society became the Bolsheviks' primary objective. If they could not create order, they would lose power. Some other governing force would seize control by challenging anarchy in the country from a different ideological premise. For this reason, the Bolsheviks almost immediately took cruel measures to suppress the mobs in the capital and quell the drunken riots.

The Bolsheviks were faced with the challenge of bringing order not only in the capital but throughout the entire country, with its millions of uneducated and angry people. While the anarchic social climate persisted, the national provinces proclaimed independence, along with many Russian regions

(V. Shlapentokh, Levita, and Loiberg 1998). The chaos in society put the very survival of the country at risk.[11] Anarchy also threatened the implementation of socialist ideals, the advancement of the World Revolution, and the survival of the Bolshevik regime. Those who predicted the imminent fall of the Bolsheviks contemplated a full collapse of Russian statehood and the disintegration of the social fabric.[12]

The Bolsheviks soon discovered that their public support from law-abiding citizens—workers, peasants and soldiers—was limited. Only a small part of the population, consisting mostly of workers, poor peasants, some ethnic minorities, and young people from various strata, supported the new power which promised the salvation of the country and a progressive society with extraordinary social mobility. The majority of the country, however, was clearly not on the side of the new rulers. In free elections to the Constitutional Assembly in January of 1918, the Bolsheviks received only 25 percent of the vote. The same lack of support was displayed in the soviets, where the Bolsheviks rarely garnered a majority. For this reason, in 1918, they began imposing stricter controls over the elections, depriving them in most cases of any democratic character. They imposed similar constraints also on other key institutions where they needed full control.

Having used the Red Guards for seizing power, they began dismantling these units in January 1918. They were eager to take these "militias of the people" apart, regarding them as too independent and prone to anarchism. Now Lenin wanted to create a normal professional army. This came only months after he had preached against the "professional army" in his book, *State and revolution*. In March 1918, the Bolsheviks abolished the election of officers and the famous Order No. 1. Two months later, they introduced compulsory military service. To the Bolsheviks' dismay, the workers and peasants were not, as they had hoped, eager to defend "their Soviet power." The people were inclined to desert their army duty at the first opportunity.[13] The Bolsheviks soon realized that without mass shootings of deserters, the Red Army could not assemble a company of troops that would readily obey orders.

Before the revolution, the Bolsheviks had advanced slogans such as "factories to workers" and had championed the idea of "workers' control" committees. On November 14, 1917, in the aftermath of the October Revolution, they went so far as to implement these committees with a special decree. However, within months they began to detect anarchic tendencies in these committees. Before long, the idea of workers' control was considered an obstacle to a normally functioning economy and a threat to Bolshevik rule. With the nationalization of industry in 1918, workers' control practically disappeared from Soviet life.

The Bolsheviks grew more and more isolated from their own social basis as they met with one confrontation after another from various strata of the population—railroad workers, printers, teachers' unions, and the Russian intelligentsia. With only a tiny minority of active supporters, the Bolsheviks were forced to reconsider their vision of the world and make a number of major changes in their pre-revolutionary ideology.[14]

The Dual Images of the Masses in the Eyes of the Leadership

From their first years in power, Soviet leaders were operating with two images of the masses: one intended for public consumption and one reserved for themselves and the party elite. In public, the Bolsheviks made hypocritical statements with flattering images of the workers and poor peasants. During the civil war they spoke about the "ruling role" of the working class, its "organizational capabilities" and "social organizational" power (Bukharin 1971; Lenin 1947–1951, Vol. 30, pp. 111–113). They ranted about the active participation of the masses in governing the country (Lenin 1947–1951, Vol. 30, pp. 111–113; Vol. 29, p. 87; Bukharin 1966, p. 23). Lenin wrote to an American newspaper in October 1919, claiming, "The Soviet government is the most democratic of all governments in the world" (Lenin 1947–1951, Vol. 30, p. 32). Rykov spoke in 1918 about the "workers and workers' intelligentsia," who successfully managed factories and offices (Rykov 1990, p. 67).

In the public eye, the Soviet leaders after Lenin maintained the ideal image of the average Soviet individual: devoted to socialism, the motherland and the state; hard-working and always ready to fulfill any assignment given by the party or the state; modest in private life and disinterested in material wealth and consumer goods.[15] Soviet leaders promoted this image of the people until the time of perestroika.[16] Soviet textbooks, and even the monographs of very respected scholars such as Igor Kon, lauded the high quality and virtue of the "ordinary Soviet citizen." Some books suggested that the people had room for progress, while others claimed that they had achieved "all-around developed personalities."[17] Many Western scholars accepted this propagandistic image at face value.[18] Adhering to Soviet propaganda, the Soviet people themselves accepted the romantic portrait of the Bolsheviks as well as the sanguine depiction of the masses until the collapse of the USSR. The utopian image of the "new Soviet man" was particularly strong among young people in the 1920s and 1930s, in spite of their rather gloomy everyday lives (Tsipko 1989a, p. 215).

The second image of the masses was concealed deep in the minds of the Soviet leaders and completely inaccessible to the public. This image depicted the ordinary Russian as prone to laziness, drunkenness, pilfering and betrayal of the motherland. Such a picture of the average citizen can be decoded from the leadership's writings and speeches, especially when the discourse was addressed to party officials. In order to avoid direct criticism of the masses, they focused their hatred and disgust on the so-called minority of people who were "influenced by hostile propaganda" and "confused by class enemies."[19]

The true beliefs of the Soviet leaders were indirectly revealed by their desire to "teach" the masses elementary virtues. From the beginning of the Soviet regime to the time of perestroika, the leadership's public speeches were inundated with recommendations, admonitions, and threats addressed to the masses.[20] The entire system of education, the media, arts and literature were all geared toward "enlightening" the masses. In January 1921, Lenin implicitly forswore his pre-revolutionary statements when he rhetorically asked his audience, "Do you believe that each worker can govern the state? Practically everyone knows that this is but a fairytale" (1947–1951, Vol. 42, p. 253). The leadership's genuine perceptions of the masses were best revealed by their actions. From the beginning, their acts were regularly at odds with the public ideology. While the ideology praised the masses, the Soviet leaders, in fact, mistrusted and feared them.[21] For this reason, they developed the political police, with its gigantic network of informers. They crushed any attempt at creating an independent organization, even for the study of Lenin's works. Almost immediately following their victory, the Bolsheviks rescinded freedom of the media and prohibited any expression of the mood of the masses.[22] With their distrust and fear of the masses, in the 1920s the Soviet leaders always favored converting ordinary citizens into soldiers. In the military, the masses were readily compelled to accept authority.[23]

With their deep contempt for the masses, the Bolsheviks looked upon the people as expendable material and were never seriously concerned about the number of human lives they sacrificed for the achievement of their goals. The idea of sacrificing one's life for the good of the motherland played an important role in the official ideology. The Bolsheviks demonstrated a grave disregard for ordinary citizens in many ways: the starvation of millions during collectivization, the deaths of a staggering number of soldiers during the civil war and WWII,[24] and the merciless neglect of 5.7 million prisoners in the German concentration camps (Stalin could have improved their plight, had he accepted help from the Red Cross and not considered all prisoners traitors) (Tepliakov 1990).

The Soviet leaders after Lenin maintained their deeply disdainful views of the masses. Stalin saw in each citizen a potential enemy and spy. Every soldier and officer was a potential deserter or traitor. He presumed that the average Soviet individual—if not a political enemy—was or could be a thief, a bandit, or a loafer. Stalin introduced several laws which "protected socialist property" and severely punished all offenders. Among those people he considered "offenders" were starving peasants who gleaned grain from the fields after the harvest. Stalin's successors inherited his negative attitudes toward the masses. As Yurii Levada put it, "From the point of view of the bosses, their subordinates were loafers who at any moment would turn to their own 'private business' instead of the implementation of the bosses' orders and plans" (Levada 1993, p. 64). In the 1960s and 1970s, Soviet sociology cast new light on the Kremlin's perceptions of the masses. In the early 1960s, the leadership began to permit sociologists to study the real attitudes and behavior of the people (with politics still a forbidden area) and publish their findings. Most described people in ways that contradicted the official image of the masses.[25] However, in spite of their distrust of sociology, the leaders never accused sociologists of denigrating "socialist reality." What is more, in the early 1980s, the Kremlin changed its public statements about the people. Andropov and Gorbachev were the first Soviet leaders to speak harshly about the masses in the public arena.[26]

Attitudes Toward the Party Rank and File

The Soviet leaders regarded the party rank and file with almost the same low esteem as the masses. At all stages of Soviet history, the party masses remained suspect in the minds of the leadership. Internal party democracy never played a serious role. At the 10th Party Congress, Lenin forbade the formation of party factions; this prohibition was equivalent to a complete ban on free debates inside the party. The alienation of the Soviet leaders from the party masses grew over time, and reached its peak during Stalin's regime, when party members and in particular party apparatchiks felt more vulnerable than the masses.[27] Both Khrushchev and Brezhnev, in the early years of their leadership, took some measures to demonstrate their respect for the party masses (for instance, giving access to some documents of the Central Committee and the Politburo), but they both ended this practice later in their terms.

Contempt for the Peasants

The Bolsheviks reserved a special brand of hatred for the peasants.[28] From their perspective, the average peasant was greedy, cruel and bound by his desire for private property. The Bolsheviks often cited Marx's notorious statement about the "idiocy of rural life."

The famous literary figure Maxim Gorky created an ugly image of peasant life in many of his pre-revolutionary stories. After the revolution, Gorky, a great admirer of cities, culture and progress, continued to see peasants as a major obstacle to Russian advancement. Gorky's position was typical of the ruling elite until the end of the Soviet regime.[29]

Stalin was notorious for his hatred of peasants. He demonstrated this clearly with the brutality he used in dealing with them.[30] Stalin's hostility toward peasants was shared by many "left" Bolsheviks, such as Zinoviev and Bukharin.[31] This hatred of peasants culminated in paranoia during the collectivization period and the ensuing famine.[32] The Kremlin attributed the urban influx of peasants from famine-stricken villages to the motivation "to corrupt and weaken the iron discipline of socialist labor" (*Pravda*, December 28, 1932). In secret telegrams to party organizations, Stalin and Molotov demanded the denunciation of the peasant exodus from Ukraine, where the famine was killing thousands of people each day; the peasants were to be treated as the enemies of the Soviet system who were abetted by anti-Soviet agitators in Ukrainian regions (Fitzpatrick 1994b, p. 94).

Fear of Public Unrest

The leaders' hostility toward the masses was to some degree nourished by their acute fear of the masses. This type of fear persisted from the civil war until the end of the regime. Fear of the masses was the main reason for the Kremlin's advancement of the gigantic network of citizen-informers and KGB agents. During the first decade after 1917, the people's hostility toward the new rulers escalated to the point where the Bolsheviks were uncertain of their own survival. The peasant rebellions, workers' strikes, and sailors' mutinies in 1918–1921 would never be forgotten by the Bolshevik rulers (Brovkin 1994; Danilov and Shanin 1994; Figes 1997, pp. 370–380).

However, as history showed, the Kremlin's fear of the masses was mostly unfounded (this subject will be discussed in detail later). In the three decades after 1953, there were only a few cases of public disruptions (these disturbances will be discussed later). As a rule, these events were kept as state secrets. The country remained virtually unaware of any public incident.

The Transformation of Proletarian Democracy

The Bolsheviks' rapid and extreme change of heart with respect to the masses forced them to adjust their ideology to a more sober perception of reality. One of the main ideological changes occurred in the political system. Before the revolution, the Bolshevik leaders had sharply denounced "bourgeois," parliamentary democracy. Quite reasonably, they pointed out the negative impact of money on the democratic process, and the gap between the elected bodies and the citizens they represented.[33] Lenin, Trotsky, Bukharin and other Soviet leaders condemned parliamentary democracy as a completely rotten institution which deceived workers and toilers (see, for instance, Lenin 1947–1951, Vol. 30, pp. 40–41, 239–240; Vol. 32, pp. 387–388, 470–472). They juxtaposed this "corrupt" form of democracy to their proletarian democracy, with its major advantages including the direct participation of the people and the unification of all three powers—legislative, judicial and executive—in the soviets.

However, almost immediately after the revolution, the Bolsheviks realized they could not trust even a modicum of power to the masses. They seized and maintained control over every organization in the country, from the soviets and trade unions to youth organizations and sports clubs. Between 1930 and 1989, not a single free election for any governmental body took place.[34]

The Bolsheviks quickly realized the dangers of the free press and media. Only two days after the coup, on October 27, the government adopted the "Decree on the press," which began the Bolsheviks' struggle against free media. By July 1918, the freedom of press had been totally eliminated. Almost simultaneously, the Bolsheviks established censorship in the person of the commissar for press affairs. In 1922, they replaced the Revolutionary Tribunal of the press with the notorious Glavlit (Blium 1994). The state's complete control of the media persisted until glasnost.

The Fate of Egalitarianism

As the Soviet leaders adjusted to the new social reality, they quickly modified their position on egalitarianism. In 1918, they began allocating special privileges to "bourgeois specialists" and party apparatchiks.[35] They mostly ignored protests against social inequality during and after the civil war.[36] The extra benefits for party apparatchiks were small in the beginning, but with each year following the civil war, egalitarianism lost ground. From the late 1920s until perestroika (with exceptions during Khrushchev's rule[37]), the Kremlin introduced new privileges for the party and state apparatchiks, the officers of the political police and army, and leading intellectuals. The Kremlin also initiated several material stimuli for managers as well as the rank and file.

Stalin drastically increased the material privileges of apparatchiks and raised managers' salaries. In his later years, he boosted salaries for scholars. He created a vast network of exclusive hospitals, stores, and resort homes for the political and cultural elite.[38] Under the influence of official policies and other factors such as semi-legal and illegal activities, social differentiation expanded in every segment of the population. Before WWII, the ratio between the lowest and highest salaries for manual workers was no less than 5 to 1.[39] In the late years of its existence, there was a high level of social inequality in Soviet society, which had a great impact on the social and political climate in the country.

The Containment of Social Differentiation

Although their secret actions contributed to social polarization, the leaders were always sensitive to egalitarian public sentiments and tried to maintain some semblance of egalitarianism in society. Compared to that in post-Communist Russia, social differentiation in the USSR was quite moderate. Contrasting these two periods lends credence to the official propaganda, which characterized the country as "a socially homogeneous society." Indeed, the USSR maintained an enormous middle class. The middle class contained a broad range of individuals, including the mass intelligentsia (teachers, doctors, engineers, and cultural workers), several other types of white-collar workers, and a large chunk of the blue-collar working class and the peasantry. According to data of the Russian Center for Public Opinion Research (VTsIOM), 43 percent of the population said that they belonged to the "middle class" (Levada 1993, p. 53).

However, in many ways, the masses were discontent with the existing social inequality in society. They were well aware of the perks and privileges of the elite. Many people despised their immediate superiors and regarded society as highly stratified.[40] Vladimir Dudintsev's book *Not by bread alone* (1956) resonated with the public primarily because it spearheaded a public discussion about social stratification.[41] In response to this discontent, in the last two decades of the regime, the leadership intensified its egalitarian policy.[42] The Kremlin's last ideological campaign took place on the eve of perestroika, when Yurii Andropov came to power. The campaign addressed many issues including social inequality. Propelled by its own inertia, the campaign did not end until the late 1980s.[43] Most importantly, this campaign reflected the general uneasiness felt by the leadership in light of the growing social differentiation in society.[44]

Yeltsin's political career as a party dissident commenced with his call for greater social equality, a call which sounded in his famous speech at the 27th Party Congress in 1986 (*XXVII s"ezd Kommunisticheskoi partii Sovetskogo soiuza: Stenograficheskii otchet*, Vol. 1, 1986, pp. 140–145). Until 1991, the future president—who would later adopt a "royal lifestyle"—turned down many perks such as special hospitals and airline flights.[45] Yeltsin positioned himself in 1987–1991 as a champion of social equality and an ardent opponent of special privileges.

Adjusting Collectivism to the Totalitarian State

The rejection of bourgeois individualism, coupled with the praise of socialist collectivism, played a leading role in Soviet ideology until the late 1980s.

The leadership endorsed collectivism in its two forms: at the micro level (i.e., "my factory," "my office," "my institute"), and the macro level (i.e., "my motherland"). The denunciation of individualism and the commendation of a life devoted to the public cause was an essential ingredient in all Soviet textbooks on philosophy, social sciences, morals, and history (Fedoseev 1985, pp. 214–216; Rumiantsev 1983, pp. 97–101; Kon 1980, 1983; Kogan 1983; Ratnikov 1978). Collectivism was glorified in numberless movies and novels.[46] The political machine successfully exploited altruism, comradeship, friendship, the human need for affiliation, respect for those in the same social surroundings, and even democratic sympathies (the obligation to obey the majority) in order to advance collectivism. The authorities benefited from the potency of collectivist morals. They understood the moral sinew of the collective and employed this influence against the perceived enemies of the state.[47]

Other factors also helped the authorities inculcate collectivism in the Soviet mind. The restrictions on free associations, groups and clubs, along with the absence of religious congregations, limited people's opportunity to interact. The official collective was the only formally organized social outlet. One's place of work was nearly the only place for social communications (along with vacation resorts). Informal groups were extremely important to the people; this type of group usually comprised one's colleagues, and less often one's neighbors and relatives.[48] The traditions of pre-revolutionary Russia, particularly the importance of "community" in rural life, also had some impact on the acceptance of collectivist ideology by the Soviet people.

While preserving the fealty of collectivism, the rulers converted it into a powerful weapon of the totalitarian state. When propaganda praised the collective, it applauded only those units (factories, large farms, schools, colleges, hospitals, etc.) that were fully controlled by the state. By prohibiting private associations and advocating the ideology of collectivism, the party leaders decreased privacy in human life and expanded the scope of public life, which made it easier to monitor society. The collective became the primary location for observing the behavior and thoughts of the population. In each factory, office and college, there was a KGB unit and a network of informers. During the typical nine-hour workday (including the lunch hour), the average worker was completely exposed to the watchful eyes of the dominant political power. Moreover, the "collective public opinion"—that is, the social pressure which emanated from one's colleagues and acquaintances— also played a major role in managing society. The authorities used this collective public opinion to control labor performance, morals inside and outside the family, and political views.[49]

The propaganda that promoted the collective over the individual was relatively successful. As several surveys showed, most Russians in the last decades of the Soviet Union accepted the importance of the collective in social life and even the superiority of collective interests over individual concerns (V. Shlapentokh 1989). Even after the collapse of the Soviet system, many Russians looked with some nostalgia to the times when "collectivism" was an important social value.[50]

Another question about collectivism concerned the degree to which individuals were ready and willing to sacrifice their material interests for the sake of collective goals. In the first decades after the revolution, this idea affected the behavior of many people, especially the youth. After 1953, the impact of the collective on real behavior evidently declined. Russian liberal intellectuals launched a crusade for "the sovereignty of personality"; they were against the idolization of the collective, and by the 1960s, subtly derogated the cult of collectivism, though they never condemned patriotism.[51] During perestroika liberal intellectuals were joined in their critique of Soviet collectivism by party officials who supported Gorbachev.[52]

Despite the privatization of Soviet society, the decline of ideology, and the liberal, "anti-collective" propaganda, the Russians maintained a high level of respect for collectivism as they entered the post-Communist period. Among the nostalgic themes in the post-Soviet mentality was the yearning for "collective values," as opposed to the "jungle individualism" of capitalist society.[53]

Conclusion

As explained in this chapter, the Soviet leadership effectively adjusted the various elements of the early socialist ideology (i.e., their attitudes toward the masses, proletarian democracy, egalitarianism, and collectivism) to the needs of the totalitarian state. The last major ideological adjustment—the compromise of the World Revolution to the needs of Russian statehood—will be treated exclusively in the next chapter.

4

World Revolution As a Geopolitical Instrument

After the Bolsheviks took power in 1917, their ideological stance on the essential issues changed rapidly and quite dramatically. As discussed in the previous chapter, their attitudes toward the masses, democracy, egalitarianism, and collectivism were transformed seemingly overnight. Changes in the last major element of the ideology, the World Revolution (WR), evolved more slowly. In fact, the concept remained mostly intact in the minds of Soviet leaders for the first two years of the new regime. However, the evolution of the WR, and its changing influence on real politics, proceeded through Soviet history in an extremely complex way. Ultimately, the Kremlin used the WR as camouflage for its geopolitical games. For this reason, the blanket statements of the Soviet leaders about the WR, as well as about the workers' solidarity, or internationalism, should never be taken at face value.[1]

World Revolution in the Early Years: Both a Means and a Goal

To understand the role of the World Revolution in Soviet politics and ideology, we must distinguish between the leadership's "goals and means."[2] Before the revolution and in the first years after it, the leaders regarded the WR as a goal per se, and anticipated the transformation of the world into a Communist paradise (see, for instance, Lenin 1947–1951, Vol. 29, p. 128). They assumed that proletarians around the globe would free themselves from the capitalist yoke and join the Russian working class in building a new society

(Trotsky 1906, p. 278). Trotsky was the most ardent proponent of the WR even before October 1917. In the first years after the revolution, the leadership adopted another fundamental goal. They wanted to create a powerful state that would build a socialist society, protect Russian independence, preserve the Russian empire and promote its geopolitical interests. These intentions functioned as the parallel goals of the ideology. In essence, each goal served as a means for achieving the other.

The WR remained a goal per se for the first years of Soviet rule, but it soon gave way to the goals of state building and high geopolitical status. From then on, the WR was regarded not as a goal in and of itself but as an instrument for achieving other goals. Until the mid-1920s, Bolsheviks (including Trotskyists) saw the WR as an essential condition for modernizing the backward society. Many Russian intellectuals and politicians believed (since the time of Peter the Great) that Russia would never catch up with the modern world without technological and cultural aid from the West. The necessity of Western aid was as clear for many Russian revolutionaries before 1917 as it was for Soviet leaders after the revolution. It was also obvious to Gorbachev and other liberals, who sought financial benefits from the West during perestroika (V. Shlapentokh 1993a, pp. 98–100).[3] The leaders also saw the WR as a shield for the Russian revolutionary cause itself. In the early years, the Bolsheviks expected intense foreign intervention. Their fears were fomented by their close study of the French Revolution (D. Shlapentokh 1999). The leaders believed that proletarians from capitalist countries would help them defend their socialist achievements and overcome the hostility of the peasants in Russia.[4] They were indeed confident that their country enjoyed the growing support of workers around the globe.[5]

There is some evidence, however, that Soviet leaders ascribed secondary importance to the WR as early as 1919–1923. Scholars who saw the advancement of the WR as the leading goal of Soviet leaders could not cite a single example of the Kremlin's sacrificing its national interests for the sake of revolution in other countries.[6] The Kremlin's aid to foreign Communist parties was reduced to rather insignificant financial donations, considering the Soviet budget (see Shishkin 2000). The political struggle between Lenin and the leftists over the Brest-Litovsk peace treaty with Germany in March 1918 clearly demonstrated the primary goal of the leadership. Leftists, headed by Trotsky and Bukharin, criticized the treaty as a "betrayal of the revolutionary European proletariat." Lenin, however, did not want to risk the Kremlin to the kaiser's bayonets. The sovereignty of Russia was unquestionably his biggest concern.[7] Lenin signed the treaty, promising a proletarian revolution in Germany in the near future. After October 1917, only a few Bolshevik extremists, mostly Trotskyists, were ready (if only verbally) to sacrifice Russia for the victory of the world proletariat.[8] Even during one of the peaks of revolutionary euphoria, around the time of the German revolution, Lenin never made any such claims, and he clearly had no intention of using a significant amount of Russian resources to aid revolutions abroad.[9] Lenin was, in fact, a Russian patriot. Appealing to patriotism, he wrote, "Only the foreign bayonet can overthrow the Bolsheviks" (1947–1951, Vol. 37, p. 216).[10] Karl Radek, a leading Bolshevik, also talked about the advancement of patriotism in the country. As quoted by British historian Geoffrey Hosking, Radek said: "Since Russia is the only country where the working class has taken power, the workers of the whole world ought to become Russian patriots" (Hosking 1992, p. 6).[11]

As will be discussed later in this chapter, the leaders clearly demonstrated their prioritization of the country's national interests when they began restoring the Russian empire under the flag of World Revolution and Communism. The only real difference between the Kremlin's initiatives and the conduct of the previous rulers was its pseudo-internationalist justification for its foreign policy. Relying on the Red Army, Moscow forced Ukraine, the Caucasian republics, and Central Asia into submission, and attempted to do the same in Poland. Moscow's use of the social demagoguery and phraseology of "World Revolution" did not deceive many experts, who understood that Communist internationalism had become a smoke screen for Russian imperial interests.[12]

Evaluating the Prospects for World Revolution in 1917–1919 and Later

In the first two years after the revolution (and in 1923, with the brief revolutionary euphoria in Germany), Bolshevik leaders believed that the fire of the October Revolution would sweep the world, particularly the advanced capitalist countries.[13] There were, indeed, some reasonable grounds for this belief. To describe the idea of World Revolution as a purely utopian myth, or an absurdity conjured up by crazy minds, would be to demonstrate a misunderstanding of historical fact.[14] Even before the events of 1917, the idea of proletarian solidarity was taken quite seriously by millions of people who belonged to socialist parties around the world, particularly in Europe. In 1914, as the threat of war loomed in Europe, socialists united in several antiwar demonstrations. European socialists saw the antiwar strike in the Putilov factory in Petersburg in July 1914 as a good omen.[15] Although nationalism and the fear of war in Europe ultimately made international solidarity impossible, it is unreasonable to evaluate the socialist leaders of the time, particularly "internationalists," as silly dreamers. The victory of the October

Revolution drew the world's attention to revolutionary socialism and prole-tarian solidarity.[16] In the next three years, several other events occurred which advanced the idea of World Revolution, including the German revolution of 1918 (despite the defeat of the Spartacist revolt led by Marxists in January 1919); the demoralization of the French army and the revolt in the French navy in 1919; the creation of the Bavarian and Hungarian Soviet republics in 1919; the revolutionary movement in the new Yugoslavia, in 1918 and 1919; and various protest actions in countries which supported Soviet Russia in 1918–1920.[17] Several other developments and projects also fueled hope for the WR. Mikhail Tukhachevsky, a commander of the Red Army (which he led to Warsaw), appealed to his troops in 1920 during the Soviet-Polish war: "Through the body of White Poland the road leads us to the world fire."[18] Tukhachevsky was clearly inspired by Lenin, who believed (along with many other leaders, with the exception of Trotsky) that the Red Army would incite the "insurrection of Polish workers" (Trotsky 1991, p. 434).

In the decade following the October Revolution, the enemies of Bolshe-vik Russia were distressed about the possible culmination of the WR. Rus-sian "counterrevolutionaries" such as Pavel Miliukov warned the outside world about the dangers of underestimating the Bolsheviks' plan to foment worldwide revolution (Miliukov 1921–1924, pp. 258–266). The ruling elites in all Western countries, including the United States, were quite concerned with the spread of Bolshevism and with the activities of the Third Interna-tional. The fact that some politicians, such as Mitchell Palmer (Woodrow Wilson's attorney general), tried to exploit this fear for political purposes makes it impossible to deny the "objective existence" of this fear.[19] In fact, the fear of revolution and the expansion of Communism haunted the West-ern ruling classes (including such experienced leaders as Britain's David Lloyd George) and influenced their foreign policy until the beginning of WWII (Harries and Harris 1997). For this reason, if one calls Lenin a "dreamer" or a "lunatic," then one must use the same terms to describe West-ern leaders who agonized over such a fanciful and inconceivable threat.[20]

At the end of 1919, the Bolshevik leaders watched the developments in the world and began to reevaluate their expectations for the WR. The revolu-tions in Europe had been crushed. The Polish campaign was unsuccessful. Lenin's *Child illness of "leftism,"* published in 1920, confirmed the erosion of the WR. In this year, the 11th Party Conference eliminated the term "World Revolution" from its lexicon and spoke only about "the unity of the working class" in different countries (*KPSS v Rezoliutsiiakh*, Vol. 2, 1953, pp. 578–588). Seemingly, the fires of WR flared again when the Kremlin created the Union of Soviet Socialist Republics in 1922. The leaders regarded the entity as "a new radical step on the road toward the unification of all countries in the World Socialist Soviet Republic" (Soviet Constitution 1924). However, the idea of the WR was on a slow but steady decline in the minds of Soviet leaders. The only substantial reversal of this trend came in 1923, when developments in Germany caused a short period of renewed revolutionary euphoria.[21] The last vestige of hope for the WR was linked to the movements in Asia. The prospects for mass revolutionary insurrection there looked rather weak, but not impossible—particularly in China, and the British colonies, such as India. Soviet participation in the Chinese civil war on the side of Chiang Kai-shek in 1926 kept the fire of socialist revolution burning. In any case, up to his death, Lenin spoke about the revolution in Western Europe and believed in the ultimate victory of socialism, although in the very distant future.[22] As the concept of WR took a less prominent role in the official ideology, some party leaders, especially those with leftist backgrounds, tried to slow this ideological change as much as possible. In 1927, still dreaming about the world socialist community, Bukharin wrote, "The World Revolution is not an instant, momentous development," but "a very complicated, heterogeneous and long process . . . an epoch in world history" (Bukharin 1990, pp. 169–170).[23]

Stalin and the WR: A Radical Shift in Ideology

Stalin played a decisive role in changing the ideological focus from the victory of the World Revolution to the development of socialism in the USSR. After 1924, Stalin regarded the WR as nothing more than a political instrument for reinforcing the regime and advancing the geopolitical interests of the USSR.[24] This was the ideological line he used in his struggle for power with Trotsky, who championed the WR during this period.[25]

With the evaporation of the revolutionary fervor in postwar Europe, Stalin believed that an ideological shift was necessary in order to maintain the regime and preserve the support of the party rank and file. The concept of WR remained part of the official dogma, but Stalin downgraded its role in the ideology, which now emphasized "the building of socialism in one country."[26] Trotsky bitterly condemned Stalin in 1928. He wrote, "The Kremlin now thinks about the world not as the arena of the World Revolution, but only as a threat of intervention" (Trotsky 1993b, p. 97). Many decades later, Zhores Medvedev said, "For Stalin, the USSR was not a torch of World Revolution, but a besieged fortress which was threatened from the West and the East" (Medvedev 1997).

The Great Depression, which began in the United States in 1929–1932 and spread around the world, did very little to resuscitate the faded concept of the WR. Even though the future of capitalism itself was being debated in the

West and some intellectuals actually doubted its survival, Stalin left the WR on the back burner of Soviet ideology.[27] Moscow's refusal to exploit this crisis reflected Stalin's deep disbelief in the spontaneous uprisings of the masses, whatever their sufferings in capitalist society.

The rise of Nazism, with its open program of expansion to the East and its methods of coping with mass unemployment, further eroded Stalin's belief in the WR. What is more, Stalin saw the fear of WR in the West as a threat to the USSR's mass import of equipment from Western countries. The USSR needed these materials for industrialization and militarization and could not risk losing the vital import of capital goods as well as the technological aid of American and German engineers.

Preserving the World Revolution for Domestic Ideological Purposes

While the WR quickly lost significance in Stalin's realpolitik, it remained useful for various propagandistic purposes and as an instrument of geopolitics.[28] Indeed, Stalin did not want to abandon revolutionary fervor completely. He only needed to make it work for his central ideological goals. Maintaining some ideological continuity with the past, Stalin introduced a less inflammatory phraseology. Instead of "World Revolution," Stalin talked about "the capitalist encirclement," "the conflicts between capitalist countries," and "the persistent class struggles in the capitalist world," which implicitly supposed the final victory of socialism in the world.

After WWII, when the Soviet Union ceased to be "the single socialist country," Stalin added new concepts to the ideological stockpile, including "the struggle of two systems," "the capitalist world as a threat to the security of the USSR," and "the permanent imperialist threat to the socialist camp." These concepts replaced the direct phraseology of the WR in Stalin's speeches and articles. The remnants of the old phraseology of the WR were also evident in Stalin's postwar works. In his book *The economic problems of socialism in the USSR* (1952), Stalin spoke about "the movement for the elimination of capitalism" (Stalin 1952a).

The idea of WR, in its various alternative forms, persisted after Stalin's death and remained in the propagandistic arsenal until the fall of the regime. Stalin's heirs continued to see Marxist phraseology as necessary for legitimizing the regime and furthering the political objectives of the state. They talked about class solidarity, the interests of the international Communist movement, and world socialism. However, starting with Khrushchev, the leadership abandoned Stalin's phraseology about the direct confrontation between socialism and capitalism. Khrushchev wanted to improve relations with the West, and he therefore proclaimed the policy of "peaceful coexistence."[29]

In their speeches and publications, Khrushchev, Brezhnev and Andropov nonetheless gave lip service to the cluster of internationalist slogans, using this terminology to substantiate their deeds in foreign policy.[30] Of these three leaders, it was Khrushchev, with his elements of revolutionary romanticism, who most often utilized the revolutionary phraseology.[31] During the first years of perestroika, the revolutionary phraseology was still visible in Soviet propaganda.[32] In his speech to the 27th Party Congress, Gorbachev talked, though in much softer terms than his predecessors, about "socialism as a real opportunity for the future of mankind," "the general crisis of capitalism" and "the contradictions between the two systems" (*XXVII s"ezd Kommunisticheskoi partii Sovetskogo soiuza: Stenograficheskii otchet*, 1986, pp. 26–42). However, by 1989, this terminology had almost completely disappeared from Gorbachev's speeches and publications.[33]

There were three main reasons for preserving the concept of World Revolution and the people's belief in the worldwide victory of socialism. The idea of the WR was particularly useful in the first years after the October Revolution. First, the WR helped legitimize the regime in the eyes of the people, especially the party rank and file. With the claims of the WR, the system represented a new and progressive society, a sort of international social vanguard and a beacon for the world.[34] The famous poem by Mikhail Svetlov, about a peasant boy who dreamed of dying for the cause of liberating Spanish peasants, conveyed the sincere and romantic anguish of many Bolsheviks, especially the youth, up until 1941. Even the liberal Soviet intellectuals of the 1960s took seriously the concepts of "the international Communist movement" and "the interests of world socialism." In his famous memorandum to the leadership, Andrei Sakharov substantiated his liberal program by suggesting that it would help the "international Communist movement" (Sakharov 1970).

Second, the leaders used the idea for sustaining optimism and encouraging productivity in the country. Between the October Revolution and the end of the war with Germany, the regime was volatile and quite insecure. The party rank and file and many party apparatchiks saw enormous obstacles on the road to socialism in Russia. World Revolution was regarded by party members as an enlightened goal, and it helped them perform the difficult tasks of industrialization and collectivization.[35] Proletarian movements in other areas of the world, especially in advanced countries, warmed the hearts and boosted the confidence of ordinary party members and the new socialist intelligentsia. In the most difficult years of the regime (from 1918–1919 until the 1930s), the Bolsheviks tried to encourage the masses with public speeches about the imminent revolutions abroad. They spoke of the "close victory of the proletariat," the spread of "Soviet power" across the globe, the growing prestige of Bolshevism, and the prominence of the Third International.[36] These harangues about the WR proved to be an effective stimulant for optimism in the country.

In the late 1920s, in spite of his sharp critique of the Trotskyist theory of permanent revolution and his focus on "building socialism in one country," Stalin continued to speak about "the coming revolutionary events" (Stalin 1946–1951, Vol. 10, pp. 215–216). Stalin presented the USSR as the center of the World Revolutionary camp in 1927 (Stalin 1946–1951, Vol. 10, p. 135). He said, "The victory of the proletarian revolution in one country is a means and prop for the development and victory of revolution in all countries" (Stalin 1946–1951, Vol. 9, p. 28; Vol. 8, p. 92; Vol. 10, p. 135). In 1929 the Central Committee described Stalin as the leader of the World Revolution (*Pravda*, December 21, 1929).

With the intensification of the fascist threat to the USSR, the belief in eventual support from the international working class bolstered the Soviet people's optimism.[37] When the USSR supported Republican Spain in the Spanish civil war in 1936–1939, the Soviet public perceived Spain as its ally against Germany and Italy (in reality, the Soviet participation in the Spanish war was dictated mostly by geopolitical considerations).[38] The medicine of World Revolution was so strong that despite the evident indifference of the working class in foreign countries, many Soviets, in the weeks after June 22, 1941, expected that the German proletariat would rise to defend the USSR against the Nazi invasion (the Nazis were a capitalist force, in the eyes of Soviet people).[39]

Third, the leadership liked the idea of the WR for purely personal (psychological) reasons. To some degree, especially in the early years, it alleviated their inferiority complex with respect to the ruling elite in the West (V. Shlapentokh 1998c). They saw themselves as champions of the revolutionary world, men with godlike powers, who could redirect the course of history. They were the leaders of the Third International, which was regarded, in the beginning, as a serious organization. The Soviet leaders believed that their international influence surpassed that of the Russian emperors of the past, even at the peak of their power. Indeed, when Moscow aided the revolutions in Hungary and Bavaria, it did so in the belief that the Kremlin one day would assume control over that area of the world.

World Revolution and Internationalism As Instruments of "Hard" Geopolitics

The idea of the WR (in all its different forms) was not only important for the success of domestic policies, but for Russian geopolitics as well. By presenting the USSR as the leading defender of socialism and the first and greatest socialist country in the world, the Kremlin justified its aggressive foreign policy and intervention in the internal affairs of foreign countries.[40]

During the civil war the idea emerged that the Red Army, and not the rebellious proletariat, would play a major role in the installation of socialist order in foreign countries. At the First Congress of the Third International in March 1919, several delegates, such as the German Communist Max Albert, asked Moscow to "ignite" the revolutionary fire in their country, using the Red Army (see Rotter 1954; Nollau 1961; Telitsyn 1999). During the Polish-Soviet war in 1920, the hopes for creating a Polish Soviet republic (as well as the extension of Sovietization to the West) rested mostly with the Red Army, which would instigate proletarian insurrection in Poland.[41] Many years before the Soviet invasion of Poland and Romania (1939–1940), Bukharin said at the 4th Congress of the Third International in 1922, "Red intervention is justified when it makes the implementation of socialism easier" (Bukharin 1924, p. 65).[42]

In Stalin's time, the idea of the Red Army as the engine of WR became a leading concept in the official ideology.[43] Before WWII, when Stalin talked about the expansion of socialism in the world, he was not referring to the Marxist dream of revolution but to the victory of the Red Army over the adversaries of the Soviet Union.[44] More and more Soviet citizens, particularly young people, supposed that a socialist victory (with the help of the Red Army) in any country meant the incorporation of this country into the Soviet Union, the first socialist regime.[45] At the beginning of WWII, and particularly at the war's end, Stalin advanced the new socialist regimes in Eastern Europe by using the crude intervention of the Soviet army and the KGB.

The concept of internationalism and class solidarity as the basis for aggressive foreign policy was fully utilized in 1939 when the USSR invaded West Ukraine and West Belorussia. The following year, the leaders used internationalism to justify the "liberation" of North Bukovina and Bessarabia. The annexation of these territories was presented as "a march for the liberation of our brothers and sisters (Ukrainians, Belorussians and Moldovans) who suffered under the yoke of Polish and Romanian landlords." Stalin wanted to use the same ideological legitimization for the Sovietization of Finland when he declared war against this country in 1939, hoping to conquer it in a brief period of time. Finland's strong resistance defeated Stalin's plan, and Otto Kuusinen's "socialist government" in the country quietly dissolved. However, in 1939–1940, during his secret negotiations with Hitler regarding the division of the world, Stalin could not and did not use revolutionary phraseology (see Sontag and Beddie 1948; see also Reshin and Naumov 1998). Under the aegis of the WR, the army "Sovietized" many countries of

Eastern Europe after WWII.[46] Stalin's heirs used a diluted version of the WR (in the form of "class solidarity") to justify their many aggressive foreign actions, from the invasion of Hungary in 1956 to the invasion of Afghanistan in 1979.

The WR and related concepts also were actively employed by the Kremlin for recruiting allies in its confrontation with the United States during the cold war. Stalin and his heirs were eager to support Communist takeovers in any part of the world as long as local Communists imitated the Soviet totalitarian system and the style of life of their masters in Moscow.[47] After 1953, Soviet leaders continued to use internationalist phraseology for their geopolitical games in the Third World. They encouraged politicians in several different countries (Cuba, Tanzania, Egypt, Congo and others) to proclaim their regimes socialist and look for support from Moscow.[48] Soviet interventions in the internal development of numerous countries were always camouflaged by slogans about "the defense of socialism" and "international aid."[49]

Many Western politicians and scholars took the leaders' words at face value. George Breslauer said that "Soviet sectarian (revolutionary) activism" was the impetus for Soviet foreign policy in Africa during the 1970s and 1980s (Breslauer 1992, pp. 202–209). John Gaddis wrote about the intentions of the aged Soviet leaders in supporting regimes like that in Cuba, saying they did so because, as "old revolutionaries," they wanted to "rediscover their roots" and convince themselves that the purposes which they had sacrificed so much for, had not been overwhelmed by "the compromises they had to make in actually wielding power."[50] Not only Western experts but also many Soviet apparatchiks, up until the end of the USSR, took the Kremlin's official declarations about its intentions in foreign policy at face value.[51]

The WR in "Soft" Geopolitics

The Soviet leaders also used the ideology of the WR and international class solidarity as a cover for their "soft" geopolitical intrigues. These concepts helped the leaders develop spy rings, undermine nonfriendly governments, and influence public opinion abroad. The Bolsheviks also used the Communist movements in other countries to further these purposes. The first evidence of the Kremlin's use of internationalism in foreign policy was the establishment of the Third International.[52] Throughout its existence, the Kremlin treated this organization as an instrument of foreign policy. In May 1919, Lenin made a rather typical statement when he suggested, "The Third International community of workers began to overlap, to some degree, with the Union of the Soviet Socialist Republics" (Lenin 1960–1965, Vol. 38, p. 303; see also Hosking 1992, p. 6; Bullock 1991, p. 128).[53] This organization became a greenhouse for Soviet agents and propagandists of Soviet foreign policy.[54] It was also a school for Communists who would later become the leaders of the new Communist states (i.e., Mátyás Rákosi in Hungary, Josip Broz Tito in Yugoslavia, Wladyslaw Gomulka in Poland, Klement Gottwald in Czechoslovakia, Walter Ulbricht in East Germany, and Ho Chi Minh in Vietnam). The Third International continued to rant about the WR until its dissolution in 1943. During its existence, all the Communist parties in the world were financed by Moscow, including the Italian Communist Party, which pretended to be in opposition to the Kremlin since the late 1960s (Lisov 1992).[55] Moscow trained party activists in special colleges (the most important was Lenin's school at the Central Committee) and regularly invited the leaders of the parties to the USSR for luxurious vacations, access to superior hospital facilities and medicine, as well as many other perks.[56] Without exception, the parties obediently performed various tasks assigned by Moscow: from direct spying to influencing leading politicians.[57] The comportment of the Communist parties following Stalin's endorsement of the pact with Hitler in August of 1939 was a remarkable example of how compliant the parties were to Moscow's command. All the parties, including the large French Communist Party, instantly changed their attitudes toward Nazi Germany and reversed their anti-war propaganda, redirecting it against Hitler's adversaries.[58]

The leadership was always seriously concerned about maintaining control of the Communist parties in other countries. For instance, in the late 1920s and early 1930s, Stalin and Bukharin refused to join the European socialist parties in their struggle against the growing danger of Nazi Germany, not because they were worried about the purity of revolutionary Marxism but because they feared losing control of the Third International (see *Stenograficheskii otchet VI kongressa Kominterna*, Vol. 3, 1929, pp. 29, 46; see also Zhuravlev 1990, pp. 187–190, 210–211).

The leadership's "soft" geopolitical maneuvers bolstered the prestige of the WR and all of its conceptual outgrowths, which in turn made it easier to recruit spies and "agents of influence" from Western countries (Courtois 1997). The "great cause" of WR gave Soviet agents ideological justification for their actions. The ideas of the WR also influenced many intellectuals, politicians with left leanings, and the general public around the world. The WR was indeed an effective instrument of international propaganda up until 1956. In every Western country—particularly France, England and the United States—there were large groups of prominent intellectuals (in the 1920s–1940s) who passionately propagated the idea of socialism as the next stage in the history of mankind (Hollander 1998; Draper 1957, 1960). Pursuing their old theses about the WR was the only way for the Soviet leaders to ensure the loyalty of Western intellectuals, who could be used as weapons against their enemies. The propagation of these ideas was particularly successful in Third World countries, inspiring revolutionary movements in Latin America, Asia and Africa.

Geopolitics and the Conflicts Between Socialist Countries

After WWII, socialist regimes emerged in several countries (some with the help of the Soviet army, and some on their own accord) with the success of national Communist parties and various liberation movements. In some ways, the first three decades following WWII were reminiscent of the first years after WWI. It looked as though the dreams of the October Revolution had finally materialized, after a 30-year delay. These were times of true revolutionary transformation in the world. However, history did not unfold according to the scenario imagined by Bolshevik leaders in 1917–1918. First of all, it became apparent to the leaders (including Stalin) that Marxist socialism, as they understood it, had no real future in socially and economically developed countries.[59] Socialism, it seemed to them, could only be victorious with the fuel of nationalism and the emblazoned struggle against colonialism.

The most significant discovery of the leaders was that Communists in other countries who had ascended to power without the help of the Soviet military could defy Moscow and conduct their own domestic and international policy. In 1948, Josip Broz Tito's Yugoslavia was the first regime with socialist credentials to defy the high command of the Soviet leaders, in this case Stalin. Relying on the West in his confrontation with Stalin, Tito challenged the Soviet geopolitical strategy in the Balkans and undermined Stalin's authority in the world. Disregarding all the ideological clichés about socialist solidarity, an outraged Stalin cursed Tito, calling him a Communist heretic and declaring a "cold war" on his country. Stalin tried every available means to eliminate the old Communist Tito and undermine his country through political and economic maneuvers. The conflict with Yugoslavia was the harbinger of a new era. In the next decades, the USSR would become embroiled in confrontations of various kinds with other socialist countries.

After Stalin's death in the late 1950s, Moscow locked horns with Mao's China, a country whose leaders claimed to be more Orthodox Marxist and internationalist than Khrushchev himself.[60] Each side denounced the other as apostates and ignored the issue of "class solidarity" completely. The Soviet and Chinese leaders clearly drew the lines of a serious geopolitical conflict, which came close to all-out war in the late 1960s. The Soviet-Chinese conflict lasted until the mid-1980s, by which time the mythology of the WR and related concepts had been totally destroyed. The prevalence of geopolitical interests was played out explicitly between these two Communist giants with their common border of roughly 5,000 miles.[61]

Conclusion

The rapid adjustment of the WR to the needs of the totalitarian state demonstrated one of the major strengths of the Soviet leadership. They bolstered their foreign and domestic policies with the valuable propagandistic resources embedded in this concept. The WR helped the leaders control the Soviet masses as well as millions of sympathetic people in foreign countries. A host of Soviet experts outside the country were duped by the Kremlin's so-called devotion to the international Communist community. While the concept itself changed in the minds of the leadership over time, the WR was seen first as the means for modernization and later as fodder for the country's geopolitical interests.

5

Open and Closed Ideologies

As the Bolshevik leaders transformed their views on many critical issues, they soon began operating with "two truths," one for the masses and one for the elite. Before the revolution, Lenin and other leaders of the party rarely lied or distorted basic facts in their public works. Although they concealed some elements of their party life—in particular, their financial resources—their pre-revolutionary writings and speeches genuinely reflected their vision of the world and their true intentions. After the revolution, Lenin and his comrades-in-arms began prevaricating and misrepresenting "reality" in almost all of their publications and speeches.

Basic Differences

The Soviet leaders based their decisions on a realistic vision of the world, while advancing an illusory world, grounded in propaganda, for controlling the masses. In this way, they developed a complex and sophisticated ideological mechanism with two components: the open (or public) ideology and closed (or private) ideology. The former dispersed information to the general public, while the latter was meant solely for the party elite and the nomenklatura.

This incongruity between the open and closed ideologies should not be considered a purely Soviet phenomenon. The same type of divergence can be found in any society, including the United States. The USSR, however, represented an extreme example because the gap between the two ideologies was so immense.

The open and closed ideologies looked similar only on the surface. While sharing some of the same elements, the ideologies differed greatly in the importance each ascribed to the given component. Some aspects of the two ideologies were completely different. The open ideology contained purely mythological values, such as the leading role of the working class, internationalism, and social and national equality, as well as pragmatic elements that overlapped with the closed ideology, such as patriotism, a high respect for the modernization of Russia (including industrialization and the development of education and science) and economic and technological progress, and a strong belief in central planning and state property as the basis for the economy. Some Soviet constructions of the external world—for instance, the superiority of its standard of living and the claim that collectivization was eagerly supported by most peasants—were complete fabrications. In the 1960s–1980s, however, the ideology allowed a more realistic depiction of life in the media, movies, novels and other forms of art and entertainment.

The closed ideology emphasized Russian national interests and was more pragmatic than the open ideology. The most important elements of the closed ideology included: the advancement of geopolitical interests in foreign policy, the high priority of defense expenditures, the low priority of the population's standard of living, the dominance of ethnic Russians in all key positions in the country, anti-Semitism (which emerged at the end of the 1930s), the prevalence of the KGB in social life, mistrust for the masses and the party rank and file, material benefits as a motivation for the nomenklatura and for high-level officers in the KGB and army, contempt for democratic procedures in any area of life, a complete monopoly on information, and party control over every institution in society.

The complexity of Soviet ideology confused many foreign experts, who were ignorant of the division between the open and closed ideologies and who supposed that the open ideology determined the behavior of the ruling elite. They evaluated the USSR on the basis of the images of socialism advanced by Soviet propaganda. They accused the Communists of failing to implant Marxist ideals. Coming from an anti-Communist, such an appraisal was like an atheist assessing human behavior by the standards of the Catholic Church.[1] The difference between the open and closed ideologies not only confused foreign experts who took the language used by the party apparatchiks at face value (Leites and Breslauer 1985; Blacker 1982; Mitchell 1982), but also confounded more experienced Russian insiders and sophisticated political dissidents such as Vladimir Bukovsky.[2]

Lies As an Essential Element of the Open Ideology

Distortion and repression of objective information as well as outright lies were vital to public propaganda. Flagrant lies were published in school textbooks, novels, plays and movies. Propaganda addressed to the public (both inside and outside the USSR) embellished data, particularly with respect to the standard of living and the quality of Soviet goods and services (Birman 1983, 1989). The magnitude of military expenditures was covered up, or fabricated (Birman 1991).

Lies were important not only for the purposes of propaganda but for the day-to-day lives of the Soviet elite. One's work performance in the various spheres of the economy was assessed on the basis of statistical reports which were regularly distorted. As a "normal" element of life, subordinates lied to their superiors. Prevarications often took on a compounding effect, because officials at any given level covered up the lies and deceptions of their subordinates so as to protect themselves from their superiors.

Another powerful stimulus for the distortion of information was the leadership's desire to obtain data that substantiated its power. This factor blurred the borders between the open and closed ideologies as well as between lies for the masses and "truth" for "the inner circle."[3] Soviet leaders were clearly predisposed to some self-deception with respect to the economy and the standard of living (this was especially true in the last years of the regime).

Stalin introduced a special methodology for measuring the production of grain on the basis of the "biological harvest." This was a highly subjective estimate that indicated the prospects of grain production before the harvest began and allowed the elite to ignore the gigantic losses. Khrushchev also is known to have elicited false reports on agricultural production. The absence of market assessments of performance and the falsification of statistics were rampant in open publications and quite pronounced even in the closed bulletins written by the central statistical board for the members of the highest political conclaves.[4]

In spite of the defects and falsifications of statistics and other forms of information, there are no grounds for claiming that the leadership did not have reasonable views about the economy. In fact, the leaders often questioned some data and looked for alternate sources of information (see Churbanov 1992, p. 76; Fetisov 1997, pp. 231–232; Vadim Medvedev 1998, pp. 94–97; Eidelman 1998, pp. 70–73). As a rule, the KGB and army intelligence played an important role, as reliable sources of information.

Differences in Propagating the Two Ideologies

In general, the leaders conveyed the two ideologies through different channels. The open ideology thrived in the mass media, school textbooks, movies, theater, poems, novels, paintings, scholarly articles, monographs, and all media materials addressed to the West. The leaders restricted the exposition of the closed ideology first of all to secret documents and memos, the minutes of closed meetings, and correspondence between members of the elite. The leaders conveyed the closed ideology to the various segments of the nomenklatura through a special system of party education (the information machine).

In some cases, closed ideological messages appeared in documents open to the public. For instance, the closed ideology was infused in scientific and party journals, or even heavily encoded in popular Russian newspapers such as *Pravda*.[5] The open speeches of the Soviet leaders also contained elements of the closed ideology. With this intermingling of the open and closed ideologies, many texts could be read on two levels. The closed messages were often encoded in open materials with an alternative lexicon that could be understood only by the party apparatus.[6] An average Soviet citizen and a party apparatchik could read the same article and take two entirely different messages from it. This multilayered style of communication allowed party apparatchiks to correspond with the masses and other members of the party elite simultaneously. Apparatchiks who could not understand the significant distinction between the two ideologies and obtusely accepted the official propagandistic dogmas at face value had no chance of keeping their position.

The texts of internal party documents and closed meetings as well as the memoirs of Soviet leaders (for instance, Khrushchev[7] or Anastas Mikoyan[8]) were jammed with such terms as "class struggle," "class enemies," "international duties," and "social equality." However, the party apparatchiks operated with very different definitions for these words. In the closed ideology, "class enemies" or "counterrevolutionaries" referred to those forces which undermined the Soviet state (not the enemies of the international socialist struggle). The term "internationalism" suggested Moscow's need to maintain control of the Soviet satellites. In the domestic context, this term often referred to the necessity of protecting the dominant role of the Russians in the national republics. Some messages of the closed ideology were passed to party officials only through oral communication. For instance, in the late 1930s, anti-Semitism became an essential part of the closed ideology, yet no documents describing the anti-Semitic views of the party leadership have been recovered. The open ideology alternately denounced or kept quiet about anti-Semitism.

The Cult of Secrecy and Special Channels of Information

With the creation of two ideologies (open and closed), it was necessary for the Soviet leaders to introduce the cult of secrecy. Created by Lenin in the early days of the regime, the cult of secrecy, with its hierarchy of secrets, developed in the early 1920s, and persisted until the end of the Soviet system (see Pavlova 1993, pp. 66–96).[9] At its peak, in the early 1950s, the most trivial data were declared classified.[10] From the middle of the 1930s until 1956, Moscow stopped publishing even small statistical yearbooks. While countries such as Britain and the United States cultivated secrecy in bureaucratic structures, no country in the world could compete with the level of secrecy in the Soviet state machine.[11]

Throughout its history, the regime spent tremendous resources on the management of secrecy. For each unit of society—that is, for each factory, office and college—there was a special department (*spetsotdel*) that protected state and party secrets and collected politically sensitive information about students and employees. This department was also responsible for issuing clearances to employees whose work required confidential materials.

Censorship played an important role in the cult of secrecy. An army of censors (employees of Glavlit) carefully read each printed word in every type of publication, ranging from local newspapers in remote villages, to the party publishing houses in Moscow. The same cult of secrecy deemed many offices and factories off-limits to ordinary people. Visitors needed special permission for entry.

The cult of secrecy helped diminish the spread of important military and technological information to foreign adversaries. For this reason, American spies in the USSR faced a much more dangerous environment than their Soviet counterparts in the United States. However, this was not the primary purpose of the cult of secrecy. Its most important objective was to prevent the people from learning about the real state of affairs in the country, particularly about the cruel actions of the authorities.

Indeed, until 1989–1990, most of the world, including the Soviet people themselves, remained ignorant of fundamental facts of life in the USSR. Until this time, the Russians did not have a clear understanding of the mass purges or of the number of victims of collectivization and of mass starvation. They knew little about the privileges of the elite, and were mostly unaware of any resistance to the system (for example, the Novocherkassk riot in 1962, or the Karaganda riot in the same year). The leaders concealed natural disasters such as the Ashkhabad earthquake in 1948, as well as technological accidents such as the radioactive contamination of Cheliabinsk in the 1950s and the anthrax epidemic in Sverdlovsk in 1979. Even during Gorbachev's regime, the Kremlin tried to hide information about the Chernobyl nuclear catastrophe as long as possible (see Yaroshinskaia 1994). The people had no comprehension of the ecological situation in the country. For instance, they were unaware of the appalling ecological state of the Baikal and Aral lakes.[12]

The cult of secrecy also helped maintain the atmosphere of fear in the country. It fomented mutual suspicions among the people, especially at the highest levels of the party and state hierarchy. Access to classified documents was one of the most significant indicators of one's status in society. Any citizen would be quite happy to receive a clearance form for visiting a capitalist country, for such clearance was an indication of their perceived loyalty to the regime. Access to privileged information tended to increase one's fear of the KGB: Many thousands of people had been imprisoned on allegations that they had divulged state secrets, and their imprisonment helped spread fear across the country.

The cult of secrecy developed a complex system for classifying information on a dozen different levels, many of which were absolutely inaccessible to the public. Classified information originated with a wide variety of sources, including party committees, the political police, and the intelligence services of the KGB and the army. Complaint letters from citizens to state institutions also constituted highly classified information.[13]

In designing methods for collecting demographic and economic information, the Soviet leaders were always concerned about the risk that their compiled data and intelligence would fall into the hands of their enemies. In many cases, they decided to sacrifice the benefits of collecting the information in order to minimize that danger. The leaders' attitudes toward empirical sociology were dictated by the desire to obtain information for "us" but not for "them." With the USSR's growing economic problems and evident failure to provide the happy Soviet life, until the mid-1960s the leadership prohibited empirical sociology. This was a rational decision based on a comparison of the benefits of the information and the risks of its disclosure (V. Shlapentokh 1987).

Having no special scientific knowledge about the validity of data (with the exception of Lenin, a great connoisseur of statistics), the leaders nonetheless had an intuitive understanding of the difference between "typical" information and irregular data on any given issue. To protect the regime's public image, they would allow the media to publish some disparaging data, but never permitted negative reports that characterized problems as typical or widespread. They clearly understood that the positive spin of propaganda did not reflect the real situation in the country.[14]

Covert Propaganda

As previously explained, the closed ideology was addressed strictly to the various levels of the nomenklatura. However, in some cases the leaders conveyed elements of the closed ideology to the party rank and file and even to the non-party masses. This situation usually occurred when the leadership could benefit from expressing its true intentions without jeopardizing the public ideology. Covert propaganda acted as a sort of bridge between the open and closed ideologies. This form of propaganda was generally disclosed through lectures and other forms of oral communication with the masses. An example of covert propaganda came in 1964 when Brezhnev unseated Khrushchev. In order to avoid damaging the party's reputation, as some leaders had in the past,[15] party officials limited their disparaging remarks about Khrushchev to indirect, oral propaganda.

Covert propaganda was also used for the dissemination of the leadership's views on the international arena. For instance, in the 1960s and 1970s, it became necessary to inform the population about the Soviet-Chinese conflicts. In the 1980s, it was important for the Kremlin to tell the people that Soviet involvement in Afghanistan was dictated not so much by the necessity of aiding "Afghani revolutionaries" in their battle against internal "class enemies" as by the USSR's geopolitical and national interests (V. Shlapentokh 1986, pp. 99–112). Covert propaganda also was used to some degree for spreading the leadership's anti-Semitic views. This was the case in the 1940s, under Stalin (particularly during the notorious anti-cosmopolitan campaign in the late 1940s and early 1950s), as well as in the late 1970s.

Changes in the Open and Closed Ideologies

While always maintaining continuity with the previous official ideology, each new regime created its own versions of the open and closed ideologies. This fact alone stands as a major contradiction to those who view the character of the Soviet leaders as uniformly dogmatic or utopian. With a comparison of the ideologies of Khrushchev, Brezhnev, Andropov, and Gorbachev, it becomes clear that each leader's ideology imposed different values and images. There were differences in the political sphere: dynamism versus stability, mass terror versus mild repressions, rotation of cadres versus life tenure, political loyalty versus competence, Russian chauvinism versus imperial impartiality, absolute control over regional leaders versus some regional autonomy. The Soviet leaders maintained dissimilar focuses in foreign affairs: aggressiveness versus accommodation with the West, harsh control over state satellites versus the concession of some autonomy. The same was true for the economic sphere: centralization versus decentralization in management, material incentives versus moral pressure and fear. rejection of all private economic activity versus the acceptance of some forms of small private business, and relative egalitarianism versus significant social inequality. A comparison between the Stalin and post-Stalin periods also shows differences in culture and morals: harassment versus cooperation with intellectuals, exclusion of religion versus some tolerance toward the church and religious people, the complete ban on criticism of Soviet life versus permission to forward some mild critiques on nonessential developments in society.

With the state's tight control of the mass media, a new closed ideology usually emerged only with the establishment of a new regime. When the closed ideology changed, the open ideology followed suit.[16] However, as a rule, the open ideology was less flexible. For propagandistic reasons, ideological changes were less visible to the public.

In the post-Stalin era, when the leaders decided to loosen some restrictions, they introduced changes in the open ideology. For instance, they adopted universal values such altruism, kindness, tolerance, prestige, and self-actualization, which previously had been considered bourgeois, abstract, and hostile to the revolutionary cause. While the leaders added some values to their ideological repertoire, they downgraded others. As explained in Chapter 4, the significance of the World Revolution as an element of propaganda declined in the 1930s. Soviet ideologists also modified the "leading role of the working class." This value nearly disappeared in the early 1960s, being replaced by the concept of the "all-people state." Then, in the late 1960s, the Kremlin started a campaign against intellectuals and restored "the leading role of the working class"; by the late 1970s, however, the leaders dropped it once again in favor of "social homogeneity" (Brezhnev 1972, 1981).

The relative flexibility of the open ideology allowed public values to change very quickly whenever necessary. In a two- or three-year period, a value might change from negative to positive in the open ideology. This occurred during the NEP, when many values related to commercial activity were at least partially rehabilitated. The same was true for the leaders' attitudes toward private agricultural plots in the mid-1970s. The Kremlin decided to change its policy and allow peasants to expand their private plots. In the closed ideology, this was a definitive policy adjustment, though it played out quite mildly in public propaganda. The expansion of private plots was not publicly praised. Rather, the leadership merely stopped attacking private agriculture as an element of the market economy and a menace to the Soviet system.

The Efficacy of the Open Ideology

Soviet and Western intellectuals mocked the open ideology (as it was reflected in the mass media, literature, arts, and the social sciences), deeming it insipid and ultimately ineffective. The author shares this view to some extent, but generally speaking, this assumption was incorrect (V. Shlapentokh 1986). The leadership successfully created and maintained a relatively effective open ideology. As will be shown later, even on the eve of the Communist collapse (despite the evident erosion of the open ideology in the last two decades of its existence), most Russians shared such values as patriotism, the superiority of an economy based on public property and central planning, and the preeminence of Soviet culture and morals. The Kremlin also effectively controlled the people's images of the external world. The official constructions about the Western world (such as its low standard of living and intensive class struggle) were deeply internalized by most Soviets.[17]

What is more, the number of Russians who "supported the system" in 1985 was much greater than in the first two decades of the regime. Conversely, the number of opponents to the system between 1917 and 1937 was higher than the number of liberal critics of the system in the early 1980s. By 1985, the masses supported most postulates of the official ideology and domestic and foreign policy. This issue will be discussed in detail later.

The great success of the open ideology came as a direct result of the leaders' strong emphasis on ideological work. They devoted the lion's share of human and material resources to this purpose. The Soviet leaders created and ran one of the most efficient ideological apparatuses in history. The most active part of the population, some 20 million people in 1985, were involved in ideological work. By the end of the 1970s, 480 million copies of newspapers and magazines containing official propaganda were being produced each day.

Conclusion

The Soviet elite operated with a very sophisticated ideological machine that separated the "closed" goals of the USSR from the tenets of the "open" ideology. The open ideology was directed toward the masses and focused on socialist ideas, while the closed ideology served the interests of the totalitarian state, particularly its geopolitical concerns. This fundamental circumstance allowed the leadership to conduct their propaganda quite successfully almost until the end of the Soviet system while pursuing their realpolitik, which had little in common with socialist ideals.

6

Policy Toward Key Social Groups
Workers and Creative Intelligentsia

From the beginning of Soviet rule, the leaders elaborated a sophisticated social policy toward the major groups of the population, combining propagandistic dogmas with pragmatic decision making. Besides the nomenklatura, the two most important groups of the population were the workers and the creative intelligentsia. Although the workers helped legitimize the regime, the leaders regarded them as the most dangerous segment of the population. Likewise, the members of the creative intelligentsia were necessary for the country's technological and scientific advancement and the maintenance of the propaganda machine; but at the same time, they were a potential oppositional force.

Special Support for Workers

Though the Soviet leaders never took the idea of "proletarian dictatorship" seriously after 1917, throughout the history of the regime, they paid special attention to the workers' influence on the existing political order in the country.[1] There were many reasons for their sapient interest in the workers. First, the leaders genuinely accepted the fundamental Marxist thesis about the decisive role of the proletariat as the "gravediggers" of the old society, the "storm troopers" against the ancien régime. During the revolution, the Bolsheviks tried to harness the hostility of the workers as well as poor peasants and disadvantaged ethnic minorities against the tsarist authorities. In the Bolshevik mind, the workers represented the foremost social basis for the fight against monarchy. In the first decade after the revolution (particularly in the first few years), the workers inspired confidence as sincere supporters of Soviet power and quelled suspicions about their possible secret collusion with the opposition. During the civil war, the Kremlin relied on workers, in particular workers from Petrograd, as their trusted vanguard in the army and the administration. Until the mid-1930s, if a conflict arose between a worker and a person with a non-proletarian background, the authorities uncompromisingly sided with the worker. As Alexander Solzhenitsyn wrote, "The workers are always right" (1973).

Supporting the workers served the long-term interests of the Bolsheviks as well. Refusing to see themselves as the usurpers of power, Bolsheviks used the workers as the legitimization of their authority.[2] By describing the Soviet Union as a proletarian state and presenting themselves as the "servants" of the working class, the leaders avoided the brutal reality of their own rule, and vindicated their power to the outside world and perhaps even to themselves.

Russian Communists were also influenced to some degree by Marxist economic theory, which suggested that the workers (along with rural proletarians) were the single creators of value (i.e., the gross national product).[3] The ruling elite saw the workers as an essential source of labor for the economy, and first of all for the military industry.

Besides being important as a source of labor, the workers as an institution were crucial for monitoring the mood of the people. The leadership supported the public's condemnation of those who did not work ("spongers") for two reasons: it encouraged production, and it discouraged activity outside the formal workplace, where monitoring the individual was more difficult.

Each Soviet leader adjusted his policies toward workers in accordance with the historical context.[4] For instance, with the strengthening of the Soviet regime after the civil war, the importance of workers as the main social basis for the leadership decreased notably.[5] Until the mid-1930s, however, the leadership continued to back the workers by blocking "non-proletarian elements"[6] from entering the party and expelling those who had falsely claimed proletarian origin. In order to maintain "the proletarian character" of the party in 1924, in the aftermath of Lenin's death, about 200,000 "genuine workers" (workers dealing with machine tools) were admitted to the party (the initial plan supposed only 100,000). This influx of workers comprised nearly half the party membership at the beginning of 1924.

In the 1920s–1930s, the Bolshevik leaders continued to regard workers as much more loyal than the members of the old intelligentsia, who were infected with bourgeois liberalism, or the peasants, who were corrupted by their yearnings for private property, not to speak of the members of the old dominant classes (i.e., landlords and capitalists as well as the bureaucracy and clergy). The Kremlin's favoritism of workers persisted until 1989. Indicatively, the relative number of workers among political prisoners in the Gulag was considerably lower than that of peasants and the intelligentsia.

In the 1920s, the leadership started training a new intelligentsia, mostly the children of working-class families and poor peasants, in the hope that it (unlike the old intelligentsia) would devote itself to the Soviet regime. This policy was only temporarily successful, in the 1930s and 1940s. Later, the leadership found the new intelligentsia with its worker-peasant background as critical of the regime as the old intelligentsia had been. Nonetheless, the same strategy of recruiting workers into the intelligentsia reemerged in the late 1960s and 1970s.

Following an evident decline in 1953, due in part to Khrushchev's flirtation with the idea of the "all-people state" (a concept that temporarily rescinded the official ideological status of the working class as the leading segment of society), in 1968 support for workers reappeared in propaganda when Brezhnev's leadership began its campaign against the liberal intelligentsia. The Kremlin lauded workers, and tried to turn them against the educated class.[7] The leaders during this period exploited workers' deeply rooted animosity toward the intelligentsia.[8]

Fear of Workers

While the leaders saw the working class as the best social basis and legitimization of their power, they also considered it the most volatile segment of the population. The political elite feared the workers more than any other group in society. The working class was a concentrated urban force that was prone to mass actions. The leaders never neglected the tumultuous events of the past, namely, the strikes and workers' demonstrations during the civil war (in particular, the strikes in Petrograd in March 1919, and in February and March 1921, and the strike of Moscow railway workers in the summer of 1918) and the NEP in 1925–1930.[9]

Stalin was less fearful of the working class. None of his successors treated workers with the rigidity and severity he did in the 1930s. For instance, he jailed workers for missing more than three days of work in a month and harshly penalized them for being late. Stalin also prohibited workers from changing jobs. The Soviet leaders after 1953, who ruled less repressive regimes, were more concerned about workers' protests and mass riots than Stalin. From their perspective, any strike, regardless of its magnitude, could trigger a chain reaction and bring many people to the streets. In 1962, the workers' strikes and demonstrations in Novocherkassk and Karaganda led to a hysterical reaction in the Kremlin. The powerful workers' movement organized in the name of "Solidarity" in Poland in the late 1970s and early 1980s unnerved the leaders to such an extent that they ordered Gosplan to revise its five-year plan for 1980–1985 and increase the output of consumer goods for the population.

Specific Policies Toward Workers

The official policy of recruiting workers into the party substantially increased the workers' chances of advancing from the factory to a career as an apparatchik.[10] Workers were promoted through official bodies other than the party as well.[11] Though they were given very little influence on decision making, their appointments to governmental bodies were real, as were the prestige, perks and benefits of those positions. In this way, the system corrupted "active" workers and prevented them from emerging as leaders of workers' movements or engaging in any other form of anti-Soviet activity.

Early in its history, the regime introduced affirmative action policies for workers and later for peasants. In the 1920s and 1930s, there were special "worker colleges" that recruited workers and their children and prepared them for advanced educations at the university level. Similar policies were quite prominent in the 1960s and 1970s.

The material life of the workers was always on the minds of Soviet leaders, particularly in the 1920s–1930s, when they confiscated the extra rooms of those with relatively good housing conditions and handed them over to workers.[12] By the end of the NEP, the "white-collar" standard of living was considerably lower, while the real salary of workers had increased by 20 to 30 percent (Khanin 1989a, p. 73). In the early 1930s, when the majority of the country (mostly peasants) was suffering from famine, especially in Ukraine and the North Caucasus, workers (and other city dwellers to some degree) were given preferential food rations. During World War II, factory workers enjoyed advantages in the supply of consumer goods over the mass intelligentsia, peasants and clerical staff workers. After the war, the major industrial centers, which contained high concentrations of factory workers, such as Sverdlovsk or Cheliabinsk, were supplied with better consumer goods than cities with lower levels of industry and fewer workers. Driven by their concern for the material life of the working class, the leadership also developed a social policy that made it almost impossible to fire a worker, evict a worker from his or her apartment, or delay his or her salary for even a few days.[13]

In any case, in 1985 the average monthly salary for an industrial worker (208 rubles) was 44 percent higher than the average salary of people working in culture, 37 percent higher than that of medical personnel, and 28 percent higher than that of teachers and employees in the retail and wholesale trade. The average monthly salary in some industrial sectors was even higher than that of scholars with doctorates. Miners and oil workers earned around 318 rubles per month, compared to an associate professor's salary of about 200–250 rubles (Goskomstat 1988, pp. 390–391).

While the workers' needs often took priority over the needs of the mass intelligentsia and the peasants, the leaders wanted to authenticate the USSR as a paternalistic state in the eyes of the masses as a whole. This could only be achieved by taking measures to satisfy the basic needs of the people, regardless of their group affiliation. The establishment of the paternalistic state was to some degree successful. No less than two thirds of the population looked to "the collective," or to some type of state organization in the case of an emergency. Millions of complaint letters poured into the various institutions of the Soviet Union, and millions of people visited state and party officials to voice their problems in person. People thought, and rightfully so, that their concerns would be heard and something would be done to alleviate their troubles. Sixty to 80 percent of the Soviet people believed that their contacts with the authorities and the media were an effective way to solve their problems.[14] To the leadership, this was a favorable system; it not only made the people completely dependent on the state but created a feeling of "belonging" in society.[15]

The life of the working class, particularly of low-skilled workers, as well as of the rest of the Soviet population, was quite dreary by Western standards. Millions of workers were prone to drunkenness and criminal activities. This is especially true in small industrial cities and in Siberia and the Far East, where the number of residents who spent time in prison reached 30–50 percent among male workers. The working conditions in most factories, which had a low level of mechanization, were abysmal. Many studies showed that around 80 percent of the Soviet people ranked "working conditions" as the number one priority in choosing a job (see Lobanov and Cherkasov 1981). Despite the attempts of the Soviet system to encourage the workers, most people regarded factory jobs as among the worst in the country. A study conducted by Vladimir Shubkin in the 1960s asked the people to rate the different occupations on a ten-point scale. Industrial workers were given a 4.0 rating, engineers got 6.5, and scholars, 6.6. Only agricultural workers were ranked lower than industrial workers, with a rating of 2.5 (Shubkin 1970, pp. 280–286). With all the real and fictitious advantages of workers in Soviet society, most people, particularly the youth, saw the life of workers as dismal. They performed physically demanding, often dirty work in a gloomy environment that gave them very little hope of improving their lives. Workers were deprived of even a slim chance to accumulate money or own a small business. All talented children dreamed of becoming a member of the party and state apparatus, joining the ranks of the creative intelligentsia, or attaining a career as an engineer or a doctor.

The Creative Intelligentsia

Starting with Lenin, the leaders paid special attention to the creative intelligentsia (a relatively small group of the highest-level scholars, writers, poets, musicians, film directors and artists, not to be confused with the mass intelligentsia). On one hand, the leaders suspected these intellectuals of undermining the regime at each turn. For this reason, many thousands of the best minds in the country perished in the Gulag, languished in internal exile, or were expelled abroad. On the other hand, the leaders of the regime regarded loyal intellectuals as indispensable for building up the economic and military might of the empire, maintaining the public ideology, and enhancing the prestige of the USSR abroad. The leadership saw the promotion and advancement of the creative intelligentsia as a very important policy for the regime.[16]

Despite the Bolsheviks' strong sense of egalitarianism, immediately following the revolution the government began granting the creative intelligentsia special privileges and a higher standard of living than the masses. Lenin aided scholars, writers, musicians, and artists during the civil war and satisfied some of their requests for assistance. Along with party bureaucrats and the political police, the creative intelligentsia benefitted from Stalin's stratification of society in the late 1920s. Though life in the 1920s and 1930s was quite harsh and many intellectuals suffered from various deprivations,[17] for those who were accepted by the leadership, living conditions were always substantially superior when compared to those of the masses (see Grigorenko 1982; Kopelev 1975; Orlova 1982). During World War II, the creative intelligentsia received favorable treatment: many were exempt from military service, and they were usually the first to be evacuated from dangerous areas. Intellectuals were also favored in the procurement system. They received better foods and enjoyed healthier diets than the working class (Berg 1983; Grossman 1980).

After the war, Stalin felt threatened by the United States, which was the only country with nuclear capability. This led to a further improvement in the living conditions of the creative intelligentsia. In 1946, Stalin raised the salaries of scholars and professors significantly. For the next two decades, they were among the wealthiest people in the Soviet Union. While the average city-dweller's monthly income during this period was about 50 to 60 rubles, a senior fellow in an academic institute, or a full professor in a university, received 400 to 500 rubles. What is more, the creative intelligentsia was given access to special hospitals, stores, resorts and cultural events. Following Stalin's death, the favored position of the creative intelligentsia persisted. In fact, their privileges increased during the late 1950s and 1960s.[18]

The creative intelligentsia enjoyed not only material benefits but a high level of social prestige.[19] In the years immediately following the October Revolution, when the egalitarian tendencies of the Bolsheviks were more pronounced, the intellectuals' official prestige was fairly low. At one point, the term "intelligentsia" was even considered pejorative (Chalidze 1981, p. 20). Then, as the new system stabilized, its leadership increased the official status and public recognition of the creative intelligentsia.

Although materially less privileged than bureaucrats, members of the creative intelligentsia were more socially visible and received more attention from the public and the media. In the 1930s, Stalin introduced scholarly degrees and numerous measures to upgrade the status of the Academy of Sciences. He created the unions of writers, painters, and actors. During this period, the government also introduced new titles for artists and musicians. A variety of competitions were conducted in the cultural fields. The winners of these competitions were awarded the title of laureate, as well as medals, financial prizes, new apartments, and valuable musical instruments. By 1984, there were 16 national titles for figures in the arts, and 20 types of medals generously used for decorating intellectuals. The high official prestige of the creative intelligentsia explained their correspondingly high prestige among ordinary people. The first Soviet sociological surveys conducted in the early 1960s revealed that the intellectual professions held nearly first place on the list of the most prestigious positions in society.[20] This level of prestige for intellectuals is unheard of in the United States.

Social Mobility

The Soviet leaders were rarely dogmatic or utopian when developing social policy. Over the years, their policies proved remarkably flexible. They deviated from their principles whenever a variation was useful for the system. As discussed in the previous chapter, the regime survived and benefited from major shifts and adjustments in both the open and closed ideologies. Another important example of the leaders' political flexibility was their policy of social mobility. As suggested in the discussion about the workers and the creative intelligentsia, there were different motives for recruiting the various segments of the population. In some cases, the regime simply required the skills possessed by specific individuals. Showing the ability to adapt their ideological tenets to the pragmatic needs of the country, only one year after the revolution, the leadership began recruiting "bourgeois specialists" (former tsarist generals and officers and former agents of the tsarist secret police) into their state apparatus. Likewise, even during the most acerbic anti-Semitic campaign in the 1940s and 1950s, they continued to use Jews in high positions in the weapons industry.

More importantly, the leaders valued social mobility as a form of political stabilization. They provided millions of people with new career opportunities, turning the young and the poor against their previous bosses. There were three major periods of intensive social mobility: in the first years after the revolution, during the mass purges in the 1930s, and after the war. In these periods, there were many new openings in the government and economy as well as in cultural and scientific institutions. Millions of citizens, particularly youth, women, and ethnic minorities, happily greeted social mobility. Young and educated people rose rapidly in the hierarchy and enjoyed a higher social status and standard of living than in the past.[21]

The memoirs of all Soviet dissidents are inundated with their hatred of the totalitarian state, yet very few conceal their elation at having been able to develop a career in the 1920s and 1930s (see Orlova 1982; Kopelev 1975; and Ulanovskaia and Ulanovskaia 1982). The same irony was discovered by a research effort known as the Harvard Project. The project studied people who had fled the Soviet Union during World War II. The respondents acknowledged that in prewar Soviet society, they had enjoyed significant career opportunities.[22] However, in the 1970s, when social mobility declined in the USSR, dissatisfaction with life was highest among the young and well-educated.[23]

Conclusion

This chapter demonstrates the rationality and efficacy of Soviet social policy. As a result of this policy, up until 1985, the working class was quite loyal to the regime. Even during the stormy years of perestroika, when the system began to crack, only the miners joined the liberals in their attack against the system. The Kremlin was less successful in maintaining the loyalty of the creative intelligentsia. Without attacking (even privately) the fundamentals of Soviet socialism, they yearned for a liberal regime. Until 1985, however, the creative intelligentsia provided the Kremlin with brilliant scholars for the military industry and enabled the regime to sustain its propaganda inside and outside the USSR.

7
The Political System
The Supreme Leader As the Major Institution

The Soviet leader was the mainstay of the regime's power and its most crucial institution.[1] As in any totalitarian society, the leader made all the strategic decisions and coordinated all spheres of social life. Each cell of the political system recognized his absolute authority. All of the main institutions—the party, the political police, the army, the ideological apparatus, the centralized economy based on state property—were supervised by the supreme leader. Strategic decisions and appointments were simply not made without his personal endorsement. Reflecting the magnitude of the leader's power, each period in Soviet history is assigned the name of one of the masters of the Kremlin.

Positing the monopoly of power in the hands of the general secretary in no way implies that he enjoyed absolute efficiency when exercising this power. In spite of his authority, he was unable to implement many of his own specified plans and tasks. Those who advocated the totalitarian model of Soviet society understood that inefficiency loomed decisively over many sectors of the country, particularly the economy. Elements of disorganization were, in fact, "normal" aspects of the system. This is not to say, however, that inefficiency undermined the totalitarian nature of the society. The Kremlin's monopoly on power persisted through the course of Soviet history, and no other center of power imposed its will against it.

The Leader As the Bulwark of Society

Lacking a market mechanism to regulate the economic and political life of the country, the totalitarian society functioned purely on the basis of a hierarchy of command, with the supreme leader at the top. Any form of "collective leadership," even within the confines of the Politburo, was dangerous for the system and presented dire, long-term ramifications. This circumstance occurred only a few times in Soviet history: during a brief period after Lenin's death in 1924, following Stalin's death in 1953, and to a lesser degree in the wake of Khrushchev's political demise in 1963.

As a rule, all Soviet leaders behaved as pragmatic, rational politicians, if we judge their behavior by their personal goals, which usually, though not always, converged with the interests of the totalitarian state.[2] As rational actors, the leaders employed an "irrational," utopian public ideology that effectively facilitated their objectives.[3]

The leaders' absolute monopoly on power allowed them to make "rational" decisions with respect to their personal interests, which appeared "irrational" in relation to the country as a whole. For instance, in spite of Stalin's failures—i.e., collectivization, and the ensuing starvation of millions of people—mass terror was useful for stifling the threat to his power; this was also true in relation to the extermination of the cream of the Red Army and the military industrial complex.[4] At the same time, the rational decisions of Soviet leaders were usually far from optimal, even if we assess them in view of their personal goals. Seemingly, even Stalin's goal to solidify his personal power did not require repressions of the magnitude of the purges in the 1930s. As post-Stalin history showed, it was possible for all Soviet leaders to keep their power intact with less severe repressions. There is no doubt that post-Stalin general secretaries learned an important lesson from Stalin's misuse of power.[5] At the same time, they benefited from the lingering effects of the fear his purges engendered in the Soviet people.

The Motivation of the Leaders

Studying the intentions of historical actors is always a difficult task because the single source of information is the actor himself, who tends to embellish his motives according to the dominant values of society. This difficulty prevails in various professional fields. For instance, marketing experts try—sometimes successfully, sometimes not—to understand consumer motivation. Politicians want to deduce the motives of the electorate. The challenge only mounts when the social actors in question reside in the distant past.

The human desire to look good and honest in the eyes of one's contemporaries as well as in the history books often makes the declarations of social actors questionable. Adding to the confusion, the actors use the mechanism of rationalization to conceal their true motives behind their secondary motives, or even purely false justifications.[6] From a retrospective vantage point, anyone can easily change (quite sincerely and without intrigue) his or her motives for past actions.[7] Moving away from the personal accounts of individual social actors does not solve the problem of spurious analysis. Outsiders who try to understand the motives of historical figures are no less affected by their own values and the need to justify their personal ideology and behavior.[8]

Many scholars believe that the best way to explain the actors of the past is to either avoid the issue of "motivation," or at least reconstruct the past using only real (observable) events and actions.[9] Indeed, most historians bypass the analysis of their subject's motivations, leaving that to the historical novelists to hash out. Defining the intentions of historical actors has been the objective of many novels, such as Gustave Flaubert's *Salambo*, Leon Feuchtwanger's *The Judea War*, Thomas Mann's *Joseph and his brothers*, Marguerite Yourcenar's *Hadrian's memoirs*, and Gore Vidal's *Burr* and *Lincoln*.

However, like several other scholars, I cannot avoid the sensitive debate about the motivation of Soviet leaders. Many Sovietologists (i.e., totalitarianists and their opponents, revisionists) accepted the goals and motives expressed by the leaders in the open ideology at face value. Some of these historians and scholars believed, for instance, that the World Revolution was the leadership's major objective throughout the regime's history. They were also quite certain that the leaders were devoted to socialist democracy, the active participation of the masses in governing society, internationalism, and ethnic equality in society. They oversimplified the motives of the leaders, motives that had evolved over the course of many years into a very complex structure.

Certainly the primary motivations of the leaders were egotistical in nature; but this could be said about any politician in any society. It would be wrong to single out Soviet leaders as especially power-hungry individuals. World leaders and politicians of all kinds have always been primarily interested in gaining, maintaining, and expanding their power, using the instruments of the given historical context. It may be said—though I realize I tread on rather fractious ground here—that each historical period demands and to some degree recruits certain leaders with special psychological qualities. Every society at any given time has a pool of personalities, ranging from the cruelest to the meekest individuals. While the existing social structure may dictate which type of individual rises to the top, the agents themselves also impact the historical process.

The Soviet leaders and the nomenklatura yearned for power and the pleasure of exercising power as most politicians in history. In their eyes, they were becoming the demiurges of history, whose decisions influenced the fate of Russia and the world, not to mention the millions of people under their rule. Like any politician, they wanted to attain a high level of social prestige (in the present and future), material comfort and wealth. The personal traits of the leaders modified the structure of society and the benefits that individuals gained from possessing power. The first cohort of Soviet leaders lived a much better life than the rank and file. However, the generations that followed made the lives of the early leadership look highly ascetic in comparison. Brezhnev began to savor not only the pleasure of power but the high style of life afforded to the general secretary.

Each politician must decide how he or she will achieve and maintain power while legitimatizing this power in the eyes of the population, particularly the bureaucracy and the most active (young and educated) people in the country. In the Soviet case, the leaders chose an ideological mixture of Marxist and nationalist elements. This mode of gaining and maintaining power was accepted by all of Lenin's successors. Russia's national interests, in particular its geopolitical dominance, became the touchstone of the leadership's foreign and domestic policy. At the same time, the leaders advanced socialist ideology, with its focus on public property, the planning system, and social equality. These elements were easily blended with Russian nationalism.

Were the Leaders Marxists?

While behaving as the champions of Russian nationalism, the leaders and members of the nomenklatura also claimed to be Marxists. Many scholars as well as ordinary people from inside and outside Russia took this claim at face value, though there were also some who sternly rejected it.[10] Lenin and to a lesser degree Stalin were quite involved in reading about Marxism and participating in theoretical debates on the subject. However, this was not at all true of the post-Stalin leaders. Nikita Khrushchev, Leonid Brezhnev, Konstantin Chernenko, and even Mikhail Gorbachev could not claim to be even moderately versed in Marxist teachings. These leaders had no serious theoretical weltanschauung. None of them, by all accounts, read serious literature on Marxist philosophy, or economic theory.[11] The leaders' aides, who perhaps had more familiarity with Marx, could not countervail the leader's personal ignorance.[12]

At the same time, all the leaders, including Chernenko (the least educated of the bunch), were "Marxists" according to the standards of Soviet textbooks on Marxist-Leninist philosophy, or "scientific Communism" (see, for instance, Afanasiev 1981a, 1981b). Their allegiance to Marxists tenets, however, should be ascribed not to their educations but more directly to the fact that they lived in a socialist society—a social framework that they did not choose for themselves. Like all Soviet citizens, they had no choice but to adjust to the given economic, political and social structures of the society in which they lived. As Henry Kissinger aptly remarked, the Soviet leaders needed "passionate belief in the system to which they owed their careers" (Kissinger 1994, p. 519).

The fundamentals of Soviet society (public property and central planning) clearly had Marxist origins.[13] Although the post-Stalin leaders did not have serious training in economics, they all believed that these fundamentals were superior to capitalist economic formations. In this respect, even without reading the four volumes of *Capital*, the leaders were Marxists, just as Western politicians should be considered capitalists even though few of them have had a serious education in the works of Adam Smith, John Maynard Keynes, or Paul Samuelson.

As a sort of "assumed" Marxist, each leader believed in the superiority of the planned economy and the fatal flaws of the capitalist economy. This set of beliefs was particularly strong in the 1930s, when many people around the globe anticipated the fall of the capitalist system. Later, in the 1960s, as the leaders and apparatchiks witnessed the great economic expansion of the United States, Germany, and Japan, their belief in the principal advantages of the central planning system was only partially undermined. The leaders and most apparatchiks still believed that the socialist economy, though less efficient than the Western economic system, was the best course for Russia and its national interests.[14]

There were other elements of Marxist folklore that the Soviet leaders accepted, including: collectivism, atheism, the predominance of science, and moderate egalitarianism.[15] Due to their beliefs in collectivism, they aggressively rejected individualism. As "materialist cynics," they assumed that material interests were the major stimuli of human behavior. They believed in several Marxist postulates, such as: conflicts are at the core of social life; the roots of all major religious and ethnic conflicts are economic; and conflicts between the classes (rich and poor), between capitalist countries, and between the capitalist and socialist systems are inevitable and uncompromising.

At the same time, the leaders relegated much of the Soviet-brand Marxism to the open ideology and used it only as propaganda. The leaders did not embrace (in their closed ideology) the ideas of socialist democracy, the dictatorship of the proletariat, the leading role of the working class, or internationalism.

The leaders' superficial Marxist educations (probably only in the first two years of their college careers) did not influence the pragmatism of their everyday politics. In all of Soviet history, there is not a single case in which

Marxist ideology stopped a leader from pursuing Russia's geopolitical interests (see Chapter 4 of this book). From the early 1930s until 1985, if a conflict arose in public discussions between a person with Marxist leanings and someone with Russian nationalist tendencies, the leaders usually sided with the latter individual.[16] The Marxist elements in the minds of Soviet leaders never stood as a major barrier to Soviet economic and cultural relations with foreign countries, regardless of the latter's political systems. These elements never obstructed them from finding common ground upon which to base their dialogue with foreign leaders if it was in their best interest to do so.[17] What is more, the highest-level Soviet apparatchiks easily adapted to post-Communist life with its democratic institutions and market economy. What was left of their Marxist beliefs did not hinder their participation in the privatization of the state, or in democratic elections (see Shlapentokh, Vanderpool, and Doktorov 1999).

How the Leaders Presented Their Motives

Whatever their links with Marxism and socialism, the leaders were preoccupied with maintaining and expanding the country's geopolitical interests and the power of the totalitarian state (along with their individual power and influence). They were rather lukewarm or even indifferent toward the life of the people. For propagandistic reasons, however, they embellished their own images to convince the people that they served noble goals such as improving the standard of living, social equality, and internationalism. In many cases, the benevolent motives that the leaders claimed for themselves were almost completely spurious.

The leaders wanted the people to believe that the standard of living was a primary policy objective, and they boasted about any progress in this realm. In 1935, when the country emerged from the period of starvation and famine, Stalin said, "Life has become better, comrades, life has become merrier" (Stalin 1952b). The same type of cheap optimism was conveyed by Brezhnev in each of his reports about the material well-being of the masses.[18] In actuality, improving the life of the people ranked quite low on the list of the leaders' political priorities, although this is not to say that they were against the betterment of their people's material well-being. The leaders were in favor of such an advance in society so long as it did not jeopardize the resources earmarked for the country's geopolitical purposes.

The leaders often tried to cover their real motives with spurious ones in their foreign policy. For example, they attributed the invasions of Hungary, Czechoslovakia, and Afghanistan in 1956–1979 to internationalism and the necessity to defend socialism. These invasions were in fact dictated only by geopolitical considerations. In this way, they substituted their genuine motives with the ideological cliches designed for public consumption.

The minutes of the meetings between Brezhnev's Politburo and the Czechoslovakian leadership following the Soviet invasion and occupation in August 1968 were indicative of the political elite's mentality. During the meetings, Brezhnev went on a tirade in his address to Alexander Dubcek and his comrades, railing about the importance of preserving socialism in Czechoslovakia. Behind the diatribes, however, was Moscow's determination to maintain its military position in central Europe. While claiming several times during the Czech-Soviet conversations in the Kremlin that the Soviet troops had come to Prague to defend socialism, Brezhnev also said that "the Czechoslovakian people lost their orientation," recognizing in this way that the masses supported the Dubcek regime. In addition, Brezhnev referred to "the friendship of Soviet and Czechoslovakian people," the hostile Western forces, "the dangerous situation on the Western borders of Czechoslovakia," and "the denigration of Soviet politics." It was clear for the participants of these talks that the last statements described the real causes of the Soviet invasion. Most scholars who read the minutes of these meetings agreed that Moscow was giving only lip service to the socialist cause in an effort to conceal its geopolitical interests.[19] This type of double-talk confused later generations of Sovietologists who focused primarily on the public statements of the elite.

The "Normal" Utopian Elements of Soviet Policy

Though the specific ideology and politics of the leaders (until the early 1960s) contained utopian elements,[20] in general, the impact of these elements on their behavior was indeed minimal. In previous chapters, I discussed how the leaders utilized the public ideology and propaganda with its highly utopian visions such as the World Revolution and the dictatorship of the proletariat to manipulate the masses and legitimize their power.[21] To cite the famous French anarchist George Sorel, the leaders used "myth" to compel the people's behavior in accordance with the formation of the new society (Sorel 1908). However, what lent credence to the complexity of the leaders' mentality and engendered bewilderment in those attempting to understand it was that some of the leaders' genuine goals and policies were "utopian" as well.[22] Stalin's famous plan of "transforming nature" was deeply untenable. One of the most quixotic Soviet leaders, Nikita Khrushchev also had ideas that were highly unrealistic (e.g., he wanted to revolutionize agriculture by making corn the leading cereal in Soviet agronomy; he also was certain that the USSR would surpass the United States in the production of meat and milk within a few years after he assumed power). Brezhnev dreamed of managing the economy with computers and optimal programming systems, an idea that may not seem utopian now but that for the times was quite idealistic. Mikhail Gorbachev tried to develop the Soviet system by introducing market and democratic elements that were deeply incompatible with its fundamentals and that led to its demise. In the early 1990s, Grigorii Yavlinsky claimed that it would take only 500 days to complete a major economic transformation, while Yegor Gaidar and Anatolii Chubais promised the Russians a better life in the next one or two years.[23]

In some cases, Soviet leaders introduced these far-fetched projects to foster an atmosphere of dynamism in society.[24] In other cases, they were simply victims of overambitious thinking, whose unreachable goals were often detrimental to society.[25] At the same time, ascribing the mistakes made by the leaders entirely to a highly utopian proclivity distorts not only the whole of Soviet history but the visionary character of all new regimes of the past. The founders of every major empire and state embraced utopian elements in their programs and set objectives beyond the constraints of *a posteriori* thinking. As their descendants would later claim, Alexander the Great, the emperors during the Roman expansion, the Oriental conquerors, and Napoleon were all driven by utopian visions and unrealistic goals. One of the most significant "utopian projects" in history was Zionism and the creation of Israel. Since its emergence in the late nineteenth century, Zionism has been regarded by many of its critics as purely utopian. Even after the establishment of the state of Israel, Zionism was still considered utopian in nature.

Consulting the annals of world history, we would find countless examples of detrimental utopian projects and wishful thinking gone bad. The decisions and actions of Western leaders would serve as no exception. If we condemn Khrushchev for his blunders in agriculture, we must, for example, reprove U.S. legislators for failing to grasp the decisive limitations of national prohibition in the early twentieth century—this being only one of the many mishaps of American domestic and foreign policy.[26]

The Pragmatism of the Leadership

As pragmatists and rational political actors, Soviet leaders understood the fundamentals of their system: the key roles of the party and state machine, the ideological apparatus and the political police. With the exception of Gorbachev, the leaders never infringed on these principles, whatever their willingness to improve the efficiency of the system.[27]

The early Soviet leaders were serious innovators. Their political and economic inventions were emulated all over the world. These innovations included the party as the basis of the state machine; the Gulag; the state's absolute monopoly on property; the planning system; the elimination of religion from public and private life; and ideological and intelligence networks that spanned the globe. The leaders made many unexpected decisions, surprising the world with their intellectual boldness. Lenin's more "rational" edicts included the recruitment of "bourgeois specialists" to work with Soviet authorities, and the development of the NEP (see Burtin 1999). Stalin, one of the most shrewd leaders in history,[28] made a number of portentous decisions during his tenure, many of which came with a very high cost for the country and the people but secured his personal power and the military might of the country. He curbed primitive egalitarianism, collectivized agriculture, advanced the well-being of scholars, abandoned socialist phraseology during the war with Germany, dismantled the Third International, fomented Russian chauvinism and anti-Semitism, and enlisted the Russian church as his ally during the war. Khrushchev radically changed Soviet foreign policy in favor of "peaceful coexistence." He also reduced the army, alleviated the tax burden on collective farmers, released prisoners from the Gulag, and denounced Stalin's atrocities.

Soviet leaders and their staffs usually possessed sound organizational skills, a necessary condition for the success of pragmatic politicians. In the very beginning of his political career in pre-revolutionary Russia, Lenin proclaimed his main goal as the assemblage of effectively organized revolutionaries (i.e., the party). He went on to create a party with thirty thousand members (February 1917). After the revolution, the leaders organized many dozens of projects, from the cultivation of the Red Army and the political police, to the development of a nuclear arsenal.

When making decisions, the leaders often demonstrated lucid foresight and considered many of objective factors, ranging from the climate of their country to the efficiency of the economy to the might of their foreign adversaries. They were also sensitive to the mood of the masses, the managers, the army, the political police and countless other important groups. A proper evaluation of the complex factors involved in decision making is an essential element of leadership, just as the miscalculation of these factors is an intrinsic phenomenon in all regimes.

While it was true that some of the leaders' oversights could be attributed to utopian leanings and wishful thinking, we must also consider the impact of simple miscalculations and human errors. Stalin, for instance, was too trustful of Hitler. He was accused of underestimating the German threat in summer 1941. However, even in this case there were rational grounds for his policy of avoiding conflict with Hitler by all means. He had a very sober estimate of the Red Army's preparedness and tried to gain time for its betterment through reforms (Glantz 1998, pp. 259–260). He also faltered in his confrontation with Yugoslavia in 1948–1949, when Tito bluntly refused to acquiesce to Moscow's influence on foreign and domestic policy. Khrushchev made a grave miscalculation when he failed to appreciate the growing opposition to his power and overestimated the support of his bureaucracy. Gorbachev fell victim to many mistakes: he underestimated the intensity of ethnic conflicts in the country, failed in his anti-alcohol campaign, and failed to appreciate the need for competition when he extended autonomy only to certain enterprises.

The Sophisticated Selection of Cadres

The Soviet totalitarian system elaborated an extremely refined mechanism for the selection of people for important positions in the party and state hierarchies. The positions of the nomenklatura were under the direct control of the general secretary or those to whom he delegated this power. The general secretary personally controlled the appointment of the members of the Central Committee, all regional party secretaries; all ministers, their deputies, and the heads of the departments of the most important ministries; ambassadors; the commanders of all military districts; and the heads of the regional KGB. The positions of the next two or three levels of the hierarchy were formally under the direct control of the secretaries of the Central Committee. Appointments at lower levels of the party and state hierarchies were controlled by the Central Committee, regional and district party committees, moving down through the hierarchy. Even the chairman of a collective farm, or an instructor of social studies in a high school was appointed by a district party committee. According to Mikhail Voslensky, there were 750,000 positions in the nomenklatura class in 1970. This number included 100,000 party and state apparatchiks of the highest level, whose appointments were made by the Central Committee and by republican and regional party committees (Voslensky 1984, pp. 180–181).

In spite of the various flaws of the nomenklatura system, under the existing conditions it worked quite well and provided the party and state apparatus with cadres who were able to perform the jobs assigned to them. The absolute majority of the most talented, educated and energetic people were ready to join the nomenklatura and faithfully serve the regime. There were very few cases—even considering anecdotal evidence—of people refusing promotions or declining job offers in the Soviet hierarchy.

The Soviet system guaranteed the supreme leader's rigid control over the party and state apparatus. When the leader decided to change the criteria for the selection of cadres (i.e., to reject Jews, individuals who spent time in German prisons during the war, and people who lived on the territory occupied by Germany), the system reacted instantly and strictly observed the new rules that dictated the selection of cadres.

The Politburo

After the supreme leader, the Politburo was the most important institution in Soviet society. It was the only body that influenced the decisions of the general secretary. This did not, however, compromise the totalitarian character of the regime, or the key role allotted to the supreme leader. Acting mostly as an advising body, the Politburo rarely challenged the general secretary.

An exception occurred in 1957 when the majority of the Politburo made an unsuccessful attempt at dislodging Khrushchev. Later, in 1964, the Politburo made another attempt at ousting Khrushchev; this time they were successful. In the first case, Khrushchev stifled the opposition by bringing trusted members of the Central Committee to Moscow. He was aided also by his complete control over all military and KGB forces (Yakovlev 1998, pp.15, 18). In the second case, Khrushchev fell victim to a conspiracy. After discovering the intrigue, he had no chance of defeating his adversaries without a bloodbath. His opponents managed to secure the support of the KGB and the army (S. Khrushshev 1990; Grishin 1996, p. 28).

The dismissal of the general secretary in 1964 was extremely unusual, and in some ways it scarred those who perpetrated it. The new leadership worried that the ousting defied the nature of the system and undermined the legitimacy of the existing political order. For this reason, it forbade the media to publish even slightly negative statements about the fallen leader. Officially, Khrushchev's resignation was ascribed to his poor health. Only in closed propaganda or encoded editorials could people find out about the accusations lodged against Khrushchev by the Politburo.

Khrushchev's dismissal was a clear deviation from the normal course of Soviet history. Even Gorbachev was never challenged by the Politburo, though he was despised by its majority. His political enemies challenged him not in meetings of the Politburo but by preparing a coup, which unlike the coup in 1964, failed.

In most periods of Soviet history, the general secretary regarded the members of the Politburo as useful advisers who would voice their concerns and yet always endorse any of his decisions. The leaders usually sought the formal endorsement of the Politburo only on serious decisions. It would be unfounded and inaccurate to suppose that the Politburo and Central Committee worked, as several revisionists have contended (see Bialer 1983, pp. 6, 35, 1980, p. 295; Hough 1980), as "collegial bodies" that discussed and made decisions democratically. In fact, as a rule, the decision was made by the leader, who consulted first with his staff, then with party officials (including members of the Politburo), and finally with experts in various fields.

Ultimately, the power of the general secretary over the members of the Politburo lay in his ability to fire (or in Stalin's times, to arrest and execute) any member at short notice. Ironically, the general secretary was elected by the members of the Politburo, with the purely ceremonial endorsement of the Central Committee. The initial role of the Politburo explains why each new general secretary usually demonstrated reverence for the members in the beginning of his term. However, this atmosphere of affable relations subsided soon after the election. Once in full control, the leader could easily suppress any aggressive move against him by the Politburo. What is more, the general secretary often followed the Machiavellian rationale, tending to replace members of the Politburo who participated in the election process, because "replacements" were always less influential than those involved in the initial election.

This was true not only of Stalin's regime but also of the regimes of Brezhnev (who had the reputation of being a mild person) and Gorbachev (who claimed to be a democratically enlightened leader).[29] Each of the Soviet leaders could easily oust Politburo members at a moment's notice. Stalin dismissed members on several occasions, many of whom were later executed. The last of Stalin's victims in the Politburo was Nikolai Voznesensky, his economic aide, who was executed in 1950.[30] Even in the last days of his rule, Stalin was not—as some revisionists have contended—"embattled" by his adversaries and scarcely able to fend off the threats of the apparatus (McCagg 1978; Getty 1985).[31] Throughout his reign he successfully maintained his hold on power.

All of Stalin's heirs (with the exception of the brief leadership of Andropov and Chernenko) removed Politburo members. Moreover, they often expelled their colleagues in the most unceremonious and humiliating ways. They behaved as if they were dismissing servants. For instance, in May of 1977, Brezhnev "relieved" Nikolai Podgorny of his duties as chairman of the Presidium and ousted him from the Politburo completely. More notably, Gorbachev removed one third of his Politburo in 1988.[32] No public explanations were given in regard to the removal of several major political figures.

At the same time, the leader, while in complete control of the Politburo's fate, paid public homage to the membership because it legitimized his power in the country. Theoretically, the Soviet system could not tolerate public discordance between the general secretary and the Politburo. Even Stalin, who after World War II never called meetings of the Central Committee or the party congresses, regularly met with the members of the Politburo. Before 1939, Stalin organized regular meetings with the entire body of the Politburo; after 1939, he met with the members on a more individual basis.[33]

The continued special status of the Politburo can be attributed to the willingness of the supreme leader to share the psychological and political responsibility for risky decisions.[34] Even Stalin asked the members of the Politburo to endorse various decisions, including the death sentences of party apparatchiks (N. Khrushchev 1970, p. 256; G. Zhukov 1989). Brezhnev appreciated the advice of Mikhail Suslov, Andrei Gromyko, and Dmitrii Ustinov; and Suslov's death in 1982 had a serious impact on political developments in Moscow (Grachev 1994, pp. 26–27). At the same time, Brezhnev disliked Alexei Kosygin, who was then chairman of the government, and often ignored him and his recommendations (Grishin 1996, pp. 39–41).

The real role of the Politburo increased when the leader had trouble making an important decision on his own. In this case, he was indeed willing to hear the views of high party officials and even to allow them to advocate different ideas. Until the final decision was made, the members were permitted to hold different views on the same subject (during Brezhnev's period, for instance, on the degree of economic centralization, or on the development of sociology). Outsiders who were not familiar with the system often wrongly perceived these differences as evidence of a factional struggle inside the Kremlin between "conservatives" and "reformers." Of course, that there were no factional struggles does not mean that members of the Politburo and other high officials did not maintain their own private opinions and values.[35]

In any case, the study of elites and the internal struggle between "reformers" and "conservatives" was a central target of Sovietologists in the 1970s and 1980s. Those who advocated the "polarized image of Soviet elites" should be quite astounded to find that even during perestroika there were no signs of real resistance to Gorbachev among party conservatives in the Politburo and Central Committee until the summer of 1990 (this issue will be discussed later).[36]

Conclusion

The Soviet leader was a major institution in the Soviet totalitarian society. He had an absolute monopoly on the decision-making process and controlled all key positions in the country. The leader was the symbol of the regime's order, unity and legitimacy. In the history of the regime, only once was a leader ousted from his position, and this occurred not through a democratic procedure but as the result of a conspiracy—which no leader, regardless of the character of his power, is immune to.

The Soviet leaders were pragmatic men whose major goals were the strengthening of the totalitarian state and the expansion of the empire. Many of the initiatives related to these goals were unsuccessful, and yet the leaders were able to cope with the existing circumstances and curb the destructive tendencies in society.

8

An Effective Political Machine

The Soviet leaders governed society with a gigantic and rather sophisticated political machine which functioned until the time of Gorbachev's reforms. The core of this machine was the Communist Party and the state bureaucracy. The machine was also supported by the vast repressive apparatus, the army, and the millions of Soviet citizens who succumbed to the pressure of fear and ideology and served as agents of the totalitarian state and as the people's supervisors and propagandists.

The Party

The party was one of the Bolsheviks' greatest political inventions. Many political parties in totalitarian and authoritarian countries (the Nazi party being foremost among them) were created in imitation of the Soviet Communist Party. This party represented the core of the state system. There were four major advantages of the party-state system as compared to a coercive regime which operated with the state apparatus alone.[1] Before explaining these advantages, it should be noted that the existence of the party and state created an overlapping, dual bureaucracy, which caused many inconveniences. The demarcation between the functions and responsibilities of the party and state was never clear in the entire history of the Soviet system. However, based on cost-benefit analysis, the Kremlin believed that the existence of the two apparatuses was quite rational.

First, with two presumably different political institutions, unlike a regime based only on direct force, the leaders maintained the image of a democratic system. The existence of both institutions allowed the Kremlin to include the crucial element of free and universal elections, even though this was only a mimicry of true democratic procedure. Elections formally included everyone (and not only party members) in the political process, and made the Communist Party look similar to parties in the West, where political leadership was decided by a "normal election process." In this way, the Kremlin substantiated the democratic character of the Soviet political system (an important postulate of the open ideology), and the system's legitimacy by Western standards. It could thus reject the accusations of anti-Soviet ideologues, who claimed that the country was ruled by the party and was not accountable to the population.

Second, the party played a vital role in the organization and function of society. It served in a capacity similar to that of the market in a democratic society. With cells in each office, plant and farm, the party was an efficient coordinating force, performing this task until its defeat in the first (relatively) free election of the Supreme Soviet in March 1989.[2]

Third, the party was responsible for the ideological indoctrination of the population. Each party committee—from the Central Committee and the regional and district committees to the committees of cities, villages, factories, collective farms, colleges, offices and residential blocks—was involved in intensive propagandistic work. They focused on literally every type of individual, from the illiterate peasant to the most sophisticated intellectual. Through the party committees the leadership controlled the media, educational and scientific institutions, publishing houses, literature and arts. With the help of the political police, the party used its army of apparatchiks and activists, along with its network of open and secret informers, to monitor the deeds and minds of each Soviet individual, from kindergartners to retirees.

Fourth, the party was necessary for the selection of cadres, who ran the bureaucratic system. The party consolidated the most active and educated citizens in the country and played a leading role in society. The party membership's high level of "human capital" greatly benefited the totalitarian state.[3] For anyone who wanted to pursue a career in the USSR, membership in the party was a prerequisite. This was particularly true in the post-Stalin period, when the party abandoned the use of terror as the main means of controlling the population. Not surprisingly, millions of Soviet people dreamed of obtaining a party card or serving the party in other capacities (i.e., as activists in the Young Communist League, in trade unions, and in numerous other governmental organizations).[4] At the end of Stalin's regime there were roughly 7 million party members; by the end of the Soviet Union, the number had risen to 18 million.

With an astronomical number of citizens aspiring to hold a party card, the leadership could easily portray party membership as a special privilege. By the end of Brezhnev's regime, there was a long waiting list for people who wanted to enlist in the party at each large office and plant. The list was indeed long because the party district committee limited the quota of new members for each unit. Professionals were especially eager to enroll in the party; although the leadership gave priority to workers and peasants, members of the creative intelligentsia "stood in line" for party membership, because obtaining a promotion was, as a rule, impossible without it. Not surprisingly, party membership was more frequent among those with advanced educations than among those with less education.[5] The proportion of party members among the employees of the Soviet Academy of Sciences (the country's scientific elite) was 70 percent in 1979 (up from 29 percent in 1948–1949). Among full professors (in the Soviet scholarly hierarchy they were known as "doctors of science"), 55 percent were party members in 1979 (in 1948– 1949, 31 percent); among those with doctoral degrees ("candidates of science"), 36 percent were members in 1979 (30 percent in 1948–1949).[6] Similarly, more than 50 percent of Soviet writers were party members. Among the participants in the Russian Writers' Congress, 87 percent were party members. Party members made up one third of all composers and filmmakers, and two thirds of all journalists (*Literaturnaia gazeta*, December 18, 1985, p. 3; *Pravda*, June 29, 1989). Millions of party members (until 1987– 1989) were proud of their membership and used it to enhance their self-respect and impress others.

In Stalin's time, if a member was dismissed from the party due to some political accusation, he was automatically at risk of being sent to the Gulag or executed. After Stalin, dismissal from the party meant a radical decline in social status.[7] The absolute majority of the rank and file were happy to be party members, even though they had no opportunity to participate in the political process. Interestingly, despite the imminent collapse of the system in 1989, the members abandoned the party rather slowly. A more significant exodus from the party began in July 1990, following the Twenty-eighth Party Congress.[8]

From the beginning of the regime until the 1970s, the leaders successfully recruited millions of Communists for various industrial and agricultural projects. There was also enthusiastic participation (particularly among the youth) during the civil war, collectivization in the 1930s, World War II, and in the postwar period.[9] The party leadership sent 25,000 Communists to carry out collectivization in 1929–1931. In 1933, they sent 15,000 to the countryside to organize the machine-tractor stations (MTS) which helped collective farms mechanize their work. In the late 1950s, when Khrushchev created regional economic councils, thousands of Communists left Moscow to work in the provinces. The party and Komsomol members were mobilized to coordinate agricultural developments in Siberia and Kazakhstan (see Shevardnadze 1991, p. 57). Hundreds of thousands of Komsomol members volunteered for various construction projects. The last such major project was the building of the Amur–Baikal railroad in the 1970s.

Though the party comprised the cream of the population, after 1917 it did not function as a true political organization. A real political party was incompatible with the totalitarian system. The members had little or no impact on the leadership's decisions and policies. Even in the early 1920s under Lenin, the rank and file did not play a serious role in shaping party policy. During this period, there were a few official and unofficial discussions inside the party, but the majority of members obediently followed the leader of the party, and the opposition had no chance of gaining power.

Through the course of Soviet history, the party remained passive. Even the original party members who had helped lay the revolutionary groundwork before 1917 never challenged Stalin. During a secret vote at the Seventeenth Party Congress, in the aftermath of collectivization, when it was evident to most that Stalin's policies had proved disastrous, the party elite did not oppose him. At best, there may have been a few dozen delegates (out of 1,059) who voted against Stalin; but their ballots were destroyed at Stalin's request, as some delegates confirmed thirty years later. Though it had been widely rumored by the Soviet people, there is no objective proof that an attempt to replace Stalin with Sergei Kirov ever occurred (see Mikhailov 1991a). The same passivity in the face of contention was evident in mid-year 1991, when the majority of the party rank and file was hostile toward Gorbachev's domestic and foreign policy. Despite this discord, there were practically no party meetings or resignations in protest against Gorbachev and his reforms.

After the late 1920s, with the party opposition quelled by Stalin, the leaders remained quite indifferent to the mood of ordinary party members. In the first years of Khrushchev's tenure, the Central Committee, as if breaking with Stalin's contempt for the party rank and file, sent some "closed letters" to primary party organizations as a demonstration of the leadership's concern for the active participation of ordinary members. This practice continued for a few years following the installation of the Brezhnev regime, but after 1968 it practically disappeared.

However, the party masses were not alone in their obscurity. The entire party nomenklatura was ignored by the Kremlin. Overall, neither the party congresses nor the Central Committee played a serious role in Soviet history. The composition of these institutions was determined by the general secretary, and with only a few exceptions neither the Central Committee nor the congresses rebelled against the party leader. One of the exceptions occurred in 1918, when Lenin was temporarily in the minority in the Central

Committee during the debates on the Brest treaty with Germany. There was also the case of the Central Committee's political struggle in 1957, when the Politburo wanted to oust Khrushchev. Khrushchev stifled the opposition by bringing trusted members of the Central Committee to Moscow. He was aided also by his complete control over all military and KGB forces (Yakovlev 1998, pp. 15, 18). However, in 1964, at the command of a rebellious Politburo, which secured the support of the KGB and the army, the Central Committee successfully removed Khrushchev without any debates (S. Khrushchev 1990; Grishin 1996, p. 28).

A more characteristic example of the party elite's impact on its leader came at the end of the regime. The impotence of the party congresses and the Central Committee was clearly revealed in 1990, when neither of these institutions, in spite of their intense hatred of the general secretary, made moves to bring down Gorbachev.

The Party and the Soviets

After the party, the second most important ruling branch in society was the state hierarchy, which was made up of soviets of different levels. The function of the state apparatus (the soviets) changed over time, but it generally dealt more with economic and social issues, leaving all political and ideological activities, including the selection of cadres, solely to the party apparatus. Ultimately, the party controlled the state apparatus in all domains, although the soviets had many important responsibilities. The executive bodies of the soviets were in charge of various departments, which oversaw numerous sectors of society (i.e., industry, agriculture, construction, education, culture, transportation, health, housing conditions, trade and others). At the level of the national republics, these departments were structured as ministries and state committees. Each department and ministry at each level of the state hierarchy was supervised by a corresponding party committee at the same level or a higher level of the party hierarchy. In this way, with the party as the major institution in society, the system maintained a high level of centralization and concentrated power over each sector of the economy, and each region, village, and city, in the hands of the party secretary.

Before 1989, any attempt to weaken the control of the party over the central and local governments was doomed to failure. The party remained the "leading and guiding" force in society. The Russians accepted the inferior role of the soviets as a "normal" phenomenon. Generally, they looked for help not to their local soviets but to local party committees, and particularly to the party's Central Committee. The Soviet system began to crumble precisely at the moment when the party lost its leading role as the coordinator of society and the soviets and the state apparatus gained autonomy. This indeed was one of the first demands of the liberals headed by Andrei Sakharov. In 1990, the famous Article 6 in the Constitution, which officially legitimized the role of the party in society, was annulled, leading to the eventual collapse of the Soviet system.

The Efficiency of Soviet and Party Bureaucracy

With a growing population, technological progress, and the increasing complexity of Soviet life, it became necessary for the leaders to delegate more and more of their power to the nomenklatura—primarily to the party nomenklatura but also to the state apparatus. For instance, in 1985, the discretionary power of a head of a department in the Central Committee was much greater than that of his predecessor in the late 1920s and early 1930s. Even as late as 1952, Stalin still held fast to the strings of power. For instance, he formally signed the decisions of the Council of Ministers in regard to the simple transfer of a single truck from one ministry to another.[10] By the mid-1980s such a case was an anachronism.

With some reservations, the Soviet bureaucracy was well equipped to manage its growing responsibilities. It consisted of highly sophisticated personnel, even by Western standards. In many respects, the work of Soviet officials was more difficult than that of their counterparts in the West. Their decisions had to be acceptable to their party superiors, the KGB, and ideologists. Soviet officials had to work in an environment with a permanent shortage of goods and services. To accomplish their tasks they had to deploy extraordinary resourcefulness. They were not, however, without deficiencies. Officials often fudged the reports on their activities, and they tended to select and promote cadres not according to their professional merits but in view of their political activism and personal loyalty. These flaws are common also in Western societies (this issue will be discussed in detail later).

The complex mentality of the elite consisted of three layers: open ideology (exhibited in public statements); closed ideology (manifested in the discourse between members of the elite); and individual values (including purely egotistical interests of careerism and personal enrichment, which were either completely concealed or designated strictly for relatives and friends). To survive as an apparatchik, they had to juggle these divergent motivations. It was imperative that their actions and behavior reflect a belief in both the open and closed ideologies simultaneously. They had to pretend not to see the differences, even when the dissimilarity was unmistakable. At the same time, they sought to minimize the distance between the three layers in order to attain peace of mind.

The Soviet political machine was most effective when apparatchiks were evaluated according to their real contributions to the goals set by the leadership. In the 1920s, the first generation of apparatchiks functioned as true "stockholders"—that is, people who took initiative in running society and who considered the society their collective property.[11] The next generation (1930s–1940s) operated as the "soldiers of the party," and readily obeyed the orders of the leadership. They rarely displayed personal initiative or argued with superiors about the rationality of their orders. They were truly devoted to the official ideology and remained motivated by ideological factors. The third generation of apparatchiks (1950–1960s), which emerged after Stalin's death, were careerists absorbed only with securing promotions by any legal means. While these apparatchiks grew increasingly critical of the open ideology (for instance, hardly anybody in the party leadership believed in the "leading role of the working class"), most of them preserved their faith in the major postulates of the closed ideology until the end of the regime.[12]

The various chronic diseases of the system worsened in the 1970s. Corruption and semilegal and illegal activities penetrated all spheres of Soviet life. During the fourth period in their evolution, the apparatchiks became increasingly involved in various forms of corruption. They not only ignored the interests of the state but often made decisions that clearly damaged the state. From "stockholders" to "soldiers of the party," to "careerists," and finally to "corrupted bureaucrats"—such was the evolution of the dominant class.

However, with all their weaknesses, in 1985 the political and economic elite were still quite professional, competent and hardworking. Numberless documents evidence the hard work of apparatchiks. This was true not only of Stalin's notably devoted bureaucracy[13] but also of the apparatus after 1953 (and up until 1985–1991), in spite of the clear decline in labor ethics in the post-Stalin period (V. Shlapentokh 1988a, pp. 33–46). Compared to Yeltsin's notorious bureaucracy in post-Communist Russia, the Soviet elite looked like a dedicated and efficient workforce.[14]

Full Control of the Province

Though the relations between the center and the provinces were quite complex, the Soviet totalitarian system managed to maintain strict control throughout the regime. In all the regions, power was concentrated in the hands of the first party secretary, who acted as the master of the region and controlled all regional institutions. The cult of the first party secretary was very strong. No one in the region dared criticize him publicly. He was so powerful and peremptory that the Kremlin, having decided to replace him, always transferred him to Moscow for permanent residence. This may be cited as another example of the rationality of the central authorities. Transferring the old regional leader to Moscow not only protected him from those who wanted revenge for his harsh rule, but also prevented him from conducting intrigues through his old camarilla against the new regional boss appointed by the general secretary. The first party secretary was a key person in the selection of the local nomenklatura (the cadres for regional offices and institutions). He could appoint them, dismiss them, and transfer them to other jobs. His major power lay also in his ability to take to task any official in his region and threaten him or her with expulsion from the party.

However, in spite of his image of power before his regional subordinates, he remained the servant of the central authorities. His major task was to implement political and economic directives sent from Moscow. He and his apparatus spent most of their time supervising major industrial and agricultural enterprises in order to guarantee the fulfillment of the plans endorsed by the Kremlin. The first party secretary was most concerned with the military industrial complex. There was no more important task for the party apparatus than enhancing the productivity of military industry. The first party secretary was also responsible for the quality of cadres (i.e., their political reliability) in his province and the implementation of various political campaigns.

The secretary's power over the selection of his subordinates and several other local officials was actually quite limited. The second party secretary, the chairman of the Executive Party Committee, the chief of the People's Commissariat of Internal Affairs (later called the Ministry of Internal Affairs and then renamed the Ministry of State Security), the procurator, the representative of the Commissariat of Procurement (later the Ministry of the Commissariat of Procurement), and the directors of large industrial enterprises of union importance were appointed by Moscow. The secretary of the regional party committee performed only a consulting function in the selection of these cadres. In addition to this ramified system of subordination and coordination, there were also commissions of soviet and party control (the Ministry and the Committee of State Control), which were subordinate only to Moscow. The task of these bodies was to monitor the fulfillment of the center's decisions on regional issues.

None of the regional secretaries saw themselves as the representatives of the region in which they governed. Rather, they almost always defended the interests of the center. Local party committees became "defenders" of local interests only in the case of food shortages, which could generate major public disturbances. In these cases they begged their Moscow bosses for favors, such as a decrease in regional agricultural quotas, or the delivery of staple foods from the central stores.

Many future regional party secretaries got their start in the Central Committee, learning what Moscow expected of its provincial cadres before actually working in the province. All of them regarded themselves as Moscow's envoys and dreamed of eventual transfer to the capital, to a high position in the Central Committee or in the government. Indeed, two thirds of all members of the Politburo in the 1970s had served as regional secretaries.

Despite the limits of his power, the regional party secretary had a high status in Soviet society. In the social hierarchy, he was equal to an all-union minister. Party secretaries of the leading regions were members of the Central Committee, and many were also members of the Control Commission of the party. As a rule, party secretaries were at least members of the Supreme Soviet of the Russian Federation, if not deputies of the Supreme Soviet of the USSR (Shlapentokh, Levita, and Loiberg 1998).

The only area where the "regional factor" influenced Soviet politics was in the selection of cadres for the highest position in the party hierarchy. Even in Stalin's time, high officials who were transferred from the provinces to Moscow tried to recruit their deputies and staff from among their countrymen.[15] After Stalin, the formation of Moscow cadres on a regional basis increased enormously.[16] However, there is no evidence that the people who had worked in the provinces used their new posts in the capital to protect the interests of their former countrymen. They all considered themselves representatives of the country as a whole.

In any case, by 1985 the periphery and its leaders had no autonomy whatsoever, and true regionalism (the tendency of a region to gain autonomy or even independence from the center) was not a factor in Soviet governance.

The Political Police

By the standards of the totalitarian state, the political police (i.e., the KGB—known in earlier years variously as Cheka, GPU, and NKVD) was a near-perfect institution. In the opinion of some American experts, the KGB consistently improved in effectiveness over the span of Soviet history, another evidence of the growing efficiency of various sectors of society (Corson and Crowley 1985, p. 29). The KGB operated efficiently both inside and outside the country (Rositzke 1981; Richelson 1986; Andrew and Gordievsky 1990; Suvorov 1984; Deriabin and Bagley 1990; Freemantel 1984; Barron 1974; Kalugin 1994). The KGB and related agencies (the Ministry of Internal Affairs) prevented the creation of any serious organization outside the system and established a network of informers which blanketed society. Among their recruited informers were several outstanding members of the intellectual community. The KGB and its predecessors supervised all areas of the Soviet population, including the church, and particularly the intelligentsia. KGB agents were omnipresent in society. With their so-called special departments in each institution, they oversaw the selection of cadres at all levels, including the appointments of graduate students. The number of traitors and defectors among cadres was relatively small, totaling several hundred.[17] Without question, the KGB was the most informed agency in the country. KGB intelligence on the mood of the people contained very little bias and was certainly more accurate than the information collected by party committees.[18]

At the same time, the KGB was not without flaws. Like most organizations, it exaggerated its role and inflated the results of its activity in order to augment its status and resources. This tendency was particularly prevalent in the 1930s, in the times of mass terror. During this period the KGB's proclivity for self-aggrandizement corresponded with Stalin's excessive demands for information on the multitude of his domestic enemies, real and imaginary.

The KGB and the GRU (the intelligence service of the army) were also successful in the international arena. The KGB's international network of direct agents and "agents of influence" spanned the world. While a performance comparison between Soviet and Western espionage remains debatable, the ability of Soviet intelligence to plant spies around the globe is an admitted fact, though the KGB tended to exaggerate its results in this area just as it did in the domestic sphere (see Andrew and Mitrokhin 1999).

The political police closely monitored the activity of Russian emigrants in Western countries. Some of their operations in the 1920s and 1930s were masterpieces of espionage; for instance, they created the pseudo anti-Soviet organization known as Trust, which successfully deceived and manipulated many leading Russian emigrants, such as Vasilii Shulgin. They also kidnapped Russian emigrants living in France (among them generals Alexander Kutepov and Evgenii Miller), and murdered other defectors, such as Fedor Raskolnikov.

KGB achievements in the realm of technological espionage would be difficult to overestimate. By 1929, Stalin had commissioned a special division in the NKVD for stealing technological secrets. The torrent of stolen technological data supplied by the KGB and the GRU lent credibility to their claims of having contributed as much to the country's technological progress as did Soviet scientists.[19] The most notable intelligence acquisition led to the country's first nuclear bomb. The father of the Soviet nuclear bomb, Yulii Khariton, publicly recognized that its development was based on data obtained by Soviet agents.[20]

Regardless of the level or degree of KGB activity, the general secretary maintained tight supervision over this organization and prevented its directors from playing political roles. Felix Dzerzhinsky, Rudolf Menzhinsky, Genrikh Yagoda, Nikolai Yezhov, and Lavrentii Beria, as well as Stalin's last heads of the KGB (Vsevolod Merkulov, Victor Abakumov, and Semen

Ignatiev) never made even the slightest attempt to show their independence in making political decisions. Stalin regularly dealt death sentences to KGB agents. As a result, the Chekists secured a place in Soviet martyrology.[21]

After 1953, the Kremlin's control over the KGB tightened. The agency was now being supervised not only by the top party leader but by party regional leaders as well. The KGB's right to monitor high party apparatchiks was restricted unless the general secretary gave direct orders to investigate a specific official.[22] Yurii Andropov, the most powerful post-Stalin head of the KGB (1967–1981), was under the full control of the ailing Brezhnev, or those to whom the latter delegated his power (see R. Medvedev 1991; see also the article by Brezhnev's personal doctor Evgenii Chasov 1991).[23] The role of the KGB as a leading actor in Soviet society has been exaggerated by several authors, including the prominent dissident Vladimir Bukovsky;[24] only a few authors have presented a well-balanced view of this organization's place in society (see Sudoplatov and Malevannyi 1998).

There was a general consensus in society (including among dissidents) that the KGB was the least corrupt state institution. One rarely heard rumors about KGB people taking bribes. The high prestige of the KGB was enhanced by the integrity of its longest acting chief, Andropov. In the early 1980s, many experts both inside and outside Russia supposed that many Russians would be discontent if a former KGB chief ascended to the position of general secretary. In fact, Andropov's appointment to the top government post had the opposite effect. His arrival in the Kremlin was greeted with sincere enthusiasm by the masses (Zh. Medvedev 1983). Even after his death and the advent of glasnost, Andropov's reputation as an uncorrupt leader flourished.[25] In general, the KGB was a professional, well-disciplined institution, with very little corruption.

The Army

In efficiency, the Soviet army as an institution clearly ranked behind the KGB, partially due to its size. In 1985, the Soviet army comprised 6 million soldiers and officers (the KGB employed several hundred thousand people). At the same time, the army proved an important instrument of the totalitarian state, which despite its various failures (for instance, the Finnish-Soviet war in 1939–1940, and the first years of the war with Germany, in 1941–1945), claimed victory in the civil war and the war against Germany (see Glantz 1998). What is more, the quality of the Soviet army (i.e., the level of education of officers and draftees and the technical level of weapons), like that of the KGB, increased uniformly over the course of history until 1985. Generally speaking, Soviet military strategies were always quite reasonable, pragmatic, and rarely influenced by ideological dogmas. As two British authors pointed out in 1986, "The Soviet generals and the officer corps are essentially practical men" and "politico-military literature is regarded far less seriously by them than it is by the military analysts in the university faculties in the Western world" (Seaton and Seaton 1986, pp. 218–219).[26] The army was not culpable for the collapse of the Soviet Union in 1991. When the country fell, its borders were safe. There were no threats to the security of the country.

The army's failure in Afghanistan (the Soviet "Vietnam") was mostly caused by political factors and the refusal of the Kremlin to wage an all-out war. Public discontent with this war on the eve of perestroika, however, had no significant influence on decision making in the Kremlin (Cherniaev 1993, pp. 120–121).

The army stood out as a well-organized force until the end of its existence.[27] It was based on the draftee system, which worked quite well and produced in the 1970s and 1980s a much better contingent of recruits than in earlier periods. In 1970, more than two thirds of conscripts (69 percent) had complete or incomplete secondary educations, against 41 percent in 1959 (Jones 1985, p. 59). By the beginning of perestroika, the educational level of draftees in 1987 had risen by at least 30 percent over that in 1970 (Goskomstat 1987). When assessing these numbers, it is necessary to consider the relatively high quality of Soviet schools and the educational focus on mathematics and science—a fact noted by American experts on the Soviet army (Jones 1985, p. 61).

Undoubtedly, life in the Soviet barracks was, as General William Odom wrote, "grim and dangerous," but it was much better than the life of Russian soldiers in post-Soviet times (Odom 1998, p. 46). In any case, on the eve of perestroika, the act of joining the army was considered honorable, though there were some cases when conscripts tried to skirt military service, particularly in the early 1980s.[28]

The army was a well-respected institution among all strata of the population. The occupation of officer was among the ten most prestigious jobs in the country. This view had already been established by the first sociological studies of male teenagers conducted in the 1960s. On a scale from 1 (low regard) to 10 (high regard), the position of officer was rated by young males with a score of 6.4 (in 1965); four years later, this number had increased to 7.5. Army officers enjoyed higher levels of prestige than the majority of occupations which demanded a college education (i.e., engineers, doctors, and teachers).[29] Among rural teenagers, the profession of officer ranked second on a list of the most favored jobs (Tarasov 1974, pp. 25–81).

By 1985, the quality of the officers corps of the Soviet army was very high. As General Odom noted, the Soviet officer was "literate and reasonably well trained in his military specialty" (Odom 1998, p. 41; see also Moynihan 1989, pp. 336–337). In comparison with the 1920s, the average educational level had risen dramatically. By 1966, 85 percent of officers had secondary military educations (Lisenkov 1977, p. 121). Military schools were extremely competitive. The training of officers was carried out in 170 military colleges around the country. One third of military cadets came from families with strong military traditions (Moynihan 1989, p. 337).

At the same time, the army had its flaws, as evidenced by cases of incompetence, nepotism in the selection of cadres, corruption, beating of recruits by officers, hazing and alcoholism (Moynihan 1989, pp. 348–350). Even during WWII, bribes were made by conscripts and their families to district military commissars in order to avoid the draft.[30] However, the number of such cases in the Soviet period is minute, compared to their frequency in the post-Soviet era.

Like the KGB, the army did not have a serious political influence on the Kremlin.[31] It would be preposterous to talk about the Soviet regime as "a military theocracy," despite the deeply militarized character of the society run by the Kremlin.[32] There was not a single military plot against Soviet authorities in the history of the country. The alleged conspiracy of Soviet commanders against Stalin in the mid-1930s was nothing more than a bluff. The Kremlin did not allow military leaders even a modicum of independence. A look at Marshal Georgii Zhukov's relations with Stalin and Khrushchev is very instructive. Stalin and Khrushchev were both intolerant of even the slightest show of independence by Zhukov. In 1946, Stalin actually fired Zhukov from his position as deputy minister of defense. Later, after being appointed by Khrushchev in 1955 as minister of defense, Zhukov was again dismissed from this position, in 1957. At the same time, there is no serious evidence supporting the theory of Zhukov's Bonapartism (see Avidar 1983, pp. 147–188). The fate of another prominent military leader, Admiral Nikolai Kuznetsov, who was rudely downgraded in rank by Stalin in 1948, confirms this rule.[33]

Marshal Nikolai Ogarkov's mild criticism of the Kremlin for its defense policy in 1981 led to his immediate "resignation" (see Ellman and Kontorovich 1998, pp. 48, 61, 62, 64). In 1987, with one stroke of the pen, Gorbachev dismissed several high-ranking army commanders, including Minister of Defense Sergei Sokolov and all his deputies; the head of the general staff and two of his deputies; and the commander and head of all Warsaw Pact troops. A total of 150 generals and officers were court-martialed. Gorbachev used the notorious Mathias Rust case in 1987 to justify these actions (Rust, a German youth, had landed his Cessna on Red Square after crossing a thousand miles of Soviet territory from Finland; see Legostaev 1998).

With the regime already on its knees, the coup in August 1991 was the single case in which the heads of the KGB and the army dared (though unsuccessfully) participate in the political struggle with their own initiatives.

The party apparatus used several tactics (most importantly, the activities of political police) to keep the army and its officials under its strict control. The KGB carefully monitored the behavior and attitudes of generals, officers, and soldiers. The KGB spread over each unit of the military, employing special officers and a vast network of informers (Mondich 1950; Seth 1967).

After the civil war, the leadership enrolled as many high-ranking commanders as it could in the party. Even a few former tsarists generals, such as Ioakim Vazetis and Sergei Kamenev, who supported the Bolsheviks during the civil war, joined the Communist Party, along with Marshals Mikhail Tukhachevsky and Boris Shaposhnikov, who entered the Central Committee (Fedotoff White 1944, pp. 37–39). Over time, membership in the party became almost obligatory for people in the military. By the end of the war with Germany, almost all officers were members of the party, which gave the commanders additional leverage over them. By 1974, almost 80 percent of the officers were party members and 15 percent were members of the Komsomol. This was a much higher proportion of party membership than among other occupations which demanded special education (Jones 1985, p. 127).

Another way in which the party exerted control over the army was through the institution of political commissars (before 1942) and of the political deputy of the commander of all army units. These political officers, with the support of party and Komsomol units, were responsible for the ideological indoctrination of all military personnel, particularly officers (see Avidar 1983, pp. 201–238). In spite of the rather unsophisticated nature of their propaganda, the campaign was quite successful. From the 1940s to the time of perestroika, almost all military personnel believed, for instance, that every great military invention (from radios and tanks to the nuclear bomb) came from Russia. Army officers were among the most loyal people in the country and completely supported its imperial and geopolitical goals.[34]

The Soviet system minimized ethnic conflicts in the army. In spite of the absolute dominance of Slavs (predominantly Russians) among generals and officers, the strong emphasis on Russian patriotism in military propaganda, and the high percentage (no less than one third) of non-Slavs among the soldiers (many of them did not speak Russian, the single command language in the army, prior to being drafted), the army commanders easily prevented serious dissent along ethnic lines among the troops. Relative ethnic harmony was achieved also by the leaders' decision to avoid non-Slavic, ethnically based combat units. In all of Soviet army history, there was not a single major rebellion by non-Russian servicemen (Moynihan 1989, pp. 337, 341, 343).

Fear As a Weapon of the Soviet State

The fear of being punished by the authorities reinforces the laws of any regime. In the Soviet Union, however, this type of fear was omnipresent. The totalitarian state could easily deprive the people of their liberty and life. The omnipresent KGB, its enormous network of informers, the internal passport system, and the permanent pressure from colleagues and coworkers generated high levels of fear in society in the first three decades of the regime. The fear was so pronounced that it passed from generation to generation. In effect, the post-Stalin leaders were able to reduce the scope of repressions while maintaining fear as a political instrument. The terror during the civil war, collectivization, the mass repressions in the 1930s, and the deportation of various ethnic groups in the 1940s, played a decisive role in maintaining fear and order in society in later decades (Luneev 1997, p. 181). The negation or underestimation of the mass repressions was a generic feature of the revisionist school and the critics of the totalitarian model. Among other things, they also underestimated the horror of collectivization.

In fact, collectivization was one of the greatest atrocities in modern history. According to one of the leading experts on collectivization, Russian historian Nikolai Ivnitsky, 1 million peasant families (a total of 5 to 6 million people) suffered in various ways under collectivization in 1929–1931 (Ivnitsky 1990, 1996). About 2 million peasants were deported. Hundreds of thousands of peasants were murdered or perished in exile. The number of deported "kulaks" does not include the many thousands of peasants who did not wait to be evicted by the NKVD and fled their villages.[35] The millions of peasants who stayed in their villages starved to death in their homes, particularly in Ukraine and North Caucasus. Russian agriculture never recuperated from the lethal blow of collectivization.[36] Along with collectivization, the Kremlin launched a campaign against the old intelligentsia in the late 1920s, holding show trials and sending hundreds of highly educated people to the Gulag.[37] These people were said to be deeply hostile to the Soviet system, but in actuality they could not be considered a real political opposition by any means.

Collectivization and the persecution of the old intelligentsia were followed by the "great terror," which brought numberless additional sufferings. As they had done with collectivization, the revisionists tried to diminish this tragedy as well.[38] According to official KGB data published in 1990, from the 1930s to the early 1950s roughly 3.8 million people were arrested and sentenced to death, internal exile, or the Gulag by extrajudicial bodies (the notorious troika). Of this group, 786,000 were executed. These figures, the compiler of the KGB data asserted, did not include the "victims of dekulakization, starvation and deportation."[39]

During the terror, the deportation of ethnic groups such as Poles and Koreans began in the 1930s and greatly increased in the 1940s. According to Russian experts, the number of people who were exiled during these two waves of deportation ranged from about 3.2 to 3.4 million; some estimates went as high as 5.2 to 5.5 million (*Istoriia SSSR* 6, 1989, p. 135; *Voprosy istorii* 7, 1990, p. 44; Tsoi 1994, p. 12; Luneev 1997, p. 172). Roughly 25 percent of those who were exiled perished along the way (*Istoriia SSSR* 1, 1992, pp. 130, 142; *Voprosy istorii* 7, 1990, p. 33).

The mass repressions of the 1940s were extended to former prisoners of war and so-called displaced people (individuals who had been displaced from the Soviet Union for various reasons and were living in West Europe after WWII). The Soviet authorities screened more than 4 million people (civilian and military) who returned to the motherland after the war. Almost all of them were discriminated against in one way or another. No less than one quarter of this group was sent to the Gulag or to "working battalions" (*Rossiia XXI* 5, 1993, p. 80).

All-Consuming Fear As the Necessary Ingredient of Soviet Normalcy

The mass repressions in the first three decades of the regime were necessary for the function of the "normal" Soviet totalitarian state. If the leaders had not resorted to these repressions, the system would not have survived even a few years. The totalitarian system was in fact essentially based on fear engendered by the state's terrorization of the populace. As Victor Luneev stated, "By 1937, the Soviet leaders created a well arranged and 'effectively' working mechanism which allowed for the elimination of any undesirable person. Any phenomenon or event which cast a shadow on the authorities had to be mercilessly destroyed" (Luneev 1997, p. 175). Without collectivization (which allowed for the exportation of grain), Stalin, Trotsky, and Zinoviev (see Tsipko 1989a, pp. 186–187) would have found it impossible to advance industrialization and the construction of the military industrial complex.[40] Collectivization crushed any peasant who was not willing to sell his grain at low prices. Without collectivization, the peasants would have remained insubordinate and unmanageable. Stalin made them into obedient servants. For many years, the peasants worked the collective farms, surviving on food from their small private plots.

The mass repressions directed against party apparatchiks and intellectuals were also an important condition for the installation of a full-fledged totalitarian society in Russia. Take away these repressions, and neither Stalin nor his heirs could have maintained their power. The system would have fallen apart as early as the 1930s. Fear was the most important element of

Soviet life before 1953.[41] Even after 1953, with collectivization and the mass repressions in the past, these events continued to be important for the stability of the system.

The Masses As Supervisors

The Soviet system, based on fear and ideological indoctrination, turned millions of people into spies, propagandists of the deceptive ideology, and supervisors of the people themselves. The leaders were able to employ these people with minimal material rewards or even no rewards at all. The inclusion of the Soviet people in the political process had nothing to do with "the participation of the masses in governing the country," as revisionists of the 1970s and 1980s contended. While conceding that Soviet mass participation in the government took a somewhat different form than its counterpart in the West, several revisionists insisted that the contribution of the masses in the Soviet political process was enormous and to some extent even higher than in a classic democratic system.

Revisionists considered the many forms of public activity in the USSR (trade union committees and conferences; the election campaigns, during which people vented their grievances to the authorities; and the people's complaints to the media and government) a sufficient alternative to free elections with more than one candidate. In order to solidify the concept of participation, some revisionists went so far as to contend that the people exercised their freedom of speech (within limits) and enjoyed the right to openly criticize and complain. These assumptions show that revisionist Sovietologists blindly accepted official Soviet data about the number of participants at various meetings, campaigns, and propagandistic actions.[42]

The torrent of new information about political life in Stalin's time, which became accessible to scholars after 1987, had little impact on the views of most revisionists, with Sheila Fitzpatrick as the main exception. In 1997, Lewis Siegelbaum continued to accept the staged constitutional debates of 1936 at face value. He did not deviate from his theory about the genuine and spontaneous character of the Stakhanov movement, which was, in fact, a mostly fictitious campaign arranged by party officials.[43]

The fact that the system included many millions of people in various state organizations is indisputable. Many people performed several public roles simultaneously. In 1982, there were 17.7 million party members, 41.3 million people in the Komsomol, 2.3 million deputies in the Soviets at various levels, 7 million members of trade union committees, 131.2 million "ordinary" trade union members, and 10.4 million volunteers in the "system of people's control" (TsSU SSSR 1982, pp. 47–51). There were also 20 million people who worked "part time" as agitators and propagandists throughout the party and state apparatus as well as in education, science, and cultural institutions (see V. Shlapentokh 1986, pp. 6–8, 167).

However, mass participation in official organizations does not mean that the people influenced domestic or foreign policy, as the "revisionists" suggested. In fact, the masses were obedient "cogs and bolts" (as Stalin called them) in the Soviet totalitarian machine. The rationale of Soviet leaders (like that of leaders of any totalitarian society) in involving people in these organizations was quite sound: Each new organization provided an additional mechanism to influence individuals' behavior; and the individual's activity, in turn, worked as an instrument for controlling others. At the same time, the participation of people as agents of the Soviet system had a conformist effect on the Russian mind-set and to some degree also on the individual's behavior toward the regime (White 1993; Friedgut 1977).

Of no less significance was the involvement of millions of people in middle- and low-level managerial work. The system employed millions of factory foremen, chiefs of laboratories, managers of educational, financial, and research institutions, and supervisors of collective farms. The transformation of up to one third of the adult population into "little bosses," who had minimal privileges or real authority yet maintained a sense of "belonging" to the dominant class, was one of the most brilliant inventions of the Soviet system.

The system also converted many citizens into informers for the political police (Felshtinsky 1995, p. 93). There are various estimates about the number of informers in Soviet society. Indirect data suggest that there were several million active informers who served either voluntarily (to demonstrate their loyalty to the regime for safety and promotion, or to settle scores with personal enemies) or involuntarily (under pressure from KGB agents).[44] In various circles (political leadership, military command, the creative intelligentsia, and the church), ubiquitous informers supplied vast amounts of reliable information about the deeds and thoughts of individuals.[45]

By enrolling a significant percentage of the adult population as informers, the regime not only obtained necessary information about potential dangers to the state but also guaranteed the people's slavish devotion to the regime.

Conclusion

Among the various elements of the Soviet system, the political machine was by far the most efficient. Essentially, the system worked as an effective tool for achieving the goals set by the general secretary and the ruling political elite. It protected the regime, maintained order and unity in society, controlled the outer regions of the USSR, ensured the country's independence and helped achieve its geopolitical ambitions. Using the political police, the system inspired fear among the people, which stabilized the political climate. It also gained the support of the most active people in the country by endowing them with various (mostly low) positions and some privileges. The official ideology, as discussed in previous chapters, blanketed the media, education, literature, and the arts, and controlled the minds of most Russians, shaping their vision of the world in an image conducive to Soviet goals. The system did not fall because of internal weaknesses, nor was it demolished by the external resistance of a discontented population, or by rival political forces. The Soviet political system was destroyed "from above." This issue will be carefully discussed in later chapters.

9
The Economy
Organic Flaws and Achievements

The Bolsheviks developed the fundamentals of the Soviet economic system almost immediately after the revolution. In spite of the evident economic changes over the life span of the regime, these fundamentals stayed largely intact after the period of "War Communism."[1] The Supreme Council of Economy (VSNKh), the future Gosplan, was created in December 1917. A number of other bodies emerged during the civil war and operated various sectors of the economy, including the Council of Labor and Defense (1919). The Bolsheviks started with the nationalization of all banks and then foreign trade. In the first half of 1918, the state took control of the big enterprises in all branches of the economy. Even during the NEP (1922–1924), private businesses, which employed hired hands, created only 9 percent of the Soviet GNP (Rumiantsev 1985, pp. 286–289).

The idea of a state-regulated economy was quite fashionable in the world, even outside the socialist movement, in the early twentieth century, particularly during World War I. This was especially true for Russia and Germany, where the state-regulated economy was a direct continuation of wartime governmental policy—for instance, in the procurement of food (Malle 1997, p. 651). After World War I, the prestige of the state as an active economic agent greatly increased in the world, with the help of John Maynard Keynes's theory and Roosevelt's New Deal. The Soviet experiment, with its planning system and five-year plans, was being watched with great enthusiasm by many intellectuals. The Nazi regulation of the German economy aroused popular support not only in Germany but also in the West. For many years after 1945 (up until the late 1970s), the state-regulated economy, as compared to the market economy, was considered by many politicians and scholars across the globe as the best instrument for rapid modernization and the prevention of economic crises. In the Russian context, the highly centralized economy was considered not only by Bolsheviks but also by many Western experts as vital for the modernization of the country.

From this point of view, it is rather preposterous to speak about the irrationality or utopianism of Soviet leaders because of their admiration for the highly centralized economy. Would a market economy have served the interests of the totalitarian system and the leaders' personal interests better than absolute state control over the economy? The leaders spurned the market not because they failed to appreciate its evident efficiency but because it was against their better interests. All of the leaders wanted to improve the command economy in one way or another, but none of them envisioned an economic revolution. Certainly, Gorbachev was closest to designing a radical economic transformation. However, even Gorbachev was reluctant to speak about private property. He did not use the term until the end of his presidency, when he was undergoing great public pressure due to the new social context.

As will be shown in this chapter, the Soviets created an original economic system. Though somewhat awkward and inefficient by Western standards, it prospered as a highly complex system, which operated with intricate mechanisms, including market instruments.

Dire Predictions and Harsh Reality

Several great scholars of the 1920s–1940s, such as Friedrich Hayek (1935, 1944), Ludwig von Mises (1951), and David Bruzkus (1995) predicted that the central planning system would fail miserably. They believed that the Bolsheviks would be unable to develop an economy that was any different from the system used during War Communism (a period in which market mechanisms were almost completely absent in the management of the economic system). This type of system, they contended, could not function over any length of time. They saw the installation of the NEP, with its focus on the restoration of the market after the civil war, as evidence supporting their prediction.

The critics were certain that the planning system was based on utopian ideas and unrealistic premises. They argued that the planned economy—which could not use free prices as the major regulator of economic decisions, which focused only on labor as the major factor of production, which ignored the productivity of capital and natural resources in the decision-making process and refused to give producers and consumers free choices—

would not generate technological progress and therefore would stagnate and inevitably collapse.[2] In many respects the critics were right.[3] Their critique, however, overlooked the system's major flaw: the ineffective mechanism for evaluating performance.

The Problematic Mechanism of Evaluation

The efficacy of any organization, individual firm, or national economy depends to a great degree on the mechanism of evaluation. The mechanism of evaluation determines the reward of actors as well as the recruitment of cadres. If this mechanism fails, the organization will eventually collapse.

The major problem with the Soviet economic system was not the lack of information about the consumer's preferences, or the production capacities of single enterprises (this criticism of the planning system was frequently voiced by Soviet economists who favored a market economy in the 1960s). Its biggest flaw was its mechanism of evaluation; the Soviet mechanism was inferior to that of the market, which utilized consumers as major actors.[4] Indeed, the relative inefficiency of the economy should not be ascribed to the central planning system per se, but directly to the lack of consumer control over economic performance. If it were possible to combine central planning with consumer control, the economy would have looked very different. The consumer can play a decisive role only when the economy has been established on market principles.

The evaluation of performance in the Soviet economy was based almost exclusively on hierarchical control. Each level of the hierarchy controlled the level below. The quality of this control depended on the competence of managers and their devotion to their professional work. Indeed, in the post-Stalin period the task of evaluating workers at all levels was taken over by people for whom career advancement and lifestyle enhancement were major priorities. Mid-level managers colluded with subordinates in order to cheat higher-level managers, the state, and consumers.[5] Apparatchiks promoted only those people who were ready to serve them rather than the state (Rigby 1990; Zemtsov 1985).

The top leaders held contradictory attitudes toward the selection of cadres and the evaluation of their performance. On one hand, Soviet leaders overvalued the loyalty of their subordinates. They regularly appointed their former countrymen and people with whom they had worked in the past to high positions, regardless of the latter's qualifications.

The "imitation" of real work became a fixture in many offices, research institutes and factories.[6] There were various forms of "imitation" as well as many ways to earn money by doing almost nothing. The imitation of work was characteristic of the post-Stalin USSR.[7]

So long as the highest managers in the country were dedicated to real economic progress, the economy could perform under the existing conditions relatively well. However, as soon as the ideological fervor, dedication to the cause, and punishment for poor work weakened, the economic system (much like any non-market sector in Western society) began to deteriorate, and effective performance declined.[8] The evaluation of performance by managers foundered because bureaucrats at various levels of the hierarchy went into collusion with each other against the consumers of the products. With this collusion of managers, the true evaluation of performance was often replaced by phony indicators as well as the imitation of effective economic activity.

The Soviet leaders were aware of the weaknesses in the mechanism of performance, the absence of consumer control, and the collusion between various levels of the hierarchy for the obfuscation of statistical data. For this reason, after Lenin died they created various external mechanisms of control. In the last two decades of the system there were several dozens of these institutions, with branches in each territorial unit, and thousands of full-time inspectors whose major goal was only to monitor and control performance. This expansion included several ministries and special party committees. By 1985, no less than 10 million people, or about 10–15 percent of all employees, were enrolled as social auditors. However, this gigantic and cumbersome system of control was almost totally ineffective, and it did not compensate for the lack of market mechanisms for evaluating performance, which give the last word to consumers (V. Shlapentokh 1988a).

The last attempt to improve economic performance was initiated in 1986 by Gorbachev, who created the state quality system. With 70,000 inspectors, the Kremlin hoped to bring about an evolution in the quality of goods. This experiment failed as had similar, previous efforts, because once again these inspectors went into collusion with managers, which aroused the hostility of the party committees (Mozhin 1998b, p. 122).

As another remedy, the leadership enrolled ordinary people as supervisors. According to official data, no less than 10 percent of those employed in the country took part in auditing activities as their social obligation. Among the members of the party, the number of "voluntary controllers," by the end of the 1970s, reached almost 25 percent (see Borev 1978, p. 33; see also V. Shlapentokh 1988a, pp. 25–26).

However, it would be wrong to exaggerate the irresponsibility of the Soviet people and depict their work as universally poor and sloppy. In fact, with the cult of professionalism in society, many people (scholars, doctors, engineers, teachers, skilled workers, and collective farmers, along with numerous managers at various levels of the social hierarchy) continued to work hard and effectively even in the last two decades of the regime.

The Negative Contribution of Ideology

The Soviet economy suffered much less from the influence of ideological doctrines than from its centralization. Most decisions in the context of the given economic system were quite rational. The ideological dogmas were used to rationalize the economic practices rather than to direct them.[9] At the same time, it would be wrong to ignore the negative impact of ideology on real economic policies.

The Marxist theory of value definitely took its toll on the economy. The major tenets of this theory—that income is generated only by labor and that the relative shortage of most resources should not be recognized—rationalized the indifference of managers to the waste of capital goods and natural resources; the loss of capital goods did not affect the financial situation of an enterprise and had no negative effect on the economic indicators used for the evaluation of managers' performance.[10] The same theory of value was used to explain why rent (i.e., the payment for production resources) was absent in official economic calculations. Likewise, time was also disregarded as an economic factor. Another drawback of this theory was that it did not recognize services (i.e., passenger transportation, retail trade, real estate services, financial institutions) as inputs of the GNP. The theory calculated the GNP using only material production, such as that of industry, agriculture, building and construction, and freight transportation.

The Marxist theory of labor value used average cost to determine prices, and rejected the consumer's evaluation of the utility of goods as an economic factor. This made it difficult for Soviet planners to take into account the law of supply and demand when setting prices. However, in the late 1970s, the Kremlin dropped some of its ideological objections against the use of "bourgeois" economic concepts. The Kremlin endorsed, for instance, the rule that made enterprises pay rent for their capital goods (Gatovsky and Abalkin 1984, pp. 539, 579–585).

The unqualified hatred of private property and the belief in the economic superiority of public enterprises over private businesses—particularly during the Stalin and Khrushchev regimes—also had a very negative impact on the Soviet economy (Lisichkin 1989, pp. 24–25).[11] However, the leaders were correct in that they understood that private property in the economy was incompatible with the political system. It would create an economic basis for oppositional activity. Of no less concern for the Kremlin was the argument that private business, however small, encouraged illegal economic activity and expanded corruption in the party and state apparatus (such was the case during the NEP, in the 1920s, when businessmen bribed the heroes of the civil war). Notwithstanding these limitations, the leadership still could have made life in the country better with a less aggressive ideological stance.[12]

Chronic Diseases of the Soviet Economy

Indeed, with the consumer playing a very limited role in the economy and with the absence of major market regulators of economic activity, the system suffered almost from the very beginning. The major chronic diseases of the system included a slow rate of technological progress, perennial technological dependence on the West, immense loss of resources, and low quality of consumer goods.

The major principle of the Soviet planning system was that production should increase each year in comparison with the previous year. The increase would demonstrate the economy's vitality and superiority over Western economies. This principle became a great obstacle to technological progress (Birman 1978, p. 153). The managers were faced with two options: either to proceed with technological innovations, which might cause production for a time to fall short of the official quota, or to continue producing old commodities at the officially prescribed rate and fall behind in technological progress. Encouraged by their superiors from the ministries, the majority of managers preferred the second option, which guaranteed a rapid rate of growth of mostly obsolete goods. As a result, the Soviet economy, from the beginning, grew extensively, due mostly to the augmentation of the labor force and only minimally to technological progress.

In terms of technology, the USSR was dependent on the West. "Soviet civilization" was technologically imitative and poised to follow the Western lead. Industrialization was carried out mostly on the basis of technology imported from the West and with the help of Western engineers. After the war, industry relied on the confiscation of German plants. The leaders later created a gigantic network of agents assigned to copy and steal Western technology. The numerous achievements of Soviet scholars and engineers (mostly in the military industry) were unable to diminish the country's technological dependence on the West. During the whole existence of the "Soviet civilization," Soviet scholars and engineers did not invent even one consumer product or service. By the end of the 1970s, it had become evident that the Soviet Union, even with the flow of information and technological secrets from the West, had to reconcile itself to a growing technological gap between it and the rest of the world. At the same time, this gap was modest apropos of military production, which concentrated the best minds in the country. The military industry was well supplied with technologies stolen from the West. Unlike the civil industry, it did not ignore the consumer of its products—generally, the Soviet army.

The dominance of public property was one of the major causes of the gigantic waste of resources (i.e., capital goods and natural resources as well as raw materials and consumer goods). Soviet industry spent two to three times more resources on the production of goods than that in advanced capitalist countries (Lisichkin 1989, p. 33). The agricultural and building industries were among the most wasteful sectors of the economy. According to official data, the annual losses of grain were calculated at 20–25 percent; vegetables and fruits, 30 percent; and milk and meat, 10–15 percent (Gvozdev 1985, p. 88). Pilfering in factories and collective farms was accepted by the population as a normal practice, and only a minority (no more than 20 percent of workers) even verbally condemned this phenomenon (Grechin 1983, p. 124).

One of the most obvious weaknesses of the economy was its inability to provide food to the people. Food shortages were a problem in the country from the revolution on. Long lines for basic staples, including bread, were constant throughout Soviet history. In the early 1960s, agricultural production was higher than in the previous years (the harvest of grain was 125.5 million tons in 1960 versus 121.5 million tons on average each year in 1956–1960), but the level of production could not keep pace with the increasing demand for food. The riots in Novocherkassk (1962) and Karaganda (1962) occurred as a result of food shortages in these cities.

While the growing food shortages made the situation dramatic, the Soviet state, without mass terror, could not guarantee the obedience of the population in the face of new sufferings. Khrushchev had this line of reasoning in mind when he decided to address the West and call for the "humiliating" importation of food.[13] The food supply, which improved in the first decade of Brezhnev's regime, deteriorated significantly again in the early 1980s. However, even with all the serious food problems in post-Stalin times, hunger was absent and the Soviet diet was in many respects quite decent, despite the tasks involved in acquiring food (i.e., long queuing lines and work in private gardens). The Soviet diet in the mid- to late-1980s was more nourishing and sustainable than the diet seven years later, after the anti-Communist revolution.[14]

The quality of consumer goods was always poor, compared with similar goods in the West (United States Congress 1981; Birman 1989). After 1953, the poor quality of goods was frequently decried in the Soviet media. Numberless actions were taken by the government in order to improve the quality of goods, but no significant success came until the end of the system. While the quality of consumer goods was poor, the products were not unfit for consumption. Some goods, though inferior, were quite reliable (e.g., refrigerators and television sets). Soviet cars were certainly substandard, yet they served as a normal means of transportation; millions of people were eager to purchase one. Not surprisingly, the highest-quality goods were produced in the military industry, where there was real control by consumers (that is, special military purchasing departments).

The Dynamism of the Soviet Economic System

With all its flaws the Soviet economy was a normally functioning system, with a history of ups and downs. As previously mentioned, this semi-cyclical movement—or almost uniform progress, in some cases—was typical also in several other key institutions of Soviet society, such as the KGB, the army, the ideological apparatus, education, and health services. Even though bureaucratic mismanagement, the waste of resources, and the low quality of products affected all periods of Soviet economic history, there was some fluctuation in overall performance. The reports made by foreigners who worked in the Soviet Union in the late 1920s and the 1930s depicted a gloomy economic picture.[15] However, after the period of industrialization, the efficiency of the economy increased. It was hardly possible to deny the significant improvements of the Soviet economy which took place in the 1950s and early 1960s and again in the mid-1970s.

The divergence of views on Soviet economic developments has stemmed to a great extent from the confusion of "objective" and "subjective" indicators of economic progress. The feebleness of the economy became a popular issue for the first time in the early 1960s. The timing of these debates had little to do with the objective processes in the economy. In fact, as Grigorii Khanin showed, the 1950s were one of the best decades, if not the best, in Soviet economic history.[16]

However, by the early 1960s, the political and ideological processes triggered by Stalin's death had radically modified the state's view of the economy. The gradual opening of the country to the West, the new knowledge about Western products, and the softening of Soviet ideology changed the criteria for assessing economic performance.[17] Paradoxically, negative views of the Soviet economic outlook emerged when the economy was in rather good shape compared to the past. The rate of growth in the 1960s and 1970s, even if we ignore the weakness of this indicator as a measurement of performance for a socialist economy, remained higher than in the United States and other Western countries. However, after 1975 the economy started to falter and entered a phase of deterioration. This decline was revealed by many "objective" economic indicators, such as the rate of growth of national income and productivity.[18]

The decline in these indicators could be partly attributed to the departure of the Soviet economy from the stage of primary industrialization and the "extensive growth" that was mostly generated by the stream of new workers in the economy. The fall of these indicators reflected, of course, the impact of various chronic diseases on economic performance. These problems included a steady decline in labor ethics, the spread of drunkenness among workers, the permanent shortage of workers, the diminution of the authority of managers, the disappearance of fear, the erosion of ideology, the falling value of the ruble, and the permanent shortage of consumer goods. Of great importance was the growing technological retardation, as mentioned before, as an inherent feature of the Soviet economy. At the same time, in the 1970s and 1980s a new factor began to affect the economy: the growing depletion of natural resources and the rising cost of extracting natural resources—particularly oil and gas.

Cruel Flexibility: Two Types of Socialist Property

While critics of the Soviet economy were right to reject Marxist claims about the planning system's superiority over the market, they underestimated various maneuvers that the leaders undertook to make their economy function. The division of Soviet agricultural enterprises into collective and state farms was a good example of rational decision making. Formally, collective farms belonged to the members of the collective farms, who elected the chairman and the board of the farm, who supposedly managed the enterprise. State farms were state enterprises run by a director, who was appointed by a minister with the consent of the local party committee. The important distinction between the two forms of socialist property—all-people's (or state) and collective-cooperative—was underscored by the ideology and official economics throughout the history of the Soviet system (see Rumiantsev 1985, pp. 316–317). This distinction was indeed advantageous for the system, though most Soviet citizens and many social scientists saw it as purely propagandistic in nature and without practical purpose (Timofeev 1985).

Both state and collective farms were controlled in the same way by the state as well as by the local party committee. The democratic character of management in collective farms was a pure fiction. The chairman of a collective farm was selected and appointed by the local party committee. Collective farms, like state farms, were obliged to deliver a planned quantity of agricultural products, and their leaders were punished for any failure to do so.

However, the separation of collective and state farms was quite reasonable from the position of the Kremlin. For Soviet leaders, the most important differences between two types of agricultural enterprise was in labor remuneration. The state guaranteed minimal wages only to state farm workers. It released itself from any obligation to collective farmers. Over several decades, collective farmers received nothing for their work, and survived only on the food from their private plots. This situation was quite satisfactory for the Kremlin. Absorbed with geopolitical interests, the Kremlin directed only meager resources to the production of consumer goods. After Stalin, when the leaders changed the distribution of national income and increased the peasants' standard of living, they began to gradually transform collective farms into state farms. The leadership's 1966 decision to begin paying collective farmers the same as state farm workers was a radical step in this direction (Shimshilevich 1969, p. 147). In 1940, state farms accounted for only 9 percent of all farmland; in 1955, the proportion was 16 percent; and in 1986, 53 percent (TsSU SSSR 1956, p. 110).

The Rationality of the Leadership

The critics of the centralized economy were wrong to reject the possibilities of improving the planning system and introducing some elements of the market. They underestimated the flexibility of the leadership and its willingness to improve the economy. Soviet leaders were in many ways satisfied with the political system, and yet quite dissatisfied with the economy. In the early 1930s, and particularly during the war, Stalin greatly increased the autonomy of the directors who ran large construction projects and military factories. Directors such as Isaak M. Zaltsman, the famous chief of the tank complex ("Tank City") in Cheliabinsk during the war, enjoyed almost total independence from local party bosses as well as from the minister who was responsible for the given branch of the economy (Zaltsman and Edelhaus 1984, pp. 76–87). The directors were subordinate only to Stalin or a member of the Politburo. Stalin used a very sophisticated bureaucratic device to guarantee the independent status of his leading "captains of industry."[19] Post-Stalin leaders were much more critical of the economic system than Stalin. They were aware of its numerous flaws and chronic diseases and looked for possibilities to increase efficiency. All of these leaders, particularly Khrushchev and Gorbachev, understood the flaws of the rigid, centralized government and tried to reconsider the relations between the center and managers as well as between the local party apparatus and managers. In the first years of his tenure, even Leonid Brezhnev—the symbol of Soviet immobilism (or "stagnation")—played with the idea of some decentralization of management with the use of market mechanisms. Yurii Andropov, with his evident neo-Stalinist orientations, also encouraged economic decentralization (Y. Andropov 1983b, pp. 4–9).

Along with administrative decentralization, the leaders had a tendency to increase the autonomy of managers from their administrative superiors, permitting them to make some modest investments in the development of their enterprises (particularly after the late 1960s). Managers were also given some leeway in their relationship with consumers and suppliers of raw materials and parts. On the eve of perestroika, the authors of an official textbook on

Soviet economics had good reason to assert that "market relations play an important role in the planning management of the Soviet economy" (Gatovsky and Abalkin 1984, p. 419; see also Hanson 1968; Birman 1983).

In the 1930s, the government accepted several instruments of the market economy, all of which were inconceivable under War Communism.[20] The role of these instruments increased until the collapse of the regime. The Soviet planning system used "indicators in kind" to determine the quantity of each good to be produced as well as "value indicators," which described the combined value of all goods in rubles, based on planning prices. These "value indicators" provided managers with some leeway in regulating the quantity of several goods to be produced. For instance, in some cases, directors could increase the production of goods with high prices at the expense of products with low prices, augmenting the general value of the product and fulfilling, or over fulfilling, the planned targets apropos of value indicators. While the military industry was pushed to meet its quota in kind (i.e., the number of tanks or planes), civilian industry was driven more by plans in rubles.

Soviet planners were never able to balance the supply and demand of goods. The demand for consumer and production goods greatly surpassed the supply. With prices set by the state, there was always a shortage of goods. Both individual consumers and managers saw the shortages as a major problem in their life and professional activity. Consumers spent hours queuing for goods, or resorted to various illegal means. Likewise, managers spent much of their working day searching for raw materials and parts for production (for a theoretical explanation of this phenomenon, see Kornai 1980; see also Karagedov 1970).

Planners tried to mitigate this imbalance in supply and demand by manipulating prices. The role of prices was particularly significant for the production and sale of consumer goods. Even Stalin, a great adversary of the market economy, publicly recognized in 1951, a few years before his death, the role of the "law of value"—that is, the role of prices in regulating the economy, particularly the production and distribution of consumer goods (Stalin 1952a, p. 17). All kinds of products (i.e., bread, milk, sugar, cheese, clothing, furniture, and cars) were purchased by citizens at state prices. On the surface, the behavior of Soviet consumers, who compared the price tags on goods, was similar to Western consumer behavior. In most circumstances, the official prices even had an anchoring effect on the prices of nonofficial (or "under the counter") goods. In some cases, the government set up prices in accordance to the law of supply and demand. For instance, it modified the prices on vegetables and fruits depending on the season. The government also curtailed the prices of some durable consumer goods (e.g., TV sets or refrigerators) when the supply was too high, and increased the price when the supply was low. The system not only used prices (in various capacities) and taxes as instruments for regulating economic activity but also relied on a developed network of financial institutions which provided long- and short-term credits to stimulate key sectors of the economy (Kuschpèta 1978; Alexandrov 1971; Garvy 1977).

Soviet planners also used monetary instruments in order to direct the supply and demand of the labor force. After 1953, when people were allowed to change their place of work, their job choice was strongly influenced by salary level. As numerous studies have shown, the level of salary was the second or third most important factor motivating Soviets to change jobs. Other factors included the lack of housing in the area and poor working conditions (see Antosenkov and Kalmyk 1970). The government augmented salaries for various occupations in different sectors of the economy, trying to attract people to jobs which demanded more effort under poorer conditions. For this reason, in 1989 the average salary in the fuel industry (coal and oil production, in particular) was almost twice as high as that in the food industry. In some cases, the necessity of recruiting people for unwanted jobs led to labor ironies (Goskomstat 1990, p. 373). For instance, a bus driver working in Moscow in the 1970s and 1980s earned twice as much as an associate professor.

The free (or collective farm) market was another important part of the Soviet economy. After collectivization, which looked like a full-scale restoration of the worst side of War Communism, Stalin allowed peasants (collective farmers and workers on state farms) to grow private plots in order to satisfy their basic needs, and even to sell some of the produce on the free market on the condition that they fulfilled their quota on the collective farm. This decision was of great historical importance, as it allowed for the survival of the peasants, who received almost nothing, or very little, for their work on collective and state farms. In 1940, almost all of the food consumed by peasants came from their own plots: 86 percent of meat, 98 percent of milk, and 97 percent of eggs (V. Ostrovsky 1988).

Moreover, the products from these private plots were also an important source of food for the urban population. In the post-Stalin era, the attitudes of leaders toward private plots oscillated. At first, Khrushchev supported private plots, but he reversed his position in the late 1950s. Then, in the mid-1970s, support for this type of agriculture returned (see Brezhnev 1981, p. 64; see also V. Shlapentokh 1989, pp. 160–162). In any case, by 1985 the owners of private plots produced 25 percent of all agricultural products in the country; what is more, they reacted to market signals when deciding what to grow (TsSU SSSR 1986, p. 185).

The private markets were initially (during collectivization, in the late

1920s) limited to peasants. In 1932, this constraint was removed and the markets were opened to everybody—"a major concession to reality on the part of Stalinist policy makers," as noted by an American researcher (Hessler 1998, p. 521). These markets were used until the fall of the USSR by the absolute majority of the population for the sale and purchase of various goods (see Belikova and Shokhin 1987, p. 7). The goods bought and sold were not only secondhand items (completely legal) but new goods as well (usually illegal and combated by the authorities with varying degrees of intensity, depending on the period). The bartering of goods between customers was another type of transaction used in these markets. Bartering was spurred by the rationing and permanent shortages of goods, particularly those of high quality.

After 1953, the importance of the private market increased enormously.[21] Several "colorful" markets emerged—"black," "gray," "pink," and "red," to use Aron Katsenelinboigen's terminology with respect to the free behavior of economic actors (Katsenelinboigen 1976; see also Belikova and Shokhin 1987, pp. 6–8). The authorities even allowed, though not officially, the activity of wholesalers in the collective farm market. Wholesalers bought the agricultural products grown by peasants on their private plots and sold them at higher prices to consumers in the marketplace.

Peasants and residents of small cities were not the only producers of consumer and agricultural products. In Stalin's times and later, millions of people worked on a private basis as tailors, builders, dentists, plumbers, mechanics, and tutors. Their activity fell in a sort of legal gray zone, though some conditions (such as a prohibition against hiring employees) were strictly enforced. This type of producer was often harassed by the authorities, usually concerning taxes of one form or another.[22]

Another important indicator of the flexibility of the Soviet economy in the 1930s–1950s was the existence of so called "industrial cooperation," or "artisanal cooperatives," which particularly flourished in the aftermath of the war, when shortages of consumer goods were acute. A cooperative (or "artel") was a small shop with a few dozen workers (formally known as members of the cooperative), which mostly provided various services, but also some small consumer items, such as buttons or clasps. The cooperative had much more autonomy in its activity than the "normal" state enterprise, particularly in obtaining raw materials, though it was always under the control of local authorities.[23] The activity of these cooperatives was strongly curtailed in 1948, with a new hardening of Stalin's domestic and foreign policy. However, it was Khrushchev, during his crusade against "the remnants of capitalism and individualism" in 1960, who abolished these cooperatives (see Hessler 1998).

Informal and Shadow Economies

The flexibility of Soviet leaders was so great that it allowed for the existence of a huge "informal economy," which helped the rigid planning system achieve the goals set by the Kremlin (Grossman 1977; Katsenelinboigen 1978). As actors in the informal economy, Soviet managers used illegal means to achieve legal goals (i.e., the fulfillment of directives from the Kremlin).

Facing the problematic shortage of production goods, managers created a network of "pushers" (supply agents), who invaded each big firm, trying to get preferential treatment in the supply of raw materials or parts for his or her company. In building favorable relationships with suppliers, managers resorted to the bartering system, in violation of planning quotas. They also used all sorts of personal connections, organized social functions, bribes, and promoted the children and relatives of those who controlled supply channels (Simis 1982, pp. 138–140).

Managers participated in the informal economy in many different ways. They violated laws and instructions when introducing various innovations (mostly of a free market character) in the company. They used illegal material incentives to improve labor. Without permission, managers sometimes sold unessential parts and equipment to firms that needed it. As a rule, the Soviet authorities turned a blind eye to these initiatives if they helped fulfill plans, particularly in the military industry.

The authorities, however, were less tolerant when a manager's innovation led to a drastic rise in employees' salaries. They regarded such an increase as a danger to the relatively egalitarian distribution of income. It could also generate inflation and encourage corruption. In some cases, the authorities even sent "innovators" to prison. For instance, the director of a Kazakh state farm, Ivan Khudenko, was sent to prison after using a new organization of work which gave generous rewards to employees and thereby increased productivity by several times (Yanov 1984). In post-Stalin times, the media as well as public opinion were energetically in favor of innovative managers and fought for the legalization of their practices.[24]

The informal economy should not be confused with the "shadow economy," even though the border between these two economies was quite vague (see Kontorovich and Shlapentokh 1986). The shadow (or "second") economy facilitated the activity of people who used illegal means to achieve illegal goals (i.e., their personal enrichment). This economy included millions of people who used state equipment (for instance, trucks) to provide various services to the population. They also developed underground factories which produced many different consumer goods, and organized teams of builders who were hired mostly by collective farms and peasants to construct buildings and houses. The Soviet authorities tolerated much of the shadow economy, with the exception of underground businesses. If such a business did not have the support of a bribed official, it could be harshly persecuted (Simis 1982, pp. 144–179).

As the informal and the shadow economies expanded, they became more efficient. At the same time, this form of privatization eroded the fundamentals of the command economy.

The Attempts to Improve the Quality of Centralized Management

While all Soviet leaders regarded decentralization (purely administrative, or based on market instruments) as the best strategy for improving economic performance, some tried also to enhance the efficiency of centralized methods of management. Such attempts were made by Stalin in the early 1930s, when he enforced strict cost accounting (*khozraschet´*). Rather than expanding the autonomy of directors, Stalin tightened constraints on the costs of production (see Gatovsky and Abalkin 1984, pp. 533–544).

Another attempt at improving the planning system was initiated during the Brezhnev period, when the Kremlin advanced the use of mathematical methods for optimizing productivity and moved toward the computerization of management (Gatovsky and Abalkin 1984, pp. 280–299). The leaders believed (or claimed to believe) that science could make centralized management more effective and enable the Kremlin to avoid the dangers of market reforms (Katsenelinboigen 1980). While the policy of *khozraschet*, which forced directors to compare the costs and the results of their activities, definitely improved economic performance, the cybernation of the economy in the 1970s and early 1980s was a complete fiasco. The Automatic System of Management (ASM) was highly praised by the Kremlin but was considered by most managers as mere lip service to "progress." They essentially ignored it as a propagandistic nuisance. They had the same lack of respect for several other pseudo-innovations which were introduced between the early 1930s and the late 1980s; the Stakhanov movement, or workers' participation in management, was a good example (see Kontorovich and Shlapentokh 1986).

The Achievements of the Soviet Planning System

Regardless of the real flaws in the system and the pessimistic prognoses in the 1920s, the Soviet economy functioned until 1989–1990 (Bergson and Levine 1983; Nove 1961; Leeman 1977). Indeed, the economy helped the leaders achieve their primary goals: modernization and geopolitical clout. The ability of the system to mobilize its human and material resources while ignoring the costs, made it possible to implement many gigantic projects, from the creation of several new industries (i.e., the automobile, air, and agricultural machine tool industries) in the late 1920s and 1930s to the development of nuclear weapons and missiles.

If the NEP had evolved into a post-revolutionary "Thermidor," the country would have been unable to carry out rapid industrialization.[25] It would have been impossible to create, in such a short period of time, a large military industry which could have provided the army with the necessary tanks, planes, cannons (including the famous Katiusha), and other weapons for the war against Germany.[26] What is more, without a centralized economy, the USSR (which was still economically far behind Germany) could not have mobilized the other resources needed to face this formidable enemy. Prior to WWII, Germany was producing three times more steel than the USSR (Harrison 1998). Reflecting on the war economy, Richard Overy wrote, "In a perfect market the Soviet Union should have been defeated and Germany triumphant" (Overy 1998b, p. 5). The same can be said about the U.S.-Soviet arms race during the cold war. A bourgeois Russia in the postwar period would have been unable to create nuclear weapons to match those possessed by the United States.

Military Parity

With all its retreats from Stalin's glorious times, the Brezhnev era witnessed moments that would have made even Comrade Stalin proud. By the mid-1970s, the Soviet Union had achieved military parity with the United States.

The first big triumphs of the post-Stalin era were the victories in space (Sputnik in 1957, and the first man in space in 1961). The Soviets stayed ahead in the space race until the Apollo 11 mission in July 1969. In the 1970s, the Soviets lost ground to the Americans in space technology generally. But the level of Russian technology in some areas was so high in 1990–1992 that, despite its crumbling economy, Russia easily found an international market (including the United States) for it.[27]

In the mid-1970s, Russia could claim to be a military power equal to the most powerful country in the world. This had been the dream of Russian rulers since the sixteenth century. With its nuclear weapons, Russia could survive in diplomatic isolation, without fear of the West or China. With its economic and military might, the USSR maintained its prominent position in the international arena.

The High Level of Education, Science, and Culture

The Soviet economy and political system supported and developed highly sophisticated spheres of education, science, and culture. The country advanced many top scholars, writers, actors, film and theater directors, and musicians.

With all of its ideological indoctrination and hostility toward independent minds, the educational system was one of the best in the world. Soviet science rapidly declined in 1991, but it previously had ranked near the top. Soviet scholars reaped fewer Nobel Prizes than their American colleagues and were clearly behind in several key fields (e.g., biology), yet they easily competed with the Americans in all areas of mathematics. Soviet theoretical physicists were also quite exceptional (though second to American physicists), allowing the state to achieve military parity with the United States. Many Soviet scholars were elected as honored members of foreign academies. The high quality of Soviet education and science became evident during the mass emigration of scholars after the fall of the USSR. These scholars easily competed with their Western colleagues for positions in the best universities in the world.[28]

The Soviet Union also produced world-class cultural figures. Since the early 1930s, Soviet musicians regularly won first prizes at international competitions. Soviet ballet, opera and dramatic theater were by all accounts excellent; artists in these fields successfully performed abroad. After 1953, the movie industry, despite the rigid ideological control, created many films of high artistic quality that gained international recognition.

A Decent Quality of Life for the Majority of the People

During the post-Stalin period, the longest in Soviet history (the revolution and civil war lasted 4–5 years; the NEP, 4–5 years; the Stalin period, 25–27 years; and the post-Stalin period, 36–38 years), the economy provided the majority of the population a relatively decent standard of living. The leadership of the post-Stalin period ended mass repressions, and the regime softened, though it remained essentially totalitarian in character and deprived the people of all political freedoms. The Soviet Union became less confrontational with the West and used more of its resources on the satisfaction of the basic needs of the population. In the post-Stalin era, the system guaranteed the people's jobs, education, health care, medicine, and basic material needs. The social impact of these positive aspects (i.e., no fear of losing employment, housing, medicine and health care, education, and culture) made it much easier for propagandists to defend claims about the good life in the USSR.

Such claims seemed plausible to people living in post-Soviet Russia. According to various polls in the 1990s, roughly two thirds of Russian people yearned for the past when comparing the old socialist society to post-Soviet

Russia. In one survey conducted in September 1999, respondents were asked about which leader they associated with "the best life for ordinary people"; 48 percent named Brezhnev, and only 1 percent said Yeltsin (Levada 1998; Fund of Public Opinion 1999, September 15). Even taking into account the human inclination to see the past as the "golden age" (especially during such a tumultuous period as post-Communist Russia), the data from surveys conducted in 1992–1994 were nonetheless remarkable.

The "Objective" Data

Compared to the 1930s–1950s, the Soviet diet in the 1970s and 1980s was quite tolerable. Meat, sugar, and milk, which were scarce in the past, became staples for the average citizen, even though millions of people spent a tremendous amount of time queuing for these goods or trying to purchase them through under-the-counter business. The elderly in the countryside probably suffered from the worst diet, but no one in the country went hungry or died of malnutrition.

There was practically no unemployment in Russia, nor were there homeless people walking the streets. The famous *propiska* (the internal passport which provided official permission to live in a given place) was a typical police procedure for a totalitarian state. The *propiska* guaranteed that each Soviet citizen had a place to sleep at night. The political culture supposed that under no circumstances could workers be denied the timely payment of salary, fired from their jobs, or evicted from their apartments. The reaction of the leadership to a delay in the payment of salaries was a good illustration of the official mentality.[29] If an apparatchik did not follow this and other norms of the political culture, he or she would be reprimanded, demoted, or even fired as a "politically immature person."

Housing conditions improved significantly in the post-Stalin era, both in the cities and in the countryside. Almost three quarters of all city dwellers lived in their own private apartments, though the typical household often included parents or grandparents (Arutiunian 1995, p. 190). Housing conditions during this period looked especially good when compared to the communal apartments of the past, which housed up to twenty people and had only one bathroom and one kitchen. Until 1985, the number of apartments in the country increased by 2 million each year, and 10 to 11 million people improved their housing conditions. The number of rural residents who lived in houses with running water and plumbing more than doubled between 1975 and 1986, from 27 to 41 percent (Artemov 1990, p. 67). By the 1980s, housing standards were higher than ever in Russian history (Goskomstat 1991a, p. 175).

The Russian people were also well-equipped with durable goods. In 1985, almost every family owned a television set (97 percent) and a refrigerator (91 percent), while two thirds had washing machines and sewing machines, and one third owned tape recorders, cameras, vacuum cleaners and other goods. Fifteen percent of all families owned a car.

Never in the past had vacations been so accessible to the masses as they were in the 1980s. Roughly 50 million people (about one quarter of the adult population) spent their vacations in various resort institutions in 1985. The majority of children spent their vacations in sanatoriums and pioneer camps (Goskomstat 1991a, p. 211).

Before the USSR's demise, the educational level was very high, commensurate with that in the United States. By the mid-1980s, 89 percent of the employed population had spent 7 years in school (in the United States the percentage was 93.1). This was a significant achievement compared to the educational level in Stalin's regime (12 percent).

Health services were free and easily accessible to the people, including in- and out-patient hospitals. Each individual had a family doctor, who visited the home of the ailing patient whenever asked. In 1987, there were 43 doctors per 10,000 people in the Soviet Union, compared to 30 in West Germany and 24 in France (Goskomstat 1988, p. 667). However, the quality of medical service for the masses was admittedly mediocre, certainly lower than in the West. It was particularly low in the countryside, where only one third of the hospitals were equipped with hot running water (Field 1991, p. 80). Medical services were always quite good for the political and cultural elite.

The Middle Class

The most important indicator of the high standard of living in Russia was the existence of an enormous middle class. The middle class contained a broad range of individuals, including the mass intelligentsia (i.e., teachers, doctors, engineers, and cultural workers), several other types of white-collar workers, and a large chunk of the blue-collar working class and the peasantry. According to data from the Russian Center for Public Opinion Research (VTsIOM), 43 percent of the population reported themselves as belonging to the "middle class" (Levada 1993, p. 53).

Notwithstanding disparities in educational background, the Soviet middle class enjoyed a similar lifestyle. Its standard of living, while in some ways inferior to that in the West, was reasonably "dignified," in spite of the lack of political freedom and democracy. The middle class had the same type of housing (usually a small individual apartment), furnishings and, of course, durable goods such as television sets (mostly in color) and refrigerators. Many

people owned an automobile, though this remained a much-envied posses-
sion throughout the 1970s and 1980s. Most middle-class families maintained
small private plots (the famous "six hundredths of a hectare"), or at least a
garden to grow fruits, vegetables, and flowers. They went on the same types
of vacations, mostly in state resort homes or as "wild vacationers."[30] Their
leisure time was also spent in much the same way, visiting friends, watching
movies and reading. Although the variance here is significant, most of the
middle class read the same periodicals. They usually subscribed to four to
six different publications (newspapers and journals). The consumption of
alcohol was common in the middle class (V. Shlapentokh 1989).

The Subjective Data

The people's perception of life before perestroika was quite positive. With
the absence of alternatives for changing their lives in the 1960s–1980s (and
earlier[31]), the people adjusted to the existing conditions. The Russians were
deeply influenced by the official ideology of the KGB. They were also largely
deprived of information about life abroad, though society in the 1960s and
1970s was much more open than it had been before 1953.

Various data collected in the 1960s and 1970s showed that most Russians
were satisfied with their lives in general as well as with most individual
elements of life. Most Russians were satisfied with their professions, jobs,
and salaries (50–80 percent).[32] In a Novosibirsk survey performed in the
early 1980s, for instance, only 8 percent complained that they lacked money
for leading a normal life (Borodkin 1990, p. 143). As various other studies
showed, when asked how much their salary should be increased, Russians
demanded no more than 10 percent, even if their salaries were among the
lowest in the country (V. Shlapentokh 1970).

In 1985, according to a survey conducted by two prominent Soviet sociologists, 52 percent of respondents who lived in urban areas were fully satisfied
with their diet; 7 percent were not (the rest had mixed feelings). The proportions reporting satisfaction or dissatisfaction with their clothing were, respectively, 36 percent and 3 percent; housing, 44 and 17; medical service, 49 and 9.
On the whole, 52 percent of these people reported that they enjoyed their life,
against 2 percent who did not (Bozhkov and Golofast 1985, p. 98). Other data
showed that the level of satisfaction with the conditions of life in small cities
and villages was even higher (Levykin 1984, pp. 90–97). This satisfaction
with life should be attributed to some extent to the people's strong feelings of
job security and to slack labor discipline; workers enjoyed many labor lenien-
cies, including the consumption of alcohol during working hours.[33]

The people's reactions to housing conditions provide an interesting example of how they adjusted. According to objective data, housing conditions in the USSR were always quite poor, especially when compared to Western standards (Morton 1987). However, in the mid-1980s, roughly 80 percent of the population considered the conditions "good or average" (Borodkin 1990). Looking back, we see that the level of dissatisfaction began to rise in the late 1950s. During this period there was a rapid increase in the number of houses and apartments being built. With the people's anticipation of improvement, dissatisfaction actually climbed even though the conditions were becoming better and better (Gordon and Klopov 1972; Grushin and Onikov 1980, p. 250; Grushin 2001, p. 129; Yadov et al. 1967; Yadov 1979, 1984; V. Shlapentokh 1970, 1975).

The national survey of the Soviet population conducted in 1976 (the author was the head of the methodology section of this project) found that on a five-point scale the Russians evaluated their life with a grade of 4. They felt certain that American life did not deserve a rating of more than 2 or 3; life in Czechoslovakia scored the highest, with a grade of 5.[34]

In the late 1970s, a study of Soviets and Americans supplied a rather interesting insight into employment satisfaction. According to the study, residents of Jackson, Michigan, and Pskov, Russia, gave similar responses to questions about their occupations. On a scale of 1 to 5 (a score of 5 represented high satisfaction and 1 represented low satisfaction), both Americans and Soviets rated their general job appreciation at 3.9. Forty-nine percent of Americans and 44 percent of Russians were satisfied with the amount of free time they were allowed. Fourteen percent of Americans and 17 percent of Russians received more satisfaction from their work than free time; the numbers for those who took more satisfaction from their free time were 29 percent and 22 percent, respectively; 57 percent of Americans and 61 percent of Russians took pleasure from both their work and free time (Robinson, Andreyenkov and Patrushev 1989, pp. 106–131).

In the late 1970s, even Soviet emigrants living in the United States evaluated their life in the USSR quite highly, in spite of several factors which led to negative responses: 59 percent were satisfied ("very" or "somewhat") with their "standard of living" in the USSR, while only 14 percent were "very dissatisfied" (Millar 1987). Most authors who published memoirs or articles about the feelings of the Soviet people in the 1960s–1980s acknowledged that "the average Soviet individual" did not feel miserable about his or her life (see Orlova 1983; Grigorenko 1982; Kopelev 1975, 1978).

Russian Complaints and Public Indifference

At the same time, most Russians were regularly irritated with several aspects of their everyday life (for instance, food shortages in state stores, particularly for meat, fish, fruits and vegetables;[35] long queuing lines, and the poor quality of consumer goods).[36] One third of the population lived in poverty (Matthews 1989, p. 68; Powell 1991, p. 187). This group included first of all the millions of retired people, particularly those who lived in the country-side, whose pensions were extremely low (no more than 20–30 percent of the average salary). Families with many children, unskilled workers, and numerous people who performed clerical work in factories and offices for meager wages were also very poor (Goskomstat 1987, p. 431; see also Starikov 1989, pp. 180–206). Alcoholism and various asocial tendencies also contributed to poverty (Zaslavskaia 1984, pp. 27–42; Matthews 1989, p. 109).

However, by the 1970s and early 1980s, despite the many complaints, quality of life was clearly not a leading problem in society. According to an analysis of letters to the editor published in major Soviet newspapers in 1985–1987, only 11 percent of the letters cited the poor quality of life; over one third of the letters were devoted to moral issues, and 12 percent called for an improvement of party life (D. Shlapentokh and V. Shlapentokh 1990, p. 175). The dissident movement almost completely ignored the standard of living of the masses in their attempts to widen their support in the country. In the post-Stalin period, the famous publications of the underground, or samizdat, were indifferent toward the material life of the people.[37] Russian literature and movies in this period (usually sensitive to human issues) were also apathetic about the material life of the Soviet citizenry (D. Shlapentokh and V. Shlapentokh 1993).

The Soviet leadership was also only moderately concerned about the standard of living, contrary to the position held by some Western authors, who spoke about a sort of social contract between the Kremlin and the masses (Breslauer 1990, p. 67). From the leadership's perspective, the discontent of the masses could not serve as a catalyst for major changes in the Soviet system.

The standard of living was not a leading item in Gorbachev's economic agenda, either. In fact, his first economic program ("Acceleration") focused on progress in the machine building industry and not on the production of consumer goods. In a long, secret memo entitled "The imperatives for political development" (Alexander Yakovlev sent this memo to Gorbachev at the end of 1985), the initial steps of perestroika were outlined, and the population's low standard of living was never even mentioned (Yakovlev 1994, pp. 205–212). In a speech to the Central Committee in April 1985 about the necessity of change, Gorbachev spoke of the standard of living, the difficulties with food shortages, housing conditions, and consumer goods and services as nonessential factors with regard to reforms. He focused rather on the anger of the masses about the neglect for the great values borne by the October Revolution and the heroic struggle for socialism (Gorbachev 1987a, pp. 152,

174). In 1985–1987, as many of Gorbachev's advisers stated, the woeful life of the Soviet people was not a major impetus for radical reforms in the USSR (Boldin 1995, pp. 97–107; Vadim Medvedev 1994, pp. 26–41).

The people themselves also did not consider it necessary to make radical changes in the country in order to enhance the quality of life. Despite the rapid decline of Soviet ideology, the prestige of socialism, and the authority of the Soviet state, even in 1989–1991 (the peak of anti-socialist euphoria) only a minority of Russians demanded radical changes in the economic order. No more than one third of Russians voted for serious modification of the Soviet economic system. According to a 1989 VTsIOM survey, only 18 percent of Russians responded to the question "What should be done for the improvement of life?" by answering, "Encourage private entrepreneurship under state control"; 50 percent demanded "firm order."[38]

Several authors who referred to the population's dissatisfaction with the quality of life confused the data from two radically different periods: before 1985, and after 1985 (H. Smith 1991, p. 16). It would be erroneous to compare the people's assessment of life in 1987–1991 to that in the period just before 1985. With perestroika, people were given life alternatives. The impact of the socialist ideology declined and fear nearly disappeared. Indeed, after 1985, with the relatively weak standard of living, the Soviet people reversed their estimates of life from mostly satisfactory to very bad. However, this change can be attributed only partially to the decline of "objective" indicators.[39]

Conclusion

In spite of the negative trends in the mid-1980s, the Soviet economy continued to function and even grew at a rate no slower than that in many Western countries.[40] The population did not feel the diminishing rate of economic growth because unemployment was absent. The number of new apartments built was another indicator of the rate of growth, yet this indicator did not change between 1965 and 1986. The people continued to increase the stock of their durable goods and they began to feel better off than they had in the past. As the polls from this period show, while the people were critical about the economy as a whole, they assessed their individual economic situation as rather good.[41]

By 1985, the Soviet economy was a very complex and sophisticated system, which focused primarily on military industry (Rees 1997).[42] While the Soviet leaders and nomenklatura were aware of the problems and inefficiencies of the economy, they decided to perpetuate the fundamentals of the given system—that is, state property and central planning. They were correct to assume that major reforms of this system were incompatible with the political regime that guaranteed their power in society. With all of its flaws, the economy served the needs and goals of the Soviet ruling elite. Among other things, it allowed for the creation and maintenance of the largest military machine in history, while providing a tolerable standard of living for most of the population.

At the same time, the Soviet economy could not close the technological gap with the West in the early 1980s, or meet the U.S. challenge in the arms race. As will be explained later, this fundamental circumstance accounted for the radical changes in the economic and political system, which in turn led to the collapse of the USSR.

10
Public Opinion
Acceptance of the Regime

After the civil war, the Soviet system had no serious political opponents inside the country and could rely on the support or neutrality of most of the population.[1] Over the course of Soviet history, public support for the regime oscillated. Contrary to the opinion of some experts, there was no systematic decline in the number of the regime's supporters since the early years of the USSR (Brovkin 1998). The number of Russians who backed the regime, or at least remained neutral, was quite high in the first decade after the revolution. Mass support declined significantly in the late 1920s and early 1930s. However, this trend changed drastically in the next decade. With the entrenchment of the regime, the growing social mobility, the continuation of repressions, the brainwashing of the people, the regime's total isolation, and some amelioration of the standard of living in the second half of the 1930s, loyalty to the regime increased. The people's support reached its peak during World War II and in the first years after the war. After Stalin's death, support for the system again began to decline. However, until the time of perestroika, the regime always enjoyed the support (active or passive) of most of the population.

The Methodological Problems

It is a mark of the totalitarian character of the Soviet Union that few surveys were conducted of the people's attitudes toward the system. Before the 1960s, there were no genuine sociological, public opinion studies. From the 1960s until 1987, Soviet sociologists were not allowed to ask direct questions about people's attitudes toward major political and social issues (V. Shlapentokh 1987). Social scientists and pollsters were barred from conducting public opinion research on the same level as their Western counterparts until midway through perestroika (Levada 1990). For this reason, well-documented and representative public opinion data from the Soviet era are sparse. The author of a rare and useful book on Soviet history (Kuleshov 1990, p. 267) wrote a special section on public opinion, but found only enough material on the people's attitudes toward Stalin's regime to fill one page.

When scholars gained access to secret archives after 1989, new sources of information about public opinion emerged. However, the archival data were mostly relevant to single cases and had been tainted by the political purposes of the compilers (the informers of the party and political police). The problems with these data were often ignored by scholars, many of whom evaluated public opinion in Stalin's time on the basis of these archival documents.[2]

When interpreting public opinion data, it is important to keep in mind, especially when dealing with totalitarian societies, the immense impact of the dominant ideology and the adaptation of the people to the society in which they lived. The adaptation of the vast majority of individuals to their existing environment and the dominant political and economic power has an enormous impact on the views of any population, particularly people living under a totalitarian regime.

The Two-Level Mentality

The Soviet people, like all other people, looked at the world through two different lenses—one pragmatic, one ideological. This subject was touched on in the chapters devoted to ideology and the mentality of the Soviet leaders. With the pragmatic lens, people make judgments about everyday life based on personal experiences or the experiences of their family and friends. With the ideological lens, people develop their picture of the external world based on secondhand information. Whereas in the first case people operate mostly with concrete facts, in the second they use generalizations.[3]

The dominant ideology is concerned mostly with controlling the ideological level of the public mind. At the same time, ideology influences the images emerging in everyday life. This sort of dual mechanism (or two-level mentality) of perception is very helpful for people living under strong ideological pressure. It allows them to keep their common sense while accepting the most absurd pictures of the world around them.

In some cases, the ideological control mechanism impacts the behavior of society even when it fails to directly change the behavior of individuals.

Those who are not influenced by the ideology often substantiate the mechanism by publicly professing official values, which influence the behavior of other, more susceptible, individuals. For instance, in the USSR many people verbally supported the various ideas of patriotism (i.e., the need to perform jobs that were useful for the country, though inconvenient for the individual; to purchase only Soviet goods; never to listen to foreign radio broadcasts) but did not behave like model patriots. However, they presumed that others might follow these principles ("values for others"), and tried to influence them to do so, often with some success.

The concept of the two-level mentality should not be confused with the approach that treats the human mind as eclectic, ambivalent, and contradictory. Such an approach does not properly explain the people's mentality, especially in a totalitarian society.[4] Certainly the minds of Soviet people, even in Stalin's time, were somewhat eclectic on both the ideological and pragmatic levels, but this eclecticism was very limited.[5] Thus, it would be incorrect to consider most Soviet citizens' complaints and requests about their everyday life, including those addressed to the authorities or the media, as critiques of the system as a whole (Rigby 1992, pp. 313–314). Most of the people who wrote complaint letters had no other social system in mind.[6]

The way in which these complaint letters were labeled by party committees and the political police is a separate matter. When Moscow assessed the efficiency of these agencies by the number of unmasked enemies, the number of complaints classified as "anti-Soviet" increased regardless of the public's actual attitudes toward authority; in fact, the people were becoming more cautious about any action that could be used against them.[7] Considering the composition of Gulag prisoners, it becomes clear that the number of Soviet enemies among the Russian population was quite small. There was almost a consensus among experts (with the exception of hardline Communists) that the absolute majority of political prisoners were "clean" by the most rigid Soviet standards—that is, they were "Soviet patriots," "true Soviet people" and "faithful Communists," whose guilt had been fabricated by the political police. The numerous publications and studies on the Gulag agree that most political prisoners were not guilty of any serious statements aimed at the essence of the system (Solzhenitsyn 1973).

In their communication with the masses, the leadership always assumed the existence of the two-level mentality. They tolerated the people's critique of individual officials and various specific flaws in everyday life, but mercilessly punished those who criticized the regime using generalizations.[8] This fundamental fact is vitally important for understanding the archival data. Casual gripes about specific flaws in everyday life should not lead one to sweeping conclusions about the public's hostility toward "the system" (Brovkin 1997).

When assessing the people's complaints, it should be pointed out that for many of them (and the number increased over time), the system was the only social reality they knew. Among other things, they saw it as "existing forever." Between the early 1920s and late 1930s, according to many sources, the number of people who anticipated the restoration of the pre-revolutionary order declined enormously, though such hopes were still strong among peasants, who could not stop dreaming about the dismantlement of collective farms (S. Davies 1997, p. 94). Even among Russian emigrants, the number of those who hoped for the collapse of the USSR decreased significantly after the end of collectivization.

The Three Mental Worlds of the Stalin Era

Throughout Soviet history, and particularly in Stalin's time, the people lived in three separate mental worlds. This phenomenon was typical even for democratic societies. In the first world, the people supported the regime; in the second, they hated it; and in the third, people tried not to think about ideological matters and spent very little time, emotion, or thought on any world beyond everyday life.

These three worlds only partially intersected. The people of each world had only a superficial idea about the minds of those who belonged to other worlds. They were often amazed when they came into contact with people from other worlds. For instance, a devoted party apparatchik simply never spoke openly with an enemy of the regime. For obvious reasons, such a meeting was impossible. Even close relatives, parents, children, brothers and sisters avoided direct debates if they harbored different political views.

Those who hated the regime lived in the worst situation (or "world"). Fear prevented them from seeking out like-minded people. They felt isolated and were extremely happy whenever they encountered someone who shared their views. In his classic work *1984*, George Orwell described this fundamental aspect of totalitarian society in the meeting of Smith and Julia. In this respect, Nazi Germany was identical to the Soviet system.

The World of Supporters and Conformists

With the prevalence of fear, the strength of official ideology, the respect for power as the counteragent to anarchy, and the material benefits provided by the regime, the majority of active people in the country were loyal citizens. Among them were millions of party members, social activists of various sorts, superiors at all levels, a considerable part of the working class, which enjoyed some privileges and was flattered by the propaganda about its hegemonic role in society, officers in the army, the political police, and all who benefited from social mobility (particularly young people). All of them were spirited supporters of the existing order and regarded their life as "normal," or even better. These people influenced their friends and relatives with their praise of the regime.[9]

Several types of sources substantiate this view. The personal diaries and private letters of ordinary people are the best source for understanding the mood in Soviet society. These materials were clearly not intended for publication or any outside audience. The authors of these diaries demonstrated their dedication to Stalin's cause.[10] For instance, with evident reluctance, the famous Russian scholar Vladimir Vernadsky wrote in his diary in 1940 that "the crowd supports Stalin" (Vernadsky 1992).

Memoirs are another important source of information. Dissidents published several books about their lives in totalitarian society in the West before glasnost, as well as numerous books after 1985 (see Orlova 1982, 1983; Kopelev 1975, 1978, 1982a, 1982b; Grigorenko 1982; Ulanovskaia and Ulanovskaia 1982; Kolodnitsky 1993). In these books, the authors described their almost fanatical support for the regime in the 1930s and explained that they enjoyed their lives despite the arrests of their friends and colleagues. Even the children of the peasants who suffered from collectivization were among those who evidently favored the Soviet regime (see Grigorenko 1982; I. Tvardovsky 1988, pp. 10–32). During glasnost, when the acrimonious campaign against Stalin was in full swing, many authors who had lived through the Stalin era still expressed positive feelings toward this period.[11]

The Soviet literature of the 1930s (i.e., the novels of Valentin Kataev, Valentin Kaverin, Yurii Olesha, Ilia Ilf and Evgenii Petrov, Konstantin Paustovsky, Ilia Erenburg, Arkadii Gaidar, and many others) also characterized this period as a "bright, radiant and heroic time, the beautiful morning of socialism." These sentiments about the mood of the masses were supported fifty years later by some of the critics of the regime (see Latsis 1989b, p. 167). Several literary works published in the 1980s, during glasnost—among them Anatolii Rybakov's *Children of the Arbat* (1988)—also described the enthusiasm of the "builders of socialism," particularly the youth in the 1930s (Laqueur 1994, p. 8). The public had an overwhelmingly positive reaction to strongly ideologized Soviet movies such as *Chapaev, Pass to life, Lenin in October*, and *The youth of Maxim*, and to novels like Nikolai Ostrovsky's *How the steel was tempered* and Boris Polevoi's *The story of an ordinary man* (D. Shlapentokh and V. Shlapentokh 1993).

The great popularity of official Soviet songs was another indirect but telling indicator of the public's acceptance of the official presentation of life in the country. The songs praised the motherland, Stalin, Moscow as the capital of the USSR, the happy Soviet life, the party, the Red Army and its generals and officers, the invincibility of the country, and the confrontation with capitalist enemies. The most popular songs had catchy melodies, always highly emotional and romantic—especially those composed by Isaak Dunaevsky, Matvei Blanter, the brothers Dmitrii and Daniil Pokrass, and a few others.[12]

The Soviet masses greeted with fervor and evident sincerity each success of the socialist motherland: the rescue of 104 passengers from the icebreaker *Cheliuskin* in 1934; the feat of polar researcher Ivan Papanin's team, which spent several months on a drifting ice floe in the Arctic in 1937–1938;[13] the first nonstop flight (Valerii Chkalov and Mikhail Gromov) from Moscow to America in 1937; and many others. Millions of people greeted the heroes; and even if all these manifestations of the people's elation were organized by local party committees, most of the participants were sincere and proud of their country.

While numerous defeatists daydreamed of the USSR's demise, most people were quite patriotic with respect to the war, supported the official foreign policy, and accepted the dogma of the "capitalist encirclement."[14] The public's fervent support of the Soviet official position on the Spanish civil war in 1936–1939, which occurred during the most sinister years of mass terror, was another indication of popular support for the regime. Millions of people ardently followed the course of the war, hoping for the victory of the Republicans and their Communist allies.[15]

The views of party apparatchiks and intellectuals in the mid-1930s were of special importance, considering the high probability of their being arrested and jailed or put to death. Most of them, even on the eve of their pending arrest, cast no doubt (either publicly or privately in communications with their spouses) on the radiant future and the official description of the past. Moreover, many prisoners of the Gulag—the so-called old Bolsheviks—remained faithful Communists with respect to their attitudes toward the past and future.[16] Nikolai Bukharin's letter to future generations of Bolsheviks, which was memorized by his wife on the eve of his arrest, demonstrated his true belief in the Communist ideology and its interpretations of the past and the future (Larina 1993).

Among the regime's supporters were many fanatics who rejected anything even remotely suggestive of defects in the Soviet system, Marxist teachings, the creative role of the party, and the wisdom of its leaders. After being sent to the Gulag, some fanatics continued to stubbornly defend the system.[17] Fanatics could be found in each group of the Soviet population.[18]

Young people formed a great reservoir of loyalty to the regime. From children in elementary schools to teenagers and young adults, the generation of youth represented one of the most dedicated sectors of the population.

Various indirect data indicate that young people passionately believed in the Communist future and eagerly looked for any sign of the World Revolution. Solzhenitsyn's biographical story "The case at Krechetovka station," describes a lieutenant who, in September of 1941, despite a German air attack, continued to take notes while reading *Capital*.

Almost all children and teenagers entered the Pioneer and Komsomol organizations with great joy and pride.[19] In most cases, parents were afraid of telling their children about their genuine attitudes toward the system. Young people were under intense ideological pressure as they moved forward through schools and colleges. The absolute majority of young people, even in families hostile toward the system, were enthusiastic supporters of the Soviet order.[20] Thousands of devoted Komsomol and party activists had been raised by so-called "bad parents," in the families of the former landlords and capitalists, deported kulaks, and executed party apparatchiks.[21] Even the German military commanders who occupied a large chunk of the Soviet territory in 1941–1942 recognized that unlike the old generation, the young people (17–21 years) were devoted to the system (see *Dialog* 3, 1994, pp. 63–64).[22]

The Attitudes Toward Mass Terror

The majority of urban citizens supported Stalin's mass terror in the late 1920s and 1930s.[23] In several cases, people were dissatisfied with "lenient verdicts" of imprisonment, preferring that the offenders be executed (S. Davies 1997, pp. 119, 132).

There is some evidence (mostly indirect, due to the lack of any representative sociological information) of "mass support for mass terror." Almost all of the memoirs written by Soviet dissidents and emigrants in the 1970s and 1980s (before the powerful anti-Communist offensive in the late 1980s and early 1990s) make clear that their authors believed in the fairness of the trials and the grounds for mass arrests. They made some exceptions for their personal acquaintances, whose guilt seemed incomprehensible.[24]

In the 1930s and even later (up until the 20th Party Congress in 1956), very few people doubted the guilt of those who were executed or sent to the Gulag.[25] People were prone to support the harsh punishments of those whom they did not know personally. Although some may have had reservations about the convictions of their neighbors, colleagues, friends and relatives, in many cases, people accepted without question the arrests of their close friends and even of their parents.[26] The cult of Pavlik Morozov, the young pioneer who reported his father to the political police as an enemy of collectivization and who was later murdered by his grandfather, reflects the mood of the country quite well. This cult was softened somewhat after 1953, with the decline of repressions (Druzhnikov 1997; see V. Shlapentokh 1986, pp. 52–54).

There were many factors that accounted for the people's acceptance of mass terror. Let us speak only about the constructions of terror and examine how it appeared in the Russian mind. First, it is necessary to make a distinction between the fear of internal and external enemies. The concept of "the capitalist encirclement" worked extremely well. The Russians were convinced of the danger and eternal hostility of foreign countries (in the West and in the East). The tendency of Russians to believe in various conspiracy theories, particularly in plots driven by foreign enemies against the motherland, was bolstered by the xenophobia left over from pre-revolutionary times.

What is more, the mass terror of the mid-1930s was directed mostly against party and state apparatchiks, and to a much lesser extent at ordinary people. For this reason, the masses often supported the leaders' treatment of the political elite and easily accepted the official accusations against these former apparatchiks as traitors, foreign agents, and saboteurs. The people's endorsement of this policy was dictated by their hatred of superiors because of the latter's luxurious lifestyles. The policy of repressions against elites was evidently employed by Stalin and repeated by Mao decades later during the Cultural Revolution (D. Shlapentokh 1991a, pp. 259–274). The repression of the elite often fell upon Jews, and even though anti-Semitism at that time was not highlighted in official propaganda, repressions against Jews enhanced the gloating among workers.

Stalin's Cult

The devotion of the Soviet people to the regime reached its zenith in the cult of Stalin. Established in the early 1930s, this cult was evidently supported by the majority of active Russians in the cities, much like Hitler's in Nazi Germany, or Mao's in Communist China.[27] It is not surprising that almost all of the outstanding writers fervently praised Stalin (some lauded him genuinely, and some, like Mandelshtam and Akhmatova, probably followed suit for fear of repression). Stalin was glorified by ordinary people even in their private communications (S. Davies 1997, pp. 155–167). The cult of Stalin penetrated the heart and soul of many Russians, from apparatchiks to ordinary citizens.[28] Stalin's authority, which was immense before World War II, increased after the war's end because Stalin himself was credited for the victory.[29] The love of Stalin reached grotesque heights in 1949, during the celebration of his 70th birthday. With the full support of its members, each administrative unit in the country sent a telegram of congratulations to "the greatest man in the history of mankind." Many ordinary people sent letters to the media and made suggestions at public meetings for historical commemorations of Stalin.[30]

The intensity with which people mourned Stalin's death on March 5, 1953 was indeed amazing. As a prominent Russian historian remembered almost 50 years later, "The grief in the country was genuine" (Pikhoia 1999, pp. 16–17). Stalin's funeral was accompanied by a stampede of thousands of people yearning to deliver their last respects. The funeral stands among the most memorable events in Soviet history (see Evgenii Evtushenko's film *Stalin's funeral*, 1990).

Behavior in Support of the Regime

The people not only maintained positive attitudes toward the regime but also behaved compliantly. The high level of labor enthusiasm in the 1930s was an important indicator of the pro-Soviet mood in the country. The people worked heroically on the major construction projects of the times—for instance, the Magnitogorsk metallurgical plant, the Turksib railway, which connected Siberia and Central Asia, and the Moscow subway.[31] The Stakhanov movement, which had been arranged by the authorities (it was not a spontaneous emergence of the people's willingness to increase personal productivity), also drew a significant number of true believers.[32]

Millions of people entered various official organizations created by the Kremlin with specific intentions to draw upon the enthusiasm of the masses. These pioneering organizations included the Komsomol, Osoaviakhim (an organization for training people for the military), MOPR (an organization that aided foreign revolutionaries), the Red Cross, and several others.[33]

Hundreds of thousands of people voluntarily served the political police as informers. However, many of them became informers only due to pressure from the political police, or for their own survival, particularly if they had "bad" social origins (see Stepan Podlubny's diary, quoted in Garros, Korenevskaya, and Lahusen 1995, p. 291).

The World of Haters

The world of haters consisted of three major groups: those who loathed the Soviet system on their own initiative, those whom the state openly saw as its class enemies, and those who emerged as enemies of the system as a result of various actions by the state.

Most in the first group were people who could not satisfy their basic needs. This group evidently increased in the late 1920s, when two trends converged: the dwindling of revolutionary enthusiasm and the deterioration of the standard of living.[34] Life during this period was particularly harsh in the countryside.[35] After the food shortages and famine in the early 1930s and the significant amelioration of life following this period, the number of "haters" decreased quite considerably.[36] This first group also included deeply religious people who saw the Soviet system as hostile to God and religion.

Among the members of the second group were those who had experienced a better life in pre-revolutionary Russia, or in some cases, in foreign countries. The leadership was right to distrust those who had been prosperous before 1917, especially the members of the old dominant classes and those who had belonged to the "middle class" (i.e., people whose lives were quite comfortable in comparison with life after 1917).[37] The authorities were well aware of their hatred. For this reason, the state agencies required everyone who applied for high-level positions to clarify in detail his or her social origin, including the positions of the parents prior to the revolution and their connections to foreign countries. In most cases, a "bad biography" would deprive the individual of any promotion. During the mass terror, any citizen who had lived abroad (even for a short period of time) became a likely candidate for being sentenced to the Gulag.

The third group of haters, which partially overlapped with the second, was generated mostly by the system itself. Vasilii Grossman noted that the Bolsheviks (as well as the Nazis) could not function without singling out part of the population as a target for discrimination (Grossman 1980). Indeed, until 1953, the regime identified certain categories of the population as its automatic enemies—sometimes with reason, sometimes not. Among those labeled as enemies were members of the former dominant classes (including the bureaucracy) and clergy, who hated the Soviet order from its inception; members of non-Bolshevik socialist parties and people expelled from the Communist party in the 1930s and 1940s; the large and diverse group of so-called special migrants—people who had been transferred against their will to the eastern regions of the country; people from the territories annexed in the 1930s (Western Ukraine, Belorussia, Bessarabia, and the Baltic republics); several ethnic minorities in the 1930s and 1950s; people who were accused of collaborating with German forces; prisoners of war; and others who simply lived in occupied territories.

The hatred of some people was so acute that they dreamed of war and foreign invasion in the 1920s and 1930s (Arzhilovsky 1995, pp. 114–128). They longed for the extermination of the Bolsheviks. They hoped for the victory of the Nazis in WWII. After 1945, some even yearned for a nuclear attack against their own country.[38]

However, it would be an oversimplification to suppose that the haters of the system rejected all Soviet values. In fact, they accepted several of these values, such as nationalized health care and education. This acceptance showed how deeply the Soviet ideology penetrated the people's minds. Fear and the Orwellian adjustment to power did not account completely for this phenomenon. Acceptance of these values was shared even among people who fled the Soviet Union during the war as well as among many dissidents in post-Soviet Russia, not to speak of the multitude of Russians in post-Communist society who voted for socialist values.

The Harvard Project—a series of studies based on surveys of people who fled the Soviet Union during the war, or who, as former German prisoners of war, did not want to return to the USSR—sheds light on the mind-set of Soviet people before the war. To be sure, the subjects of this project did not represent the whole population.[39] This special universe contained a disproportionately high ratio of people who for one reason or another held a grudge against the system and were afraid to return to their motherland.[40] What is more, the respondents were inclined to please the American interviewers at a time when the cold war was at its peak.[41]

To the credit of this survey, it should be pointed out that the respondents were finally living outside the realm of the totalitarian system and were relatively free to express their true views about the USSR. All other sources on the views of the Soviet people from inside the country (i.e., letters in the media, or even party and police reports) were infected with much greater bias.

Keeping in mind both the advantages and disadvantages of the Harvard Project, it was amazing that on average one third of the respondents reported that they "once were in favor of the regime" (Inkeles and Bauer 1968, p. 47). Extending this question to the entire Soviet, prewar population, it would not be so daring to suppose that the number of those "in favor of the regime" would be much greater than one third. Eighty to 90 percent of all respondents in the Harvard Project supported state ownership of "heavy industry" and "transport" as well as the "cradle-to-grave welfare program." Two thirds of the respondents approved of Soviet educational and health services. The majority of respondents hailed Soviet cultural achievements (for instance, literacy increased to 83–97 percent by the early 1940s; see Inkeles and Bauer 1968, pp. 234, 236, 238–239). The majority (70–80 percent) favored a "basic socialist economy as in the NEP period," while only about 5–28 percent preferred "capitalism" (Inkeles and Bauer 1968, p. 243; for an analysis of these data, see Lukin 1996).

Three decades later, another large group of Soviet citizens found themselves in the West. This time they were émigrés, mostly Jews, who had left Soviet society for different reasons than those who fled as displaced persons. These people openly expressed their unwillingness to live in Soviet society. Like the respondents of the Harvard Project, they were free from the Soviet authorities and wanted to please the American interviewers with negative attitudes toward the USSR. However, surprisingly, most of them characterized life in the USSR in the 1970s (the survey was conducted in the early 1980s) in rather positive terms. Indeed, of the 2,800 respondents, only 14 percent assessed the life they left behind as "very dissatisfying." Adding those who were "somewhat dissatisfied" (25 percent), the proportion of those who were critical of their life in the Soviet Union (39 percent) was still much less than half. The number of those who were "very dissatisfied" with their job was only 6 percent (Millar 1987, p. 33). This was a rather fantastic indicator, considering that it came from people who emigrated from the USSR.[42]

The World of Philistines

A significant number of Soviet citizens, despite the barrage of propaganda, remained deeply indifferent to politics. They suppressed their political sympathies and antipathies, and showed neither the ability (most had very poor educations) nor the desire to deliberate on political issues. Understanding clearly that it was dangerous to speak openly on these issues, they abstained from reflections beyond their everyday concerns, as though they had extirpated "the ideological layer" from their brains.[43] Soviet propagandists in Stalin's times denounced these people as "philistines," and viewed them with suspicion. This attitude changed in Brezhnev's era, when the Kremlin, facing various internal dangers, realized these people were innocuous with respect to the regime.

Considering the advocates, the haters, and the philistines, it was estimated that 50 to 70 percent of people in cities and probably 10 to 20 percent of people living in the countryside had a positive attitude toward the regime in Stalin's time.

The Three "Worlds" During World War II

The war offered many Russians and non-Russians the opportunity to say "yes" or "no" to the Soviet regime. During the war, the people's behavior seemingly revealed their true attitudes. With this reasoning, some anti-Communist authors described any action against the USSR (on its territory, or in the German POW camps) as evidence of hostility toward the regime. These authors did not, however, treat patriotic behavior during this period as evidence of popular support of the regime. They saw this behavior simply as a by-product of the people's fear of the KGB and other institutions.[44] The assessment of behavior during the war was indeed a difficult task. Both the admirers and the critics of the system used the war experience to support their views.

In my opinion, it would be shortsighted to explain the behavior of the absolute majority of the population as dictated only by fear of the authorities. Certainly, fear played a significant role. Arrests and absurd accusations, along with the heavy recruitment of informers, were ever present during this period.[45] The special government decree issued in July 1941 assured the punishment of individuals who "spread false rumors." The whole system of the KGB with its army of informers was fully operational.

At the same time, the war was decidedly a people's war.[46] The people were given a kind of freedom of choice in that they could perform feats of heroism, or refrain from such actions. There were in fact numberless acts of heroism. What is more, the war allowed people to display their initiative in new ways.[47] By all accounts, this patriotic fervor was dictated not so much by a desire to protect the existing political regime as by a willingness to fight an aggressor who wanted to enslave the motherland.[48] For this reason, Stalin changed the official ideology, drastically increasing its Russian nationalist elements. Vasilii Grossman, a shrewd observer of the war, wrote that during this period there was an "awakening of Russian national self-identity" (Grossman 1970).

Most people accepted the system and its leader as the champion of the country and the defender against Nazi aggression. Contrary to the argument that Soviets had no choice but to accept the system, Russian emigrants in the West, including the most ardent anti-Soviets such as Pavel Miliukov, saw the Kremlin in the exact same light. Even more telling were the patriotic feelings which prevailed among many prisoners of the Gulag.[49]

The sincerity of millions of Russian soldiers who crawled from the trenches and propelled themselves forward during attacks, exclaiming "For the Motherland! For Stalin!" cannot be doubted, even if some veterans many years later denied that this slogan was used frequently. In post-Communist Russia, some people tried to dilute the importance of this fact by placing the focus on another very important fact: the role of special police units, which were positioned behind the front line, where they mercilessly shot any soldier who fled before the overwhelming might of the adversary or evaded the hopeless and extremely costly attacks ordered by Soviet commanders who were almost indifferent to human losses.

The attitudes of Soviets who lived on the territory occupied by German forces were more complicated. In this case, a distinction should be drawn between the different periods of the war. In the first months, many people, particularly in Ukraine and especially in the countryside, vented their anger against the Soviet order and accepted the occupying power with mixed feelings. The memories of collectivization and mass repressions were still fresh, and many people greeted the Germans as liberators from the Soviet yoke. Thousands of people who had fled from Soviet prisons migrated to the occupied territory. Certain that the Soviet order was doomed, more and more chose to adapt to the new political power. In an effort to "normalize" the world around them, they deported themselves as committed enemies of the Soviet system. Many of these people (according to Volkogonov, 800,000) served the Germans in various capacities (see Kalinin 1998). Collaboration with the occupiers was common in most countries seized by the Nazis (see Mazover 1999). However, watching the cruelty of the Germans and their evident unwillingness to endow the Soviet people with any rights and observing at the same time the increasing might of the Soviet army, most people on the occupied territory soon became clearly hostile toward the Germans (Marples 1992, p. 80; Goebbels 1982). The guerrilla activity in much of the occupied territory was supported by most people.

Overall, however, it can be said that many Soviet citizens demonstrated their hatred of the Soviet system during the war. Between 5 and 6 million Soviets found themselves in Western Europe after the war. Most had been brought west by the Germans for forced labor or as prisoners of war. Hundreds of thousands did not want to return to the USSR. There were many suicides among those whom the Allied authorities forced to go back to the motherland (Dallin and Nikolaevsky 1947, p. 284).[50]

Another revealing fact about the attitudes of the people toward the Soviet authorities was the mass exodus of people (Ukrainians, Russians, and others) who retreated along with the German troops, though some fled simply out of fear because they had collaborated with the enemy in one way or another. Many non-Russians (e.g., Tatars in Crimea, Chechens, Ingushes, and other people in the North Caucasus) supported the German troops and clearly demonstrated their hostility toward the regime.[51] There were also many Soviet people far from the front line who harbored anti-Soviet feelings. In 1990, a Soviet author reported that he had found about 6,000 letters, mostly unsigned, that had been sent in 1942 to the local newspaper in Ivanovo. This area was a poor, working-class region, known for its discontent with the Soviet order (*Komsomol'skaia pravda*, May 5, 1990). Many of the letter-writers expressed hope that, with the victory over Nazi Germany, Stalin would soften the existing regime.[52]

In the end, the war proved a great political asset for the system. The prestige of the USSR was very high during this period, both inside and outside the country. The war engendered a sense of unity between the people and the regime. This assertion was noted by many foreign observers during and after the war (Smith 1976). Most Soviet people felt that the victory over Germany was a triumph not only for Russia but also for the Soviet system as a whole. The war inspired many non-Russians and non-Slavs (Tatars from Volga, Georgians, Kazakhs, Uzbeks, Armenians and many others) to fight side by side.

Attitudes Toward the Regime in the Post-Stalin Period

The attitudes of the Soviet people after 1953 were shaped by several new developments including the disappearance of mass repressions against loyal Soviets. Though the fear of the political police was still quite strong, repressions were directed only against people who were indeed involved in some sort of anti-Soviet behavior as it was defined by the authorities. The individual critiques of the regime that had served as the basis for an arrest in the past were now documented by the KGB, but without major reprisals. The private life of the citizenry was respected by the authorities and nobody was persecuted for any ideas expressed inside the family. Some of the restraints on media, literature, film and other arts were lifted, as long as the material did not challenge the official ideology. The quality of life improved radically for the majority of people.

The country was gradually opening to the West. With access to foreign radio and some opportunities to travel abroad, the people became better informed about life in the West, though the picture of foreign life was still quite distorted and contained elements of propaganda. The post-Stalin era brought a decline in prestige for the official ideology and for labor ethics, as cynicism began to spread about the regime's claims to superiority.

In 1985, however, the majority of Soviets still supported a variety of official dogmas including Soviet and Russian patriotism, the supremacy of socialism, social equality, the obligation of the state to guarantee the basic needs of the people, the superiority of public property over private property, the central planning system as superior to the market economy, and Soviet-Russian culture and moral superiority over the West. The people saw the Communist Party as the true leading force in society and accepted the images of the world which the leaders imposed on them.[53] The leadership controlled images of the past as well as images of foreign countries.[54]

In spite of their criticism, the people trusted the leadership and strongly supported almost all of its domestic and foreign policies (Grushin 2001, pp. 92, 109, 125, 138). Most Soviets backed the invasions of Czechoslovakia in 1968 and of Afghanistan in 1980 as well as the shooting-down of the Korean airliner in 1983. The absolute majority of Soviets either condemned the behavior of dissidents or simply did not know anything about them.[55]

Many people listened to foreign radio broadcasts (by the Voice of America, the BBC, and Free Europe).[56] However, contrary to both the fears of Soviet leaders and the expectations of liberal intellectuals, access to foreign radio did not change the views of the masses. The positive attitudes of the people toward the system were impervious to new information which was deeply at odds with official information.[57]

A powerful argument for the efficacy of the ideology in the post-Stalin period was its influence on the behavior of the masses. This ideology definitely played a part in motivating young people to take part in the implementation of projects such as the construction of the Baikal-Amur railroad. These people lived for many years in very difficult conditions in Siberia and the Far East. The party could always find workers who were willing to make sacrifices not only for material advantages but also for the sake of the country and their own patriotic urges.[58]

In 1989, when the official ideology was being derogated and berated, the people considered Lenin the greatest man in Soviet/Russian history (according to a survey conducted by VTsIOM). Lenin took 70 percent of the vote, while Peter the Great came in second with 40 percent. Marx took 38 percent; Engels, 20 percent; and Einstein 8 percent. In the same VTsIOM survey, 24 percent of respondents answered the question "What are you most proud of?" by pointing to their own "patriotism" (a relatively high percentage, considering that by 1989, people could freely answer any question without fear of reprisal). This survey question was set up so that the respondents could select only two of twenty alternatives. Overall, in first place among the things Russians were most proud of, "children" garnered 43 percent (Levada 1993, pp. 176, 202–203). Even in 1990, when the media fiercely attacked egalitarianism, most survey respondents expressed their support for the system.[59] In the same year the majority still believed that the state bore responsibility for the well-being of its citizens (Levada 1993, p. 62).

In the last years of perestroika, Dmitrii Volkogonov—then a leading detractor of Soviet ideology—wrote, "All we believed in for several decades was the 'historical advantages of socialism,' 'the saving role of proletarian dictatorship,' 'the complete lack of rights and freedoms for the workers in capitalist countries,' 'the inevitable demise of capitalism,' and 'the triumph of Communist ideals in the whole world'" (Volkogonov 1995, p. 211). Volkogonov and a host of other liberals (the future political activists in post-Communist Russia) contended that they had entered the period of perestroika as true believers in the Communist ideology.[60]

The Transformation of Two Fundamental Values

Private property and religion were two central values in pre-revolutionary Russian society that dissolved during the Soviet era. Indeed, not only were the Communists the first people in world history to destroy the foundation of traditional private property, but they convinced the people to loath this form of property. This was a grandiose ideological success, even taking into account that some "communal traditions" existed in Russia before 1917. In the late 1990s, after the people had been bombarded with anti-Communist propaganda since 1989–1991, more than 50 percent of Russians still demonstrated in various polls their allegiance to the ideas of socialism and public property.[61] They advocated public property for large enterprises and a regulatory state role in the economy, while expressing suspicion of private property and private businessmen.

The Communists were also quite successful in downgrading the importance of religion in Soviet society. There are widely divergent views on the degree of religiosity among Russians before the revolution (from the praise of pre-revolutionary Russians as "the single God-bearers in the world" to the assertion that they had always been indifferent toward Christianity). However, it can hardly be denied that the church played a significant role in the lives of most Russians before the revolution.

In the 1920s and 1930s, the Bolsheviks managed to recruit hundreds of thousands of Russians to destroy many thousands of their churches. With their educational system and propaganda machine based on the glorification of science, the Bolsheviks greatly eroded religious beliefs in the public mind. In the 1970s, according to a sociological study, no more than 25–30 percent of the population (mostly old people) considered themselves religious.[62] In comparison with that in the mid-1930s, this proportion was two times smaller. According to the national census in 1937, the proportion was 57 percent (Zhiromskaia 1998). Besides the energetic atheist propaganda, the worldwide trend of secularism was also accountable for these changes and the dominance of atheism in the country. Those who were developing careers in the Soviet Union adapted to official atheism extremely quickly (after 1991, the same people declared themselves religious).[63] People with higher educations in the USSR were less likely to hold religious beliefs.[64]

According to Yurii Levada's study of the Soviet people's religious views in 1989, "en masse nonbelief in God surpasses belief in God," and "it is possible to speak of the nonreligiosity of Soviet society." By 1989, it was understood by the people that their religious feelings would not hurt their social status. In fact, many in the media favored religion. And still, 35 percent of Russians declared themselves nonbelievers; less than 20 percent reported that they followed religious rituals (Levada 1993, pp. 216–218).

Moderate Optimism

In general, the Soviet people entered perestroika with a relatively optimistic view of the future. The mood of the people in the 1980s looked especially optimistic when compared to the people's gloomy attitudes in the 1990s.

The official ideology succeeded in implanting optimistic images in most of the population. From the early years of the new regime until 1987, most Russians believed that their lives had improved from one period to the next. This evaluation of life prevailed even in the 1930s, when the country was suffering from hunger and mass terror. In the 1930s, millions of Russians, particularly the youth, were enthusiastic about the future. They believed Stalin's famous statement: "Life has become better, more merry." Indirect data substantiate the conclusion that the urban population strongly supported the regime and "sincerely" believed that their life was better "now" (i.e., at each new period in Soviet history) than in the previous period and would be much better in the future.[65]

After Stalin's death, there was some erosion of the official ideology, and the future was no longer described in such glowing terms. Nearing the end of the Soviet system, the notion of a Communist paradise had almost disappeared from the media. It was replaced by mature, or developed, socialism, which had already provided people with a better style of life than in the West (Kim 1983; Vishnevsky 1989; Glezerman, Rutkevich, and Vishnevsky 1980). However, the leadership was still quite concerned about maintaining some degree of optimism in the people's perspective on the future (see Grushin 2001, pp. 96, 191). Any attempt to introduce even slightly pessimistic elements into the official vision of the future was quashed. Even purely theoretical, scientific debates about the eventual end of the earth or universe could not be published.[66]

Russian intellectuals, including dissidents, were in a dour but not an apocalyptic mood in the 1970s and 1980s. They believed that the existing mode of life, regardless of its shortcomings in their estimation, would survive for decades without any cataclysm (V. Shlapentokh 1990).[67] In any case, the mood of the Russian intellectuals by the mid-1980s was no worse than the psychological climate in many empires long before their collapse. In the Ottoman Empire, for instance, gloomy predictions started in the sixteenth century, almost four centuries before its demise. The *fin-de-siècle* mind-set was typical also in many other societies which would not collapse for many decades or centuries.

Resistance to the Regime

Popular resistance during Stalin's reign was minimal, especially when compared to the rebelliousness of workers and peasants during the civil war and its aftermath (see Pavliuchenko 1997, pp. 141–153; Osipova 1997, pp. 154–176; Velidov 1991). The Tambov peasant uprising in 1920–1921 and the Kronshtadt sailors' rebellion in 1921 were significant events. However, nearly seventy years would pass before another major mass movement would influence the masters of the Kremlin (i.e., the miners' strike of 1989 and the national movements in Armenia and the Baltic republics in 1987–1989).

In the early years after the Bolshevik revolution, workers displayed their discontent with strikes. In the 1920s, and particularly in 1925–1929, strikes spread throughout almost all branches of industry (notably, mining, metallurgy, and textiles). According to Brovkin's data, from January to March 1927 the number of small local strikes fluctuated from fifty to seventy each month (Brovkin 1998, p. 183). There were also textile strikes caused by food shortages in Ivanovo-Voznesensk in the spring of 1932 (*Svobodnaia mysl'* 17, 1991, pp. 71–78).

Other data show that acts of protest generally were minimal and inconsequential. For instance, protest leaflets might be circulated at a special shop for the elite in Ivanovo-Voznesensk with little effect (R. Davies 1997, p. 191). Whether absenteeism, turnover, and slowdowns were forms of protest against the repressive apparatus, as has been suggested by some authors (see Kotkin 1995, p. 223), is debatable.

There were a number of peasant protests in the 1920s, but no mass action forced the leaders to change their social policy. Typically, resistance emerged in the countryside, where bands of peasants devised political assassinations and committed arson. In January 1925, 160 cases of resistance were reported in the Volga basin and Siberia; in February, there were 125 (Brovkin 1998, p. 163). This was a relatively small figure, taking into account the well-known tendency of the political police to inflate the proliferation of anti-state activity and treat cases of nonpolitical violence as factional insurgency. Following collectivization, even the number of actions registered by the GPU was limited; peasant resistance was rare and in some areas unknown. Collectivization destroyed the traditional life of most of the population and led to the cruel deportation of millions of peasants. Yet, while most Russian emigrants living abroad expected a sort of Pugachev rebellion,[68] there were only a few isolated local riots.

In her book *Stalin's peasants*, Sheila Fitzpatrick wrote about "passive resistance," which, in the context of her book, quickly degraded into a catch-all phrase for so-called protest actions such as the slaughter of livestock; "the apathy, inertia, and spirit of independence"; the spreading of various rumors by old peasant women; "rural hooliganism"; and "heavy drinking" (Fitzpatrick 1994b, pp. 66, 208, 214, 235). Fitzpatrick and several other authors who wrote on topics such as slavery, serfdom, and workers in Soviet and Western society, eagerly cited "the refusal to work" as political resistance (James Scott 1985). In the Russian case, people's refusal to work (or their insistence on working poorly) cannot be considered political defiance. Unlike veritable cases of political resistance (for instance, the civil rights movement in the United States), uncooperative Soviet peasants did not necessarily have an organized list of objectives, or even a unified will to protect and further their interests. In the absence of work incentives, a refusal or reluctance to perform should not be embellished to the level of political defiance.

The peasant resistance also was very limited. In 1931, local riots of exiled peasants ignited in Siberia. The disturbance lasted a week and was characterized by Russian historians as "more of an organized attempt to flee than an uprising in the full sense of the word" (R. Davies 1997, pp. 128–138). Sheila Fitzpatrick described a riot in a village in the Astrakhan region on February 22, 1930 as "a drunken crowd of several hundred people." During the riot, the dekulakization commission was attacked. Fitzpatrick also discovered some archival data on individual acts of violence against Soviet activists (Fitzpatrick 1994b, pp. 65–66; see also Viola 1996). In this period, the highest level of resistance amounted to people tearing down official pro-collectivization posters and leaflets in Nizhnii Novgorod in 1931 (Ivnitsky 1995). In his memoirs, Nikita Khrushchev (1970, p. 731) recounted only a few secondhand stories about small disturbances in the country (one in Krasnodar in 1932, another in Ukraine the same year).[69] The famous Russian economist Nikolai Shmelev noted that the peasants maintained only one of the necessary conditions for mass insurrection: "the feeling of desperation" (Shmelev 1989, p. 69). Among other things, they lacked political organization and confidence in their own power. After the war, cases of resistance in the countryside were extremely rare.[70] The peasants patiently endured collectivization and the great hunger. This sort of tolerance would be remembered six decades later, in 1992, when many Russians suffered from the loss of their life savings, hyperinflation, and long delays in the payments of their salaries. In spite of the hardships, there were no major demonstrations or strikes in 1992.

The workers' strikes and peasant riots in the 1920s marked the end of mass protest actions in Stalin's times. The two main exceptions were the rebellion in the Vorkuta concentration camp in 1942,[71] and the uprising of the prisoners who worked on railroad construction in the North Urals in 1948 (see Dobrovolsky 1999). Resistance now came only in the form of individual actions which demanded extraordinary courage.

Public actions such as the dissemination of leaflets were extremely risky in the face of the political police.[72] Sarah Davies discovered documents in the archives which showed that after the issuing of the notorious labor decrees of 1938 and 1940 (the decrees banned the change of jobs and introduced draconian measures against absenteeism), leaflets with anti-Soviet appeals and calls for strikes spread throughout Leningrad. No serious public actions came to fruition, however. Brave indeed were the people who disseminated leaflets protesting the mass purges and show trials (S. Davies 1997, pp. 47, 122–123).

The public declaration of one's dissenting views on substantial ideological matters was also quite dangerous. The famous scholar Ivan Pavlov once sent an unprecedented letter to Molotov, blasting Stalin's regime, comparing it to "ancient Asiatic despotism" (*Sovetskaia kul'tura*, January 14, 1989). Few people living in Stalin's time had ever depicted the regime so boldly and uncompromisingly. Miraculously, the letter did not impact Pavlov's fate. Had Pavlov not been world famous, his punishment would have been severe. Indeed, the risk for ordinary people who sent letters to party committees and media was much higher.[73]

As is only natural for a totalitarian system, the letters sent by citizens to the media and authorities were carefully studied by the KGB and its predecessors throughout the life span of the Soviet Union. The KGB was aided by workers from the "department of letters" (Avzeger 1993, p. 56).[74] In spite of the KGB's monitoring, the Soviet people (as mentioned earlier) sent millions of letters to the media and various institutions, with complaints and in some cases reactions to current events. Many people expressed their discontent during election campaigns. As a party official from the Novgorod region said in February 1946, the people "criticized the Soviet election system, or used the shortages of food, housing and other difficulties to couch their complaints and blame the Soviet government" (Glavatsky 1995, pp. 289–290). In effect, the people's myriad letters eased the workload of the KGB. To some extent, the KGB simply supervised the great numbers of citizens who reported themselves. However, in most cases, people were discreet in their letters and avoided complaints that could be interpreted as anti-Soviet.

Individuals also criticized the regime in their personal diaries and private discussions.[75] The number of people who took the risk of keeping a diary was surprisingly high.[76] Some wrote long manuscripts with blatant anti-Soviet content. In 1939–1940, Lidiia Chukovskaia wrote a novel-length diary about the terror in Leningrad (Chukovskaia 1998).[77] Even bolder were those who sent private letters to friends or relatives with some critique of the regime; practically everybody assumed that these letters would be scrutinized by the KGB or other state agents.[78] Many were arrested for sending prohibited materials through the mail. In 1945, Alexander Solzhenitsyn was arrested for writing a letter in which he criticized Stalin, after which he spent eight years in prison and labor camps, and three years in internal exile.

These forms of resistance all had an individual character. After the 1930s, there were a few cases where students became involved in some form of collective action. They organized circles in which they discussed the ideas of socialism and Leninism and opposed them to Stalin's tyranny. Some of these groups emerged after the war. None did anything more than talk. In all cases, if a group was discovered, it was cruelly destroyed. Its members were shot, or at best sent to the Gulag. The Alliance of the Struggle for the Revolutionary Cause in Moscow consisted of sixteen teenagers who were applying for admission to Moscow University. Three of the leaders were executed (Rumer-Zaraiev 1996; R. Medvedev 1974, pp. 974–975). Another group emerged in Voronezh, also in the first postwar years. Its members were arrested and sent to the Gulag (Zhigulin 1988).

The party membership and loyal intellectuals accepted the repressions against its ordinary members and even leaders without a hint of public resistance. Stalin easily expelled Trotsky to Alma-Ata in 1928, and to Turkey in 1929, without any serious demonstration. A small protest action by Trotsky's followers in Moscow on the eve of his exile to Kazakhstan entered history as the single event of this sort. Later, Stalin would murder thousands of leading party members and people from the army and the state apparatus without being challenged.

A number of glasnost-era writers described a group established by Martemian Riutin, who wrote a declaration "To all members of the VKP(b)" in 1930. The declaration circulated among dozens of party members and eventually brought about Riutin's arrest and execution in 1937 (see Borshchagovsky 1990a, 1990b).[79] As another example of resistance inside the party, Soviet historians in 1990 cited an anonymous document entitled "The voice of the masses" (1929), in which the authors revealed their despondency about the internal party struggle as a waste of energy, accused party officials of being careerists, and demanded Stalin's resignation (Kuleshov 1990, pp. 290–291).

Virtually no one in the party leadership dared to defy Stalin, even on their deathbeds. Many party leaders refused to defend their friends and colleagues. Some who had been sent to prison participated obediently in the show trials. They confessed to every imaginable crime against the revolution and the motherland. However, two party leaders stood out for their bravery: Pavel Postyshev defended himself during the meeting of the Central Committee when Stalin cast doubt on his "Bolshevism." And Nikolai Bukharin skillfully responded to prosecutor Andrei Vyshinsky's questions during his trial in 1938. (Bukharin was nonetheless sentenced to death on March 13, 1938.) Nikolai Krestinsky, another defendant in the trial of 1938, bravely retracted his guilty plea in court.

A note of dissent with policy can be found in some letters written by middle-ranking party officials. Some even risked publishing relatively bold articles in the media which they supervised.[80] These cases were more frequent after World War II, when there were feelings in various strata of the population that Stalin was more trustful of his people (the victors) and would therefore mollify his rigid control and allow more freedom of expression for the sake of progress.[81]

There were also cases of intervention by loyal intellectuals. For instance, Mikhail Sholokhov sent a deeply critical letter about collectivization to Stalin. Another famous writer, Maria Smirnova, sent Stalin a gloomy letter about the situation in the countryside after the war in 1952 (Aksenov 1991, pp. 202–203). The young, promising physicist Lev Landau was among those intellectuals who were "fairly" arrested and sent to the Gulag in the mid-1930s. In 1938, Landau participated in the writing of an anti-Stalinist flyer that accused "the great leader" of betraying socialism. Landau, who was also accused of "wrecking activity" in the Kharkov research institute, was released from prison at the request of Piotr Kapitsa. For the next three decades of his life, Landau steered clear of politics, remaining politically passive even during the thaw (Gorelik 1992, 1995, pp. 11–16).

Like the party leaders and intellectuals, army personnel and officials at all levels were passive with respect to the regime. In order to save the prestige of the Russian army, Marshal Sergei Akhromeev asserted that in the 1920s–1940s there were two trends: Stalinist and anti-Stalinist. He contended that these two "stormy" trends struggled for power in the party (see Cherkashin 1990; see also Volkogonov 1991). There is no evidence, however, that the Soviet generals who were executed by Stalin in 1937 had been embroiled in any conspiracy against Stalin. Despite the efforts of post-Communist historians to find an example of resistance to the bloody despot, none has been found in the military.

In all of Soviet history, there was only one case that may be treated (with great reservations) as potentially dangerous for the regime. Georgii Zhukov, a glorious commander during the war with Nazi Germany, was seemingly considered (probably without grounds) a potential "Bonaparte" by Stalin and then Khrushchev. In connection with Zhukov, whom Stalin evidently planned to arrest in 1945–1946, the KGB arrested numerous people close to him, and some of these individuals did harbor anti-Soviet views (Zhukov 1992). Colonel General Vasilii Gordov was one of them. Gordov had served as commander at the Stalingrad front. In several telephone conversations with his aide and wife in December 1946, he criticized Stalin and the regime and praised Western democracy. The conversations had been taped by the political police. Subsequently, Gordov was arrested. He was executed in 1950 (Maximova 1992).[82] There is no evidence, however, to substantiate allegations of an attempted terrorist attack against Stalin or his lieutenants.[83]

Stalin's death stimulated some active resistance, though most of it was spontaneous and unorganized. The most serious acts of defiance took place in the Gulag, where inmates rebelled against the administration of the camps. These uprisings can be considered a form of resistance to the regime. The most important incidents occurred in the concentration camps in Norilsk in May

1953 and in Kengir in 1954. In Kengir, the prisoners made several demands, including the radical improvement of their living conditions, the firing of several officers, and even negotiations with a member of the Soviet leadership. After some hesitation, the riot was put down by force (see Solzhenitsyn 1973; see also *Otechestvennye arkhivy* 4, 1994, pp. 33–87; *Komsomol'skaia pravda*, July 17, 1991).[84]

After Stalin's death, it took several years for people to free themselves from the nightmare of mass terror and start resisting the system. The Russian intelligentsia was the most active in challenging the status quo, though even at their finest moments they did not present a significant threat to the system.

With the retreat of mass terror in the 1960s, members of the Soviet intelligentsia, and particularly intellectuals (primarily scholars and writers), began to criticize the Soviet regime (V. Shlapentokh 1990; Tökés 1975; R. Medvedev 1980; Spechler 1982). They were joined by non-Russian nationalists (Ukrainians and Lithuanians). The intelligentsia resorted to various actions that revealed their discontent with the regime. They published protest letters, disseminated samizdat literature, and published their works abroad. Some of them even planned demonstrations and meetings. The latter culminated in a five-minute demonstration by seven intellectuals in Red Square, protesting the Soviet invasion of Czechoslovakia on August 25, 1968. In the 1970s, despite the political reaction, the opposition of intellectuals went so far as to create the first oppositional organizations in the Soviet Union. The first two major groups were the Human Rights Committee (1970) and the Moscow Helsinki Group (1976).

However, between 1967 and 1975, only 1,583 individuals (less than 200 per year) were sentenced for such "anti-Soviet activity" (including those who were persecuted for nationalist and religious activities).[85] By Vladimir Bukovsky's estimate, which was based on KGB documents from the post-Stalin era, 6,000 people were sentenced for political crimes (Bukovsky 1995, p. 130). According to Andropov's analysis of anti-Soviet activity, between 1967 and 1975, 50 percent of the punishable offenses against the state were "calumnious or politically damaging statements." The second category in importance (about 8 percent) consisted of "calumnious or politically damaging documents"; the third group (about 6 percent) included other "antisocial, hippie-type actions. The people who committed the most terrible deeds "attempted to contact or contacted anti-Soviet centers abroad." All of these cases together accounted for only 0.4 percent of repressions by the KGB between 1967 and 1977 (Bukovsky 1995, p. 139).[86]

Notwithstanding the increased resistance, the oppositional activity of the intelligentsia and other groups of the population (with a few exceptions, including Solzhenitsyn's deeds) never challenged the fundamentals of the regime and never presented a serious threat to the Kremlin. The number of people who were ready to sign open letters of protest against the regime did not surpass a few hundred. On December 5, 1968, the number of people who participated in the Human Rights Day demonstration was 100–200 (Alexeeva 1984). Keep in mind that in order to demonstrate their importance to the Kremlin, the KGB was on the lookout for the slightest manifestations of hostility toward the regime.[87]

It is also important to note that the majority of dissidents only wanted to humanize the regime. In Andropov's analysis of the ideological affinities of those who were sent to prison between 1967 and 1977, he found no enemies of socialism. More than 50 percent were accused of bourgeois nationalism (including 17 percent who were "Zionists"); 35 percent were evidently supporters of socialism, because they were described as bearers of "revisionist and reformist ideologies"; and 8 percent were labeled as advocates of "religious ideology" (Bukovsky 1995, p. 140).

On the whole, the dissident movement—quite strong in the 1960s and 1970s, though it recruited only a few thousand intellectuals and was ignored by the masses—was almost totally decimated by the beginning of the 1980s. Resistance groups existed in Russia only as long as the Kremlin tolerated them. The hesitation of the leadership with respect to the best political course, particularly given its growing concern about international public opinion, is the main reason why these groups were not stifled immediately. The regime decided to eliminate the intellectual opposition in the late 1960s, and resistance was fully extinguished by the early 1980s, only a few years before perestroika.[88] The absolute majority of the regime's critics quickly were transformed into loyal Soviet citizens. It took significant effort on the part of Gorbachev to arouse critiques of the Soviet system in 1985–1987.

While the intellectual opposition was quite weak, the conduct of other classes and groups was even more obedient. A careful study and collection of data was conducted by Ludmila Alexeeva between 1953 and the early 1980s with the purpose of finding any sign of resistance to the regime. The study did not overturn this general conclusion about the universal compliance of the Soviet people in the post-Stalin era, even when the number who challenged the local authorities on nonpolitical issues increased—an unheard-of trend since the early 1930s (Alexeeva 1984).[89] There were disturbances in several cities (most of which were directed against the local police) in the late 1950s. Such disturbances continued to occur until the mid-1960s, then subsided.[90] According to former KGB chairman Vladimir Kriuchkov, one thousand people were involved in these actions (Kriuchkov 1996). However, there were only a few public disturbances that had real political resonance (i.e., the riots in Karaganda and Novocherkassk in 1962, and the riot at the sports stadium in Tashkent in 1973). Public disturbances of this kind were so rare that when such an event occurred, it drew the complete and immediate attention of the Kremlin.[91]

Similarly, only a few of the brief workers' strikes had political overtones (Alexeeva 1984). For instance, after the Soviet invasion of Prague (as can be seen from the secret documents published after 1991), the protests of a few dozen nonintellectuals never went beyond one or two sentences uttered in public or in private conversations, and even these rebukes were most often expressed in a state of heavy drunkenness (see Novikov and Shinkarev 1992; Bukovsky 1995).

In the last two decades of the Soviet regime, the army was as politically passive and loyal to the regime as it had been in previous periods. The rebellion of Valerii Sablin, the deputy commander of political education, was unique in the whole of Soviet military history since the Kronshtadt rebellion in 1921. With the support of a few officers and sailors, Sablin organized an insurrection aboard his ship *Storozhevoi* in the Baltic Sea in 1975. The protesters demanded access to radio in order to publicize their program, which proclaimed that "Great Russia should become a vanguard democratic and law-abiding state instead of a hungry and backward country under the guidance of the Central Committee and Brezhnev." The rebellion was easily quelled and Sablin was executed on direct order of the Politburo (see Alexeev 1995; Urusov 1995; Cherkashin 1990; see also *Komsomol'skaia pravda*, March 3 and December 26, 1990).[92]

The KGB was also impermeable to dissent in the post-Stalin era. The single known case of internal dissension involved Victor Orekhin, who worked in the KGB's Moscow directorate. In the mid-1970s, he began informing dissidents about planned actions against them. He was arrested and spent eight years in prison (Khinshtein 1994).

Conclusion

At all stages of its history, the Soviet regime enjoyed significant public support. Respect for the regime and its ideology—a blend of socialism and Russian nationalism—remained strong in Russia even after the fall of the Soviet Union. As the available data show, the regime always enjoyed the active or passive support of the majority of the young and educated. After the civil war, most of the population (with various limitations) adjusted, materially and psychologically, to the regime. They saw it as a force that guaranteed order in society, protection from foreign enemies, and some degree of social and economic progress.

11

The Regime and the Empire
A Complex Relationship

There was a radical difference between the Soviet regime and the empire. This contrast corresponded to the distinctive roles played by Russians and by non-Russians in society. The regime was mostly associated with the Russian segment of the population, which constituted the core of the empire (the metropolis), while the empire administered the non-Russians in the provinces. Throughout Soviet history, the leaders of the party and state, along with their apparatuses, were always concerned about the ethnic factor, and closely examined the differences between Russians and non-Russians when establishing policies and strategic decisions.[1]

Utopians Turned Machiavellian

Before the revolution and for a short period after it, the Bolsheviks harbored some illusions about ethnic issues. Prior to 1917, they assumed that the proletariat would unite the country, including poor peasants and non-Russians. Non-Russians would support the revolution and take part in running the new society. Following the *Communist Manifesto*, Lenin and his comrades believed that the ethnic factor would dissolve before the coming solidarity movement in all countries around the world. Lenin wrote in 1906, "The proletariat of all nations in the course of the revolution will unite more and more in the common struggle" (Lenin 1947–1951, Vol. 10, p. 138).

The Bolsheviks were confident about the strength of internationalism and the solidarity of toilers in all nations. Before 1917, they resolutely supported the idea of self-determination of all countries. They were certain that the "free nations" would join the Communist brotherhood at the first opportunity. For this reason, Lenin attacked Rosa Luxemburg, who expressed doubt about the application of the principle of self-determination in the aftermath of the socialist revolution (Lenin 1947–1951, Vol. 22, pp. 306–344). The Bolsheviks thought they could use the hatred of non-Russians toward tsarism as a weapon for destroying the Russian monarchy without jeopardizing proletarian internationalism.

However, very soon after October 1917, the Bolsheviks were disappointed not only by the Russian masses but also by the non-Russian nations' immediate proclamations of independence. Even Ukrainians, the ethnic group closest to Russians, joined the crusade against Russia. The idea of internationalism (vital to the Bolsheviks before the revolution) was discarded almost completely from the closed ideology, while remaining a crucial feature in the open ideology, particularly when it was addressed to non-Russians. Lenin and his colleagues quickly realized that "nationalist feelings" were stronger than "class feelings," and they took this into account when developing and implementing policy.

In the first two years of the regime, the Bolsheviks acquired new insight into the ethnic issue and began to behave not as utopian leaders aloof from reality but as Machiavellian politicians. They quickly realized that the elite of the army and political police should comprise numerous non-Russians (in the case of some units, the majority), who harbored no sympathy for the old Russian regime. While we must discard the theory that the Soviet system was created by Jews, it is impossible to deny that Jews played a prominent role in the state and party apparatus. The same was true of various non-Russian ethnic groups: Georgians, Armenians, Poles, Latvians, Chinese, and several others.[2] The Latvian and Chinese regiments were often considered by the Kremlin as the most reliable of military forces. They proved their reliability during the rebellion by the left wing of the Socialist Revolutionary Party in July 1918, when Lenin's power was severely threatened.

Imperial Policy: Three Strategies

The rulers of empires have always understood that they must recruit local elites from the indigenous populations and that the loyalty of these elites is paramount for their empire's survival. This loyalty depends on the status of local elites in comparison to the elite of the dominant nation and their chances of obtaining positions in the metropolis. However, the cost of total equality among local and central elites is quite high, as such equality leads to a weakening in the loyalty of the elite of the dominant nation.

The rulers had three strategies for developing the empire: universal, ethnic, and mixed. The first strategy completely disregarded ethnic origins and re-cruited elites universally (an internationalist, inclusive strategy and "pure" imperial, universal policy). Internationalist empires included the Roman em-pire in the last centuries of its history, the Austro-Hungarian empire, and the Chinese empire during the Qing Dynasty. These empires attempted to recruit political elites of various ethnic origins.[3] Another example of this type was the Moghul empire of the sixteenth through the eighteenth centuries. It was estab-lished by Moghuls from Central Asia who conquered India.[4] They broke rela-tions with their native region, established a Muslim dynasty in India, and claimed all the peoples of the empire as their subjects, regardless of religion.[5]

The second type of imperial strategy was chauvinistic in nature and re-cruited the central elite from the dominant ethnic or religious group. The rulers sent the members of this group to the provinces as supervisors of the local elite. The Russian empire was an example of this type. The preponder-ance of Russians in the administration was absolute. The Russian elite made some exceptions for foreigners (primarily Germans and various ethnic groups of Eastern Orthodox religion, such as Armenians and Georgians), allowing them to hold some high positions. Muslims and Jews were almost totally excluded from leading positions in society. The priority of Russians in the official ideology was evident, and the idea of their exceptionalism and even their missionary role in the world was strongly supported by official propa-ganda and the Orthodox church.[6]

The Arab empire at the time of the Umayyad dynasty also belonged to this type, though with several qualifications. While most caliphs were quite liberal and tolerant toward other religions, and non-Arabs could improve their material status by converting to Islam (for instance, gaining exemption from some taxes), the Arabs made up the ruling class and regarded their non-Muslim subjects as second-class people. Even highly educated individuals who had converted to Islam were rarely admitted to high society. Non-Arabs —especially Greeks and Persians—who maintained high positions in soci-ety were gradually replaced by Arabs.[7]

The third imperial strategy combined the strategy of giving advantages first to the dominant national or religious group with the strategy of eliciting the active involvement of local, indigenous elites in the ruling of the provinces, even with some moderate chances for them to reach the apex of power. Most empires in history followed the third pattern of policy. Among them were the Roman empire (throughout much of its history),[8] the Abbasid empire, and the Ottoman empire in the first centuries of its existence.[9] In almost all continental empires in history, the central elite oscillated among the three strategies, though it is possible to discern a single, dominant strategy in each empire.

The Rational Imperial Policy of the Soviet Communists

In the Soviet Union, the rulers employed all three strategies with respect to imperial policy. As previously explained, as early as 1918 or 1919 Lenin and his comrades evidently were intent on making Russia the center of the world.

In the view of many Bolsheviks, the universal strategy was ideal for three reasons. First, it helped garner the mass support of non-Russians who had been discriminated against in the past and therefore were more loyal to the new state. Second, it helped assimilate non-Russians into the mainstream (Russian) culture and interests. And third, it bolstered the official ideology with its focus on internationalism. At the same time, while the tenets of this strategy were indeed vital, clearly the Russian segment, which constituted the largest ethnic population and possessed the highest level of education and culture, was destined by design to figure most prominently in the Soviet empire.[10]

By the mid-1920s, however, the empire had shifted from the first to the second strategy. The Russians began replacing non-Russians, especially Jews, in the imperial governing bodies. This process remained quite invisible until the late 1930s, when Stalin removed the leaders of almost all the non-Russian republics, on charges of nationalism (Zotov 1989, pp. 267–268). In the same years, Stalin started to foment state anti-Semitism. Russian chauvinism advanced after the beginning of the war and reached its peak in the last years of Stalin's rule, when the Russification of the party and state apparatus was universal.[11] Any manifestation of the non-Russian national conscience was mercilessly extirpated by Stalin. At his order, many non-Russian nationalists were sentenced to the Gulag and execution.

After Stalin's death, the imperial policy moved to a new strategy that corresponded most closely to the third type. In the 1960s-1980s, the dominant position of the Russians (as "senior brother") in the Soviet empire was indisputable. The Russian language prevailed in all provinces. Russian was the official language of all higher educational institutions. Russians continued to hold key positions in all ethnic provinces. However, the number of apparatchiks with local origins was still quite high, and their importance increased significantly after 1953.

The mixed strategy followed by the Kremlin after 1953 was not stable, and the proportion of its chauvinistic and internationalistic components fluctuated until 1987–1989. In May 1953, Lavrentii Beria made an attempt to diminish radically the chauvinistic element; but after his fall from power, Khrushchev restored the concept of "senior brother." At the same time, Khrushchev increased the significance of the "pure" internationalist imperial factor in domestic policy. The role of "the Russian factor" increased during Brezhnev's rule but diminished during Andropov's short tenure in 1982–1983.

The Regime and Empire in the Open Ideology

The essential difference between the regime and the empire was manifested clearly in the open ideology. As previously explained, by the early 1930s, the open ideology consisted of two independent elements: socialist ideas and nationalist slogans. After WWII, this was also the typical blend of tenets employed by the socialist states that were independent from the USSR (i.e., China, Vietnam, Cuba, Albania).

The central leadership accentuated the socialist side of the ideology whenever they addressed the local ethnic elites and the rest of the indigenous population. In the provinces (first and foremost, those in Central Asia), the socialist ideology pushed for the modernization and even Westernization of life. Indeed, the regime relied on the socialist ideology for the restoration, expansion and maintenance of the Russian empire until 1985. Socialism turned out to be an excellent imperial ideology—not so much for the Russians as for their non-Russian counterparts. In the national republics, the open ideology praised the empire as well as socialist ideals. Moscow tried to suggest that the provinces not only had the advantage of socialism but a great empire as well.

While the open ideology addressed to non-Russians clearly emphasized the socialist component, it conveyed a somewhat different message to the Russians, particularly in oral propaganda as well as in literature and movies. Russian patriotism, Russian culture, and Russian moral and spiritual superiority were advanced, and the socialist elements, pushed to the background.

As the empire was being dismantled, respect for the empire and its ideology was replaced by contempt and hatred. The growing freedom of information and expression was also a powerful factor that explained the drastically changing attitudes of non-Russians after 1989.[12]

The Dominance of the Russians

In fact, in all of Soviet history, particularly since the early 1930s, Russia was obviously the dominant nation in the USSR, even if the degree of its supremacy changed over the seven decades of the empire (Khazanov 1995, pp. 4–5; Hajda and Beissinger 1990, p. 307). A number of facts confirm the Russian dominance in the Soviet Union until 1989.

Official ideology unequivocally presented Russians as "the senior brother" and all other nations and ethnic groups as "junior." Official history since the early 1930s praised the expansion of the Russian empire in all areas: in Europe (Tatarstan, Ukraine, and Moldova); in Siberia and the Far East; in the Caucasus and Central Asia. Russian tsars and commanders—tyrants such as Ivan the Terrible and General Alexander Ermolov—were commended as great statesmen, and their monuments were preserved intact (since revolutionary times) in the capitals they had conquered (for instance, the monument to Ivan the Terrible, in Kazan, and that to Ermolov, in Grozny). At the same time, the national heroes of non-Russians—such as Ivan Mazeppa (Ukraine), Timur (Central Asia), and Shamil (North Caucasus)—were treated negatively (Khazanov 1995, pp. 8–9).

The Russians held the leading positions in the party and state apparatus. Eighty-three percent of the ministers and 88 percent of the top military command were Russians. While the Kremlin's cadre policy for the national republics changed over the years, the Russians always played a primary role in governing the country.[13] For instance, if the local first party secretary was not an ethnic Russian (as was often the case in Stalin's time), the second party secretary and the head of the KGB were always Russian.

The Russian language and culture were propagated throughout the USSR from its very beginning to its last decades. In 1979, 62 percent of non-Russians were fluent in Russian.[14] The Kremlin strongly encouraged the use of Russian as the main language of communication inside the empire. With the help of the authorities and some support of non-Russians, the language circulated quite successfully through the "small" national republics (i.e., Chuvashia, Bashkiria, Kalmykia, North Ossetia and others).[15] However, the linguistic policy of the Kremlin was not, as will be explained later, hostile toward non-Russian languages in "big" national republics, and it supported the use of these languages in secondary schools and the media.

The Russians also developed a strong presence in all parts of the empire. During the 70 years of the Soviet empire, the migration of Russians to the provinces significantly increased in comparison with the pre-revolutionary times, when colonization of the provinces by Russians also had been intensive. In 1926, 5 million Russians lived outside the Russian Federation; by 1989, this number had increased to 25 million (Ostapenko and Subbotina 1993, p. 286).

The emigration of Russians to the national republics was partially spontaneous (industrialization demanded Russian cadres, especially professionals and workers), and partially directed by Moscow, which saw the Russification of the regions as a remedy against the threat of local nationalism. The mass evacuation of the population from the territories occupied by Germany during WWII also accounted for the shift of the Russians toward the national republics, as did the wholesale deportation of several ethnic groups (i.e., Kalmyks, Crimean Tatars, and others) and the mass exile of people from the Western parts of the Soviet Union (Ukraine, Moldova, and the Baltic republics) for alleged collaboration with the Nazis.[16]

Most Russians (like the British and French in their respective empires) enjoyed the USSR's imperial character, with its many nations and ethnic groups. The Russians were well aware of their dominant role in the empire. They saw the Soviet Union as "their" state, but they stayed in line with the official ideology, viewing other ethnic groups as the "junior brothers" and themselves as their benefactors. Yurii Levada found that as late as 1989, the Russians still exhibited the imperial syndrome and strongly admired the Soviet empire (Levada 1993, pp. 175, 181).

The imperial mentality was not, however, strictly a Russian phenomenon. The empire played an eminent role in the mind-set of many non-Russians, and not only Slavs.[17] Several non-Russians were convinced that it was quite convenient for small nations like Estonia to live under a mighty empire that provided them a ready market for their goods, and a strong national defense.[18]

At the same time, the difference between the Russians and non-Russians in their attitudes toward the Soviet state was gigantic. This was clearly revealed in a survey conducted by VTsIOM in 1989 in which respondents' level of personal identification with the state was assessed. The survey found that the number of ethnic Russians who identified themselves as Soviet citizens was 3 to 4 times higher than the numbers of Ukrainians, Lithuanians, and Kazakhs who did the same; it was 4 to 5 times higher than that of Moldovans, and 9 to 14 times higher than that of Georgians and Armenians. The number of Russians who identified with "the concrete territory" (a euphemism for the national region) was 2 to 3 times less than the numbers of non-Russians. The number of Russians who identified with the USSR was 57 percent. Three percent of Estonians, 8 percent of Armenians, and 39 percent of Uzbeks identified with the USSR. Forty-two percent of Russians in another survey (August 1990), reflecting the dismantlement of the empire, openly bemoaned "the loss of the leading role of Russia" in the Soviet Union.[19]

The data about the attitudes of Russians versus non-Russians with regard to religion also showed a radical variance. The number of believers among non-Russians was much higher than among Russians. Religion played a very important role in the national and cultural survival of non-Russians. While 35 percent of the Russians living in Russia (25 percent in Siberia and 32 percent in Moscow) saw themselves in 1989 as religious people, 74 percent of Lithuanians and 84 percent of Uzbeks considered themselves religious (Levada 1993, p. 231).

Even though they represented the dominant nation in the empire, many ordinary Russians were discontent with their status and perceived themselves as "neglected in their own country." They were dissatisfied with their status in the Soviet empire during the internationalistic stage and in the times of the mixed strategy.[20] The discontent of the Russians was exacerbated by the developments after 1989 when many ethnic groups were able to express their hostile attitudes toward the empire.[21]

The discontent of the Russians with their status in the empire and the strong belief in the subvention of the provinces played an important role in the demise of the Soviet empire. Yeltsin used this discontent as a major instrument for the removal of Gorbachev in 1991. This will be discussed in detail in the next chapters.

The Important Role of the Ethnic Elite

While endowing Russians with the dominant role in the central elite, the empire energetically promoted the national elites in all the provinces, using "affirmative action." Special quotas were used in admissions to higher educational institutions in Moscow and Leningrad, especially to party colleges, in order to accelerate this process. The Russians held most of the key positions in local party organizations and particularly in the KGB, but Moscow soon filled many bureaucratic positions with local people. With the relaxation of the regime, the role of the local elites in the administration of local business grew considerably. In Brezhnev's times, the first party secretaries in all the provinces were virtual satraps, ruling their own people yet always observant of the strict constraints imposed by the center: no open nationalism, and no interference in military and foreign affairs or security matters (Rigby 1990; Conquest 1986a).

In general, the Kremlin's policy toward the ethnic elites was successful, not unlike the British policy in India and other colonies. However, while the central elite was able to control the local elites, these "obedient servants" were ready to betray their masters at the first opportunity.

The Jews and the Empire

The complex relationship between the regime and the empire in many respects shaped the fate of the Jews in the Soviet Union. It is difficult to underestimate the Jewish role in the creation of the regime as well as the empire.[22] Most Jews identified with the socialist transformation of the country and with the Russians and did not consider themselves members of a non-Russian ethnic group. In the first decades after the revolution, they were considered loyal minions of Moscow and Russia (to some degree the same was true of Jews in East European countries such as Poland, Hungary, and Czechoslovakia). The key role of Jews in the party and state apparatus in the first two decades after 1917 has been well documented (see Pasmanik 1923; Frumkin, Aronson, and Gol'denveizer 1968; Schwarz 1951).

The active and highly visible role of Jews in the party and Soviet apparatuses as well as in science and culture only enhanced the deeply rooted anti-

Semitism in those who bore animosity toward the regime, particularly in Ukraine. Anti-Semitic feelings were manipulated by the political opposition. The Bolsheviks' adversaries, particularly the monarchists, claimed that the high proportion of Jews in major institutions was proof of the anti-national character of the regime.[23] At the same time, anti-Semitism, in spite of the official policy in the 1920s, was also quite intensive among ordinary people as well as among party members who yearned for the positions held by Jews.[24] Ethnic Russian Bolsheviks ascribed many anti-socialist qualities to the Jews which went along with their general anti-Semitic images, such as the reluctance to work hard (particularly in physical trades and manual labor), the love of money, and the attempt to dominate the political, economic and cultural elite. The large number of Jewish defendants in the show trials of the mid-1930s was used by party loyalists to justify their anti-Semitic stance (S. Davies 1997, pp. 84–85, 87). At the same time, Jews were accused of the opposite flaws (i.e., supporting the revolution), and many ordinary people identified them with the dominant power and political police, combining the traditional hatred of Jews with their ingrained hatred of bosses.

As mentioned above, in the late 1920s, party attitudes toward anti-Semitism began to reverse. In the beginning, the reversal was covert, but gradually it became more open. In the late 1930s, Moscow closed Jewish schools and started to restrain the access of Jews to the nomenklatura. This policy was advanced further after the pact with Hitler in 1939 (Skoczylas 1965; Ro'i 1995; Ginzberg 1999). During the war, the anti-Semitic policy was openly discussed (probably for the first time) at meetings of the Central Committee. The party leadership, in an effort to render the Nazis' anti-Semitic propaganda impotent as a weapon for turning the Soviet people against the Soviet regime, issued commands to restrict the access of Jews to various institutions and positions. They also recommended that Jews be replaced by Russians in the most politically sensitive areas.[25] The momentum of Stalin's anti-Semitic policy culminated in 1949–1952, on the eve of his death in 1953, when several hundred Jews were arrested, many dozens were executed, and thousands lost their jobs. The policy appealed to millions of Russians in addition to the individuals who filled the posts of ousted Jews in the party and state apparatus. Jews were gradually removed from the army, the KGB, and the Central and regional party committees; their access to science, culture and industry was limited and sometimes prohibited (Kostyrchenko 1995).

After Stalin's death in 1953, this policy, though in a softer rendering, remained intact, and discrimination against Jews became a "normal" phenomenon in Soviet life. While some Jews still worked in the party apparatus and army, their numbers in science and culture dropped decisively. In 1949, Jews constituted 14 percent of scholars who worked in the Academy of Sciences;

by 1980, the proportion was half that.[26] Anti-Semitism was one of the most influential parts of the closed ideology. It was the subject of numerous private debates among party and state apparatchiks, particularly in the 1970s and early 1980s. Rude anti-Semitic jokes were a fixture at private gatherings of apparatchiks and among non-Jewish intellectuals of the 1970s. Without some demonstration of anti-Semitism, a successful career in any prestigious sphere of Soviet life was impossible.

Most of the Soviet population in the post-Stalin era supported state-sponsored anti-Semitism. Negative attitudes toward Jews were universal. The Jews had a sort of unifying effect on the empire because all other ethnic groups (except perhaps Germans) considered themselves in a better position. The officials in almost all non-Russian republics demonstrated their contempt for Jews. Ukrainian bureaucrats and intellectuals surpassed their Moscow colleagues in their hatred of Jews. Remarkably, anti-Semitism did not stunt the internationalist fervor of the Soviet people, who easily combined it with friendliness toward other peoples.[27]

In spite of the strong anti-Semitic undercurrents in the Soviet Union, the rulers remained quite rational in their dealings with Jews. Even at the peak of anti-Semitism, the Kremlin used numerous Jewish professionals, who loyally served the regime even to the point of denying that discrimination against Jews existed. There were some who not only enthusiastically worked in the military-industrial complex (for instance, Yulii Khariton and Vitalii Ginzburg, who were both members of the Soviet Academy of Sciences) but fervently participated in the most heinous political campaigns, including those with evident anti-Semitic overtones (such as journalist David Zaslavsky in the 1940s and early 1950s, and writer Alexander Chakovsky in the 1960 and 1970s).

With good reason, most Jews welcomed perestroika and actively participated in the destruction of the Soviet system and the totalitarian state. Gorbachev himself was more than reticent on the issue of anti-Semitism and never explicitly condemned it. In the mid-1980s, no one could have imagined the position of Jews ten years in the future. With the post-Communist revolution in August 1991, Jews returned in throngs not only to the highest positions in the economy but also to the "commanding heights" in media and even in the government. As the Russians grew disillusioned with liberal capitalism, some Jews even restyled themselves as Russian nationalists (D. Shlapentokh 1998, p. 107).

The Best Years of the Empire

Retrospective analysis suggests that the Soviet empire was a rather successful enterprise. Indeed, the legitimacy of the entire imperial structure lay precisely in the expansion of the empire and the defense of its spoils. These goals dominated the official rhetoric and propaganda of all empires, including the Soviet empire. Extending the empire and controlling the provinces were goals familiar to practically all dignitaries, from the master down to the lowest official. Unlike other objectives ascribed to the empire's elite, these goals were explicitly formulated in official policy. The Soviet empire was quite successful in pursuing these goals. It reached its peak, in the eyes of its contemporaries, in the late 1940s, when it dominated most of Eastern Europe and saw as its vassals socialist Asian countries such as China and North Vietnam; later, it took control of several regimes in Africa (see Besançon 1984; Bialer 1980; Brzezinski and Huntington 1964; Matlock 1995; Ionescu 1965; Gwertzman and Kaufman 1992; Wolf 1986; Abbott 1882; Carrère d'Encausse 1993).

The Soviet empire civilized many national provinces, particularly the republics of Central Asia and the Caucasus, where industrial and cultural levels by 1985 were much higher than in neighboring foreign states such as Afghanistan, Turkey, Iran, and China.[28] The industrial production in most republics grew immensely and was higher than that of the country as a whole. According to official data, between 1913 and 1987, the industrial production of Russia/USSR increased by 213 times. In Tadzhikistan, industrial production increased by 205 times; in Georgia and Kazakhstan, 318 times; in Moldova, 419 times; in Kirgizia, 494 times; and in Armenia, 576 times (Goskomstat 1987, p. 17).

The Soviet leadership could also be proud of the cultural and educational progress in all non-Russian republics. The level of education in all republics improved enormously. In 1939, the number of people with higher education in the Uzbek Republic was 55 per thousand; by 1986, it was 698 per thousand. The respective numbers for Kirgizia were 46 and 679; for Belorussia, 92 and 674. Educational progress was also quite pronounced in Latvia and Estonia, where the level of education was already high in 1939, compared to that in the USSR (176 per thousand in Latvia, and 161 in Estonia, compared to 108 in the USSR). By 1986 these indicators reached 716 in Latvia, 701 in Estonia, and 701 in the USSR (Goskomstat 1987, p. 525).

No less remarkable was the success of Moscow in establishing a relatively stable ethnic climate in the country—even if the might of the totalitarian state and the fear that it engendered accounted for much of this success. In spite of their complex and sometimes condescending attitudes toward non-Slavs, the Russians maintained friendly attitudes toward all ethnic groups in the USSR (with the clear exception of Jews). Despite the evident dominance of the Russians in society (as "senior brother"), their relations with non-Russians never degraded to offensive levels, even in the Baltic republics and in Central Asia, which did not share Russia's Eastern Orthodox religious heritage (as did Ukraine, Belorussia, Georgia, and Armenia). Social relations between Russians and non-Russians were decent almost everywhere, and public ethnic slurs were a rare occurrence.

In turn, non-Russians, at least on the surface, behaved amicably toward Russians and other ethnic groups. However, the positive attitudes of Estonians with respect to Russians, and of Armenians with respect to Azerbaijanis, were primarily the result of people adapting to the dominant conditions, which punished individuals who violated the rules of "politically correct behavior" in ethnic relations.[29] The relations between groups that would fall into serious conflict after 1985 (i.e., Armenians and Azerbaijanis, Tadzhiks and Uzbeks, Kirgizes and Uzbeks, Tatars and Bashkirs) were relatively peaceful. The relations between various non-Russian ethnic groups inside the national republics (where the situation was indeed quite tense) were an exception. In each republic the dominant group used its position to gain advantages over other ethnic groups. As a result, Uzbeks felt uncomfortable and disadvantaged in Tajikistan, and Armenians felt the same in Azerbaijan. In general, however, direct, public hostility of one ethnic group against another was unusual. Violent actions inspired by ethnic hatred were rare. "The friendship of Soviet people" was a real fact, and not at all a "fraud" as contended by Walter Laqueur after 1991 (Laqueur 1994, p. VII). Certainly, the data from Soviet surveys on ethnic relations should not be taken at face value in view of the impact of desirable values on people's responses. Even so, however, they convey the general idea that the ethnic factor in human relations was quite tolerable. According to these surveys, about two thirds of the people in various regions of the USSR claimed to have friends among people of other ethnic groups and to have no objections to having them as colleagues (Drobizheva 1978, pp. 157–158; Payin 1999).

One indicator of Soviet accomplishments in interethnic relations was the significant number of mixed marriages in the USSR. These marriages took place not only between Russians and other nationalities but also between members of non-Russian ethnic groups that had previously experienced fierce conflict, such as the Armenians and Azerbaijanis, and the Uzbeks and Tadzhiks (Chuiko 1974; Fisher 1980).[30] The ethnic conflicts and fierce hatred of the 1990s (for instance, between the Russians and "people of Caucasian nationalities," or "darks," as they were dubbed by Russians) were unimaginable by the standards of ethnic relations in the early 1980s. In the 1990s, the Moscow police regularly harassed people who came to the capital from Caucasian regions, especially Chechnia and Azerbaijan.[31]

While pursuing its policy of Russification and mildly encouraging non-Russians to send their children to Russian-only schools in non-Russian republics, Moscow also supported the national languages at the level of secondary education. In Georgia, Moldova, and Turkmenia, about two thirds of secondary educational institutions used the national language (Riabushkin 1978, p. 148). Non-Russians were not targets of discrimination in educational and cultural policy. The Soviet system accepted their national cultures as long as they did not encourage anti-Russian nationalism. The decline in the use of non-Russian languages in the last two decades of the empire did not represent a reversal in Soviet policy. Rather, this decline was the result of the willingness of many non-Russians to offer the Russian language to their children. The imperial language offered many more career opportunities on the vast territory of the USSR than the local languages. The same phenomenon occurred in the colonies of the Western powers. For this reason, in the last decades of the Soviet empire the number of secondary schools that used the national language declined dramatically in many republics, particularly in Slavic republics such as Belorussia, Ukraine, and Moldova, and in the "small" national republics of the Russian Federation.[32] Similarly, the use of indigenous languages in periodicals also dwindled over the years of Soviet rule. Between 1940 and 1986, the circulation of periodicals in Russian increased by almost 5 times; periodicals in the Ukrainian language increased by only 1.9 times; in Uzbek, by 3.0 times; and in Kazakh, by 2.5 times. However, the circulation of periodicals in Georgian and in three languages of the Baltic republics increased as much as, or more than, publications in Russian (Goskomstat 1997).

The Soviet successes in national politics were manifested in intensive cultural exchange between republics. The exchange was real and not simply a myth of propaganda, though it was certainly trumpeted in propaganda as much as possible. Books written by non-Russian authors were translated into Russian and read throughout the country. The names of writers such as Chingiz Aitmatov, of Kirgizia, and Ramsul Gamzatov, of Dagestan, were very popular across the USSR. Georgian, Armenian, and Lithuanian movies; Armenian, Ukrainian, Moldovan, Estonian, and Georgian musicians; Lithuanian and Kazakh theater directors and actors; and Armenian and Georgian painters all enjoyed the respect and admiration of the entire country.

At the same time, it would be inaccurate to depict ethnic relations in the USSR in a purely Arcadian style, as did the "revisionists" of the 1970s. The peaceful relations of various ethnic groups and the acceptance of the Russians as "senior brother" coexisted with suppressed enmity, first of all against Russians; with the dream of independence; and with hostility toward some other ethnic groups. We also can observe the suppression of ethnic and racial animosities in democratic countries.[33] True, the Russification of the empire, the complete control of the Kremlin over the media, education, culture and science, and frequent migration from one republic to another all created a sort of "new Soviet nation." This thesis was first launched by Soviet ideologues in the 1970s. It was not a simple ideological artifact, as several liberal intellectuals of this period contended (Fedoseev 1985, pp. 305–306).[34] The thesis was later linked to the concept of the Eurasian nation, which supposed the unity of Russians and Asians and opposed Eurasia to Western Europe and the United States (Kara-Murza 1994b, p. 52). However, as soon as the coercive element of "love thy brother" disappeared (along with the empire), the ethnic elite in each region fomented deep feelings of ethnic hatred and revenge, primarily against Russians. The repressed factors of culture, religion, lifestyle, and particularly the ambitions of the ethnic elite to take full control over their territory, suddenly reemerged.[35] The collapse of the Soviet Union (like that of Yugoslavia) opened an era of aggressive nationalism and discrimination against "others" in each ethnic unit of the former empire (Toshchenko 1994, pp. 31–37).[36]

Conclusion

In the historical context, the USSR as an empire was a controversial success. The policies that supported Russian dominance and coercive Russification, along with the imperial ideology and the suppression of autonomous tendencies, molded the relationship between the core and periphery and secured the Pax Sovietica on the vast Eurasian territory. The suppressed separatist feelings and the animosity against Moscow had a relatively weak impact on life in the Soviet province. At the same time, Moscow played an active role in promoting the economy and culture in non-Russian regions, particularly in Central Asia. By 1985, the empire was strong, and nothing portended its demise in the years ahead.

12

Reforms
Alternatives in History

When a society becomes aware of its chronic diseases and inborn defects, it usually advances people to improve the system and defend it against revolutionary demolition. However, while struggling against the flaws of the system, the reformer may endanger the functionality of individual sectors and put the entire system in jeopardy. This danger often causes a division between different types of leaders and officials. Those who struggle for change assume that there are alternatives to the given social structure. Those who oppose change assume that the society is too rigid and incapable of withstanding the risks of reform. To predict which position is best for the given society at a given historical moment is very difficult.

Alternatives in History

Indeed, at each moment in the historical process, almost all societies have several alternatives for the future. The range of these alternatives depends on the rigidity of the structure. There are objective constraints (i.e., geographical, historical, cultural, economic, and other) imposed on each society. The number of alternatives expands when a society is in the state of "soft structure." Soft structure usually emerges during times of social turmoil, changes in leadership, and particularly when the legitimacy of the regime is in question. This state of society can be called "anomic," because in these times old norms are disregarded by the majority of the population. When a society is in a state of "soft structure," the role of individual events and political actors expands. Within this structure, small factors have a greater potential for making significant changes in the course of history.[1]

The "alternative approach" (or "counterfactual history") is tightly inter-connected with so-called revisionist history (in French, *histoire événementielle*), which has become quite popular among historians in the past few decades, though we can find many advocates of this approach in the more distant past as well (see Renouvier 1901; Squire 1931; Ferguson 1998; see also Tucker 1999; Waller 1998). These historians object to the underestimation of the role of "agent." The concepts of "agent" versus "structure" in historical causation separate historians into two groups: "splitters," who focus on multifarious-ness and complexity, and "lumpers," who tend to "look for large patterns of recurrent forces" (to use J. H. Hexter's categories; see Gray 1998). Splitters stimulate new approaches to the study of events such as the British revolution and the civil war of the seventeenth century,[2] the French revolution in 1789,[3] the American civil war (Macksey 1995; Ward 1995),[4] World War II (Macksey 1995; Dick 1988; Harris 1992; Gingrich and Forstchen 1995),[5] and various developments in Mao's China,[6] by focusing on the importance of single events and individual persons whose absence could have radically changed the course of history (Cust 1991, p. 325).

The contemporaries of a given event perceive the event in a much differ-ent light than do historians in later generations. Looking back on history, scholars tend to consider the various developments as almost unavoidable and preordained. They are exposed to what Henri Bergson called "the illu-sions of retrospective determinism" (Bergson 1960). At the same time, the contemporaries and particularly those who were active participants in the given event remain certain that the course of history could have been differ-ent if the main actors had made different decisions or if some external factor (which had nothing to do with the internal logic of developments) had inter-vened. I am more inclined to trust the judgments of contemporaries than the interpretations of those outside the context of the historical event.[7]

The alternative vision of the past is particularly interesting for the study of Russian history. Several Western scholars have mused about the potential alternatives at different moments in Russian history, especially during the Soviet era.[8] The contemporaries of various crucial events in Russian history also vehemently debated the possibilities of alternatives depending on many factors, some of which had seemingly minor importance. The contemporar-ies of the February Revolution did not consider this event inevitable. Many of them (e.g., Vasilii Shulgin) pointed to several factors that could have changed the course of events (Shulgin 1990). The main figures of the Octo-ber Revolution were confident that the victory of the Bolsheviks was contin-gent upon many circumstances. Lenin and Trotsky insisted that many different circumstances could have transformed the course of history in October 1917 (Trotsky 1960).

After Russia became a totalitarian state, the debates on the alternatives in Soviet history disappeared almost completely from both public and private discourse. The Marxist paradigm about the objective and deterministic laws of the historical process conquered the minds of intellectuals in the Soviet Union as well as in Eastern Europe—even of Polish intellectuals, who were the most hostile toward Moscow (Milosz 1953), and even of intellectuals in France and in New York between the 1930s and the 1950s (Abel 1984; Barrett 1982; Glazer 1984; Hellman 1976; Howe 1982; O'Neill 1982; Pells 1985; Perry 1984; Phillips 1983; Podhoretz 1979). Several generations of Soviet intellectuals were taught to believe in strict, objective social laws. The cause-and-effect relationship, in their interpretation, did not allow for many alternatives. In this way, the diversity of historical processes was obscured. It took a great amount of effort for liberal intellectuals after 1956 to release themselves from the spell of Marxist determinism, which they found extremely attractive, with its "scientific approach to history" (V. Shlapentokh 1990).

With the onset of glasnost, intellectuals began discussing historical alternatives to both the Lenin and Stalin regimes as well as to the February and October Revolutions. In 1989, A. Chubarian praised "the alternative analysis of history" (*Nedelia*, December 31, 1989). During this period, liberals and to some degree neo-Stalinists popularized a theory regarding possible alternatives to historical development. They suggested that Russian history could have taken other courses following the October Revolution and Lenin's death. Mikhail Shatrov, through his historical plays about the events of 1917–1924 (for instance, the play "Further, further, further . . ."), was the most eloquent propagandist of this theme. Shatrov's plays described the liberal (Bukharinian) and bureaucratic (Stalinist) alternatives following the October Revolution (Shatrov 1988; Afanasiev 1987a, 1988a; Burtin 1998a, 1998b; Butenko 1988; V. Kiselev 1988).[9]

A few liberals (especially Igor Kliamkin) opposed this view, contending that under the existing historical conditions both Stalin and his policies in the city and the countryside were unavoidable in one form or another. Those who shared this view often pointed to the lack of democratic traditions in Russia as a decisive factor that predetermined Stalinism (I. Kliamkin 1987; Gal'tseva 1988; Ovrutsky 1988).

Ironically, with the gradual demolition of Marxist ideology in the last years of perestroika, liberal intellectuals started to move from the alternative approach to a sort of liberal determinism. They began to see the Western model as the only alternative. In fact, the first book published by the leading liberal intellectuals bore the title *There is no alternative* (Afanasiev 1988b; see also Borodkin, Kosals, and Ryvkina 1989; Kazakov 1989a, 1989b; Protashchik 1990). Francis Fukuyama's book *The end of history and the last man* (1992), which predicted the universal victory of liberal capitalism, was very popular among Russian liberals.[10]

After the demise of the USSR, however, an interest in alternativism returned to the intellectual landscape in Russia. The victory of liberal capitalism had not materialized. Instead, a blend of feudalism and untamed "nomenklatura capitalism" reigned. Against these developments, Russian intellectuals began again discussing the various alternatives that faced Russia in 1989–1991 and in the next years. A growing number of authors have analyzed these historical events and looked for moments when an alternative political decision could have changed the course of history (Sobchak 1991, pp. 73–74).

Two Types of Reforms: Alternatives to the Status Quo

The alternative approach allows us to look for processes in society that could have led it toward recovery from its various chronic diseases—or toward a different outcome. In the Soviet case, the chronic diseases of society (first of all, its economic problems) could have been treated with two types of reforms: the first was to improve the system by expanding freedoms and decentralization (liberal reforms); and the second was to enhance the government's control over individuals, institutions, and the provinces (authoritarian reforms). Reforms can be undertaken at various stages of chronic disease, and for different purposes: as a response to a real event (reactive reforms), or as preventive measures to protect society (preventive reforms). All the reforms of the nineteenth and twentieth centuries in pre-revolutionary Russia were of the reactive character. The reforms of Alexander II in the 1860s were a direct result of the Russian defeat in the Crimean War. The reforms of Nicholas II, in particular his October manifesto in 1905, were proclaimed under the influence of Russia's defeat in the Russo-Japanese war and the ensuing revolution (Lincoln 1990; Sakharov 1996; Eklof, Bushnell, and Zakharova 1994).

Contrary to the pre-revolutionary reforms, most reforms in the Soviet Union were of a preventive nature.[11] Lenin's NEP, however, was an exception. In this case the Soviet leader insisted on the reforms because of the danger of mass riots (i.e., the Kronshtadt sailors' rebellion in 1921, and the Antonov peasants' riot in 1920–1921). Stalin's military reforms during the war with Germany also were a reaction to the defeats of the Red Army in the first years of the war. Apart from these measures, most innovations advanced by Stalin, Khrushchev, and Gorbachev were of a preventive character. The major stimulus for the Soviet leaders' preventive reforms was their concern for military and economic development ("productive forces," in the official terminology). Stalin's economic reforms in the 1930s, Khrushchev's reforms in the late 1950s, Andropov's initial steps in 1982–1983, and Gorbachev's economic reforms in the mid-1980s were motivated by the desire to expand the economy and accelerate technological progress for military purposes.

Another stimulus for reforms was the fear of mass discontent, though resistance to Soviet power was quite weak. During Stalin's times, at the height of mass repressions, this stimulus had no effect, though it played a role both before and after Stalin's rule. The post-Stalin leadership effectively maintained the apparatus of repressions and mass ideological indoctrination. These leaders were much less concerned about riots than Lenin had been in the early 1920s, yet they remained distrustful of the masses and closely monitored the mood of the people. They were worried that even a modest riot such as the revolt in Novocherkassk in 1962 could produce a chain reaction. The leadership's concern for mass discontent increased during transitional periods when power moved from one leader to the next. For this reason, the new leaders after 1953 began their rule with a number of actions designed to improve the standard of living for the masses. The leadership's fear of the masses reached its apex at the end of Stalin's rule in 1953–1954 and gradually decreased to almost nothing on the eve of perestroika.

In 1953, Khrushchev and his supporters were sure that without mass repressions the people would revolt against the regime unless the standard of living was improved. Brezhnev was afraid of the reaction of the masses during the ousting of Khrushchev in 1964. Moreover, the Kremlin was thinking seriously that the rebellion of Polish workers against Wladyslaw Gomulka's regime in 1970 could spill over into Russia. This prompted Brezhnev to revise the five-year plan radically in order to increase the production of consumer goods. Andropov, as soon as he became leader in 1983, started a campaign for "social justice," with the purpose of mitigating social differentiation in the country and averting anti-state activity. Gorbachev and his colleagues in the Politburo in 1985–1986 also knew that political stability in the country should not be taken for granted. However, their worries about military and technological retardation were much stronger.

Reforms: Always a Big Risk

As described above, the Soviet leaders (with the exception of Stalin in the postwar period) were all aware of the chronic diseases in society.[12] Indeed, their general picture of society was quite accurate (Khanin 1998, pp. 94–95). With the defects of society in mind, they also understood the dangers of reforms and the risks of introducing serious changes in the country. If Brezhnev was the shyest of the leaders in this respect, Gorbachev was the boldest, despite his cautious political behavior in the first years of his tenure (Gorbachev 1995, 1998).

History lends ambivalent lessons to those who want to preserve the fundamentals of a given society. Some lessons suggest that reforms helped the society survive and expand; others suggest the opposite. Looking back, historians rarely agree about the ultimate effect of reforms on the longevity of a social organism. Russia has a long history of reforms with different outcomes. The reforms of Alexander II, in the opinion of many historians, prolonged the life of the Russian empire. Although the reforms were inconsistent and eventually aborted, they probably increased the Russian empire's economic and technological growth. Moreover, the military (and other) reforms benefited the Russian empire by allowing the emperor to increase the empire's size and continue its expansion in Central Asia and the Far East. At the same time, however, the reforms clearly unleashed forces in Petersburg and in the provinces (the terrorist Populist movement and the Polish rebellion of 1861–1963 were serious omens) that were intent on destroying the tsarist regime. For this reason, it is difficult to evaluate the counterreforms later initiated by Alexander II and continued by his son Alexander III. Before 1917, Russian liberal historians denounced the inconsistencies of Alexander II's initial reforms and eventual counterreforms (official Soviet historians, of course, followed the same line). By contrast, conservative historians before 1917 praised the conservative course of the tsars as having been necessary to stave off anarchy and chaos. This view was later echoed by dissident Soviet historians with Russophile tendencies.[13] The struggle between reformers and conservatives was the central development in the empires of the nineteenth and twentieth centuries (i.e., the Austro-Hungarian, Ottoman, and Chinese empires).[14]

The Totalitarian Leader: The Motor or Evader of Reforms

The outcome of the struggle between reformers in totalitarian and authoritarian societies was usually determined by the leader of the country in the context of "objective" constraints, including the psychology of elites and the masses, not to mention economic and foreign circumstances. With respect to decision making, we should think of the leader's command as a highway with numerous exits. The driver can choose among different paths of development. The driver's options for changing routes is determined by objective constraints—that is, the number of exits on the given stretch of interstate. While the circumstances and conditions of the road may change, only the driver can choose which exit to take. When one driver or ruler is replaced by another, the conditions of the road often change dramatically and the choices of the potential driver or the new leader usually increase. In other words, the death or ousting of a dictator creates a situation with multitudinous potential outcomes. A larger pool of opportunities has a greater impact on the new ruler's choices.

Soviet history is ideal for implementing alternative methodology. It demonstrates the importance of a change in leadership in times of soft structure. These sensitive junctures occurred in 1924–1926, 1953, 1964, 1982–1984, and 1985. The change of leadership always modified the direction of Soviet development. Throughout Soviet history, the vector of transformation might have changed if the leaders had been different men. It is wrong to assume that all potential leaders after Lenin would have pursued the same policy as Stalin. Such an assumption is an evident tautological error. Indeed, the historical process of Stalin's goals first required "a Stalin." Trotsky or Bukharin were not committed to the same exact society as Stalin. Had they taken power, things may have been different. We can suppose, along with Stephen Cohen, that Bukharin might have led Soviet society in a different direction, and perhaps even toward its downfall as early as the 1930s (Cohen 1973).

In 1985–1991, the "structure" was especially "soft," and several hidden alternatives emerged. It is impossible to exclude the possibility that Grigorii Romanov could have taken the position of general secretary rather than Gorbachev. He had some chances of ascending to this position.[15] World history would have taken a different course, and the Soviet Union might have survived past December 1991. Alexander Yakovlev (an active participant in the election of the new leader after Chernenko's death in March 1985) talked about the importance of Gorbachev's favorable relationship with Andrei Gromyko, the minister of foreign affairs and the most respected member of the Politburo. Gorbachev had promised Gromyko the position of chairman of the presidium of the Supreme Soviet. This was a crucial factor in Gorbachev's rise to power (Yakovlev 2000).

With Gorbachev at the helm, the Soviet empire traversed many crossroads and landmark decisions where historical developments could have changed drastically. After 1989, the structure was still mutable. If Yeltsin had not been summoned by Gorbachev from Sverdlovsk in 1987, history would have been very different. There were no other potential leaders with personalities as rebellious as Yeltsin's.[16] Several Russian authors have conjectured about the circumstances that might have impeded Yeltsin's advent to Moscow and his promotion as head of the department of the Central Committee.[17]

Several other individuals and groups also had a great impact on the course of Soviet history: the Minister of Defense Dmitrii Yazov and the KGB Chairman Vladimir Kriuchkov decided not to assail the White House in August 1991; Yeltsin, Leonid Kravchuk, and Stanislav Shushkevich dismantled the Soviet Union in December 1991; the miners in July 1989 started a strike to support the democrats; the population of Ukraine voted for independence on December 1, 1991. Some of these social actors emerged on the political scene by the force of accident, but all of them could have altered the course of history had they acted differently.

The individual characteristics of politicians, and particularly the leader of the country, are often strong determinants of future developments. The character of the leader narrows the number of alternatives in the decision-making process. Even secondary factors (for instance, the health of the leader[18]) can influence the alternatives, especially when the leader maintains the concentrated power of a dictator. At the same time, the notion of "errors" made by historical actors is almost meaningless. It is nonsensical to speak about the mistakes of Lenin, Stalin, Gorbachev, Napoleon, Hitler, or Roosevelt. Each historical actor behaves according to his own personality, which determines his perception of and reaction to historical events. In this case, we focus not so much on the deterministic influence of the social environment (though it is very important), but on the "deterministic" feature of the personality of the historical actor.

The Soviet Leaders As Reformers

Soviet history can be seen as an arena of activity of three types of leaders: conservatives who were against reforms, liberal reformers, and authoritarian reformers. The Soviet Union knew only two periods of relative stability: the last stage of Stalin's rule, in the postwar period (1945–1953), and Brezhnev's period (1964–1982). During these times the leaders did not change the major institutions of society.

A need for reforms emerged in Soviet society immediately after the end of the civil war. Lenin, seemingly against the will of the majority of the party, decided to implement the NEP. The fledgling Soviet society, with its institutions still flexible and with the mentality of the masses still linked to the past, combined with the existence of private property and the market, was much more responsive to Lenin's liberal economic reforms than was society six decades later.

Were Lenin's reforms useful for the Soviet system? When the reforms began, many people, Communists as well as their opponents, believed that the *embourgeoisement* of society would lead to the regime's degeneration and demise. However, soon after the NEP was implemented, contemporaries accepted the idea that Lenin saved the regime (future historians would agree). The reforms allowed him to gain the time necessary for strengthening the system. Starting in the late 1920s, Soviet society was again forced to experience new changes, this time authoritarian (Stalinist) reforms. Stalin liquidated private business in the country, recentralized the state's control over industry, collectivized agriculture, and expanded mass terror to its limits. He introduced fear of the political police as an essential element of Soviet life. Stalin's reforms were extremely successful in that they were carried out with virtually no resistance from any segment of the population. Even the peasants, who fell victim to starvation en masse, did not revolt. When Stalin, in his speech at the 8th Congress of Soviets, asserted that society in 1936 was radically different from what it had been ten years earlier, he was absolutely correct (Stalin 1952b, p. 546).

The impact of Stalin's reforms on the Soviet regime is a controversial subject, even among some pro-Communist historians. The so-called neo-Leninists were critical of Stalin's innovations; they considered them damaging to the regime as it was shaped by Lenin. However, without Stalin, the Soviet Union as a social system may not have survived through the late 1920s and 1930s. As the experience of other socialist countries independent of Moscow showed, the strengthening of totalitarianism in all spheres of social life was essential for the survival of the given social system and its leadership. Good examples of this are evident in Cuba, Vietnam, and China. Watching Stalin's transformation of the country, particularly collectivization, many Western observers predicted that Stalin's actions were counterproductive to his own system and would destroy it. The opposite occurred and Stalin's accomplishments became clear as the Soviet system demonstrated its viability over the next several decades.

At one point, Stalin even seemed to be moving toward a mild liberalization of society. During the war, many of Stalin's actions (i.e., the selection of cadres for the army and military industry based on merit, the softening of attitudes toward the Orthodox church, the abandonment of Communist propaganda in media, the improvement of relations with Western countries, and the rise of outspokenness in the country) had clear liberal overtones. The liberal tendencies in wartime policy were perceived by many Russians as harbingers of radical changes after the grandiose victory of the Soviet Union over Germany. Millions of Soviet soldiers and officers had the opportunity to see Eastern and Western Europe, which only enhanced the yearning (particularly among intellectuals) for liberal reforms (Arkadievich 1990). In reaction to these dreams, Stalin responded with a harsh, chauvinistic ideological offensive and a new expansion of terror. Mass terror as an institution continued to function, and arrests remained a fixture of Soviet life.

When Stalin died, the country was as calm as it was in 1985, on the eve of Gorbachev's radical reforms. In 1953, there were no threats to the regime, just as there were no threats 32 years later. Following Stalin's death the political elite, which had experienced no serious public ideological disputes since the late 1920s, almost immediately split into factions of hard-liners and liberals. Although these factions agreed to eliminate mass terror as the main instrument of control, they disagreed about the proper political course for the future.

The hard-liners evaluated the country as fairly healthy, while most liberals disagreed, citing technological and military retardation, the low standard of living and the frighteningly poor state of agriculture. Georgii Malenkov, Lavrentii Beria, and Nikita Khrushchev believed that the likelihood of mass riots would intensify if the existing standard of living continued and the state did not resort to mass terror. At the same time, neither they nor their opponents in the Politburo wanted to continue the Stalinist repressions. This mentality emerged primarily because they understood that all but one—the victor of the internal party struggle—would fall under the wheels of the new political juggernaut (N. Khrushchev 1970).

Malenkov evidently wanted to humanize Soviet domestic policy. He advocated the increased production of consumer goods at the expense of capital goods. He was also in favor of increasing the role of peasants' private plots in agricultural production. In addition, he wanted to weaken party interference in the economy, and he was the first Soviet leader to proclaim that nuclear war could destroy not only capitalism but all of civilization (Paschal 1958; see Malenkov 1992).

Much less is known about Beria's plans. However, well-known facts showed that Beria was quite interested in changing the Soviet system. Beria initiated the revelation of the notorious "doctors' plot" as well as Stalin's murder of Solomon Mikhoels, a famous Jewish actor. He practically eliminated the cult of Stalin. He reduced the number of people imprisoned for petty crimes, and prohibited the use of torture in prisons. He demanded a shift in the country from the party to the government (Knight 1993, pp. 183–194; Bezirgani 1999; Mikhailov 1991a, 1991b; Starkov 1993, p. 6; Shpakov 1990; Naumov and Korotkov 1994).[19] His most daring attempts at change fell in the realm of national policy. Beria evidently intended to soften Russification in the national republics by replacing Russians with indigenous people in the leading party and state positions there.

Nikita Khrushchev was probably the most significant reformer in Soviet history before 1985. His major innovations included the elimination of mass terror in domestic life, the release of hundreds of thousands of people from the Gulag, and the weakening of the role of fear in society. He made radical changes in Soviet science and culture, and partially opened the country to the West. The International Youth Festival in Moscow in 1957 was an extraordinary innovation because it permitted ordinary Muscovites to have contact with foreigners. Soviet scholars were now allowed to travel abroad, while Soviet publishing houses started to translate novels written by a number of foreign authors. The journal *Inostrannaia Literatura* ("Foreign Literature") appeared in 1955, reacquainting Russians with the Western literature and culture they had lost touch with in the early 1930s.

Khrushchev created regional centers of economic management (*sovnarkhozy*). This was a significant step toward the decentralization of the economy. Another innovation was the split of party regional committees into two types (industrial and agricultural). Of course, behind these innovations lay Khrushchev's willingness to undermine, to some degree, the position of the conservative nomenklatura, forcing them to leave Moscow and go to work in the province in new economic agencies. He also restrained the power of regional party secretaries by assigning two bosses with equal power to each region. Probably even more important were Khrushchev's innovations in the material life of the masses. He introduced cash salaries for collective farmers (before, they received only agricultural products as their income) and a relatively decent pension for state employees. Both measures were genuinely revolutionary.

Initially, Khrushchev's approach was successful. Technological progress seemed to accelerate, agricultural production rose dramatically, and intellectual activity increased. In the late 1950s, the United States saw the Soviet Union as a tremendously dangerous enemy that had pulled ahead in several important areas. The uproar over the Soviet Sputnik program reflected this feeling (see Wolfe 1979).

Khrushchev's reforms were strongly supported by party liberals and most intellectuals, who sincerely espoused liberal Leninism and refused to recognize the problems of the Soviet Union as chronic (Karpinsky 1972; Kopelev 1978). They were certain that with a modicum of liberalization, more rational and fewer ideological approaches to solving problems, and a better selection of cadres, they could radically improve life in the country and surpass the West economically (Crankshaw 1966). However, the liberal intellectuals, like Khrushchev, overestimated the flexibility of the system. This lack of flexibility was better understood by the conservative members of the political elite, who believed that continuing the liberal reforms would prove catastrophic for the Soviet system (indeed, the developments of 1989–1991 confirm their beliefs). In 1964, the conservatives succeeded in regaining the party throne.

The new regime under Leonid Brezhnev initiated counterreforms, proclaiming the restoration of stability as its first priority. With the exception of mass terror, the Stalinist model was substantially reinstated (R. Medvedev 1990a, p. 3; Latsis 1993). The new regime also attempted a number of economic reforms. In 1965, the so-called Kosygin reform was instituted, to increase the autonomy of enterprises and increase the role of economic regulators of the economy (profit and prices, among others). Brezhnev, however, effectively blocked this reform because its implementation supposed a significant reduction of party interference in the management of the economy, particularly in the so-called branch departments of the Central Committee, which supervised single sectors of the economy.

By the end of the 1960s the leadership seemingly had abandoned the idea of reforms; this term was even deleted from the political vocabulary.[20] The structural reforms for improving the economy were replaced by a plan to computerize economic management. This plan failed to boost economic performance. The last known case of economists attempting to persuade the leadership to introduce modest innovations took place in 1979, spearheaded by Vladimir Kirillin (chairman of the state committee of science and technology). The committee's report was a relatively sound analysis of the deteriorating economy, but it was discarded by top officials with demagogic arguments. The Brezhnev model went unchallenged in both the center and the provinces, and remained in place until 1982, when Brezhnev died.

Yurii Andropov came to power in November 1982, after Brezhnev's death, with a determination to change many things in the country (Zh. Medvedev 1983; Semanov 1995; Doder 1986; I. Andropov 1994). In his initial statement as general secretary, he said, "We do not know the society we live in" (Y. Andropov 1983a). Several authors suggested that he wanted to rid the bureaucracy and party apparatus of corruption (in this, he was quite successful[21]), improve discipline, increase the role of intellectuals in social life, and even take some steps toward democratization—for instance, to include several candidates on election ballots (Arbatov 1992; Chebrikov 1998; Volkogonov 1995).

Conclusion

There were many junctures in Soviet history when the course of events could have changed radically in spite of the existing structural constraints. Under different circumstances, the USSR could have collapsed decades before or decades after 1991. From Lenin to Gorbachev, the Soviet leaders as the single motors of change in society tried to improve the system. For this purpose, they used either authoritarian reforms, which made the system more rigid and repressive, or liberal reforms, which introduced some elements of freedom at various levels of society. Until 1987, no reform in Soviet history had been aimed at changing the fundamentals of the system, including the core of the official ideology, the leading roles of the party and the KGB, the militarization of society, and the drive toward geopolitical expansion. In an attempt to improve the efficiency of the economy, between 1985 and 1987, Gorbachev initiated reforms that shook the pillars of Soviet society. These reforms were radically different from Deng Xiaoping's in China, where major changes were made in the national economy but the ideological and political institutions of the totalitarian state remained untouched.

13

Reforming the System, Destroying Its Fundamentals

Since 1991, analysts advanced several theories about the origin of perestroika and the collapse of the Soviet Union. In many cases, their theories did not distinguish between the causes of these two very different events. The collapse of the Soviet Union should be regarded as a two-step process. First, the Kremlin decided to launch perestroika and the restructuring of society. The second step brought the negative consequences apropos of the economy, the state, its official ideology, the level of order in the country, and the mood of the masses, all of which resulted from the leadership's initial decision to restructure.

Chronic and Lethal Diseases

Before 1985, Soviet society faced many problems, but most of these difficulties did not jeopardize the existence of the system. Likening the problems of the country to diseases in a living body, it is important to distinguish between chronic and terminal illnesses. Terminal diseases incapacitate the system and lead the society toward immediate collapse. The developments born of perestroika destroyed the regime in a short period of time. Perestroika afflicted the official ideology, the legitimacy of the system and its socialist framework. In the place of these structures emerged free political organizations, and full access to the West. The diseases that brought about this transformation were indeed terminal.

On the other side of the spectrum, chronic diseases should be understood as long-lasting processes that may be very negative and dangerous for the survival of an empire, but only in the long term.[1] The Byzantine empire, for example, as well as the Habsburg and Ottoman empires, lived for centuries while battling several chronic diseases. Chronic diseases should be considered independently of the process of disintegration when analyzing an empire's deterioration and death. No one social organism is "perfect" from any point of view. Each society, including liberal capitalist societies, possesses some organic features that weaken its performance throughout its life span.

Another distinction should be made between "subjective" and "objective" chronic diseases. "Subjective diseases" reflect the people's mind about the health of the social organism in which they live. The people's attitudes toward the disease develop in two ways. First, people sometimes become aware of the "objective diseases" and the decline of their country. Second, they may apply new standards to their assessment of the state of affairs in the social organism; that is, people gain access to data about the situation in another country, which had been closed to them. Quite often contemporaries exaggerate the scope of diseases, or reevaluate a so-called illness as serious when they regarded it as innocuous in the past. The Roman, Arab, and Habsburg empires weathered multiple periods of decline; these empires stand as reminders that every gloomy season does not necessarily bring about the fall of an empire.[2] This was certainly true for the Soviet empire. In the 1960s and 1970s, many observers exaggerated the scope of the country's problems.

Beginning in the late 1950s, various "objective" as well as "subjective" chronic diseases afflicted Soviet society. As in other empires, intellectuals were among the first to discuss the society's various chronic diseases and bring the issues into the open (see Dudintsev 1957; Yashin 1954). By the late 1960s, a feeling of malaise had swept the country. Andrei D. Sakharov's manifesto diagnosing the country's condition was received by an intelligentsia eager to discuss this topic (Sakharov 1970). By the 1970s, analyses of Soviet society's various diseases and how to cure them became the major topic of samizdat.[3]

The following discussion will include an analysis of the various theories for the origin of perestroika, including the one I consider most plausible.

The Public Discontent Theory

The most popular theory suggests that the economic deterioration in the second half of the 1970s and early 1980s, and the economy's inability to satisfy the basic needs of the population, were the main causes of perestroika.[4] Without question, the economic system suffered from many essential flaws, particularly in production, and was much less efficient than the Western market economy. In the last decade of the USSR, the rate of economic growth steadily declined, the quality of goods deteriorated, and technological progress slowed.

According to the "public discontent theory," with its focus on economic failures of the system, perestroika was essential for calming a dissatisfied and potentially hostile population. While many Russians were in fact dissatisfied with several aspects of life (namely, food shortages, long queuing lines, and poor quality of goods), several surveys conducted in the 1970s and 1980s showed that most people actually gave a positive assessment of their material life (as discussed in previous chapters). As previously noted, in the early 1980s, there was no sign of any serious protest movement in the country. The public discontent theory was particularly amusing in light of the profound passiveness in the dismal post-Soviet period.[5] There is no evidence to support the claim that the people's discontent in the 1970s and 1980s pushed the leaders to reform society. Moreover, most Russians were against the economic reforms when they began. Despite the fast decline of the state, the ideology, and the prestige of socialism, in 1989–1991 (the peak of anti-socialist euphoria) only a minority of Russians demanded radical changes in the Soviet economic order. No more than one third of Russians voted for serious changes in the economic system. In a VTsIOM survey in 1989, only 18 percent answered the question "What should be done for the improvement of life?" by saying "Encourage private entrepreneurship under state control"; 50 percent demanded "firm order."[6]

All of the data show that in 1985, in spite of their hatred of the local bureaucracy, most Russians (save for a small part of the intelligentsia) still accepted a variety of official dogmas, including the preeminence of Soviet and Russian patriotism, the supremacy of socialism, social equality, the obligation of the state to guarantee the satisfaction of the people's basic needs, and Soviet social and moral superiority over the West. In addition, they saw the Communist Party as the leading force in society.[7] The Russians fully supported the Kremlin's foreign policy, including the invasions of Hungary, Czechoslovakia, and even Afghanistan.

The Demoralization Theory

There were two popular theories for the origin of perestroika that focused on the Soviet ruling class. The first theory pointed to the demoralization of apparatchiks, their corrupt activities and the ensuing degradation of the entire political system ("the weakening of the centralizing role of the Communist Party and the disintegration of the state," to use the words of the prominent

Soviet economist Yurii Yaremenko).[8] In spite of the increased level of education among apparatchiks in the 1970s and 1980s, according to this theory, there were major negative changes in the morals and motivation of most apparatchiks.[9] Though minimal in Stalin's times, corruption in the bureaucracy reached a high point in the last years of Brezhnev's regime.[10] The public regarded corruption as a universal phenomenon and could not imagine that in post-Communist Russia the problem would only grow worse.[11]

Corruption indeed demoralized the whole society and probably had a tremendous impact on the future life of the country.[12] It led to the "imitation of real work," which became a norm in society, along with the gradual decline in the professional work ethic in many areas. This led to decreasing quality and productivity among the cadres in science, industry, culture, and other areas, and accelerated the process of moral degradation throughout the 1970s and early 1980s. Alcoholism and criminal activity reached new heights, as did moral cynicism and lying (Segal 1990; G. Kiselev 1992).

At the same time, this evidently negative trend in the last period of Soviet history should not be exaggerated. In 1985, the political system was essentially intact. There were still numerous apparatchiks who fulfilled their state and party duties and worked as competent and energetic managers.[13] The level of corruption in the party apparatus, particularly in the Slavic and Baltic republics, was quite low (if measured by the standards of post-Soviet Russia) and kept under control by the leadership. In the early 1980s, the Kremlin undertook a series of actions against corrupt officials (this was a serious anti-corruption campaign, compared to the post-Soviet Kremlin's refusal to prosecute bureaucrats who were evidently steeped in the most heinous activities). Corruption flourished in the 1970s and 1980s in Central Asia and to some degree in the Caucasian republics.[14] As problematic as corruption was, however, it did not threaten the Soviet state.

During this period, the KGB and the high military command were almost totally free from corruption. The leadership maintained its absolute monopoly on all strategic decisions in the country. Even during perestroika, until 1989–1991, there were no other groups in society that could impose their will on the general secretary. The party continued to control the everyday activities of all institutions at the central and local levels. The Central Committee, via its various departments, was still the main supervisor of all ministries. Local party committees oversaw the work of all factories, offices, and colleges. Several highly trained and talented managers successfully implemented major national projects during Khrushchev's rule and even under Brezhnev. Discipline in the party and state apparatus endured the rise of cynicism and careerism. The army and the KGB were well-organized, effective structures.

The Privatization Plot Theory

The second theory that focused on the Soviet ruling class assumed that the apparatchiks were greedy thieves who dreamed about living the Western style of life. Accordingly, the nomenklatura, who longed for private property rights, advanced perestroika, knowing that it would lead to great riches in the wake of the Soviet collapse.[15]

The main problem with this theory is that prior to perestroika the apparatchiks were not even close to advocating the idea of privatization. In fact, even during perestroika and up until 1989–1990, there were no Moscow officials who thought seriously about privatizing state property. Most party apparatchiks were deeply hostile toward privatization. Gorbachev avoided the use of this term until the last year of his rule.[16] In 1985, the political elite was pursuing its egotistical interests more than its predecessor had in Stalin's time, yet it remained concerned with the strength of the state, the party, and Russia's geopolitical interests.

The Dissident Theory

The claim that the dissident movement pushed the Kremlin toward reforms is inaccurate for one very simple reason: At the time, the dissident movement barely existed (see M. Berg 1995; Bukovsky 1995). By the early 1980s, Andropov's KGB had more or less destroyed the movement. Almost all of its leading figures were in the West, in prison, or in exile. Even the samizdat movement was on the verge of collapse.[17] The number of people who were sentenced for anti-Soviet views in the early 1980s, on the eve of perestroika, was insignificant (35 in 1980, 39 in 1981, 26 in 1982, 44 in 1983, and 25 in 1984; see Luneev 1997, p. 186). Compared to the numbers arrested in Argentina, Chile and Brazil during the dictatorships in these countries, the level of anti-Soviet activity looks quite low. Moreover, in order to demonstrate their own importance to the state, the KGB had to look for the slightest manifestations of hostility toward the regime so as to substantiate their vigilance.

By 1985, the liberal intellectuals were so demoralized that they were in no hurry to support a new, evidently reformist, leader.[18] Gorbachev had to drag them into public activity. It was not until 1987–1988, when the system was moving toward self-destruction, that dissidents became serious actors in political life.

Gorbachev's Democratic Design

A few authors (in 2000, Alexander Tsipko distinguished himself as one of them[19]) advanced the theory that perestroika had been a preconceived plan to destroy the Soviet totalitarian state and install a democratic society. There is not a single empirical fact that supports this theory. All the available data suggest, as will be shown later, that Gorbachev entered the political stage as a moderate totalitarian leader, and spent almost the first two years of perestroika trying to implement neo-Stalinist reforms. After 1995, Gorbachev and Yakovlev, contradicting their previous statements, tried to romanticize their motives for perestroika as if they had been moved only by the ideas of democracy and freedom.[20]

The Imperial Theory

A number of authors advanced what we might call the imperial theory, maintaining that the reforms were necessary in order to overcome the alienation of non-Russians and prevent the disintegration of the empire as a result of separatist forces. As the Moscow political scientist Algis Prazauskas wrote: "The Soviet Union will be doomed to collapse first of all because it forcibly united completely alien people with different cultural traditions, with different orientations toward the centers of different civilizations and with different political cultures" (Prazauskas 1993). Another author believed that Gorbachev started his reforms to benefit the new generation of Soviet bureaucrats, the "republic elites" (Shevtsova 1997, p. 71).

Throughout history, separatist movements in the province have posed a major threat to empires. For instance, the Austro-Hungarian and Ottoman empires suffered from internal conflicts of different types, including those between the center and the province. The Soviet Union, however, does not belong in this category of empires. In 1985, when Gorbachev initiated his reforms, the provinces were quiet. The ethnic peace persisted until 1987 when war between Armenians and Azerbaijanis in Nagorno-Karabakh triggered an era of interethnic conflict on the territory of the Soviet Union. Nationalism was deeply rooted in the mind of intellectuals in all republics, particularly in the Baltic republics, Ukraine, and Georgia. Many nationalists, particularly Lithuanian and Ukrainian intellectuals, were sent to the Gulag. However, even in the Baltic republics, the nationalist movements did not represent a serious threat, and most Baltic citizens loyally served the Soviet empire. The true decline of the empire began in 1987–1989, when the regime started to lose its totalitarian character.

No Dangers from Abroad

All empires in history have faced external enemies (openly hostile or potentially so) which used every opportunity to exploit their internal weaknesses, curtail their role in the international arena, and swallow parts of their territory. Military defeats brought about reforms in many empires in the past. Perestroika, however, was not provoked by the threat of foreign invasion. During the last four decades of the Soviet empire, there was no real threat to its sovereignty, nor were there any experts who predicted its fall as a result of military defeats. The only exception was Andrei Amalrik, who prophesied the collapse of the Soviet Union during a war with China (see Amalrik 1970; see also Andrei D. Sakharov 1970; Solzhenitsyn 1975; Bukovsky 1979). There was also no threat from the West. In fact, Western politicians wanted to preserve the Soviet empire.[21] U.S. President George Bush's famous speech in Kiev in May of 1991 was an eloquent example of the West's support for the Soviet empire. Among other things, Bush asked the Ukrainians to cooperate with Moscow.[22] Even in 1991, when Russia was at its weakest, the country's major antagonists (the United States, its Western allies, and China) never planned an attack on the USSR or plotted to take over its territory. Its potential adversaries were concerned only with coexisting peacefully with the USSR, a superpower that could destroy the entire world. Its nuclear shield eliminated the possibility of foreign invasion. What could the world have done in the face of a zealot regime in Moscow, even if its nuclear arms were relatively obsolete compared to Western technology? In the late 1980s, only one or two years before its demise, everyone was confident that the USSR would persist for many years.[23]

The CIA Theory

Among the most ludicrous theories for explaining perestroika and the country's collapse were those advanced by the Communists and nationalists in the mid-1990s. The advocates of "the CIA theory" suggested that perestroika and subsequent events were designed by the American secret services in order to secure world dominance and turn Russia into a raw-material-supplying appendage to the Western world (see N. Yakovlev 1996; Zinoviev 1992, 1994).

Most advocates of this theory participated in the coup in August 1991.[24] Among them were the leaders of the nationalist and Communist opposition to Yeltsin's regime.[25] Other advocates of this theory included various writers in *Den'* (renamed *Zavtra* in 1993), *Pravda*, and *Sovetskaia Rossiia* in 1991–1999,[26] and some who belonged to the liberal camp in 1991–1995 but who began to play the nationalist card in politics in 1996.[27] Among the most well-known theorists of the Western conspiracy theory was Alexander Zinoviev.[28] The conspiracy theorists suggested that the master plan for the destruction of the Soviet Union started in the West no later than the 1970s. With great attention to detail, these people depicted the Western program to crush the Soviet Union.[29]

Military Parity as the Motivation of Reforms

If perestroika was not initiated owing to the lack of order, the faltering economy, the discontent of the masses, ethnic conflicts, separatist movements, conspiracies, or military defeats, what then led to the emergence of these reforms?

The real cause of perestroika stemmed from the leadership's ambition to preserve the military parity between the USSR and the West, which had been attained in the mid-1970s. By the early 1980s it became evident that the growing technological gap placed this parity in serious jeopardy. The chief of the General Staff, Marshal Nikolai Ogarkov, expressed his concern about this gap in open publications starting in the late 1970s. In his articles, Marshal Ogarkov demanded a radical revamping of the Soviet economy in order to meet the needs of the military (see Ogarkov 1981, 1982, 1985). President Ronald Reagan's Strategic Defense Initiative (SDI, or "Star Wars"), though not the first signal, was seen by many Soviet generals as a major indicator of the military imbalance between the USSR and the West. Whatever its actual feasibility, the Kremlin perceived the SDI as a direct threat to the geopolitical status of the USSR.[30] While military experts in Moscow may have doubted the viability of creating an impervious shield against all incoming nuclear missiles, the Kremlin believed that Reagan's SDI, regardless of its success or failure, would mobilize and integrate the technological resources of all major Western countries.[31] In effect, the SDI would act as a springboard for Western technological advancements in all military areas. Yurii Andropov, as the master of the Kremlin in 1982–1983, was the first Soviet leader to identify the SDI and related projects as a direct threat to the USSR's military parity with the West. In a special declaration, Andropov characterized Reagan's SDI as a program "aimed at the disarmament of the Soviet Union"; he vowed never to allow the United States to gain military superiority (see Y. Andropov 1983a, p. 250; see also Dobrynin 1995, p. 528; Boldin 1995, pp. 97–107; Vadim Medvedev 1994, pp. 26–41). Following a trip to the United States, Victor Afanasiev, editor in chief of *Pravda*, wrote, "Star Wars was a way for the USA to gain complete and enduring military and technological superiority over the Soviet Union" (*Pravda*, February 12, 1986). It should be understood that *Pravda's* editor could not stray from the views of his masters in the Kremlin. Gorbachev himself said practically the same thing, though in a less direct way, in his first speech as the new leader: "The achievement of military-strategic parity with the aggressive NATO was a great historical accomplishment of the fraternal socialist countries. It was necessary to maintain this parity by all means, because it held down the aggressive appetites of imperialists" (Gorbachev 1987a, p. 167).

How would the Soviet Union match the great leap forward in Western technology? In the time of Stalin, when the postwar nuclear arms and technology race began, the leadership completely ignored the basic needs of the people and mobilized the country's material and labor resources in order to keep pace with the United States. Forty years later, Stalin's harsh totalitarian regime was gone, and still the Soviet leaders were faced with the same daunting question, but now with a much weaker state machine at their disposal. By the early 1980s, the Soviet leaders were forced to make a very difficult decision. They must either relinquish the USSR's status as a superpower—one of the greatest achievements in Russian history—or adopt the social and political measures necessary to accelerate technological progress and prevent American military superiority. Mikhail Gorbachev was chosen by the party leadership to initiate the latter choice.

Numerous Russian authors and intellectuals have supported the view that "perestroika began with the Soviet defeat in the arms race . . . after 'Star Wars' was initiated, and not with the 'reforms' of Gorbachev and Yakovlev" (Zolotusky 1998). This opinion was shared by another author, who claimed that "the attempt to modernize the military-industrial complex" under threat from the SDI marked "the beginning of perestroika" (Novikov 1995). But Gorbachev and other ideologues of perestroika never publicly acknowledged that the SDI was the impetus behind Soviet reforms. "The first impulse for the reforms," Gorbachev stated to Margaret Thatcher in 1990, "was the lack of freedom." Countering the general secretary's rhetoric, Thatcher responded forthrightly, "There was one vital factor in the ending of the cold war: Ronald Reagan's decision to go ahead with the Strategic Defense Initiative."[32] The concerns surrounding the SDI explained the abrupt change in Soviet policy toward the missile crisis in Europe, and Gromyko's offer of negotiations in 1983 during his unexpected visit with Reagan (who was despised by the Soviet political establishment).

Technological retardation and slow economic growth (and not the standard of living, economi- structural reforms, and democratization) were the main topics of Gorbachev's major speeches until June 1987. He focused on these topics in his speech at the April meeting of the Central Committee, only a few days after his new appointment (Gorbachev 1986, pp. 152–173). In his report to the 27th Party Congress, Gorbachev acknowledged the ineffectiveness of Soviet science during the Brezhnev era (Gorbachev 1986). All the high officials agreed with Gorbachev and his complaints about the technological and scientific retardation of the Soviet Union (*Pravda*, February 27, 1986, p. 5).[33] Gorbachev's first program was suitably called "Acceleration." The program aimed at accelerating economic growth and technological progress mostly through radical advances in the machine-building industry and through decentralization of economic management (Gorbachev 1985; *Kommunist*, Vol. 14, 1985, pp. 3–40; Aslund 1989; Gustafson and Mann 1986, pp. 1–2; Hough 1987, pp. 21–43; Nove 1989). Had the Soviet leadership abandoned its goal of military parity with the West and focused only on protecting the status quo, the empire could have persisted for many years with its inefficient yet "normally" functioning economy.

A Call for Reforms: Neo-Stalinist or Liberal?

While the necessity of reforms was obvious, in the late 1970s it was unclear which type of reformer would win the battle with the conservatives: the neo-Stalinists or the liberals (V. Shlapentokh 1988a). Neo-Stalinists regarded administrative measures and radical improvements in discipline (for bureaucrats and the masses alike) as the cure for the country's ills. The liberals saw liberalization and partial democratization as the most efficient means by which to avert the USSR's transformation into a Third World country.

Gorbachev, as a relatively young party apparatchik and Andropov's pet, was seemingly elected as the leader who would pursue Andropov's neo-Stalinist agenda. His election was endorsed by those who saw him as an advocate of the neo-Stalinist policy, even if he was also known for being relatively liberal. Gorbachev was supported by the Politburo, the KGB, and most of the regional secretaries (the more conservative part of the party apparatus[34]), and was given a mandate to modernize the Soviet economy and maintain military parity with the West.[35] In the first two years of his tenure, Gorbachev looked in many respects like an "enlightened Stalinist" (see Hosking 1991, pp. 139–141). He was far from the Prague Spring ideology of 1968, although he did communicate with Zdenek Mlynar (the movement's future leader) during their university years.

Gorbachev's Personality: A Crucial Factor in Russian History

During his presidency, Gorbachev's personality had a peculiar mix of traits. He was a believer in the advantages of socialism over capitalism (much more so than most members of the Central Committee). He hated violence and the spilling of blood, yet he was unable to predict the elementary consequences of his deeds.[36] At the same time, he was absorbed with the preservation of his power and seemed comfortable in the role of totalitarian leader. He was often cruel to those around him; and he replaced the entire Politburo and most of the Central Committee with new members.[37]

While maintaining an awareness of the intrigues of the party apparatus, Gorbachev and his colleagues had seemingly little understanding of the social consequences of expanding the freedom of human behavior.[38] He sincerely believed in some of the dogmas of Soviet propaganda, particularly the deeply rooted friendship between different ethnic groups. Perhaps, as contended by one Moscow author in 1995, if Gorbachev had not been a believer in the potential of socialism and had been more aware of the risks of reforms, "we would still be living in the realm of mummies" (Pumpiansky 1995, p. 25). Vadim Bakatin, a close aide to Gorbachev, said in 1995, "Perestroika did not set the social, economic, and political goals for the transformation of our society and state . . . rather, it aimed at cosmetically revamping our socialism" (Bakatin 1995). Certainly, if Gorbachev had understood the complexity of ethnic relations, he might have been better prepared for his mission to transform the Soviet Union.[39] He might have begun transforming the USSR into a true federation much earlier, thus postponing the disintegration of the Soviet empire.

Gorbachev's misconceptions about the economy could only lead to economic crisis. Gorbachev came to power with a strong belief that given the "correct" policy, the powerful state machine could solve any economic problem. His faith in the socialist state and its leaders was combined with a conviction that no actor on the political or economic scene (including political figures, political parties, and the masses) could successfully challenge the will of the Kremlin. Like many of his countrymen, Gorbachev believed that only the political theater was important, that there was only one script writer, and that only one actor ever took the stage.

Gorbachev and his colleagues in Moscow had a superficial understanding of Western society (probably similar to their Western counterparts' knowledge of the Soviet Union). This misunderstanding of the West greatly contributed to the tribulations of the Soviet Union and post-Soviet Russia.[40] If Gorbachev's reforms had been based on a more comprehensive comparison and evaluation of Western economics and society—its strengths, weaknesses, and applicability to the USSR—perhaps he would have modified the liberal reforms with a greater concern for the authority of the state.

At the same time, Gorbachev was a totalitarian leader who was personally against the use of mass repressions. When it became evident that the reforms were not successful and that this failure presented a direct threat to his power, Gorbachev hesitated; but in the end, he refused to use violence to bolster his power and return to the old totalitarian order. The use of such violence would likely have prolonged his tenure for many years (Zh. Medvedev 1987; Doder 1990; McCauley 1998a).

The Single Motor of Initial Change: Gorbachev

After being elected general secretary, Gorbachev gained monopolistic access to the prerogatives of power.[41] His opponents were able to obstruct the implementation of his policy, but they could not initiate new policies. With his enormous power and his determination to change the country, Gorbachev was (until 1989) the motor of all changes in the USSR.[42]

From the moment Gorbachev came to power, he craved the intelligentsia's support for his innovations. While the intellectuals remained passive and shy, mistrusting the Kremlin and fearful of a trap, Gorbachev quickly initiated contacts with prominent intellectuals in both camps (liberals and Russophiles), such as Yevgenii Yevtushenko, Valentin Rasputin, and others.[43] In 1986, having strengthened his political position, Gorbachev was able to release Andrei Sakharov from exile and make several other conciliatory gestures toward the intellectuals.

The liberal intellectuals' influence on Gorbachev, however, should not be exaggerated.[44] Though he was the most highly educated Soviet leader since Stalin, he was completely unfamiliar with the major Russian liberal works of the 1960s. According to his memoirs and other sources, it was not until later in his life, after he became general secretary, that he digested the ideas of the 1960s (i.e., the role of public opinion, the independent mass media, and the concept of a decentralized economy).[45] To Khrushchev's famous "Thaw" (which occurred when Gorbachev was a student at Moscow University) Gorbachev devoted only a half page in his memoirs (Gorbachev 1996; see also Boldin 1995, p. 132). More serious was the influence of his travels abroad (Italy, France, Belgium, West Germany). His future liberal views were also influenced by Alexander Yakovlev, who metamorphosed from orthodox party hack to fiery democrat (Gorbachev 1996, pp. 99–103, 148–150, 159–162). According to the presumptions of his close aide Anatolii Cherniaev, Gorbachev was not familiar with Western scholarly or political analyses until he became the master of the Kremlin.[46] Gorbachev's most important and most specific ideas (i.e., privatization of the Soviet economy and pluralism in political activity) were for the most part absent from samizdat materials of the 1960s and 1970s and probably were not discussed at private meetings as having practical relevance for the country. It can be supposed that both of these ideas, privatization and political pluralism, came to the Kremlin directly from the West, which Gorbachev visited on a few occasions, without Soviet intellectuals as intermediaries (V. Shlapentokh 1990).

First Steps As Andropov's Heir

Gorbachev's first economic initiatives (some decentralization of management; the introduction of some elements of market regulation, with the dominant role being preserved for the planning system; the improvement of worker discipline and morale; and the war against inefficient bureaucracy) were neo-Stalinist in character and strongly resembled ideas expressed by Andropov and his aides in the early 1980s. In 1984, a large-scale economic experiment aimed at giving limited autonomy to enterprises began. This action was smoothly incorporated into Gorbachev's economic reform plan for 1985–1986 and 1987 (Prostiakov 1998b, pp. 100–105; Yun 1998, 108–116). During the 27th Party Congress, however, Gorbachev and other leaders continued to praise central planning as "a great triumph and a fundamental advantage of socialism" (see Ryzhkov 1986; see also Gorbachev 1987a; 1987b, p. 213).

Even Gorbachev's new policy of involving the intelligentsia (particularly creative intellectuals such as scholars, writers, and filmmakers) was in consonance with Andropov's legacy.[47] Gorbachev saw the intelligentsia as a crucial ally for the implementation of his liberal neo-Stalinist reforms.[48]

In 1985–1986, Gorbachev followed Andropov's lead, concentrating on administrative actions designed to force the Soviet people to work harder. He launched (or at least supported) a harsh anti-alcoholism campaign and a campaign against the debauchery of party apparatchiks (see White 1996; Treml 1991, pp. 119–136, 1987, pp. 151–162). He lauded the "socialist collective" as a force able to make all its members work efficiently. He also started a campaign to eliminate all "nonlabor income" (May 1986)—a campaign which was extremely painful for the Soviet people.[49]

With special vehemence, Gorbachev followed Andropov's precepts about the necessity of cleaning up the party bureaucracy, a campaign which started in May 1986.[50] These and other measures introduced by Gorbachev (including the extension of a measure of autonomy to enterprises) also played a part in the agendas of all Soviet leaders since Stalin.[51] Gorbachev created "work teams" which were supposedly self-managed in order to stimulate worker productivity. In November 1985, he reorganized (as had his predecessors) the bureaucratic management of agriculture; and in January 1987 he initiated state quality control in industry and called for the election of managers by workers (Gorbachev 1987a, p. 163). A decree setting up a multi-shift work schedule in industry and another for the regular election of managers (February 1987) were the last of the neo-Stalinist economic reforms.

In the first two years of his rule, Gorbachev filled his speeches and articles with Soviet postulates of neo-Stalinist character. He ordered a celebration on September 1985 to mark the 50th anniversary of the Stakhanov movement, one of the major symbols of Stalin's times. Inviting the veterans of the movement to the Kremlin, he referred to them as a good example for the people and talked about workers as "masters of their enterprises." He praised socialist emulation as a crucial instrument for technological and economic progress.

Gorbachev also attacked the notion that material incentives were important for increasing productivity. He declared, "For the vanguard worker, the moral stimulus is not less but more important than the ruble." This speech could have been made by Andropov or any of his followers. Gorbachev's statements about democracy in 1985–1986 also had typical Soviet qualities. Gorbachev, like his predecessors, continued to speak about the "further development of Soviet democracy," and "the seasoned principles of democratic centralism" (Gorbachev 1987b, pp. 8, 13, 235–240).

The Radical Jump Toward Liberalism in 1987

By the beginning of 1987, it was evident that the authoritarian reforms in the economy had failed and in fact had made the situation even worse.[52] Several innovations (among them the election of managers and the development of Agroprom, a bureaucratic system for the control of agriculture and related industries) adopted in the first two years were later dropped. In the second stage of perestroika, Gorbachev moved from neo-Stalinist actions toward real liberalism and even democratization. It was evident to him and his close aides that it was much easier to implement radical change in politics (domestic and international) than in the economy. What is more, they believed that the essential modification of the Soviet political system would make progress in the economy possible.[53] Under these circumstances, by the middle of 1987 Gorbachev left Andropov's track and started to look like a "liberal Communist" and an advocate of "socialism with a human face" (see Gorbachev 1987a, pp. 422–431; V. Shlapentokh 1985a, 1988b). Gorbachev's turn to political reforms rather than economic reforms was quite similar to Khrushchev's advancement of de-Stalinization in 1962 after his attempts at economic progress had failed. However, contrary to Khrushchev, who never threatened the fundamentals of the system, Gorbachev was so confident of his ability to control the political process that he undermined the pillars of Soviet society and took the risk of going against the official ideology and then against the party and state apparatus. Khrushchev was far less aggressive, yet was considered by the party apparatus—and not without grounds—a threat to the survival of the Soviet system. The most successful reformers of a totalitarian society, the Chinese leaders headed by Deng Xiaoping, were far more cautious in dealing with the ideology and the state and party machine.

The Assault On the Totalitarian State: Denigration of the Official Ideology

Having decided to abandon the neo-Stalinist reforms for liberalization and democratization, Gorbachev and his team delivered one blow after another to the totalitarian state and ultimately, Russian statehood. The Soviet state was destroyed by Gorbachev's changes in the official ideology, the planning system, and the major institutions of the state.

From mid-1987 on, the Kremlin combined liberalization of the economy with a frontal offensive against its own ideology. This contradictory initiative was extraordinary and had very few precedents in history. So enormous was the task of reversing seventy years of Soviet history that only the supreme leader could have been its initiator. Had this fundamental critique not originated with Gorbachev but with some other oppositional force, the liberal reforms would have had much less impact on society. Indeed, neither samizdat nor the foreign radio stations that became accessible to the people after 1953 had seriously undermined the people's belief in the major official values. The intellectuals were mobilized by Gorbachev and his closest colleague Alexander Yakovlev to tear down the official ideology, which was still supported by the majority of the population.[54]

In 1985–1988 (as during the Thaw in the late 1950s and the early 1960s) the public critique of Soviet society was based mostly on neo-Leninist ideology (i.e., Lenin was great; Stalin made some bad mistakes). After 1987, the Kremlin allowed an all-out attack on Stalin and the society he built. It was possible to say (with the complete endorsement of Gorbachev and Yakovlev) that the society which emerged under Stalin's guidance was completely removed from the true socialism Lenin dreamed of. Liberals and to some degree also Russian nationalists started condemning almost every event and development of Stalin's time. Collectivization was the first target of the acrimonious critique; it was declared the greatest crime in history (Mozhaev 1988; Burlatsky 1987; Chernichenko 1988; Tikhonov 1987). The post-collectivization Soviet order in the countryside was "feudalistic." Stalin's industrialization was criticized as another cruel enterprise (see Antonov 1987). Stalin's critics rejected the arguments of those who defended industrialization as a necessary condition for winning the war against Hitler and pointed out that Russia's economy would have developed rapidly even without Stalin (Aitmatov 1988). The critics of Soviet ideology in 1987 and also in 1988 continued, however, to defend socialism as Lenin saw it before his death, as the highest ideal for Russia and for other countries. They spoke of the Soviet society as "totalitarian" socialism, "barracks socialism," "feudal socialism," "state socialism," "bureaucratic socialism," "state bureaucratic socialism," the "Thermidorian" degeneration of the revolution (Afanasiev 1988b; Butenko 1988; Karpinsky 1987). Writers reacted with a special enthusiasm when called on by the Kremlin to attack the Stalin era.[55] They were joined by outstanding scholars, economists,[56] philosophers, and historians,[57] as well as by some journalists, as heralds of the new Kremlin policy.[58]

The next targets were the October Revolution and the civil war. With the full endorsement of the Kremlin, liberals depicted the October Revolution as "a great bloody scuffle, and a meaningless collapse" (Gefter 1988, p. 310; Tsipko 1989b, pp. 43–44). They denounced the dismantling of the Constitutional Assembly by the Bolsheviks in 1918 (Vasiliev 1990), and bluntly depicted the horror of the "red terror" during the civil war (Seliunin 1988, pp. 164–167). In these years, the Kremlin allowed the publication of works that had been banned for decades for their descriptions of the mass terror, the civil war, collectivization and the great purge.[59]

From 1985 to 1989, prominent liberals talked about their true opinions of Lenin only in private conversations; publicly, they continued to use Lenin as their ally for liberal reforms (see Popov 1990, pp. 203–204). But the number of those who believed that Stalin was genuinely Lenin's heir and that Lenin bore the original responsibility for the cruel society created by the October Revolution clearly had increased (see Shatrov 1988, p. 14).

In 1989–1990, a few liberals began to denounce the sacred image of Lenin. The bravest of them began the demythologization process by portraying Lenin as a leader who made mistakes, such as misunderstanding the role of the state after the revolution, overestimating the revolutionary potential of the working class in 1920, embracing the ideas of War Communism, and underestimating the market's role in the years immediately following the revolution. Other authors identified Lenin as the originator of an administrative and nondemocratic model of Soviet society, despite the fact that he did not abuse his power (*Moskovskie novosti*, November 15, 1987; Batkin 1988, p. 176; Gefter 1988, p. 311; I. Kliamkin 1989; Seliunin 1988; Tsipko 1989b; Popov 1987). In 1991, the Kremlin went a step further and permitted the critique of Marxism and of socialism.[60] Gorbachev's "new thinking" discarded Marxist socialism as a concept, emphasized "the values of all mankind" and adopted other such notions as "the present human civilization" as the goal for Soviet society (*Pravda*, July 14, 1989). The attacks on Marxism and socialism meant a final break from the official ideology. This break was supported not only by liberals but also by a number of Russian nationalists who hated the Soviet system.

In these years, the empire opened itself to foreigners and allowed citizens to travel to the West. Russians returned from Western countries and shared their experiences with their colleagues. The travel exchange of Soviet and Western intellectuals and officials increased dramatically as well as the number of joint Soviet and Western projects. The Soviet mass media began disseminating objective information about foreign countries, which significantly contributed to the destruction of official myths. The final opening of the empire to the West accelerated its disintegration—an event which had several precedents in the history of other empires.[61]

The Apologia for Liberal Capitalism in the Soviet Context

After defeating the old official ideology based on Marxist ideas, the liberals began propagating the ideology of liberal capitalism. Creating a new mythology, several Russian economists and political scientists in 1989–1991 praised liberal capitalism and promised economic miracles within one to two years after economic liberalization.[62] Belief in economic miracles increased as the economy deteriorated. In 1990, a leading enthusiast of liberal capitalism, Larisa Piasheva, promised that within three years the people would "feast and remember the past as a bad dream." She claimed: "Private farmers will assert themselves, new houses will be built, as well as new roads. During this time normal supplies of all goods . . . will be set up." In 1991, Piasheva said that these changes would take only one year to implement (Piasheva 1990d, 1991).[63]

The liberal media in 1990–1991 highlighted the advantages of liberal capitalism while condemning the Soviet ideology. The public was bombarded with repeated assertions that only privatization could save the country in a brief period of time. Many propagandists of liberal capitalism suggested that the destruction of socialism would make the people the owners of the means of production.[64] The newspapers and weeklies that opposed these views reached a much smaller audience than did their ideological adversaries (V. Shlapentokh 1990, pp. 265–266).

The Anti-State Ideology

The advocates of liberal capitalism in the Soviet Union became committed enemies of the state.[65] In their articles and papers, they ignored the positive economic aspects of the state and other public agencies. In fact, they completely denounced the state without making a distinction between the state in a socialist society and the state in other societies (see Seliunin 1990a, pp. 146–150). Their "ideal economy" was driven by the following principles: "Investments are shaped as the result of a multitude of private acts of investment; prices flow from the interaction of supply and demand; labor resources freely flow from unprofitable branches of the economy toward profitable branches; raw materials are sold on the free market; and wages are shaped through the process of negotiation" (Piasheva 1989, pp. 264–271; 1990a). When the ideologues of privatization mentioned the state, they talked about it only as a force inimical to the economy. The state was never discussed as an important agency for establishing and enforcing the rules of the new economic landscape (particularly in fighting monopolies and enforcing laws); it was never seen as a promoter of science, education, technological progress, and the arts, nor as an institution necessary for supporting some sectors of the economy that were important for satisfying public interests (i.e., transportation).[66] Some of these writers, in the frenzy of privatization, also denounced the state's welfare functions. Piasheva condemned the social function of the state and called for the privatization of all public services. This author explained that with economic progress, "social expenditures should dwindle," and people should pay for education as well as medicine and health care directly (Piasheva 1989, pp. 266–267, 271). The liberal ideologues never mentioned the state helped generate the economic miracles in South Korea and Taiwan. They looked down on the federal government of the United States, which they saw as too interventionist. Even among the most conservative American economists, it was difficult to find persons as "anti-institutionalist" as some of the liberal Russian ideologues of the late 1980s and early 1990s.

Blows to the Command Economy

As the new ideology evolved, Gorbachev declared a war against the Soviet totalitarian state on many fronts. First, in late 1986 he began reversing his neo-Stalinist ideas (i.e., the enhancement of discipline with the help of some material stimuli) and moved toward the market economy.[67] In November 1986, the Kremlin passed a new law that legalized individual entrepreneurship. The state also began curtailing its own monopoly on foreign trade. The next decrees included, "the enterprise law," which expanded the autonomy of production units (June 1987); a law allowing for the creation of independent cooperatives (June 1988); and agrarian reforms that initiated individual farming (March 1989). The radical break with the planning system took place in 1989 when the Kremlin publicly accepted the market economy as its near-term objective.

On July 1, 1990, the Soviet parliament adopted the law "On Property." The law explicitly introduced public property and "collective property"—which implicitly included private property. In 1991, the all-Union and national parliaments passed several laws that fostered privatization and private business activities. By 1990–1991 the role of the state as the main economic agent had decreased significantly. Commands from the government and Gosplan were systematically ignored. The central administration lost control of enterprises, even in the spheres where they intended to maintain control (see Freinkman 1998, pp. 187–190). At the same time, the state economic machine was not replaced by a new economic mechanism (i.e., market regulation). The economic system fell into chaos; money almost ceased to play a serious role, and barter became the dominant form of exchange. To a great extent, many elements of the Soviet economy in 1990–1991 were transferred to the post-Communist economy.

The destructive economic processes were caused by inadequate attention to political, social, and legal conditions. There was an absence of a highly elaborated strategy in the Kremlin for replacing the centralized economic controls (Mozhin 1998b). In 1986–1988, leading Soviet economists such as Vladimir Mozhin, the head of the economic department of the Central Committee, "were not yet ready to discuss a transition to the market mechanism based on private property, unregulated prices, and no centralized planning" (Mozhin 1998c, p. 137). Moreover, many "innovations" were in fact fraudulent from the start. Gorbachev's team had inherited the tendency of "show" modernization from the Soviet past.[68]

Several ideas advanced by Gorbachev and his economic aides (Abel Aganbegian, Leonid Abalkin, and Stanislav Shatalin) "came from the blue," and were often empirically unfounded and irresponsible. With these ideas the Kremlin sought to create an impression of dynamism.[69] Some ideas were based on a belief in miracles and were openly adventurous.[70]

The Assault on the Party: First Steps Toward Democracy

The totalitarian society could function only if the state and the party played the leading roles in society. The destruction of these two mechanisms was quite dangerous for the existing system because it could have engendered disastrous tendencies in the country. Despite the dangers, after 1986 the Kremlin first tolerated and then encouraged attacks against the party apparatus. Even in the first years of perestroika the attacks against the party bureaucracy and its numerous privileges were quite serious and could be treated as a part of the neo-Stalinist, Andropovian crusade of cleansing the party and refurbishing its reputation among the masses.

Yeltsin's famous speech at the 27th Party Congress against the perks given to apparatchiks, followed by his rejection of privileges as the party boss of Moscow, was an important episode in the attack on the bureaucratic machine.[71] In 1987–1988, the attacks against the nomenklatura were carried out by Yeltsin and the liberals with democratic slogans. Until 1991, the future Russian president, who would epitomize the "royal lifestyle" in the years to come, turned down many perks such as a special hospital, a house in the country, and access to special planes.[72] Gorbachev himself, though not as fervently as Yeltsin, also participated in destroying the authority of the central state apparatus and to a lesser extent also the regional party committees (Ryzhkov 1995, p. 352). Gorbachev, however, kept his distance from Yeltsin's egalitarian slogans and tried as much as possible to defend the elite's privileges.[73]

The next blow to the party's authority was delivered by the Kremlin's decision to permit so-called informal organizations; this was a radical step away from the Soviet policy in effect since the civil war, which did not tolerate even a semblance of independent organization. Thousands of informal organizations, which pursued various goals (i.e., human rights, democratic freedoms, national autonomy, protection of the environment), emerged in 1988 and swelled in 1989 (Pechenev 1990; Sedaitis and Butterfield 1991; Smith 1991; Tolz 1990; Babosov 1990). In 1989, workers entered the political arena for the first time. The nationwide miners' strike convinced a frightened yet fascinated country that a new political force had emerged.

In this year Gorbachev instituted new procedures for the election of the Soviet parliament, providing for the nomination of more than one candidate per seat in many cities and regions. The election, which occurred in March of 1989, had a revolutionary impact on the future of Russia and marked the beginning of the disintegration of the Soviet empire. Its results were totally unexpected by the Kremlin and party apparatchiks across the country. The election swept across the USSR like a tornado. The people seized this new opportunity to express their discontent with local party bosses whom they held responsible for the long lines for goods, the bad housing conditions, and the high level of corruption. In Leningrad, Kiev, and other republican and regional centers, 37 key party bosses were defeated in the election. In most cases, insult was added to injury because those who were defeated had run unopposed. As it turned out, they could not garner the required 50 percent of the vote to be elected. In fact, in 275 districts (almost one fifth of all districts), the candidates, most of whom had been nominated by the party apparatus, were rejected.[74]

After the October meeting of the Central Committee in 1987, Yeltsin, then the secretary of the Moscow party committee, confronted Gorbachev, a formidable enemy.[75] Gorbachev could have easily sent Yeltsin into political oblivion by transferring him either to the provinces or abroad as an ambassador to a small country. Instead, Gorbachev fired Yeltsin as Moscow party secretary, but allowed him to stay in Moscow as a member of the government. It was, however, clear that Gorbachev could have taken more serious measures; Yeltsin implicitly acknowledged his political vulnerability when he publicly asked forgiveness at the meeting of the Moscow party city committee. Almost one year later, Yeltsin was still claiming to be a good Leninist, and again asked the party for forgiveness, begging for the restoration of his "good name as a Communist" (see *XIX Vsesoiuznaia konferentsiia Kommunisticheskoi partii Sovetskogo soiuza, 28 Iiunia–1 Iiulia 1988, Stenograficheskii otchet*, 1988, Vol. 2, p. 36; see also Vadim Medvedev 1994, p. 77).

When Yeltsin entered the parliamentary election campaign in the winter of 1989, Gorbachev could have thwarted his participation and thereby prevented his decisive victory (he took 98 percent of the vote).[76] Gorbachev had many opportunities to stall Yeltsin's move to the peak of political power; he used some of these opportunities, but always irresolutely and inconsistently. If Gorbachev had behaved like a consistent leader of a totalitarian system, he would have prevented Yeltsin's election as chairman of the national Russian parliament in 1990.[77] However, after the election, he could not have removed Yeltsin from his position as chairman of the Russian parliament in February–March 1991 unless he was ready to spill blood. The miners' strikes in support of Yeltsin on March 1 promised a real civil war. Considering Gorbachev's indecisiveness and his sentiments against mass repressions, he could not take drastic measures against the miners.[78] Gorbachev had even less chance of undermining Yeltsin's election as the president of the Russian Federation in June 1991, although he did make an inconsistent and weak attempt to do so.[79] Nor could he prevent the election of the anti-Communist mayors in Moscow (Gavriil Popov) and Leningrad (Anatolii Sobchak).

Gorbachev could not stand up to Yeltsin's strong personality; this circumstance alone had a major influence on Russian history.[80] In any case, in 1990–1991 Yeltsin created a second center of power in the capital, which was contrary and damaging to the totalitarian system. The election in March 1989, and even more so the elections in the republics one year later, led to the emergence and strengthening of Yeltsin and several other independent political actors, which deprived Gorbachev of his monopoly on political decisions in the country. The emergence of "the interregional group" of parliamentary deputies meant the appearance of a political party that was able to challenge the Communist majority in the Soviet legislature.[81]

At the same time, the newly elected national parliaments became arenas of intensive political struggle, even if in most of them Communists still maintained control. In 1990, the ideas of political pluralism and the multiparty system became dominant in the country. Gorbachev yielded to the liberals and took the next step of concessions: the abolition of Article 6 of the Soviet Constitution (about the leading role of the party); this decision went into effect in March 1990.

In 1990, a considerable number of ordinary people joined the political activists in their fight against the Kremlin and the party. Official data indicate that between January 1 and February 23, 1990, 6.4 million people participated in political meetings across the country. Attendance at mass meetings peaked on February 24–25; and in March, despite the Kremlin's frenzied opposition, more than 1 million participated in meetings and demonstrations. In the end, the Kremlin could only watch, with anger and despair, the mass movements that *Pravda* characterized as "dangerous and destructive" and "destabilizing and explosive."

However, most of the population (even in Moscow) was passive. If Gorbachev had decided to stop the process of democratization, he would have been fully supported by the army and the repressive agencies, as developments during the coup in August 1991 showed clearly. The provinces were almost totally silent, and even in Moscow only a small minority, mostly the intelligentsia, took part in the defense of Yeltsin's headquarters and the White House. The situation in Leningrad was anomalous: There several hundred thousand people took part in a demonstration in support of democracy (Sobchak 1995, p. 35).

Denigration of the Empire's Major Institutions

Having lost control of the country in 1989, Gorbachev could not prevent the crusades launched by liberals against the fundamental institutions of the empire. In 1989–1990, the party remained the target of systematic denunciations. The prestige of this organization dropped during these years, and party committees were deprived of their power in many regions of the country.

In 1989, the army became the target of liberal attacks. The mass media discovered various flaws in the army such as hazing, the corruption and incompetence of generals, and the inefficiency of military organization. Russian liberals blamed the army for using military force against the nationalists in the republics (i.e., Tbilisi in April 1989, Baku in 1990, and Vilnius in January 1991). The prestige of the army and its commanders fell precipitously. The political split between officers intensified. These developments impacted the events of August 1991, when a demoralized Russian army could not be used to curb the emerging regime.

Cautiously, the liberals also began condemning the KGB, its past and present activities. The fear of the KGB, which had served as the foundation of the Soviet empire since its inception, dissipated in 1989–1990. Soviet people now spoke freely in public meetings. The old borders between public and private life had almost disappeared.

Conclusion

Most of the Soviet ruling elite understood the serious dangers of trying to radically reform the rigid Soviet system. At the same time, they were aware of the growing technological gap between the USSR and the United States. In order to preserve the geopolitical status of the Soviet Union, the leadership advanced reforms. In the beginning, the reforms were purely neo-Stalinist in nature. Shouldering responsibility for restoring military parity with the West and accelerating technological progress, Mikhail Gorbachev resorted first to liberal economic reforms, followed by reforms of the political system. These policies had a dramatic impact on the fundamentals of the Soviet system (i.e., the party, ideology, army, and the KGB). With its strong hierarchical, totalitarian order, the system was not prepared to defend itself against the attacks of its own supreme leader.

14

Consequences

Although controversy surrounds the causes of perestroika, very few people dispute the causes of the Soviet collapse in 1991. The main objective of perestroika was to strengthen the might of the state. What ensued as a result of Mikhail Gorbachev's initial reforms was a brutal irony. Within a few years, the fundamentals of the totalitarian society were demolished. Several different actors delivered the fatal blows to the USSR—actions that had nothing to do with the origins of perestroika. These political and economic actors included intellectuals, Russian and non-Russian nationalists, the nomenklatura, and individual politicians—chief among them, Yeltsin.

The Soviet system, a rigid hierarchical organism, turned out to be defenseless against the actions of its leader, who undermined its vital mechanisms. By definition, the system could not resist the directives of the general secretary. Watching this process of self-destruction, it was amazing to witness the system's inability to stop the gradual decline of its own ideology, the Communist party, the repressive apparatus, the command economy, and the imperial structure.

Ideological Collapse

The deliberate and rapid destruction of the dominant ideology along with seventy years of Soviet traditions greatly impacted the mentality of the political elite and the masses. The sudden changes undermined the entire country's belief in the nomenklatura, Soviet managers in industry and agriculture, and all levels of the leadership hierarchy, as well as the ideological and moral legitimization of their power. The changes destroyed people's confidence in the future, not to mention the very model of Soviet society. Among many ordinary people, the obliteration of official Soviet dogmas created a vacuum of social values and promoted asocial behavior directed against the state. In these years, the Russians were in complete ideological disarray, which persisted in the next decade after the fall of the Soviet Union. Polls conducted in 1990–1991 suggested that only a minority supported any cohesive social program, whether based on socialist or liberal capitalist myths. Most Soviets considered all these programs ineffective and all the options (socialism or capitalism, planned economies or market-regulated economies, public or private property, totalitarian or democratic order, the preservation of the empire or its disintegration) fatally flawed.[1]

The Destruction of Statehood

As the Soviet Union entered the period of disintegration, it could no longer maintain the institutional supports that were necessary for preventing the disarray in 1991. State discipline at all levels declined. Local bodies, enterprises, and state farms refused to obey Moscow's command, and ordinary Russians rejected the orders of their superiors. The ultimate cause of the state's disintegration was the collapse of the Communist Party (the core of Russian statehood). The prestige of the party plummeted. In two years it lost almost all of its legitimacy in the eyes of the absolute majority of the population; in 1990, no more than 10 percent of Russians believed in the constructive role of the party (Levada 1993). Without the support of the party and the army, the KGB could not play a serious role in the salvation of the regime and the empire. In 1989–1991, Gorbachev's prestige also declined significantly. The father of reforms steadily lost control of the country and proved, in the people's eyes, incapable of running society under the new rules of the game.

The Political Consequences

The political reforms, combined with the intentional demolition of the official ideology, brought the system to the brink of total collapse. The crumbling of the party and state apparatuses began gradually after the 19th Party Conference in June–July 1988, and accelerated following the election in March 1989. The next blow was delivered by the 1990 abolishment of Article 6 of the Constitution, which had guaranteed the party's leading role in society. Then came the mushrooming of informal organizations (Cherniaev 1993, p. 240). The widespread defections from the Communist Party, which began in 1989, burgeoned in 1990, leaving only a few party organizations intact. Perhaps the most telling indicator of the party's popularity crisis was the destruction of monuments to Lenin in many Soviet cities in 1990–1991, an unimaginable event at any other stage in Soviet history.

Boris Yeltsin played an instrumental role in the destruction of the Soviet system. The soft structure that emerged with the gradual decline of the central government allowed the individual qualities of politicians such as Yeltsin to greatly impact the historical process. If Yeltsin had not been such a daring person and if his hatred of Gorbachev had been less intense, developments in 1990 and 1991 might have been radically different. Moved by his determination to replace Gorbachev in the Kremlin, Yeltsin played the "Russian card"; this was seen as bold defiance of those who were proud of the Russian empire in both its pre-revolutionary and Soviet forms. Yeltsin's campaign for Russian sovereignty was the first lethal blow to the Soviet Union, followed by the Ukrainian referendum for independence on December 1, 1991 (Zdravomyslov 1994, p. 174; Tsipko 1990, p. 7; Dunlop 1993; Fitzpatrick 1994a, pp. 62–63, 170–172; Shlapentokh, Levita, and Loiberg 1998, pp. 79–127).

By announcing the crusade for Russian sovereignty, Yeltsin exploited Russian nationalism in an unexpected way. He used the Russian nationalists' complaints about the exploitation of the Russian people by the non-Russian republics for his own political purposes. Yeltsin's slogan "Sovereign Russia" also attracted democrats who saw the Kremlin as a major obstacle to reforms and were ready to use any means available to crush Gorbachev. In any case, Yeltsin's call to achieve the "independence of the Russian Federation" was the core of his political activity in 1990 and 1991.[2] He encouraged various industries to emancipate themselves from the center's yoke and "come under the jurisdiction of Russia." He declared that Russian laws were superior to all-Union laws, sealing the Russian empire's fate in a political move that caught even the liberals by surprise. Yeltsin tried to pit Moscow against not only the "big" Union republics, such as Ukraine and Uzbekistan, but also the "small" non-Russian republics inside the Russian Federation. Looking for additional allies in his fight against the Kremlin, Yeltsin encouraged each ethnic region, particularly Tatarstan and Bashkortostan, within the Russian republic "to take as much sovereignty as possible"—an offer he came to regret one year later (see *Sovetskaia Tataria*, August 8 and 12, 1990; *Sovetskaia Bashkiria*, August 14, 1990; and *Ural'skii rabochii*, August 16, 1990; see also Gulbinsky and Shakina 1994, p. 90).

In combating Yeltsin, Gorbachev actually contributed to the destruction of Soviet statehood. He did not object to the call for sovereignty of many autonomous republics in the Russian Federation, such as Tataria, Bashkiria, Kalmykia, Mari, Chuvashia, and even small national districts (see Baturin 1994, pp. 212–221; Veber et al. 1985, pp. 172–184).

Yeltsin's "Russia card" was extremely successful. The belief that Russia was being exploited by the non-Russian Union republics was accepted almost unanimously by the Russian people. Yelstin also used the growing economic difficulties in the country to his advantage. He promised to radically improve the standard of living as soon as he gained control. Yeltsin, for instance, espoused Yavlinsky's program "500 days," which was rejected in the fall of 1990 by Gorbachev as foolhardy. Gorbachev could not stop Yeltsin, who capitalized on his role as underdog and rose to immense popularity. This renown played a decisive role during the crucial days of August 1991, when the Soviet state was ultimately demolished after the failure of the coup.

The Expansion of Crime and Corruption

The weakening of the state, the party, and the official ideology, along with the legalization of private property and the lack of control over the process of privatization, led to an eruption of crime and corruption. The major elements of the criminal society emerged during perestroika. The drastic decline in the authority of the state, and the people's fear of the police and other official bodies, stimulated an expansion of criminal elements in Soviet behavior. Between 1985 and 1990 the number of registered crimes increased by 30 percent, while the relative number of crimes whose perpetrators were never identified increased drastically, from 18 percent in 1985 to 49 percent in 1988 and 63 percent in 1989 (Luneev 1997, p. 65).

The fear of crime in the streets had been relatively weak in the Soviet past, particularly in big cities. However, in 1989–1990, a crime wave swept the nation and became a main topic in the mass media (see *Izvestiia*, November 2 and 15, 1989; *Izvestiia*, October 18, 1994; *Sovetskaia kul'tura*, September 30 and October 21, 1989; *Sovetskaia kul'tura*, January 27, 1990). Muscovites who once had looked down on crime-ridden cities like New York and Washington, D.C. were now afraid to take a taxi from the international airport at Sheremetevo to downtown Moscow because they were afraid of being robbed or murdered.

In the late 1980s, there were about 35 million ex-convicts in the Soviet Union.[3] The existing climate in the country strongly encouraged these people to resume their criminal activity (*Pravda*, October 2, 1989; *Izvestiia*, November 22, 1989). People with criminal pasts streamed into the private business sector. The focus became short-term rather than long-term interests, and trade instead of production; instead of a new business ethic, businesspeople developed a disregard for laws and the interests of other parties (*Ekonomika i zhizn'* 48, 1990; Myslovsky 1991, pp. 10–18).

Even more significant than the explosion of criminal activity was the outburst of corruption in the bureaucracy. With the collapse of the official ideology and the state's authority, apparatchiks at all levels felt free to enrich themselves and their relatives and friends. This tendency emerged in spite of the anti-corruption drive that had been launched by Andropov and continued under Gorbachev. In the first years of perestroika, Gorbachev focused this campaign on Central Asia, where he replaced nearly 80 percent of Central Committee members between late 1985 and to early 1986. The "cotton affair" in Uzbekistan and the fight against corruption in Moscow (centered around Moscow Party Secretary Victor Grishin) represented the peak of this campaign. In the end, however, the anti-corruption drive proved incompatible with the weak state and party, and it gradually sputtered to a standstill (see Analytical Center of *Izvestiia* 1994; Gurov 1995, pp. 204–218). The appearance of private businesses, particularly cooperatives that could use their profits as they pleased, fueled the illegal collusion between directors of state enterprises and apparatchiks, and opened numberless avenues for getting fantastically rich.[4]

At the same time, bureaucrats and emerging private businesspeople began collaborating with criminal structures on a full scale. The traditions of the illegal economy of the past were instantly expanded and utilized by all the actors of this period. One of the most unexpected developments was the almost immediate corruption of the local authorities who had been elected on a relatively democratic basis in 1989 and 1990.

Another Criminal Consequence: Wild Privatization

Full-scale privatization began in 1989–1990. Contrary to the claims of its apologists, privatization evidently damaged the economy and led to a general moral decline. The apologists of privatization were sure that state property would fall into the hands of "effective owners," efficient managers and active investors. As it turned out, these so-called effective owners were often the very members of the nomenklatura (party apparatchiks and bureaucrats in various bodies) who had directed the economic transformation. In short, they used their connections and status to turn the state's property into their own.

Most types of "wild privatization" (also commonly called "party privatization," "state privatization," and "managerial privatization") were economically ineffective because the new private or semi-private organizations maintained a monopoly on the market. What is more, instead of expanding their firms, they began reducing production, selling off equipment, dumping products in the global market, and renting their premises to various other commercial organizations. The new owners neglected their entrepreneurial destiny and became money-hungry barons who disregarded the long-term interests of their enterprises (see *Komsomol'skaia pravda*, August 3, September 26, October 3 and 29, 1991; *Nezavisimaia gazeta*, October 19, 1991; see also V. Shlapentokh 1992, pp. 75–95). Wild privatization highjacked the economic transformation. The new magnates operated with very few real legislative or social limitations.

The Economic Consequences

The gradual decline of major institutions coincided with a steady economic decline.[5] The economy could not function without the party and state apparatuses (see Kuznetsov 1998, pp. 190–210). Meanwhile, the main motivation of perestroika identified by Gorbachev was economic development. The population accepted this thesis, which only led to increased dissatisfaction with the developments that followed. The intelligentsia was more or less the only group that evaluated the new regime in terms of political liberalization and glasnost. Most of the population assessed Gorbachev's regime on the basis of economic indicators such as the consumer market.[6]

The failure of Gorbachev's liberal economic reforms (and not the failure of the Soviet planning system as it functioned before 1987) undermined Soviet power and opened the gates for an anti-Communist revolution. The failure of Gorbachev's economic innovations robbed the spirit and confidence of the ruling elites and deprived the masses of their respect for the Kremlin. It is important to note that the ultimate failure of the system was not caused by the intrinsic tendencies of the economic reforms (privatization and marketization) but by the social context (that is, the state's lack of authority and full disrespect for law) which resulted from the Kremlin's failed policies in ideology and politics. Within the given social context, the directors of state enterprises became almost independent from the state as well as from the market, and freely enriched themselves at the state's expense.[7]

The decree that gave enterprises the right to set their own prices had a particularly nefarious impact on the Soviet economy. In effect, the decree increased profitability but did not necessarily help the economy. Inflation accelerated immensely and gradually swept consumer goods from legal commerce. At the same time, labor discipline declined, and the pilfering of production expanded even beyond previous levels.[8] The one good economic decision (the cut in military expenditures and the redistribution of investments in the heavy and military industry to consumer production) could not reverse the damage of the Kremlin's other decisions.

In 1989, the destructive processes brought on by Gorbachev's reforms culminated in an unprecedented decline in industrial and agricultural production. The production of 64 different goods, out of the 144 goods that were monitored by the Central Statistical Committee, dropped (*Ogonek* 12, 1990, p. 13). The fall in production was especially significant in the extractive industries (oil, coal, and iron ore) as well as in other sectors of the heavy industry (steel, pipes, tractors, cars, bikes), and the food industry (fish products, canned food; see *Pravda*, January 28, 1990).[9]

According to official data, only in 1990 did the national income decline in comparison with the previous year; this decline was quite significant, at 4 percent. For the first time since 1985, investments ceased to grow, while the construction of apartments declined by 8 percent (Goskomstat 1991a, p. 7).[10] Before perestroika, the Soviet Union was virtually free from foreign debts; by 1991 the debt reached $80 billion (Latsis 1995). The Soviet system was incapacitated to such a degree that it could not cope with the rich harvest of 1990.[11]

In 1989 and 1990, there was an acute shortage of several products (paper for newspapers, petrol, electricity, basic medicines, iron for the steel industry, and many others). Of special significance were the major shortages of many consumer goods, which can be ascribed to inflation.[12] The decrease in the production of potatoes, Russia's "second bread," was one of the first danger signals in the food supply. In 1986 the country produced 87 million tons of potatoes; in 1987, 76 million; and in 1988, 60 million. The decline of potato production greatly impacted the overall food shortage in the country, even in regions that had been the traditional producers of the product (*Pravda*, November 22, 1989). The production of bread decreased by 9 percent, making it more and more difficult to purchase bread in city markets around the country.[13] The bread crisis was accompanied by a huge deficit in the tobacco supply, which irritated millions of smokers and created a tense atmosphere in several cities, some with ensuing riots (for instance, Cheliabinsk).[14] The rationing of major consumer goods since 1988 (in this year the rationing of sugar was initiated in Leningrad, though the shortage had already impacted the whole country), and particularly in 1990, was widespread, as was the hoarding of goods.[15] Moscow authorities in 1990 made it impossible for nonresidents to buy food in the city, allowing only those people with Moscow identity cards access to stores (Popov 1994, pp. 96–97).

Along with the growing shortages of goods, many problems emerged in transportation. Railroad stations and sea ports were often bottlenecked. It sometimes took weeks and even months to unload freight trains and ships, despite the acute shortage of goods. This became one of the most serious national problems in 1989, demonstrating the inability of the state and party to cope with economic issues. The problems in the transportation and freight industries emerged in the national post office as well (see *Literaturnaia gazeta*, October 18 and November 1, 1989; *Moskovskie novosti*, November 19, 1989). Some regional authorities, in total disregard of national interests and longstanding divisions of labor, refused to obey the orders of the central authorities to send their products to other regions. In 1989, for example, agricultural regions ignored their obligations to the Urals, the industrial backbone of the USSR, thus triggering the country's first real food riots.

Perhaps the most dangerous consequence of the low work discipline was the increasing number of major technological disasters in the country. In June 1989, in Bashkiria, hundreds were killed in a gas line explosion. The next year, sloppy management at a petrochemical plant resulted in the poisoning of the water supply of Ufa, a city with one million residents.

Serious declines in the authority of the central government led to genuine feudalization, which clearly aggravated the country's increasingly chaotic conditions. Following the lead of the Baltic republics, several regions and cities (including Ukraine, Moscow, and Leningrad) introduced the use of coupons for goods, sold excess goods only to those able to prove permanent residency, and prohibited the sending of parcels of food to other regions.

The value of the ruble in 1988–1989 also changed drastically. A visitor in Moscow in 1989 found a different country, compared to 1988.[16] The devaluation of the ruble led to the emergence of barter exchanges in each village and city (*Pravitel'stvennyi vestnik* 6, 1990, p. 6).

The people's disappointment in the economy was extremely high. In July 1991, only 23 percent of the Soviet people said that they "would have supported the changes in 1985 if they had known what would happen to the country"; 52 percent said "definitely not" (*Moskovskie novosti*, September 22, 1991). In answering the question, "What are the main causes of the current difficulties?" only 24 percent of respondents in a December 1990 survey pointed to "the nature of socialism," while 45 percent chose the alternative which blamed "the leadership of perestroika" (*Obshchestvennoe mnenie v tsifrakh*, Vol. 8, Part 1, 1991, p. 9).

The failures of Gorbachev's economic reforms did not mean that reforming the command economy was impossible. The Chinese experience proved quite the opposite. It is possible that with some other strategy Gorbachev could have improved the economy without destroying the system.

The Consequences for the Empire: The Unexpected Outburst of Nationalism

The nationalists in the provinces, as well as Russian liberal intellectuals, reacted to the new course of liberalization and the weakening of the Soviet state with some hesitation. However, even in 1987 they realized that their time was coming and they would be able to change the ideological cassette in the mind of the masses in the national republics from internationalist to nationalist. The political elite and intellectuals in each ethnic region used the reforming central administration to establish a course toward autonomy and then independence. With the weak ideology, the rapidly degrading party apparatus, and the lack of will on the part of the Kremlin to fight the enemies of the empire, the USSR's decline accelerated.

The December 1986 revolt of Alma-Ata students, instigated by Kazakh nationalist intellectuals and politicians who were against the appointment of a Russian apparatchik as Kazakhstan's leader, was the first sign of major troubles for the empire. However, in the next year the revolt in Nagorno-Karabakh against Azerbaijan's authorities was even more portentous for the empire. For the first time in Soviet history an ethnic group, which had been provoked by Armenian politicians and intellectuals, decided to change its administrative status in the empire and challenge not only the power in Baku but also that in Moscow. In late 1987, they demanded that Nagorno-Karabakh, the Armenian enclave on the territory of Azerbaijan, be included in their republic.[17] If Gorbachev had crushed this revolt in the traditional Soviet style, the disintegration of the empire would have been frozen for years. In this case, even the Baltic intellectuals would not have made much progress in their nationalist movements. Gorbachev still had the opportunity to stop the process by arresting only a few nationalist leaders. He did not act, and the empire continued its decline.[18]

The first relatively free elections of 1989–1990 greatly empowered the nationalists in the provinces. The Baltic republics were the first to start the fight for independence. In 1989–1990, several other republics joined them in the struggle for the same goal. However, while the nationalist movements in the Baltic republics were actively supported by the masses with their deeply rooted hatred of the empire and the Russians, in other republics, particularly in Belorussia, Ukraine, and Central Asia, the movement was much weaker. Nationalism did not have the same hold over people's hearts here, and could have been easily controlled in 1989–1990 with commanding actions from Moscow.

The strongest blow to the empire was not delivered by the Baltic republics (their departure from the Soviet Union did not preordain the dissolution of the USSR) but by the core of the empire. Yeltsin mobilized the nationalist feelings of the Russians and pit them against their own empire, leading a political crusade against the USSR in 1990–1991.[19] In his struggle for "Russian sovereignty," Yeltsin supported the nationalist movements in all of the Soviet republics. For this reason, he was met in Vilnius, Kiev, and Alma-Ata as a hero and a friend of local nationalists. Moreover, Yeltsin asked voters to reject Gorbachev's referendum on March 17, 1991 that called on the population to declare its support for the Soviet Union as a federal state.

The decline of authority in the Kremlin also allowed the escalation of fierce animosities among non-Russians. The Armenians triggered a chain of inter-ethnic conflicts. Clashes between various ethnic groups began in other regions of the empire, including in Baku in January 1991. The bloody events in Baku were soon followed by nationalist riots in Dushanbe, the capital of Tadzhikistan. In 1990–1991, ethnic conflicts raged in Yakutia, Moldova, Uzbekistan, and Tuva. During this period, the center tried to save the empire by inciting ethnic minorities in the national republics against the dominant nationalist movements, but it was too late (see Guseinov and Dragunsky 1990).[20]

In contrast, Moscow quickly reconciled itself to the loss of its East European external provinces in late 1989. The "velvet revolutions" swept Eastern Europe because Gorbachev wanted to accommodate the West with his foreign policy.

The explosion of nationalism and the Kremlin's failure to unify the empire underscored once again that the empire was ultimately based on coercion and fear of the center. A similar resurgence in nationalism and separatism occurred in other empires (Roman, Arab, Habsburg, and Ottoman) as soon as the center began to weaken. The national Communist elite turned their back on the Soviet empire. They almost immediately changed colors and joined new nationalist leaders (this was equally true of Baltic, Armenian, and Georgian Communist apparatchiks), or tried to outrun them in their confrontations with the empire (for instance, Communist leaders in Ukraine, Azerbaijan, and Uzbekistan). The triumph of nationalism in the Soviet empire brought the defeat not only of Marxist internationalist ideology but also of the idea of assimilating small nations into the empire.

The hard-liners' coup of August 1991 was directly related to Gorbachev's signing of the new All-Union Treaty. A result of increasing popular support for national separatism, this treaty was an attempt to preserve the Union by means of a compromise giving the republics greater autonomy. The Soviet political elite staged its coup not so much against the liberal transformation as to prevent the signing of the treaty, which they believed would shatter the empire.[21]

The Consequence for the National Mood: Pessimism in the Empire

The disorganization of the economy; the significant drop in the standard of living; the destructive processes in science, education, culture, health services, and welfare; and the drive of non-Russian republics toward independence generated deep pessimism. Many of the best professionals and intellectuals left the country. Gloom pervaded the metropolis and the empire on the eve of collapse. The Russians were more dissatisfied with their lives than they had been in Soviet times. They tended to judge the current conditions as worse than they actually were. According to a 1989 survey conducted by the Moscow Center for Public Opinion Studies, 77 percent of the respondents said that they "look to the coming winter with alarm or fear," and only 3 percent expressed "confidence in what the next day will bring." The polls revealed that much of the population foresaw various disasters, including big technological catastrophes such as the tragedy at the Chernobyl nuclear power station in 1986 (up to 66 percent, according to the Moscow Center of Public Opinions Studies), the collapse of the economy (50 percent), the coup in the Kremlin (40 percent), and the civil war (about 33 percent). Only a tiny minority (no more than 10 percent) of the people held optimistic views of the future. No less than 50 percent of young people reported that they planned to leave the country, permanently or temporarily (Popov 1990, pp. 786–787; Levada 1990).

In spring 1989, the people flocked to the polls, vigorously supporting the liberals and spurning the apparatchiks and their socialist slogans. One year later, however, the Soviets were apathetic and indifferent; they supported neither socialist nor capitalist orientations. In Leningrad (the vanguard of the fight against Communism), only 20 percent of the voters made it to the polling booths. Moscow voters were equally passive. Ideologues of every major political party joined the ranks of the pessimists. Despite their passionate speeches and tough talk, Soviet politicians sounded compelling only when arguing against the programs of their opponents. When presenting their own platforms, they sounded muddled, haphazard, and far less persuasive.

The gloomy mood in society generated widespread beliefs in various miracles, such as nontraditional medicines (the medical charlatan Anatolii Kashpirovsky enchanted TV viewers in 1989–1990 with his "curing" sessions), mysticism, and exotic philosophical concepts, mostly with Oriental origins.[22] Traditional religions, in particular Orthodoxy and to some degree also Islam, made sweeping comebacks as the leading spiritual and even political forces in the empire. The popularity of religion grew rapidly in 1989–1991, and politicians tried to adjust to the new trend. The Orthodox church took back its confiscated property and became active in political gatherings and events and in the mass media and education. However, seven decades of atheistic education probably dampened the influence of religion; in any case, the people's infatuation with religion did not prevent the demoralization of the empire.[23]

The Soviet Nomenklatura Could Not Defend the System

The nature and composition of the ruling class developed over decades under the powerful and pervasive Soviet system. In the end, it was the very nature of the nomenklatura that rendered it unable to defend itself against the liberal reforms.

The ruling elite had a very specific relationship with their leader. The elite, particularly the Politburo, could influence the appointment of the leader; but as soon as the general secretary gained access to the buttons of power, he became the master of the country and the nomenklatura. In most cases, the nomenklatura was helpless apropos of the leader, who could murder members or fire them at any moment. The successful plot against Khrushchev was an exception in Soviet history.

By 1987–1988, the nomenklatura realized that Gorbachev's perestroika was leading the empire toward collapse. Hatred for Gorbachev brimmed in each party committee, first in private conversations, and later at public meetings. The nomenklatura tried (always shyly and timidly) to attack some liberal developments and sabotage them,[24] but they never assailed the leader. Nina Andreeva's notorious article in *Sovetskaia Rossiia* was an exception, and probably represented the peak of nomenklatura resistance before 1989.[25] Andreeva's article had been published while Gorbachev was away from Moscow. When he returned, he used his dictatorial authority to force the conservative majority in the Politburo, which had supported the article, to endorse a publication in *Pravda* that denounced both Nina Andreeva and her article (Remnick 1993b).

Later, in 1988–1991, party apparatchiks made several attempts to confront Gorbachev, but never directly; they did not openly demand his resignation (Boguslavsky 1991). In 1990 and in the first half of 1991, when the assaults against his policy intensified, Gorbachev's power remained unscathed. Only Boris Yeltsin dared (on February 19, 1991) to demand Gorbachev's resignation (Cherniaev 1993, p. 431). In April 1989, Gorbachev forced 100 members of the Central Committee to vote for their own expulsion from this body. In 1988–1990, Gorbachev forced the members of the Politburo, whose majority evidently hated him, to oust three conservative members of this body, a decision which was easily endorsed by the Central Committee (Vadim Medvedev 1994, pp. 79, 93, 119). The second Party Secretary Yegor Ligachev was deeply dissatisfied with Gorbachev's leadership. By the end of 1987, he often criticized Gorbachev's policy; but it was not until 1990, at the 28th Party Congress, that he dared to publicly confront the general secretary (Ligachev 1992, pp. 230–233).

The developments around the 19th party conference in mid-1988 were quite significant. The conservative majority in the party apparatus could not prevent the election of Gorbachev's supporters as delegates of the conference. During the conference, the members of this conservative majority criticized glasnost and a few other liberal developments, but did not touch even remotely Gorbachev himself. They also endorsed Gorbachev's plan for free elections to be held in 1989.[26] During several meetings of the Central Committee in 1988–1989, the nomenklatura attacked Gorbachev's policy, yet almost unanimously endorsed all of Gorbachev's proposals. Later, the growing disarray in the country and the increasing dissatisfaction of the population encouraged the conservative majority to be more bold in their critiques of the liberal reforms in 1990–1991.[27] However, when the conservatives faced two major forces (the Moscow liberal activists and the pro-liberal Russian miners, particularly in Kuzbass), they retreated. The fear of mass riots against the Kremlin was acute among conservatives, who were certainly impressed by the televised firing squad execution of Romanian President Nicolae Ceausescu and his wife in August 1989.[28]

The Constituent Congress of the Russian Communist Party convened in June 1990, a few days before the All-Union 28th Party Congress, at which hard-liners publicly attacked the general secretary. It looked as though the conservatives would be able to demote Gorbachev.[29] Encouraged by their success at the congress of the Russian Communist Party, they continued to attack Gorbachev personally at the All-Union 28th Party Congress. Only one third of the deputies pledged their support for Gorbachev's policies. Once again, however, they were not daring enough to remove him from office. The hostility of Muscovites and the miners' strikes dampened their motivation (Lopatin 1993, pp. 16–17). Gorbachev was elected general secretary by the conservative apparatchiks—a stinging blow to Yegor Ligachev, the champion of the conservatives.

It was not until the April 1991 meeting of the Central Committee that many speakers called for the general secretary's resignation. However, by the end of the meeting, when Gorbachev announced his decision to resign, the members of the Central Committee got scared and implored Gorbachev to stay in his position.[30] At the June 1991 meeting of the Supreme Soviet, Prime Minister Valentin Pavlov, Minister of Defense Dmitrii Yazov, and KGB chairman Vladimir Kriuchkov attacked Gorbachev's policy, but not him personally; several conservatives also demanded Gorbachev's resignation to no avail (Gorbachev 1996, pp. 394–396; Cherniaev 1993, pp. 441–443; Pavlov 1993, pp. 76–78). By July the nomenklatura was in great despair, seeing Gorbachev's invulnerability and the country's slide into chaos.[31]

In August 1991, the conservatives finally decided to take action. At this time, there was a high probability that almost all of the major figures in government, who were all opponents of Gorbachev, would lose their positions during the transformation of the Soviet Union into a real federal state, which meant the end of the Soviet empire.[32] But even then the ambition and courage of the putschists vacillated. Instead of fiercely denouncing Gorbachev, they proclaimed him physically ill and therefore unfit to lead the country.

The apparatchiks fully demonstrated their inability to defend the Soviet

Union. As previously explained, there are no grounds for describing the apparatchiks as prescient adventurists who had planned perestroika knowing it would lead to "nomenklatura capitalism." The Soviet nomenklatura descended into catastrophe as a helpless social animal; its real adjustment to post-Soviet Russia began only after the August Revolution. As a whole, the Soviet nomenklatura was one of the most craven dominant classes in history.[33]

Most Soviet apparatchiks, even in the early 1980s, were efficient managers in the execution of orders from above. But they had been trained since the beginning of their public activity to forsake their individual role as autonomous political actors. In a time of crisis, the system needed individuals who not only had organizational skills but also had the initiative to reverse negative trends. It was only natural for the system to demand that all apparatchiks abandon their self-respect and permanently grovel before their superiors. To keep their position, or get promoted, they had to be ready to commit any act commanded by their superiors. Apparatchiks took their positions voluntarily and accepted the state's control over their family life, their children and spouses, friends, their religious feelings, reading materials, and travel habits. They acquiesced to the ban on informal groups inside and outside the party apparatus. With such a toleration for any disgrace, they were unable to organize public debates or protest the policies of the Kremlin. The further the Bolshevik Revolution faded in history, the weaker and less daring they became.

The October 1964 coup which ousted Khrushchev succeeded as a palace coup. The coup was carried out by a dozen members of the Politburo, who secured the support of the KGB and the army although they knew well that the sympathies of the party apparatus would be on their side. The party barons of 1964 were very different from their counterparts of 1991. Khrushchev was removed by people who had been raised in, and had achieved leading political positions in, Stalin's era. They were extremely self-confident, believed wholeheartedly in the legitimacy of their cause, and were merciless to their enemies. By contrast, those who planned the 1991 coup were, like everyone else in the country, influenced by the recent processes in the Soviet Union. They had lost much of their faith in the legitimacy of the Soviet system (there was not a single comment about socialism in their emergency declaration). They spoke of preserving the empire, but mentioned no ideological underpinning (they avoided Russian chauvinist terminology). They also reluctantly accepted the rules of the democratic game (they even tried to present their coup as perfectly constitutional), and hesitated in the face of spilling too much blood.[34] In the late 1950s (the time of the first thaw), liberal intellectuals, and then the rest of the population, viewed the bureaucracy as the cause of, and the main impediment to, healing the Soviet Union's chronic diseases. The bureaucracy was consistently seen as egotistical and concerned only with maintaining its privileges (see Andreev 1989, pp. 546–560). After the events of August, however, the bureaucracy became a laughingstock, unable even to carry out a coup.[35]

Had the bureaucracy been less shortsighted, fickle, and craven, it could have chosen among a few alternative actions. It could have offered the empire a chance to modernize, to adopt the social democratic model of society, which had been advocated by party intellectuals like Shatalin and Burlatsky.[36] They also could have removed the reformer, or persuaded or forced him to change his policy and go back to Andropov's course. Had the nomenklatura successfully persuaded Gorbachev to halt the process of disintegration, history may have taken a different course. In fact, there were some chances for such a reversal in the fall of 1990 and in March 1991. It seemed that Gorbachev was contemplating a partial restoration of the Soviet order.[37] Gorbachev's behavior on the eve of the coup also looked quite peculiar to many observers; his acts suggested the possibility of radical policy changes in favor of the enemies of perestroika.[38] A major policy reversal could have prolonged the empire's existence. The empire could have relied on two very powerful forces: its nuclear shield and the KGB. In the end, the party apparatchiks failed to seize either alternative, and they left the historical stage, in disgrace.

Conclusion

Though the introduction of perestroika in the 1980s was in no way inevitable, once set in motion, the decisive consequences of perestroika could not be avoided. The anti-establishment forces unleashed by Mikhail Gorbachev attacked the Soviet ideology, party, KGB, and army. The preservation of the regime and empire as they functioned in 1989–1990 soon became a lost cause. Instead of a single totalitarian leader governing the country with the help of a few advisers, now many thousands of people were mapping the course for Russia's political development. Under these circumstances, only a murderous, conservative coup could have returned the Soviet Union to totalitarian rule.

Conclusion

The vision of the Soviet Union as described in this book helps us better understand the major events of the twentieth century. With all of its human horrors and economic flaws, the USSR was a normal society because it functioned and reproduced itself over a long period of time. The Soviet Union had tremendous impact on the world, whatever the assessment of this influence. Its rivalry with the West deeply affected Western economic and political developments. It is enough to mention Sputnik's effect on American science and education in the 1960s. The Soviet Union not only shaped its satellite regimes but greatly influenced the formation of independent Communist countries such as China, North Vietnam, North Korea, Albania, and Cuba. The USSR also inspired many changes in the political, social, and economic processes of several developing countries, the so-called Third World. The legacy of the USSR will continue to affect the world for many years in the twenty-first century.

The concept of the Soviet Union as a normal totalitarian society is important for the analysis of post-Communist Russia. Today, many Russian and Western experts regard Russia as abnormal. They predict radical changes or even disintegration of the country in the near term, basing these assumptions on empirically observed facts such as the low productivity of the Russian economy and the severe influx of crime and corruption in all spheres of society. In their opinion, Russia must build a law-abiding, liberal capitalist society or perish. In fact, Russia is not threatened by collapse. With its rampant crime and corruption, and regular violations of democratic rules, post-Communist Russia is very different from Western democracies. Nonetheless, Russia emerged as a new social organism that will continue to function as it does today, for many years (see V. Shlapentokh 1998d, pp. 9–34; 1996, pp. 393–411).

The interpretation of the USSR as a normal society is important not only to the study of post-Communist Russia but of many other countries as well. This definition is a powerful argument in favor of the civilizational approach in social science advanced by prominent scholars such as Arnold Toynbee and Samuel Huntington. The approach rejects the labeling of societies as good or bad based on religious, cultural, political, or economic criteria.

Moral judgements hovered over the ideological debates of the past century. Those who considered liberal capitalism the "peak of history," and those who ascribed this role to socialist society, struggled for ideological dominance during these years. At the end of the century, the ideologues of liberal capitalism seemingly emerged as victors. The collapse of the Soviet Union and the ensuing euphoria in the West strengthened the belief in the hierarchical approach and the liberal model as the "radiant future" for all mankind.

However, despite all the wishful thinking of Western experts like Francis Fukuyama, only a tiny minority of countries in the world meet the requirements of the liberal model: a competitive market, effective democracy, and the observation of law in society. Countries such as Turkey, Mexico, Pakistan, Belorussia, Uzbekistan, Burma, and Nigeria simply cannot pass these tests. However, these countries functioned and reproduced in the past and will continue to do so in the future, using the same political, economic, and social structures. In some ways, these countries are just as "normal" as was Soviet society. A sober social analysis demands that scholars avoid their personal values as much as possible in their examination of the specific structures of a given society that account for its ability to function and reproduce over a long period of time.

Notes

Notes to Introduction

1. The *Great Soviet encyclopedia* states: "Objectivism is a world view hostile to Marxism, because it preaches the rejection of the class analysis of social phenomena and is oriented toward cognition based on social and political neutrality" (Prokhorov 1973, p. 911).

2. Sober and objective analysis of Soviet society can be found in the work of liberal social scientist Anatolii Vishnevsky (see 1998) as well as in some articles by the conservative writer Sergei Kara-Murza (see 1997a).

3. Several ideas in this book were first developed in "A normal society? False and true explanations for the collapse of the USSR," *Times Literary Supplement* (V. Shlapentokh 2000). See also "The Soviet Union–a normal totalitarian society" (V. Shlapentokh 1999b, pp. 1–16).

Notes to Chapter 1: Theoretical Concepts

1. Discussing his research in Moscow after 1991 and the access he gained to the secret Central Party Archives, Richard Pipes wrote that this access "enabled me to modify and amplify certain parts of my narrative, but in not a single instance did it compel me to revise views which I had formed on the basis of printed sources and archives located in the West" (Pipes 1993a, p. XVIII).

2. *Society* is here defined as a "nation-state" formation (Frisby and Sayer 1986).

3. Richard Pipes, for instance, subscribes to the concept of "normalcy" in its ethical connotation. He has suggested that until Russians become aware of the changes they need to make in their own culture, it is unlikely that they will have a "normal society" (Pipes 1996, pp. 31–32).

4. The concept of normalcy developed in this book is quite close to the ideas of Emile Durkheim. In a special chapter called "On the normal and pathological" in his book *The rules of sociological methods*, he focused on the ability of a social organism to survive as the criterion of normality (Durkheim 1938, pp. 47–75). See also Katsenelinboigen 1990.

5. Some authors said that Soviet society began its consistent decline, if not immediately after the October Revolution, then after the civil war, or after Lenin's death in 1924. Other authors, mostly Stalinists, ascribed the beginning of the decline to other events, such as Stalin's death in 1953, the failure of Khrushchev's reforms in the early 1960s, "stagnation" in the middle of the 1970s, or the beginning of perestroika in the mid-1980s.

6. Pipes wrote that "tsarism—which survived not seven decades but seven centuries —presumably so popular, collapsed in a matter of days" (Pipes 1993a, p. 512).

7. Eduard Shevardnadze, who is considered by many one of the destroyers of the Soviet empire in 1991, noted two years later that if the end of the empire had come a decade later, "we would have encountered much greater cataclysms. In this case we would have had to deal with the explosion in Georgia, Ukraine, in Central Asia and we would have faced an armed insurrection" (see his interview in *Moskovskie novosti*, June 6, 1993).

8. This view of the system is very close to the explanations developed by Vasilii Grossman in *Life and fate* (1980) and by Alexander Zinoviev in *The yawning heights* (1979).

9. Walter Laqueur contended in 1992 that "although much maligned by Sovietologists in the 1970s and 1980s, totalitarianism has proved to be the most fruitful of the paradigms" (Laqueur 1994, p. 83). It is also remarkable that as soon as they acquired the freedom of speech, Soviet intellectuals immediately adopted the totalitarianists' evaluation of Soviet society. David Remnick aptly noted that *The origins of totalitarianism* (Arendt 1951) was one of the most popular books among Russian intellectuals during perestroika (Remnick 1994), many of whom also identified Pipes and Conquest as their intellectual heroes. Perhaps the historical victory of the totalitarianists over the revisionists was partially explained by the critical spirit of their works.

10. In the mid-1960s, Brzezinski wrote: "In the past, the key groups that had to be considered as potential political participants were relatively few. Today, in addition to the vastly entrenched institutional interests, such as the police, the military, and the state bureaucracy, the youth could become a source of ferment, the consumers could become more restless, the collective farms more recalcitrant, the scientists more outspoken, the non-Russian nationalities more demanding" (Brzezinski 1967, p. 9). By definition, Brzezinski separated the following groups: "political groups," "Moscow/Leningrad intellectuals," "economic commutator," "agronomists" and others (1967, p. 10).

11. Discussing the revisionist school, Peter Kenzer pointed out that this "new cohort" of Soviet researchers denied "the extraordinary nature and importance of state intervention" in Stalin's era, tried to "de-demonize Stalin and his Politburo," and made their politics look like "humdrum politics," as though the government was "just like any other government operating in difficult circumstances" (Kenzer 1986, pp. 375–384; see Fitzpatrick 1986, pp. 357–373). Likewise, Geoff Eley aptly noted that the revisionists' perspective had been infused with the pluralist model of politics, thus creating a provocative and unwarranted assertion of similarities between Stalinism and pluralist democracy (Eley 1986).

12. Regarding the abstract character of the totalitarian model as a major drawback, revisionists ignore the equally abstract nature of the democratic model. Moreover, they neglect the fact that all political science textbooks published in the 1970s and 1980s used the "totalitarian versus democratic dichotomy" as a fundamental concept (see, for instance, Macridis 1986; Nagle 1985; Curtis et al. 1990, pp. 3–15).

13. Ulam was correct when he pointed out that Lenin, in the aftermath of the revolution, "enunciated what would become the pervasive characteristic of Soviet society and Communism" (1998, p. VII).

14. Seventy-five years later, after the August Revolution of 1991, a new post-Communist Russian society was born with the same speed. I believe that in the next few decades Russia will not differ greatly from the Russia we saw in 1992–1993.

15. Some authors distinguished between the "nation" and the "empire" rather than the core and the empire (see Kara-Murza 1994b).

Notes to Chapter 2: Two Components of Soviet Ideology

1. As another example, the ideology of Zionism propagated the creation of the Jewish state based on socialist, collectivist principles.

2. For postwar works on the history of socialism in the nineteenth and twentieth centuries, see the balanced studies on the role of socialist ideas in the world, conducted by Crozier and Seldon 1986; Beer 1957; Sédillot 1977; Lerner 1982; Lichtheim 1969, 1970; Morris and Bax 1893. Other less objective works on the subject, which belittle or derogate socialist ideas, include Burbank 1986; and Brovkin 1998.

3. Figes was correct when he wrote: "By 1918 most European socialist parties subscribed to the view that capitalism and imperial competition was the fundamental cause of the war and that to prevent another war like it they would somehow have to be swept away." It seemed to them, in short, that the old world was doomed, and that only socialism, in the words of the Internationale, could "make the world anew" and eliminate wars from human society (Figes 1996b, p. 823).

4. Scholars and historians, in their analysis of the Soviet system, often disregarded the fact that after the Franco-Prussian war in 1870–1871 (and on the eve of and during WWI) socialism was widely considered the antidote against wars launched by capitalists (on the role of socialists in the antiwar movement, see Martin Du Gard 1933). The Bolsheviks' appeal to stop the war, which by 1917 had claimed millions of victims and had left the Russian economy in shambles, played a decisive role in their victory (see Ioffe and Korablev 1989, p. 41; Gimpelson 1995, p. 11). It also generated support from socialists across the world (Ulam 1992a, p. 8).

5. It would be wrong to negate the role of socialist ideas and deem them nothing more than a smoke screen for Russian authoritarianism. Richard Pipes did just that when he disregarded the socialist dimensions of the October "coup" and the importance of socialist ideas in Soviet development (see Pipes 1984, pp. 17–24).

6. American intellectuals' infatuation at this time with Marxism and Soviet socialism was later derogated by several authors who underestimated the influence of socialist ideas in the world (Hollander 1998).

7. Most "old Bolsheviks" (prisoners of the Gulag), like Maria and Nadezhda Ulanovskaia (1982) and Evgenii Gnedin (1982), broke with the ideology they had passionately espoused in their youth. However, several of them, despite or because of their Gulag experience, continued to regard post-Stalin, Soviet society as true, "normal" socialism (see Blinkova 1983).

8. The neo-Leninist view of Soviet society, which emerged after 1953, recognized many elements of contemporary Russian society in the 1960s as "normal" for countries with a socialist order. At the same time, the holders of this view found several abnormal traits in their society, traits that they wanted to eliminate in order to

achieve a more perfect society, as it was under Lenin. Some neo-Leninists labeled the system "state capitalism." The most authoritative mouthpiece of the neo-Leninist ideology was Alexei Rumiantsev, who, as a high party dignitary, represented party liberals until his dismissal in 1972 (Rumiantsev 1965, 1970; see Tvardovsky 1974, 1985; Kopelev 1978; Karpinsky 1972; Karpinsky under pen name Zimin 1981, pp. 144–146; Grigorenko 1982; R. Medvedev 1974).

9. His first samizdat publication, "A Reflection on Progress, Peaceful Coexistence, and Intellectual Freedom," was a manifesto of liberal socialism that called for the elimination of the imperfections of Soviet socialism (Sakharov 1970, pp. 51, 64, 73, 79, 161, 170, 181). Many of Sakharov's later written materials (the memo to Brezhnev in 1970, the interview with Swedish radio and TV in 1973, the article on Solzhenitsyn's "Letter to the Leaders" in 1974, his Nobel lecture in 1975, the article "About the Country and the World" in 1975, the article "The Alarming Times" in 1980, and several others) described in detail the concept of liberal socialism as it was perceived at the time.

10. Several groups of "young Marxists or Leninists" whose members saw the system as "abnormal" existed even in Stalin's times (Zhigulin 1988). Among the critics of socialist abnormality in the 1930s was the future Nobel Prize winner in physics Lev Landau. For more about young believers in "good socialist society," see Kopelev 1982b, p. 42; Pimenov 1972, pp. 105–108. As former inmates in the camps pointed out, the Gulag of the post-Stalin era was filled with committed young followers of Leninism. Former camp inmates have described curious scenes in which prisoners requested copies of Marx's *Capital* or Lenin's works, and other similar works for study—works that the KGB officers had never read (Gideoni 1980, pp. 164–165; Ginzburg 1985; Vail 1980).

11. Reflecting on the 70th anniversary of the October Revolution, Mikhail Gorbachev noted that it was "the most grandiose attempt to elevate the country with one powerful leap to another civilizational level, make it economically and technologically powerful," and "create a new social system which would confront capitalism and surpass it" (see Gorbachev 1997c). Gorbachev was seconded by the liberal political journalist Alexander Bovin, who underscored in his article, "The Great Revolution," that "The revolution elevated the country to the orbits of superpower" (Bovin 1997). Gavriil Popov, one of the most active politicians during perestroika, also agreed with Gorbachev's assessment of the revolution (1998a).

12. Lenin rejected Western parliamentarism as a tool of the bourgeoisie, and espoused the idea of dictatorship more vigorously than Marx or Engels. Although his contemporaries (including Marxists in Western Europe, such as Eduard Bernstein and Karl Kautsky, along with the entire German Social-Democratic Party) abandoned this concept in the late nineteenth century, Lenin boldly praised a future revolution that would permit the creation (for a short time) of a dictatorial state machine controlled by revolutionaries and their party, with the full support of the absolute majority of the working masses (see, for instance, Lenin 1947–1951, Vol. 25, pp. 389–398).

13. Historically, the Russian elite maintained a complex and often contradictory standpoint toward the West. Despite public harangues about Russian exceptionalism and superiority over the West (because of Russia's Orthodox religion or its Communist ideology), the elite fostered an inferiority complex with respect to Western countries. The conflict between Westernizers and Slavophiles in the nineteenth and twentieth centuries could not eclipse the deep envy of the Russian elite. The elite had always dreamed of reaching a level of personal equality with the ruling classes in

France, England and America—countries which served, at different times, as models for Russia. This longing was evident even if the wealthy, profligate landlords of the nineteenth and early twentieth centuries claimed to be on a par with the Western elite. For some of the most recent works on this debate, see Paramonov 1996, pp. 11–40; V. Shlapentokh 1990.

14. In 1913, Lenin contended, for instance, "The backwardness and lawlessness of Russia are outrageous" (1947–1951, Vol. 20, p. 293). Russia was "the most backward capitalist country in the world" (ibid., p. 256), "more backward and reactionary" than Republican China (Vol. 19, p. 213); agriculture in Russia was run not in "a European way" but as in old China and Turkey (Vol. 19, p. 168). For more of Lenin's sharp denunciations of Russian backwardness, see 1947–1951, Vol. 19, p. 253; Vol. 33, p. 73; Vol. 19, p. 117. See also Rykov 1990, p. 365.

15. Many Sovietologists—mostly conservatives—disregarded or dismissed the role of modernization in Bolshevik ideology. In his book *Russia under the Bolshevik regime* (1993), Richard Pipes attributed the emergence of the Bolshevik Revolution to the "belligerent intelligentsia," which "was bent on toppling the government and using Russia as a springboard for World Revolution," and to Lenin's and Trotsky's "yearning for power" (p. 497). Pipes ignored the issue of modernization. Martin Malia labeled what happened in Russia "pseudomodernization" and "mis-industrialization" (Malia 1992, p. 9). Adam Ulam also downgraded Soviet modernization (1997, p. 14). Only a few authors in the post-Communist era focused their attention on this important issue (see Kara-Murza 1997b; Figes 1996b, p. 814).

16. All of these elements could be found in any general text on modernization (see Alford 1963; Lipset and Rokkan 1967; Moor 1979; Levy 1996; see also Dmytryshyn 1974).

17. In 1939, Stalin accused his political enemies (the followers of Trotsky and Zinoviev) of "groveling before foreign countries and for their slavish feelings before each foreign clerk." Asserting Russia's cultural and scientific superiority over the West, Stalin advanced as examples such pseudo-scholars as Trofim Lysenko, who "surpassed" Western science with their "revolutionary innovations" based on "materialist theory" (Stalin 1952b, p. 630; see Korolev 1999).

18. This type of inferiority was revealed by Khrushchev in one of the first meetings of the Central Committee under his guidance in 1955, and by Gorbachev in 1986. This issue will be discussed in later chapters.

19. Richard Pipes downgraded the significance of the Russians' fear of foreign invasion from the West. He contended, in fact, that such fears were unfounded. Thomas DiMaggio rebuked Pipes's position, rightly underscoring the fact that these fears—however they were exploited by the political elites—were based on historical facts. In his rebuttal to DiMaggio, Pipes seemed unwilling to accept even Napoleon's invasion as an example of Western hostility, on the grounds that in the eighteenth century Russia conducted various aggressive wars in the West. For more on the debate between Pipes and DiMaggio, see Pipes 2000a, 2000b; DiMaggio 2000.

20. For an analysis of the Soviet media during the crisis of Soviet-British relations in 1923 and 1927, see Brooks 1999.

21. Yulii Khariton (along with his coauthor, physicist Yurii Smirnov) cited another "father" of nuclear weaponry, Andrei Sakharov, as having said in his greeting to Edward Teller in 1988: "I and all who worked with me were absolutely convinced of the vital necessity of our work." In 1994, Khariton continued to insist that "the security of our motherland and its people" as well as the dangerous American monopoly on this

weapon fully justified their work even if "the leadership of the country was Communist" (Khariton and Smirnov 1994). Evgenii Velikhov, a famous Russian nuclear physicist with liberal credentials, was closely involved in the Soviet nuclear program. Velikhov also asserted that the danger of an American nuclear attack was completely real (Velikhov 1999).

22. In his book *The birth of a superpower*, Sergei Khrushchev showed (probably unintentionally) how in the late 1950s and early 1960s his father systematically created serious international tensions in various corners of the globe, particularly in Berlin and Cuba (S. Khrushchev 2000, pp. 389–568).

23. With the Kremlin's seemingly firm control over much of the Third World, coupled with Stalin's strong belief in the might of his regime, in the last years of his life Stalin made a number of demonstrative moves to underscore that his empire was a continuation of the Russian empire. He introduced the same types of uniforms worn in the pre-revolutionary monarchy by personnel in the army, railroads, legal offices, and several other institutions. He replaced the Soviet anthem, the "Internationale," with a new anthem of clear imperial character. Stalin also restored the old policy of separating boys and girls in schools.

24. Even Gorbachev rejected the idea that the USSR was an ordinary empire dominated by one ethnic group, in this case, Russians (see Gorbachev 1987b).

25. Gavriil Popov wrote about the success of "state socialism" as being able "to preserve the integrity of the Russian state," while "all the big empires of the twentieth century collapsed" (Popov 1998a; see also Lisichkin 2000).

26. For the views of the nationalist school with respect to the Soviet and Russian empires, see Dugin 1998; Agursky 1980; Yanov 1988.

27. Geoffrey Hosking was one Western scholar who understood the close link between the Russian and the Soviet empires. He also saw Soviet ideology as a tool for achieving Moscow's imperial goals. He wrote: "There was a Russian imperial subtext to Bolshevism, almost from the moment the Bolsheviks seized power" (Hosking 1992, p. 6). The same views were shared by Alain Besançon (1986, p. 5). Richard Pipes, however, disagreed. In his four major books on Russian history (1974, 1989, 1990, 1993a), Pipes avoided the discussion about the continuity between the Russian and the Soviet empires. Analyzing the civil war in his *Russia under the Bolshevik regime*, Pipes wrote about "the Red empire," but disregarded "the Russian factor" and refused to see the subjugation of Ukraine, Caucasia and Central Asia as the Kremlin's determination to restore the old Russian empire (1993a, pp.141–165). In his analysis of the commonalities between the Communist regime on one side and the Fascist and Nazi regimes on the other, again he did not mention a word about the imperialistic character of all three regimes, nor about their full militarization (1993a, pp. 240–281). In his *Russia under the old regime* (1974), discussing the nature of the Russian monarchy, he almost completely ignored "the imperial factor." Only in his book published in 1982, at one of the peaks of the cold war, did Pipes take a more realistic stance. He wrote that "Communist ideology and the interests of the nomenklatura reinforced the expansionist traditions making Russian imperialism more aggressive and more persistent than ever before." However, even in this work, Pipes is far from considering Russian nationalism as the major motor of the Soviet state, its modernization and imperial drive (Pipes 1984, pp. 12, 42, 470–475). Disregarding the importance of Russian nationalism, and rejecting the continuity between the Russian empire and the Soviet empire, Pipes was joined by post-Soviet, Russian "totalitarianists," such as Irina Pavolova and Galina Kurskova. Pavlova's interesting analysis of Stalinism

completely ignored the nationalistic component of the Soviet ideology as Stalin shaped it in the early 1930s. She explained that the Soviet empire emerged only with the creation of the USSR in 1922 (Pavlova 1993, p. 166). She never mentioned that the Red Army reconquered Ukraine, the Caucasian republics, and Central Asia in 1918–1922. Kurskova also ignored the role of Russian nationalism in Soviet history. In her book about the USSR, she never talked about the "Soviet empire," ethnic relations, nor Russification in Soviet society (Kurskova 2000).

28. See the discussion of Lenin's glorification of violence in Ioffe and Korablev (1989, pp. 82–83).

29. For more about Lenin's attitude toward the Soviet state and his praise of violence as the means for forming a new society, see his writings in Pirozhkov 1987. Lenin's position was seconded by Trotsky, who described the state as "the greatest means of organization, disorganization, and reorganization of social relations" (Trotsky 1917, p. 35).

30. In 1939, in his report to the 18th Party Congress, Stalin openly proclaimed the cult of the state and criticized anonymous individuals who "underestimated" the importance of the state (including major state institutions, such as the army, "punitive agencies and the intelligence service") "in the process of moving toward Communism" (Stalin 1952b, p. 646).

31. For more about the popularity of the interventionist state in the twentieth century, see Yergin and Stanislav 1998.

32. Noting that militarization had been a typical feature of the pre-revolutionary Russian state since its formation, Vladimir Starostin (a Moscow author) wrote: "After the revolution, militarism was enhanced immensely even by Russian standards." He pointed to the 8th Party Congress, which in 1919 set itself the task of creating "the most powerful army which ever existed in the world" (Starostin 1999).

33. Clifford Gaddy aptly summarized: "For nearly sixty years, the Soviet Union had the most militarized large economy the world had ever seen" (1996, p. 1). See also Conquest 1993, p. 4; Katsenelinboigen 1990; Overy 1998a, pp. 3–14.

34. Many of the radios and televisions manufactured in the 1980s were made by enterprises which formally belonged to the military-industrial complex (see Katsenelinboigen 1990).

35. See, for instance, movies such as Grigorii Chukhrai's *Ballad of a soldier* (1959), Mikhail Kalatozov's *Cranes are flying* (1957), and Nikita Mikhalkov's *Kinfolk* (1982).

Notes to Chapter 3: Adjusting the Revolutionary Ideology to Totalitarian Goals

1. In his pre-revolutionary works, Lenin wrote with enthusiasm about the "conscientious and cultured workers," especially in Petersburg, where the people supported the Bolsheviks, "understood the Marxist teachings on their own," rejected religion and devoted themselves to "the fight for a better life" (Lenin 1947–1951, Vol. 10, p. 66; Vol. 20, pp. 273, 338, 361). For more about Lenin's admiration of the Russian working class, see Akhiezer 1991, pp. 30–35.

2. One of Lenin's best polemics against his critics (for instance, Kautsky, after the revolution) was to promote the dictatorship of the proletariat (as though it was widely supported by the people) by focusing on the antagonism between the minority of exploiters and the majority of those who were exploited (see Lenin 1947–1951, Vol. 37, pp. 256–312).

3. For more about the pogroms and other forms of violence in 1905–1907, see Dubnow 1916, p. 115; Miliukov 1955, p. 224; Vandervelde 1918, p. 106; Woytinsky 1924, p. 325; Ascher 1988, pp. 133–141; see also D. Shlapentokh 1991b, pp. 465–467, 1994; Smith and Christian 1984.

4. As many contemporaries noted, the pogroms were sponsored by the monarchy, not only to direct the people's wrath against Jews but also to demonstrate the dangers of provoking mass disturbances (see *Revoliutsiia v materialakh i dokumentakh: Khrestomatiia, 1901–1905,* 1924, p. 188).

5. Interestingly, the Bolsheviks' vision of military structure reemerged roughly three decades later, in Israel.

6. Fear of catastrophe has been used by politicians in democratic and semidemocratic societies in order to win popular support. This was particularly true of the Russian political opposition, which used fear in their programs and presented themselves as the sole saviors of the nation. In post-Communist Russia, the Communist and nationalist oppositions similarly tried to play on people's fears (see V. Shlapentokh 1997b, 1998e, pp. 161–176).

7. The anarchy which followed the February Revolution was described in hundreds of books and articles. Among Western authors, see Ross 1918, pp. 239–40; Dorr 1917; Poole 1918; Houghteling 1918. Among Russian authors, see Shidlovsky 1923; Lobanov-Rostovsky 1935; Spiridovich 1960–1962; Sorokin 1950; see also Lincoln 1986; Fitzpatrick 1982.

8. See the resolution of the 8th Party Congress, in *Kommunisticheskaia partiia Sovetskogo Soiuza v rezoliutsiiakh i resheniiakh s"ezdov, konferentsii i plenumov TsK* 1953, p. 436.

9. As Soviet historian Eric Zhagar contended, they even came close to murdering Lenin in the train that transported the Soviet government from Petrograd to Moscow in March 1918 (Ioffe and Korablev 1989, p. 670).

10. The absenteeism rate for each worker was 22.7 days per year in 1917, and 71 days per year in 1920 (Yarov 1997, p. 614). For more on labor desertion, see the materials of the 8th Party Congress in 1919 (*Kommunisticheskaia partiia* 1953, p. 488).

11. As a Russian historian said nearly eight decades later: "In the national sense, the Communists not only halted the chaotic collapse of Russia, but also restored the unity and the territorial integrity of the country and mobilized the people, even if using ruthless methods, to build up a great country" (Kortunov 1998).

12. Observing the dangerous anarchic tendencies in post-Communist Russia, a prominent Russian journalist of the 1990s described the Bolsheviks' policy for "restoring unity in the country" as "consistent, smart and cruel" (Tretiakov 1998).

13. For more about the people's attitude toward serving in the army, see Stalin's speech at the 8th Party Congress in 1919 (Stalin 1946–1951, Vol. 10, p. 43; see also Lenin 1947–1951, Vol. 29, pp. 425–427).

14. As a matter of fact, Lenin slowly began to change his views on the masses in the fall of 1917, on the eve of the October coup (see Lenin 1947–1951, Vol. 24, p. 315; see also Koenker and Rosenberg 1989, p. 97; Clements 1989, p. 115).

15. For more about the model Soviet individual, see V. Shlapentokh 1989.

16. See, for instance, Leonid Brezhnev's appraisal of his compatriots in Brezhnev 1976, pp. 46–47; 1981, pp. 83–84.

17. See the following textbooks on historical materialism, published on the eve of perestroika: Fedoseev 1985, pp. 389–391, 402–405; Klementev 1984, p. 28; Pazenok

1983; Rumiantsev 1983. Only a few authors claimed that "ordinary Soviet people" had not yet achieved the ideal level (see Kon 1983, p. 193; Dontsov 1984; Krutova 1985; Kogan 1983).

18. Robert Conquest, for instance, was sure that the Soviet leaders were obsessed "over the experiment's seventy-odd years" with "the attempt to transform the human mind" (Conquest 1992, p. 7).

19. Lenin believed, for instance, that the workers who were against the system were "unconscientious people," who, like the peasants after the elimination of serfdom, yearned for the past, along with a tiny minority of people who served the capitalists (Lenin 1947–1951, Vol. 29, pp. 9–11).

20. The first Soviet leaders were somewhat more cynical than their descendants. Bukharin was not afraid to alert his colleagues about "the necessity to belabor human material," "to force people to understand," and "to press on the masses and involve them in the struggle" (Latsis 1989b, p. 113).

21. Pipes was right when he wrote that Lenin "did not believe in the revolutionary commitment of the working class in Russia or elsewhere. In this disbelief lay the kernel of his future Bolshevik dictatorship and terror" (Pipes 1998).

22. In the 1920s, Alexander Miasnikov, a worker and party activist, described the negative attitudes of the Bolshevik leaders toward the masses, especially the workers, demonstrating that workers as well as peasants were completely deprived of the freedom of speech (Gimpelson 1995, pp. 176–177).

23. After the civil war, Trotsky and other party leaders advanced the idea of turning each factory into a military unit and each worker into a soldier. The Central Committee (in the texts of the 9th Party Congress) openly called for the militarization of the economy, arguing that "transition toward a planned economy is unthinkable without measures for coercing social parasites as well as the backward elements of the peasants and the working class" (*Deviatyi s" ezd RKP (b) Protokoly* 1960, p. 556).

24. Trotsky (during the civil war) and Zhukov (during WWII) were notorious for characterizing the masses as expendable material. For more about Trotsky's style of military command, see Volkogonov 1990.

25. Sociological studies in the 1960s showed that most Russians were not at all "ready to work wherever the motherland asked them to work." They were always looking for better jobs and better places to live. They considered pilfering from state enterprises "normal," and they were not concerned about the stability of the Soviet family, or the increasing divorce rate (V. Shlapentokh 1986, pp. 83–86; 1990, pp. 20–22).

26. Much like the Bolsheviks in the aftermath of the October Revolution, Russian liberals in post-Communist Russia also changed their attitudes toward the masses. On the eve of the anti-Communist revolution of 1991, and for the two years that followed, the liberals believed in the wisdom of the masses. By 1994–1995, however, they had concluded that ordinary Russians did not understand what was in their best interest and that the country should be governed by authoritative rule, perhaps even by monarchy. After 1995, many Russian liberals expressed (mostly privately) their skepticism about the ability of the masses to make correct choices during the elections. In 1992–1998, the liberals claimed that the masses themselves were responsible for their plight. Victor Loshak, the editor in chief of the liberal weekly *Moskovskie novosti*, went on a tirade, accusing the Russian people of "looking for any explanation to justify their inability to work" (*Moskovskie novosti*, August 1998). Another article in this newspaper, written by Yeltsin's former press secretary, Viacheslav Kostikov, blasted the Russian people for their narrow understanding of the past as "historical mythology with the images of

heroes and scoundrels." He wrote, "The people can be seduced and frightened, but to think the people have a sound historical memory is no less naive than to think a rural accordion player can execute a passage from Schnitke" (a highly sophisticated postmodern composer) (*Moskovskie novosti*, September 13, 1998). Alfred Koch, the former vice prime minister, made one of the most disparaging remarks. Speaking on an American radio program, he declared, "The Russians deserve their miserable fate." Koch was blunt in his assessment of the Russian people: "They suffer from their own guilt. Nobody occupied them, nobody conquered or subjugated them. In the Soviet times, they informed on each other, herded each other into prisons and shot each other at the firing squad." He spoke of the Russians turning into "homo sovieticus, who does not want to work but keeps his mouth perpetually open and wants bread and entertainment." See the text of this unusually revealing speech in Minkin 1998; see also V. Shlapentokh 1999a.

27. Victor Zemskov's archival data show that in Stalin's time there were more political prisoners in the Gulag with a higher education (mostly party members) than with a basic or mid-level education (mostly non-party members). This proportion increased from 1934 to 1941 (see Zemskov, Getty, and Rittersporn 1993, p. 1030).

28. In the 1920s, Soviet economist Boris Bruzkus, who understood the essence of many of the country's economic and social problems, wrote about the party's (and the left opposition's) special hatred of peasants (Bruzkus 1995, pp. 23, 119). Yurii Burtin, referring to Lenin's NEP, agreed with Bruzkus about this particular hatred of peasants among Bolsheviks (Burtin 1999).

29. The theory that peasants were the cause of repressive policies in the 1930s was quite popular in the Soviet Union from the 1960s to the 1980s. According to this theory, if the workers with long proletarian records had not been replaced during industrialization by peasant boys who lacked proletarian ideology, Stalin would have been unable to carry out his policy of mass repression. Otto Latsis, a well-known party liberal in the 1980s, openly defended this theory (1988, pp. 155, 170), as did Leonid Gordon and Eduard Klopov, who praised "the workers of big industrial centers . . . for their strong traditions of proletarian discipline, political activity, and the willingness and skill to defend their interests and contain the pressure of bureaucracy" (Gordon and Klopov 1989, p. 129). For more about the adulation of the working class, see Tsipko 1989b, pp. 176–177.

30. For documented examples of Stalin's hatred of peasants, see his 1946–1951, Vol. 10, pp. 196–197; see also Tsipko 1989b, pp. 187–188.

31. In his book *Economics of the transformation period*, Bukharin wrote, "The proletarian coercion of peasants, in all its forms (from execution to forced work), can be regarded as a sound method for creating Communist material from the human material of the capitalist era" (Bukharin 1971, p. 168).

32. Several historians, particularly those of Ukrainian origin, believed that Stalin purposely created the famine in Ukraine in 1932–1933 in order to prevent mass riots of Ukrainian peasants against collectivization (see Conquest 1986b).

33. See, for instance, Lenin's famous article "Proletarian revolution and the renegade Kautsky" (1947–1951, Vol. 37).

34. The election in the countryside in 1925, when the Bolsheviks launched the campaign "Face the village," was an exception to the rule, being a relatively free election (Brovkin 1996, pp. 71–80).

35. See the new data about the material privileges of party apparatchiks during Lenin's rule in Vlasov 1996; for more about their style of life in the late 1920s and 1930s, see Ginzburg 1985; Leontiev 1998.

36. The protests against the privileges of the party elite were quite significant during the 9th Party Conference in 1920 (*Deviataia konferentsiia RKP (B): Protokoly* 1972, p. 149).

37. Khrushchev curtailed some of the apparatchiks' privileges. For instance, he cut the so-called envelope money, the additional salary that was typically handed out to the nomenklatura in envelopes.

38. For more about the nomenklatura's privileges, see Ginzburg 1967; see also Pavlov 2000.

39. See the data related to the industrial workers in Leningrad in 1936 in S. Davies 1997, p. 24.

40. This hatred of superiors was revealed in my 1968 survey of the readers of *Pravda*. In response to the open-ended question, "Do you have any additional thoughts or wishes?," one third of respondents expressed their resentment of the bureaucratic machine and the high standard of living of their superiors (V. Shlapentokh 1969b).

41. Much of the controversy surrounding the book revolved around the problem of social inequality. One of the more publicized events of the late 1950s was Konstantin Paustovsky's lecture at the Writers' House about the social differentiation among passengers on a European cruise.

42. First, they tried to appease workers by paying engineers relatively low salaries. A content analysis of 500 letters sent in by the readers of *Literaturnaia gazeta*—the readers took part in the discussion "Engineers and Society," which focused on work environments and was organized by the research unit I headed at the Institute for Concrete Sociological Studies—revealed that almost half of all participants said that the engineers' wages were generally lower than those of skilled workers.

43. Vadim Rogovin was one of the most prolific and outspoken authors writing about the social ills of the 1980s. Following the events of 1991, he openly proclaimed his Trotskyist leanings (Rogovin 1984, 1991, 1992, 1993).

44. Social inequality did not trouble Russian liberals and dissidents of the 1960s to the 1980s. Paradoxically, the ruling elite, which enjoyed enormous material privileges, was more concerned about this issue than liberal intellectuals. As a group, the dissidents were oblivious to the material well-being of the masses and the problems of social inequality. While I generally disagree with the outspoken chauvinist Leonid Borodin, I admit that Borodin had a point when he wrote that the dissident movement of the 1960s was completely unresponsive to the "plight of the people" who lived in so-called doomed villages, to the size of the pensions paid out by collective farms, to problems faced by veterans, and to corrupt practices in the armed forces (Borodin 1998, p. 172).

45. As Moscow first party secretary, Yeltsin's refusal to use the special hospitals reserved for the nomenklatura was one of his most famous demonstrations against the party apparatus. However, comparing the gigantic budget of the presidential medical center in 1998 to the medical services for the masses, one Moscow journalist noted, "In our country the difference between the standard of living of bureaucrats and the people has never been so high" (*Novaia gazeta*, August 17, 1998). For more on the president's lifestyle, see *Moskovskii komsomolets*, March 14, and June 6, 1998. See also the book by the president's longtime employee Alexander Korzhakov (1997, pp. 156–200).

46. See, for instance, such movies as Nikolai Ekk's *Pass for life* (1931); Evgenii Gabrilovich's *Communist* (1958); Iosif Kheifits's *The big family* (1954); Lev Kulidzhanov's *House I live in* (1957); and Andrei Mikhalkov-Konchalovsky's *Siberiade* (1979).

47. The importance of the "collective" for many Russians, particularly youth, declined in the last two decades of the Soviet system, but still remained quite high. For survey data on this issue, see Babosov et al. 1985, pp. 52–54, 137; Sokolov 1981, p. 267; Blinov and Titma 1985, p. 12.

48. Forty percent of Soviets married colleagues from their place of work or from their colleges, in the early 1970s (Kharchev 1976, pp. 215–216).

49. There are numerous examples of Soviet surveys which inquired about the respondent's influence or control of their colleagues (Changli 1978; Plaksy 1982; Smirnov 1971).

50. According to surveys conducted in 1996–1999 by the directors of the project "Fears in the Post-Communist World" (Vladimir Shlapentokh was the principal investigator; Vladimir Shubkin directed the Russian part of the project), two thirds of Russian respondents expressed regret (with differing intensities) about "the loss of feelings of collectivism and mutual help and the increase of individualism." The same number of people bemoaned the decline of "collectivism" in other countries, including Ukraine, Lithuania and Bulgaria (see Shubkin and Ivanova 1999, pp. 31–37; Shubkin 1997; Mitev, Ivanova and Shubkin 1998).

51. See, for instance, Roman Balaian's movie *Day and night dreams* (1983); Sergei Mikhailin's *Fell in love on one request* (1982); and Leonid Zorin's *Kind people* (1980). During perestroika, Soviet collectivism became a direct target of liberal intellectuals (see, for instance, Rolan Bykov's *Scarecrow* 1984).

52. The party media in 1985–1986 started to denounce "collectives" as mafia-like organizations that mishandled production. They accused these organizations of protectionism and embezzlement, and labeled them "Cosa Nostra" (see *Pravda*, July 20, 1985, and March 11, 1986; *Nedelia* 21, 1986, pp. 15–16; *Sovetskaia kul'tura*, June 28, 1986).

53. Only 2 percent of Russian respondents to a 1998 survey mentioned the "priority of the individual's interests" among the major principles of new Russia; 27 percent pointed to "order," and 22 percent said "social justice" (Fund of Public Opinion, *Bulletin*, www.fom.ru/, November 27, 1998).

Notes to Chapter 4: World Revolution as a Geopolitical Instrument

1. Some scholars did, in fact, take the Soviet leaders' statements at face value. For instance, Adam Ulam wrote: "No sooner did the rulers of the Soviet Union explicitly abandon the mission of remaking the world in a Marxist-Leninist image than power began to slip from their hands" (Ulam 1992b, p. 344). Ulam's idea that the Soviet leaders saw the WR as a primary goal was supported by Robert Conquest and several other Western scholars in the latter years of the twentieth century (Conquest 1993; McCauley 1998b, pp. 96–97). This position was also maintained by several Russian scholars with strong anti-Communist leanings. Yurii Afanasiev believed that the Kremlin maintained its allegiance to world Communism even after 1991 (Afanasiev 1998).

2. The use of "goals and means" as a paradigm for explaining human behavior has been discussed in philosophy and sociology for many years. In spite of the weak spots of this paradigm, it has been widely employed by many authors in various sociological theories. See, for instance, the works of Max Weber (1978, pp. 24–26, 65–69) and Talcott Parsons (1954; Parsons and Smelser 1956).

3. In 1906, Trotsky wrote: "Without direct state support of the European proletariat the working class of Russia will not maintain its power and will not transform its temporary dominance into a long-term socialist dictatorship. It is impossible to doubt this for even a second" (Trotsky 1906), pp. 277–278). After the October Revolution, he continued to assert that "saving the Russian Revolution means expanding it to the whole of Europe." Speaking about the views of Bolshevik leaders during the civil war in 1923, he wrote that if the European proletariat took power, it "will help us technically and organizationally, give us the opportunity to correct and change the methods of War Communism and build up a true socialist economy" (Trotsky 1923, p. 16; see also R. Medvedev 1990a, p. 104).

4. See, for instance, Lenin's important brochure "The successes and difficulties of Soviet power," published in 1919 (1947–1951, Vol. 29, p. 40).

5. In one of his public speeches in 1919, Lenin contended, "The revolution can be victorious in its final form only if it embraces all or at least some of the most advanced countries" (1947–1951, Vol. 29, p. 314; see also Vol. 30, p. 103; Rykov 1990, p. 90).

6. According to Geoffrey Hosking: "There was a Russian imperial subtext to Bolshevism, almost from the moment the Bolsheviks seized power" (Hosking 1992, p. 6). Il'ia Mogilevkin, a Moscow historian, seconded the British scholar when he wrote: "As soon as they came to power, Soviet leaders . . . considered the WR their most important geopolitical component. The Bolsheviks' strategy supposed the destabilization of society in the countries—their adversaries by all means—by political and economic strikes, terrorist acts, guerilla warfare and military insurrections" (Mogilevkin 1999).

7. Gavriil Popov, a prominent Russian liberal, described Lenin as a true Russian patriot. He wrote: "After a few acts of classic Marxism (like the granting of independence to Finland), already in early 1918, Lenin signed the Brest Peace Treaty which advanced not the World Revolution, but the preservation of Russian sovereignty as his main priority. Then Lenin sent the Red Army divisions not only to 'take the Far East by force,' but also Central Asia, Ukraine and the Caucasus" (Popov 1998b).

8. After the October Revolution, Russian nationalists denounced the first Soviet leaders, particularly Trotskyists and Jewish revolutionaries, for their plans to sacrifice Russia for the victory of the WR. In 1995, Vladimir Soloukhin wrote that these people "hoped to use the colossal riches of Russia, its immense potential resources and ultimately its human material for the achievement of this crazy idea." In Soloukhin's opinion, Trotsky was not interested in Russia; the country was "no more than an armful of wood to be thrown in the fire of the World Revolution" (Soloukhin 1995, p. 6). Gennadii Ziuganov went even further, presenting the advocates of the WR (primarily Trotsky and Zinoviev) as haters of Russia, who sought insidiously to exploit "revolutionary romanticism and the expectations about the World Revolution" in the implementation of their "anti-state and anti-Russian views" (Ziuganov 1999).

9. Lenin greeted the Socialist Republic of Bavaria on April 29, 1919, with a plethora of recommendations, but said nothing about possible aid (1947–1951, Vol. 29, pp. 298–299; see also Vol. 29, p. 128).

10. On the role of patriotism in Soviet propaganda during the civil war, see Ioffe and Korablev 1989, pp. 126–127.

11. Even the universalist Trotsky eventually tamed his views with respect to sacrificing purely Russian interests for the WR. In the early 1930s, he vehemently denied Stalin's accusation that Trotskyists were "ready to sacrifice the interests of the USSR for 'permanent' revolution" (R. Medvedev 1990a, p. 155).

12. Mikhail Agursky, a noted expert on Soviet history, contended that even before the revolution the German social democrats suspected the Russian Bolsheviks of harboring imperial ambitions and camouflaging them with socialist terminology. This circumstance explained why the German socialists emerged not as Lenin's allies but as his adversaries (Agursky 1987).

13. Speaking about the revolutionary developments in Hungary on March 13, 1919, Lenin said, "We are telling you again with full confidence that victory on the world scale is insured for us" (see Volkogonov 1995, p. 146). See also Lenin's speech on May 1, 1919 (1947–1951, Vol. 29, p. 301). The logic of propaganda pushed Lenin and other politicians and ideologues to the verge of fantasy. For instance, they believed that soviets would emerge in the United States in 1919 (Lenin 1947–1951, Vol. 29, p. 2).

14. Dmitrii Volkogonov exploited Lenin's obsession with the WR, treating it as one of Lenin's numerous ill-fated predictions. Volkogonov saw it as a highly utopian idea, and did not understand how the WR and the Comintern served the interests of Russia for 80 years (Volkogonov 1995, pp. 64–87).

15. Roger Martin Du Gard has described the widespread expectations of an insurrection among socialists in various European countries (Martin Du Gard 1993).

16. Evidently, the Bolsheviks had some chance (slim, but not insignificant) of instigating insurgence in some Western countries in 1918–1919. Had they succeeded, Russia would have taken control of the new regimes.

17. Analyzing these events, the Western scholar Stephen White recognized the realistic elements of the WR (White 1993, p. 186).

18. As Grigorii Zinoviev, a Soviet leader, recollected: "With trembling hearts," each morning the delegates of the Second Congress of the Communist International marked flags on a large map of "the World Revolution," tracking the progress of the Soviet offensive in Poland. They viewed Berlin as the ultimate goal of this march (Sirotkin 1992).

19. The Red Scare in the United States was quite serious after the October Revolution as well as after WWII (see Powers 1995; Bartlett 1984; McCormick 1997; Coghill 1970; Selvern 1968; Tannenhouse 1999, pp. 46–47).

20. The twenty-eighth U.S. president, Woodrow Wilson (1913–1921), was described by many authors as a politician who combined love of power and self-righteousness with high-minded idealism, some of which looked like pure utopianism, particularly in the area of foreign policy. However, as American scholar Ronald Steel has noted, Wilson's idealism affected the course of history, especially in international foreign relations (Steel 2000; see also Auchincloss 2000).

21. Grigorii Zinoviev, who chaired the Comintern in 1923–1924, asserted "The developments in Germany, Poland and Bulgaria which occurred in May–November of 1923 opened a new chapter in the history of the international movement" (*Pravda*, February 7, 1924).

22. Speaking at a meeting of the Comintern executive committee on July 17, 1921, Lenin said, "Only stupidities can prevent the victory of Communism in France, England and Germany" (Volkogonov 1995, p. 84). As some authors contend, Lenin's belief in proletarian internationalism was so strong that he reduced the size of the Red Army after the civil war by ten times. This allowed the Soviet foreign minister to claim in 1928 that Soviet military expenditures were the lowest in the world (see Sirotkin 1990a).

23. In the second half of the 1920s, Bukharin still talked about "our party" as "the party of the international revolution" and predicted "the victory of the proletariat in a few capitalist countries" (Bukharin 1990, p. 95; see also Zhuravlev 1990, pp. 32–33, 38–39).

24. Debates about Stalin's interest in the WR persisted in the 1990s. Several authors continued to take Stalin's statements of devotion at face value. Edward Radzinsky said that Stalin "wanted to create the world state of workers and peasants" (Radzinsky 1996, 1997). On the other side of the debate, some authors insisted that Stalin resolutely adopted a policy of Russian nationalism and had no interest in the WR after 1924. Vladislav Zubok and Konstantin Pleshakov (1996) showed that during the postwar period, Stalin "wanted to confront the West" and pursue his geopolitical goals in Europe and Asia. Il'ia Mogilevkin asserted that Stalin's vision of the world was purely geopolitical (1999). See also Kara-Murza 1995a, 1995b; Zh. Medvedev 1998; Korolev 1999.

25. Indeed, Trotsky and his followers continued to see the WR as a key issue for the Soviet leadership in the 1920s and even later. At the end of the 1920s, he was still confident that "the building of socialism is the competition of the Soviet state not with the internal bourgeoisie, but with the international one." He believed that without the WR, socialist Russia would not survive. He considered the revolutionary developments in different countries (China, Germany, even Estonia) extremely important for the USSR. In 1928, he contended, "There will be no shortage of revolutionary activity in the next decade, just as there was no shortage in the previous decade" (Trotsky 1993a, pp. 70, 93, 96–102).

26. Yurii Zhukov, the Russian historian who first gained access to the archival materials on Sergei Kirov's assassination, speculated about why Stalin used Kirov's murder on December 1, 1934, as a pretext for the almost immediate (December 16) arrest of Grigorii Zinoviev and Lev Kamenev. He wrote: "The time came to change drastically the foreign and domestic policy, and Stalin saw Zinoviev as an obstacle. In 1934, Stalin ultimately moved to the position of statist. He abandoned the idea of the World Revolution and focused on the national interests of the country. The Zinoviev opposition continued to see the goal and meaning of their life as the Bolshevik World Revolution" (on Zhukov's research, see Polianovsky 1999).

27. Six decades later, Martin McCauley wrote, "There was a real chance that capitalism would not survive the 1930s" (McCauley 1998b, p. 93).

28. According to Brooks's analysis, from 1924 to 1927 *Pravda* devoted nearly two thirds of its editorials to foreign affairs. The percentage dropped to one third in 1928–1929, decreased to less than one fifth between 1930 and 1933, and then fell to almost zero for the rest of the 1930s (Brooks 1999).

29. After 1953, Georgii Malenkov was the first official who wanted to soften Soviet foreign policy for fear of a third world war. At the time, Viacheslav Molotov, in defense of Stalin's heritage, rebuked Malenkov, claiming that in the case of a third world war, only capitalism would die. However, all of the Soviet leaders followed Malenkov's line (see Openkin 1991, p. 220).

30. See, for instance, the reports of the party congresses made by post-Stalin leaders, as well as the resolutions of the party congresses and the Central Committees. Each of these materials contained a special section devoted to the international Communist movement, with optimistic declarations about its bright future (Khrushchev 1961; Brezhnev 1972; see also the Central Committee's text about the 100th anniversary of Lenin's birth in *KPSS v rezoliutsiiakh i resheniiakh s" ezdov, konferentsii i plenumov TsK*, 1986, pp. 497–510).

31. As Volkogonov noted, "Khrushchev never spoke about 'the world proletarian revolution,' but believed in the possibility of the victory of socialism on this planet by peaceful means" (Volkogonov 1995, p. 416). In Khrushchev's eclectic mind, the revolutionary idea along with the "class struggle on the international scene" coexisted

with the geopolitical ideology. However, it was the second and not the first which determined his real deeds. In his memoirs, Khrushchev recognized that when the USSR invaded Hungary in order to defend the achievements of the workers' state, its major adversaries were Hungarian workers, particularly those from the Chepel (Khrushchev 1970; Volkogonov 1995, pp. 335–436).

32. The Central Committee of the Communist Party issued the following statement on the 70th anniversary of the October Revolution: "The forces of the international proletariat with their Marxist-Leninist, Communist and workers' parties have multiplied. The mass democratic, anti-imperialist, and antiwar movements have been extended. The global crisis of capitalism is deepening" (*Trud*, March 14, 1987).

33. See, for instance, Gorbachev's report to the First Congress of People's Deputies of the USSR in his *Izbrannye rechi i stat'i* (Gorbachev 1990, pp. 558–590).

34. The Soviet victory in the war against Germany partially replaced the WR as the ideological legitimization of the regime. Soviet propaganda heralded Russia as the force that single-handedly saved the world from German enslavement. It was more than coincidental that the Third International was dissolved in May 1943, following the Stalingrad victory in February of the same year.

35. Talking about the second generation of party apparatchiks, Russian historian Vladimir Alpatov wrote, "The basic postulates in their education as party members were the ideas of the World Revolution, internationalism and extremely negative attitudes toward pre-revolutionary Russia" (Alpatov 1998).

36. See, for instance, Lenin's speeches at the meetings of the Petrograd Soviet on March 12, 1919 (1947–1951, Vol. 29, pp. 2–40), and at the Narodnyi Dom in Petrograd on March 13, 1919 (1947–1951, Vol. 29, p. 34).

37. An antifascist poster from 1935 showed workers' fists smashing fascist columns labeled Finland, Romania, England, Poland, Germany, Italy, and America. The caption read: "The imperialists prepare Fascist Bands for intervention against the USSR—We will bring Millions of Toilers to the Defense of the Homeland of the World proletariat" (Brooks 1999).

38. Gerald Howson noted that the USSR tried to extract material benefits from its commerce with Republican Spain by overcharging its ally for useless materials (Howson 1999).

39. In Kiev, at the start of WWII, I remember how an old family friend, Mr. Zaretsky, a low-level party apparatchik, persuaded us that the German proletariat would soon rise to defend our socialist country.

40. Most Western scholars believed that the USSR championed the WR throughout its history. George Kennan considered "the triumph of socialism" as the "central" element of the Soviet view of the world (Kennan 1961, p. 389). Martin Malia wrote that unlike the tsarist empire, which was a relatively normal state, the Soviet Union was "a Party-empire that existed not for circumscribed Russian national purposes, but for the internationalist task of building socialism" (Malia 1994, pp. 142, 126, 288, 295). Robert Conquest wrote in 1993 that until "Shevardnadze's stint as Foreign Minister, Moscow was fundamentally committed to a view of the world as an arena for battle between socialism and capitalism; between proletariat and bourgeoisie" (Conquest 1993; see Ulam 1992a, p. 344; Service 1998, p. 548; Courtois 1997; Gaddis 1997, pp. 32, 187, 189–221, 261–262; see also Judt 1997, p. 43).

41. In June of 1920, when the Red Army started its counteroffensive against Poland, Julian Marchlevsky created "the Polish Revolutionary Committee," which became the nucleus of the future puppet government. The meeting of the Petrograd

Soviet, at the suggestion of Zinoviev, endorsed the resolution, which rejected peace with Poland unless a Soviet republic was installed (Dan 1959, pp. 116–117).

42. Bukharin's position was repeated in the so-called Brezhnev doctrine, which legitimated Soviet intervention in East European countries in the 1960s.

43. The leaders of other totalitarian countries pretended to take the threat of international Communism seriously in order to justify their own propaganda against neighboring countries. For instance, Nazi Germany, fascist Italy and imperial Japan concluded the anti-Comintern pact as a cover for their war preparations against not only the USSR, but also Western countries. The pact was concluded first between Germany and Japan (November 25, 1936) and then between Italy, Germany, and Japan (November 6, 1937).

44. The manifest role of the Red Army in the victory of socialism in Europe was a dominant theme in Stalin's speech at the Politburo on August 16, 1939. Seemingly, Stalin was hoping that a prolonged war between Germany and the Allied forces would eventually allow Moscow to intervene decisively and promote Soviet regimes in Europe with the strong arm of the Red Army. One week later (August 23), Joachim von Ribbentrop arrived in Moscow for the conclusion of the German-Soviet treaty. See Carl Gustaf Strom's article "Stalin's strategy for war and peace," which relates the content of this speech by Stalin, which Strom discovered in a Soviet archive (1996).

45. Before the war, several young poets, including Mikhail Kulchitsky, Pavel Kogan, Iosif Utkin, and Il'ia Selvinsky, devoted their best lines to praising the liberation of mankind from the capitalist yoke by the victorious Red Army, under the guidance of mother Russia. Reflecting on this train of thought, the then famous poem "The Lyrical Digression" by Kogan read: "But we will reach the Ganges River and we will die in fights, but our motherland will glow from Japan to England" (see Shokhina 1995). This subject was absent from the work of the new generation of poets. Poets like Alexander Tvardovsky, Boris Slutsky, Alexander Mezhirov and Semen Gudzenko disregarded the WR and focused only on Soviet and Russian patriotism (see Tarasenkov 1966).

46. With internationalism as a pretext, Stalin was close to expanding his "external empire" into Greece, where the Communists were quite prominent after the expulsion of the Germans in 1944. They had ample opportunities to seize power. Only British intervention on the side of the royal troops, and Stalin's neutrality (he did not want to spoil relations with the Allies before the end of the war), prevented the Communists from doing so in 1944. The Communists renewed the civil war in 1946, but with limited support from Stalin, who was afraid of taking major actions in this first period of the cold war. The active intervention of the West on the side of the Greek government (the famous Truman doctrine) finally dashed the hopes of Moscow for the expansion of its empire in this part of the world (Volkogonov 1995, p. 237).

47. For more on this issue, see Voslensky 1984, pp. 452–453.

48. In the middle and latter decades of the twentieth century, the USSR participated in military conflicts in almost twenty different countries. In each case, it used official ideological slogans related to the concept of WR and the solidarity of the workers to justify its actions. These cases include: Korea (1950–1953); Algeria (1962–1964); Angola (1975–1979); Afghanistan (1978–1989); Vietnam (1965–1974); Egypt (1962–1963, 1969–1972, 1973–1974); Mozambique (1975–1979); Syria (1967, 1973); Ethiopia (1977–1978); Yemen (1962–1963); Mongolia (1939); Spain (1936–1939); China (1924–1937); Cuba (1960–1963); Libya (1969); Somalia (1969–1977); Iraq (1980–1988); and Cambodia (1937–1942 and 1945).

49. Marxist ideology functioned as a mask for dictatorial power in less-developed

countries. This fact was mostly disregarded by "utopian totalitarianists" such as Conquest, who believed, for instance, that Ethiopian officers (after they seized power in 1974) collectivized agriculture because of "their acceptance of Marxist ideology" and not because they wanted absolute control over the country (Conquest 1992, p. 7).

50. John Gaddis also believed that Khrushchev favored Fidel Castro because of Castro's enthusiasm for Marxism-Leninism (1997, pp. 181, 187).

51. Some Soviet generals were also unable to separate ideological clichés from the Kremlin's genuine geopolitical interests. After 1991, General Makhmut Gareev, former deputy chairman of the General Staff, still believed that "our ideology dictated that once we instituted a socialist state in our country we should spread it throughout the world" (Ellman and Kontorovich 1998, p. 61). General V. Shlykov, a leading official in the GRU, talked about "promoting the cause of the revolution" as the major goal of the International Department of the Central Committee (Ellman and Kontorovich 1998, p. 42).

52. For more about the history of the Third International, see McDermott and Agnew 1997; Broué 1997.

53. Russian Mensheviks knew that Moscow controlled the Third International. The Menshevik leader Martov, as early as 1920, had no illusions about the purpose of the Third International. He saw it as Lenin's tool for expansionism. He wrote this in a letter to Kautsky (see Brovkin 1994, p. 259). In 1922, David Dallin wrote: "The extreme internationalism of the Communist International was a weapon of Russian national politics" (Dallin 1922, p. 18).

54. From this point of view, it seems Pipes was not quite right when he wrote, "The record of the Comintern . . . is one of unrelieved failure" (Pipes 1993a, p. 236).

55. On the secret financial transactions with the Italian Communists, see the party documents published by Bukovsky (1995).

56. For more about the perks of foreign Communist leaders, see Klehr, Haynes and Anderson 1998, p. 152.

57. For more on the activities of the Communist Party in the United States, see Klehr, Haynes, and Anderson 1998; Haynes and Klehr 1999; Weinstein and Vasiliev 1999; Radosh and Joyce 1997, pp. IX–XXX, 54–57; Tannenhouse 1999; Isserman 1999; Howe and Coser 1957; Draper 1960.

58. For the reaction of the Communist parties to the Hitler-Stalin pact, see Broué 1997; Courtois 1997.

59. As previously explained, the hopes for a socialist transformation in advanced capitalist countries were abandoned in the 1920s, though some hope was rekindled after WWII. Stalin dreamed briefly about such a course of events in the first postwar years in Europe, particularly in Italy and France, with their large Communist parties. However, as Russian historian Mikhail Narinsky contended, "Stalin never posed the question about the seizure of power by Communists either in the period of the liberation of France or in 1947, when there were intensive social and political battles in France" (Narinsky 1996).

60. In the 1960s, socialist Albania also challenged Moscow's supremacy and joined sides with China in the latter's conflict with Moscow.

61. For more about the Soviet-Chinese conflict, see Rozman 1987; Thornton 1972; Westad 1998.

Notes to Chapter 5: Open and Closed Ideologies

1. Martin Malia, for instance, accused the regime of compromising "the moral idea of socialism" and failing to bring about "the fullness of human equality." Malia

lamented, "The Party had built socialism, and it turned out not to be socialism" (Malia 1994, p. 224; see also Malia 1993, pp. 86–90). Even the otherwise sober historian Richard Pipes argued that the Soviet leaders "distorted Marxism in every conceivable way" (Pipes 1993a, p. 501). Referring to Ronald Reagan's speech in 1982, Pipes wrote that Reagan resorted to "Marxist terminology" when he "predicted the collapse of Communism on the grounds that its political system no longer conformed to its social and economic base, which to those familiar with Marxism spelled revolution" (Pipes 1999, p. 107). Critiquing the Soviet system from the perspective of "true socialism" was also typical for several post-Soviet, Russian critics (see, for instance, Pavlova 1993, pp. 19, 23, 166).

2. In the aftermath of the anti-Communist revolution in August 1991, Vladimir Bukovsky acquired a copy of the minutes from the Politburo meetings in the 1970s and 1980s. He devoted a special chapter in his book, *Jugement à Moscou* (1995), to the mentality of the Soviet leaders. In this chapter, Bukovsky acknowledged that his findings were difficult to comprehend (p. 214). It seemed absurd to him that a person as intelligent as Andropov could use paranoid terms (in the 1970s and 1980s) such as "class enemies," and other Marxist jargon. Bukovsky could not grasp the mentality of these leaders because they used Marxist terms to cover their cynical totalitarian and imperialist ideology and to present themselves as the "good guys."

3. For many years it was believed that two ledgers were used by Gosplan (the State Planning Committee) and the Central Statistical Board: one for the public, and one for the government. As it turned out, this was incorrect. While the public received very little information, the government also had no accurate data on mass consumption.

4. The calculations made by Grigorii Khanin and a few other economists showed that by using various techniques the Soviet Statistical Board overstated the growth rate of production in the country by two to three times its actual amount (see Seliunin and Khanin 1987, pp. 181–192; Khanin 1991, pp. 139–166; Khanin 1993; Eidelman 1998, pp. 70–76).

5. A survey I conducted among readers of *Pravda* in 1968 found that a significant number of Russians consistently read the editorial section of the newspaper. It had been assumed by liberal intellectuals and even by the journalists of *Pravda* itself that very few people read this section because of the dryness of the material. The survey also discovered that no less than 80 percent of *Pravda*'s readers (most of whom were party apparatchiks of various levels) read these editorials because they were looking for encoded instructions from the Kremlin (see Yevladov, Pokrovsky and Shlapentokh 1969).

6. I once knew a mid-level party apparatchik (he was the deputy editor in chief of the highly ideological journal *Voprosy filosofii*) who read *Pravda* with an assortment of colored pencils, each color indicating a different type of hidden message. He paid special attention to the editorials, the speeches of the general secretary, and the resolutions of the Central Committee and party congresses.

7. Khrushchev's description of the Hungarian revolt in 1956 in his memoirs (1970), as well as the texts on Brezhnev's conversations with Dubcek in 1968 (*Nezavisimaia gazeta*, August 19, 1998), were typical in this respect. In both cases, we see a remarkable potpourri of socialist slogans and declarations on Soviet geopolitical interests with an evident focus on the second, while the first functioned only as propaganda. See the book *Nightfrost in Prague* (1980) by Zdenek Mlynar, who was present at Brezhnev's meeting with Dubcek in 1968.

8. In his memoirs, Anastas Mikoyan described his work as the first party secretary of Nizhny Novgorod in the 1920s. He did not see any contradiction between his

Bolshevik convictions and his description of the hostility of the population, including the working class, the repressions against them, and their apparent fealty to the major dogmas of the open ideology (Mikoyan 1975, pp. 65–68).

9. For more about Lenin's obsession with secrecy, see Volkogonov 1995, pp. 115–120.

10. I started my professional career as a statistician in the Kiev regional statistical state agency in 1949 (as a Jew, I had no prospect of entering a graduate program or a research institute). In this position I quickly realized the vast dimensions of secrecy. Even the number of trucks in a given region was classified. I often needed special clearance to conduct my work. My next encounter with the cult of secrecy was in the 1960s and 1970s, when I conducted surveys for major Soviet newspapers. The editors of *Pravda* released only a smattering of the data I had collected. Most data, including the evaluation of *Pravda*'s articles by readers and the readers' attitudes toward different authors, were considered by *Pravda*'s bosses as secret (see Yevladov, Pokrovsky, and Shlapentokh 1969).

11. For more about the cult of secrecy in England and the United States, see Vincent 1998 and D. Moynihan 1998, respectively.

12. In the 1960s, the Kremlin permitted a degree of debate on ecological issues. *Literaturnaia gazeta*, a liberal weekly, was allowed to publish some ecological data. Discussion of environmental problems was also permitted in movies such as Sergei Gerasimov's *Zhurnalist*. However, in the late 1960s, censorship was stiffened, and even the most innocent ecological data were classified.

13. Gorbachev mentioned that as a young member of the Politburo in the late 1970s he had access to various pieces of military information.

14. The Soviet leaders and the editors of periodicals, for instance, were well aware of the selective character of the "letters to the editors" which appeared in the most popular newspapers. Apparatchiks often gave direct instructions to journalists about "the organization" of the people's "response" to various events, emphasizing "the support" of official policy. In many cases, journalists simply invented letters to the editors. Stalin himself published a few letters under a fake name (for instance, see his reaction to a book by Vilis Lacis, *Towards new shores*, 1958 (1948). For more about letters to the editors in the Soviet media, see V. Shlapentokh 1969b; Grushin and Onikov 1980; Verkhovskaia 1972; D. Shlapentokh and V. Shlapentokh 1990.

15. In 1956, Khrushchev had exposed and repudiated Stalin's purges.

16. Depending on the circumstances, the leaders changed the priorities ascribed to the various goals of the regime. For instance, the well-being of the population fluctuated on the list of the most important Soviet goals. Usually, the leaders treated the population as a relatively low priority. Sometimes it assumed third or fourth position, behind goals such as "the development of productive forces," and the advancement of Communist education and state security (Stalin 1952a, p. 614; Khrushchev 1961, p. 51). In the early 1970s, under pressure from events in Poland, Brezhnev elevated the well-being of people to a higher position (Brezhnev 1972, pp. 38, 50). However, by 1977 the ideology had returned the priority of the population to its previous position.

17. Some social scientists in post-Communist Russia denied the fact that most Russians believed in many Soviet dogmas. Referring to a litany of Soviet propagandized ideals, Igor Kon wrote, "Needless to say, hardly any Soviet person took this ideological fiction seriously" (1997, p. 193).

Notes to Chapter 6: Policy Toward Key Social Groups

1. For more about the leaders' complex attitudes toward the working class, see the analysis by Russian historian Sergei Yarov (1997, p. 607).

2. The proportion of workers in the Communist Party was a subject of constant debate from the inception of the party in 1902 (see Latsis 1989a, pp. 141–154). The debates reflected the perennial concern of the political elite about the legitimacy of their power (see Gimpelson 1995, p. 21).

3. The Marxist theory of value influenced many economic decisions and attitudes of the leaders, including their willingness to increase the relative number of workers directly involved in "material production" in all sectors of the economy, their negative attitudes toward so-called ancillary personnel who helped workers in production, and their ambivalence toward engineers.

4. See the speech by Mikhail Tomsky, the head of the Soviet Trade Union, at the 14th Party Congress in 1925 in *XIV s"ezd vsesoiuznoi Kommunisticheskoi partii: Stenograficheskii otchet*, 1925, p. 125.

5. The decline in the importance of workers as the major social basis of the new regime was quite conspicuous in the first decade after the civil war, when the economy was in shambles and workers left their factories en masse and moved to the countryside for survival.

6. My father, whose parents had been wealthy before the revolution, had to wait several years for admittance to medical college.

7. The campaign began in May 1968 when two party officials, Richard Kosolapov and Pavel Simush, published an article in *Pravda* stating that the Soviet intelligentsia was in need of the "guiding and educative influence" of the working class (May 25, 1968). The campaign gained momentum, and Brezhnev himself began to take an active part in lauding the working class. He offered a portrait of the advanced worker, who was clearly superior to any representative of the intelligentsia (Brezhnev 1972, p. 483–484). Throughout the next decade, subsequent publications on the working class followed this pattern (see, for instance, Bliakhman and Shkaratan 1973). Even in 1989, during perestroika, two respected sociologists, Leonid Gordon and Eduard Klopov, contended that workers were "the major social basis for the developments of socialist democracy," with their "strong proletarian traditions, conscious discipline, political activity, willingness and ability to defend their rights and oppose offensive bureaucratism" (Gordon and Klopov 1989, pp. 129, 133).

8. The existence of hostile sentiments among workers toward the intelligentsia was revealed in my 1968 survey of the readers of *Pravda*. The final question of the survey was: "Do you have any additional remarks or comments?" About one third of the respondents replied to this question. Of those who responded, a significant proportion expressed animosity toward both intellectuals and bureaucrats.

9. For more about the workers' strikes and other public disturbances during the civil war and in the 1920s, see Yarov 1997, pp. 613–614; D. Shlapentokh 1991a, pp. 262–264; Carr 1964, p. 393; Dolgorukov 1964.

10. In early 1918, 57 percent of the members of the Bolshevik party were workers, 22 percent were employees and 15 percent were peasants (Malle 1997, p. 648).

11. There is substantial evidence that Soviet leaders were concerned with the presence of workers in governmental bodies. In 1922, Lenin wrote a special letter to the Central Committee on the eve of the 11th Party Congress, suggesting special measures

to guarantee that those who claimed to be workers (so as to be admitted into the party) indeed had a "proletarian record" (Lenin 1960–1965, Vol. 45, pp. 19–20). In his report to the 5th Congress of the Comintern in June 1924, Rykov declared, "The party considers the attitudes of the machine tool workers as a main political barometer and the single check for party policy as well as its single unshakable social basis." He added, to applause, "We will make no exceptions," and "Even when the whole of our intelligentsia is red Communist, the major class mainstay for the party will still be the workers of machine tools, and not the intelligentsia" (Rykov 1990, p. 371).

12. In 1933–1934, my grandfather, who owned a few pharmacies before the revolution, lost two of the four rooms in his apartment in Kiev. The family that moved in were Ukrainian factory and railroad workers.

13. In the opinion of General Makhmut Gareev, former vice chairman of the Soviet General Staff, the regime's concern for workers was one of the causes of the country's collapse. In the 1970s and 1980s, the Soviet leadership refused to curtail the mass production of obsolete weaponry (particularly tanks) and shift resources toward the development of advanced microelectronics because this shift could jeopardize the jobs of many workers (see Ellman and Kontorovich 1998, pp. 48–49).

14. In a five-year period, no less than one third of the Soviet population addressed complaints to the authorities or the media at least once, through various means (usually by letter or in meetings with officials); and one quarter of the population made complaints 3 to 4 times a year (see Grushin and Onikov 1980, pp. 376, 379). The newspaper *Izvestiia*, with a circulation of 8.6 million, received about 500,000 letters from its readers in 1967 (see V. Shlapentokh 1970, p. 148). For more about the role of letters to the editors in the life of the people, see Verkhovskaia 1972; Grushin and Onikov 1980; D. Shlapentokh and V. Shlapentokh 1990.

15. When, in 1992–1993, appeals to the authorities and the media for help became useless, one of the fundamental bonds connecting Russian society broke, leaving the people to fend for themselves. When asked in 1994–1995, "Who do you look to for support during difficult times," 75 percent of the respondents answered, "I count only on myself" (see VTsIOM 1994, 5:58, and 1995, 1:11; see also Riabushkin and Osipov 1982).

16. An analysis of Stalin's position presents a good example of the dual character of the Soviet system's treatment of intellectuals. On one hand, Stalin was directly responsible for the persecution and elimination of thousands of intellectuals (see the list of outstanding intellectuals killed by Stalin in R. Medvedev 1989, pp. 151–156). Stalin was often extremely critical when intervening in scientific matters, and brutally persecuted scholars who held dissenting opinions. On the other hand, he was compelled by economic and military considerations to behave quite differently toward some intellectuals, such as Sergei Korolev (who would later organize the Soviet space program), Lev Landau (a future Nobel Prize winner in physics), and Alexei Tupolev (a leading figure in the development of Soviet aviation). Stalin released these men from the Gulag. During World War II, he created the famous *sharashki*, special prison camps where intellectuals were interned and fared much better than inmates in ordinary camps (for more about *sharashki*, see Solzhenitsyn 1968; see also *Moskovskie novosti* 48, 1987; Kopelev 1975). Stalin never lashed out against the intelligentsia as a group. Only in the early 1930s did the mass media attack "bourgeois" conservative engineers and scholars, going so far as to accuse some of them of sabotage; by 1939, however, these overtones had vanished completely. Moreover, in his various speeches of the late 1930s, Stalin demonstrated respect for the intelligentsia (Stalin 1952b, pp. 550–551).

17. For more on the lives of Soviet scholars and writers during this period, see Berberova 1983.

18. For more about the material privileges of Moscow actors, see Vishnevskaia 1984, pp. 84, 206, 226, 326; for the privileges of composers, see Goldshtein 1970, p. 103–108; about musicians, see Ashkenazy 1985; Reznikov 1984, p. 109. The organization of life in "scientific towns" exemplified the privileges bestowed upon intellectuals. These towns were constructed in the late 1950s and 1960s, the most famous being Academic Town (Akademgorodok) in Novosibirsk. Residents of Academic Town enjoyed a much higher standard of living than did residents of Novosibirsk and other Siberian cities. When I lived in Acadmic Town, in the 1960s, the food supply and housing conditions available to scholars there seemed almost miraculous in comparison to the other cities and villages where I had lived before (for more detail, see Josephson 1997). The same was true for other scientific towns, such as Dubno (Polikanov 1983), Chernogolovka, and Pushchino.

19. Along with their willingness to accept workers into the party, the Soviet leaders, particularly after 1953, made efforts to recruit the creative intelligentsia. In the early 1980s, 50 to 70 percent of the creative intelligentsia were party members (*Sovetskaia kul' tura,* June 8, 1985).

20. According to Vladimir Shubkin's data from the early 1960s, on a ten-point rating scale of prestige, male graduates from secondary schools in Novosibirsk assigned scholars an average score of 6.61. Engineers received an average score of 6.55, workers in industry scored 4.01, and agricultural workers 2.5 (Shubkin 1970, p. 280–286).

21. After the anti-Communist revolution in 1991, the same situation was repeated. Again, the young and educated benefited most from the new regime (V. Shlapentokh 1997a).

22. The Harvard Project also discovered a correlation between the respondents' hostility toward the regime and their level of education, their age, and their social status. Among the intelligentsia the number of people with strong hostility toward the Soviet system was 12 percent; among white-collar employees, 16 percent; skilled workers, 20 percent; ordinary workers, 34 percent; and collective farm peasants, 36 percent. Hostility toward the system was inversely proportional to occupational satisfaction. Among the members of the intelligentsia who were highly satisfied with their jobs, only 20 percent expressed "some hostility to the Soviet system"; of those who reported low satisfaction, 45 percent reported the same. Among ordinary workers the respective percentages were 35 percent (satisfied/less hostile) and 63 percent (unsatisfied/more hostile); and among collective farm peasants, 32 percent and 65 percent, respectively (Inkeles and Bauer 1968, pp. 27, 36, 260–261).

23. The people's average level of satisfaction with the standard of living (using a four-point scale in which 1 represented the highest satisfaction and 4 the lowest) increased uniformly with age: respondents under 31 years of age reported a score of 2.59; people over 54, 2.28. The same was true with respect to one's level of education: people with higher educations reported an average satisfaction rating of 2.55; those with lower-level educations rated their satisfaction at 2.04 (Millar 1987, p. 33, 36).

Notes to Chapter 7: The Political System

1. Each leader assumed the cult of leadership, that is, the glorification of his personality through propaganda in all educational institutions, media and the arts.

This was true for all the Soviet leaders, even the most liberal leader, Mikhail Gorbachev (see the memoirs by his lieutenant, Cherniaev 1993).

2. Weber's concept of rationality (and not Pareto's notion of "residuals") serves as the best explanation of Soviet leaders' conduct. For other useful comments on rationality, see Goodin 1976, pp. 9–18; and Sica 1988, pp. 5–7.

3. Malia believed that the Soviet Union was a utopian construction, built like a house of cards, by dreamers and lunatics. He talked about "the fantastic and surreal Soviet experience." Among other things, Malia characterized the society as "wrong from the start," "a social theater of absurdity," the "grim mistake of Columbus," and "the greatest triumph of ideology over real life" (1994, pp. 7, 9, 14–15). For other works that presented Soviet history as an era of utopianism, see Heller and Nekrich 1982; Bauman 1976.

4. The same event occurred during the Cultural Revolution in China (1966–1977), which damaged China's economy, education, culture, science, and international reputation. This revolution was necessary for Mao to destroy his enemies inside the party, who had tried to use the failure of Mao's "Great Leap" in 1956 to remove him from power. As in Stalin's case, no social groups in China were demanding this action from Mao, even if some benefited from the turmoil in the country (see Joseph, Wong, and Zweig 1991; Barnouin and Changgen 1993).

5. I thank Galina Firsova for developing this idea.

6. The case of General Dmitrii Volkogonov (along with several other ideological turncoats in the last years of perestroika and in post-Communist Russia) was a good example of the rationalization of motives—in other words, the replacement of one's primary motives with secondary or even purely spurious motives for the sake of one's best interest. Volkogonov served as the deputy chief of the political directorate of the Soviet army (1984–1988). He was responsible for the ideological indoctrination of the army and the population. He was also the director of the ideological Institute of Military History (1988–1991). From 1984 to 1991, before the victory of the liberal course in Russia, Volkogonov published dozens of aggressive anti-Western and anti-liberal publications (see, for example, his *Kontrpropaganda: Teoriia i praktika* 1988). As one of Gorbachev's aids recounted, even in 1987 Volkogonov demanded that the Central Committee harshly punish "ideological deviationists" (Cherniaev 1993). In the late years of perestroika, however, Volkogonov literally changed his views overnight. He became a leading figure of perestroika. Later, he said that his motivation to change his role was dictated only by his sudden enlightenment about the nature of the Soviet regime. Volkogonov explained that he had started studying archive documents from the late 1980s. Apparently, his experience of Soviet life and his full access to all sorts of critical literature about the system were not enough to change his mind earlier and enable him to join the hundreds of thousands of liberal intellectuals in the 1960s and 1970s (see his articles, with an introduction by his daughter, in Volkogonov 1998a, pp. 10–12).

7. As will be discussed later, after 1991 Mikhail Gorbachev's expressed reasons for starting perestroika jarred with his actions in the first years of his tenure as general secretary. Many of Russia's new "liberals" had fervently served the Soviet regime only a few years back. After 1991, however, they declared that they joined Yeltsin's administration because they had "always" hated the Soviet system.

8. The debates about the attribution of motives have been ongoing in social psychology since the late 1950s (see Ross and Fletcher 1985, pp. 73–122; see also Zimbardo and Leippe 1991).

9. For more on the study of human motivation, see Jones and Davis 1964; Harvey, Ickes, and Kidd 1976; see also Pittman 1998.

10. In his monumental work, Pipes devoted only a few perfunctory sentences to Marxism, and paid little attention to Lenin's views on history, economy, and politics. Lenin's relations with Marxism were treated as irrelevant to his seizing power. Pipes mostly dismissed the ideology of the Soviet Communists as a "subsidiary factor" in the formation and development of Soviet society (Pipes 1993a, pp. 500–502).

11. One Moscow author wrote that after 1953, the Soviet leaders had no "serious theoretical vision of the world" (Utkin 1997).

12. One of the major guardians of Soviet ideology in the postwar period was Mikhail Suslov. He became an important ideological figure in the late Stalin period and the main ideological watchdog in the times of Khrushchev and Brezhnev.

13. Dismissing the role of Marxist ideology in the Soviet Union, Pipes cited Raymond Aron as having remarked at a Harvard seminar in the 1950s, "'Ideology' in the Soviet Union boiled down to two propositions: that Communism is good and capitalism is bad: and that Communism will vanquish capitalism" (Pipes 1999, p. 107). They both underestimated the role of this ideology in the creation and perpetuation of state property and central planning in the Soviet system.

14. This trend in the mind of Soviet leaders explains why textbooks on Marxist philosophy and "scientific Communism" in the 1970s and 1980s ceased to promise the economic victory of the USSR in its competition with the West in the near future (see, for instance, Fedoseev 1985, pp. 249–255).

15. Nikita Khrushchev was probably the single Soviet leader who tried, if very superficially, to introduce some elements of classic socialism, as depicted by the open ideology, in his domestic policy. He initiated the creation of "voluntary teams of workers" for the maintenance of order in cities and villages; he also launched the "people's theaters," which only supposedly competed with professional theaters. He made some decisions which encouraged the use of collective cars and country houses. After his dismissal, his attempts to introduce genuine socialist ideas disappeared almost instantly. In his foreign policy, Khrushchev twisted the public ideology as much as necessary. He referred, for instance, to Soviet actions to quell the insurrection in Hungary in 1956 as an action to assist "the Hungarian working class," even though it was Hungarian workers who made up the core of the insurgents. He went so far as to say that "with the suppression of the Hungarian counterrevolution," Soviet Russia had paid its debt to Hungary for tsarist Russia's having crushed the Hungarian revolution of 1848 (see Khrushchev 1970, pp. 2–63, 223, 247).

16. For instance, in 1972, Alexander N. Yakovlev published an article in *Literaturnaia gazeta* that critiqued Russophile literature from a Marxist perspective. He was immediately demoted from his leading position in the Central Committee and later was sent abroad as an ambassador (see Yanov 1978, pp. 49–52, 57–60).

17. Henry Kissinger's lengthy book *The White House years* (1979) covers the period of 1968–1973, when Soviet-American relations were crucial for the White House. In his description of this period, he almost completely ignored the ideological factor in his intensive contacts with the Kremlin, for instance, in the negotiations on the ABM and SALT treaties (pp. 534–557). What is more, when he described the function of the highest echelons of power in Moscow, Kissinger never even mentioned ideology (pp. 526–527). He also ignored ideology in his description of Brezhnev's personality (pp. 1137–1144). Anatolii Dobrynin, the Soviet ambassador to the United States, also disregarded ideology and described Soviet-American rela-

tions in the 1970s and 1980s almost from the same geopolitical perspective as Kissinger (Dobrynin 1995). Interestingly, it was Ronald Reagan, not Brezhnev and Dobrynin, who operated with ideological clichés. According to Dobrynin, Reagan believed that "the American people regarded as their main threat the principal political idea of the Soviet Union which was based on the fundamental Marxist-Leninist teaching that the world would surely become Communist" (1995, pp. 519, 556).

18. See, for instance, his report to the XXIII Party Congress in *XXIII s" ezd Kommunisticheskoi partii Sovetskogo soiuza: Stenograficheskii otchet*, 1966, pp. 71–73.

19. See the article "Peregovory v Kremle, 23 and 26 August 1968" (*Nezavisimaia gazeta,* August 19, 1998).

20. Here, I am using "utopian" to describe unrealistic or adventurous plans, putting aside the more rigorous definition of the term as "an ideal society able to satisfy the needs of all its members" (see Mannheim 1929; Nozick 1974, pp. 297–335).

21. Utopianism in the minds of the masses was quite pronounced during the revolution and in the first decade of the regime. Andrei Platonov described this predilection in his novels of the late 1920s. Platonov depicted how people with good common sense could be brainwashed with the most absurd utopian ideas (see Platonov 1978, 1996; see also Batalov 1989, pp. 18–19).

22. With his ideas about the militarization of the economy, particularly agriculture, Trotsky was among those Soviet leaders whose belief in utopianism was quite strong. However, even his seemingly absurd ideas about agriculture were implemented by Stalin ten years later. Moreover, it is hardly reasonable to identify collectivization as a highly "utopian project."

23. For more about the mythology of privatization, see V. Shlapentokh 1993b.

24. This tendency of using utopian projects to increase dynamism was particularly typical for Brezhnev's period of "stagnation." Many innovations during this period were false initiatives. For more about the pseudo-innovations of the Brezhnev era, see Kontorovich and V. Shlapentokh 1986).

25. Khrushchev's encouragement of the propagation of corn in all regions of the country regardless of climatic conditions, and his enthusiastic personal support of various agricultural methods (for instance, a specific formula of cattle feed, and techniques of raising cows), hurt the agricultural sector (see McCauley 1976).

26. U.S. President Woodrow Wilson (1913–1921) has been described by many authors as a politician who combined a love of power, and self-righteousness, with high-minded idealism which verged on pure utopianism, particularly in foreign policy. Yet, as American scholar Ronald Steel noted, Wilson's idealism greatly influenced the course of history, especially in international relations (Steel 2000, pp. 19–21; see also Auchincloss 2000).

27. Leszek Kolakowski, in spite his approach to the study of Soviet society as a product of utopian ideas, wrote that Lenin was "an extremely sober politician" (Kolakowski 1992, p. 5). Ulam persistently described Lenin in his monumental work *Bolsheviks* (1965 and 1998) as an extremely rational politician (see pp. 389, 393, 394). The famous Soviet dissident Andrei Siniavsky also described Lenin as an extremely rational leader "who approached any task—economic, military, organizational—as a subject for research" (*Nezavisimaia gazeta–Khranit' vechno,* June 2, 1998). However, several other authors described Lenin as a leader who lacked "political realism" (see Gray 1998, p. 3).

28. As Abraham Brumberg noted, Stalin "was au fond going about his job of crushing millions of people in pursuit of eminently rational objectives" (1998).

29. One of Brezhnev's closest aides, Georgii Arbatov, wrote, "Without resorting to

conflicts and stresses, or bloody repressions, or even demanding public obedience, Brezhnev secured for himself whatever he wanted: submission, docility and even fear" (Arbatov 1992; see Aksiutin 1992; see also Ovrutsky 1992).

30. As Khrushchev recounted, Stalin not only sent some members of the Politburo to their deaths but treated all of them extremely rudely and unceremoniously (N. Khrushchev 1970, pp. 44, 46–48, 85, 278– 279, 281–282, 289).

31. In their attempts to destroy the totalitarian model and discover political plural-ism in the USSR, revisionists looked to the Politburo to substantiate their views. Lewis Siegelbaum, for instance, maintained this view in the late 1990s, even after numerous documents had been published without lending a single piece of evidence to his theory. He extended his discourse to the different factions in Stalin's Politburo, with Kirov as a leader of the "moderate" faction and Yezhov as a politician with "his own agenda." Siegelbaum evidently supported John Arch Getty's theory of the origin of "the Great Purge" as a result of the "failure of two campaigns to renovate the party" (Siegelbaum 1997, pp. 311–313). However, in their 1999 book, Oleg Naumov and John Arch Getty said of the Stalin period: "We found no documentary evidence of the existence of anything like stable elite factions or groups in the available archives" (Getty and Naumov 1999, p. 575).

32. Gorbachev ousted three conservative full members of the Politburo: Vladimir Shcherbitsky, Victor Nikonov, and Victor Chebrikov. Before this purge, the eleven-member Politburo—the USSR's highest political body—had been dominated by its seven conservative members (Lev Zaikov, Yegor Ligachev, Vitalii Vorotnikov, and Nikita Sliunkov, in conjunction with the three members removed on April 21).

33. Until the late 1930s, the members of the Politburo were treated in official propaganda as *vozhdi* (leaders), and their pictures (along with the pictures of regional party secretaries) were almost as ubiquitous as Stalin's. From the early 1940s until 1985, pictures of the members of the Politburo were displayed only during demon-strations on the major Soviet holidays. I remember collecting pictures of *vozhdi*, in-cluding members of the Ukrainian Politburo, when I was a boy.

34. Such was the case in 1969 when the Politburo discussed whether or not to publish an article in *Pravda* about the 90th anniversary of Stalin's birth. According to the minutes of the meeting, the subject was indeed hotly debated among the mem-bers. Brezhnev sided with the majority view, and instructed *Pravda* to publish a posi-tive article about Stalin. The article was published on December 21, 1969 (see Pikhoia 1999, pp. 16–17).

35. The case of Alexei Rumiantsev, who simultaneously held various high posi-tions in the party hierarchy (i.e., head of the department of science at the Central Committee of the Communist Party, *Pravda*'s editor in chief, vice president of the Academy of Sciences), is instructive. In the second half of the 1960s, before "the Prague Spring"—when Brezhnev's domestic policy was quite ambivalent—Rumiantsev was active in promoting a liberal ideological policy. However, when Brezhnev moved toward a harsher, antiliberal policy, Rumiantsev quickly was dis-missed from all his positions, even as director of the sociological institute (V. Shlapentokh 1987).

36. Counterfactually, revisionists have described the Politburo in the 1970s and early 1980s as an arena of conflicting ideas and elitist democracy. Dozens of leading scholars and Ph.D. candidates have studied factions in the Politburo in the 1960s–1980s. Some have discovered as many as five factions in the eleven-person body (Rutland 1993, p. 115).

Notes to Chapter 8: An Effective Political Machine

1. Questions about the dual party-state system began to baffle Soviet political scientists in the 1960s, when it became permissible to discuss (though cautiously) theoretical issues in social science. They started to advance differing theories about which entity served which—whether the party served the state or the state served the party (see Burlatsky 1970).

2. When the Communist Party went on trial in the Russian Constitutional Court in the summer of 1992, Sergei Shakhrai, speaking on behalf of Yeltsin's government, proclaimed that the party was an unconstitutional organization, and accused it of performing the functions of a state. Interestingly, this was exactly what the mission of the Communist Party in the Soviet Union had been. The last Soviet Constitution, the so-called Brezhnev Constitution (1977), stated in article 6 that the party played "the leading role in Soviet society," as did the Stalin Constitution (1936) in Article 126 (see *Pravda*, July 18, 1992).

3. Alexander Zinoviev aptly noted in *The yawning heights* (1979) that party members were superior to their colleagues without party cards in every possible way: in education, professionalism, and even moral standards.

4. This was true even in Stalin's times, when party members, particularly those holding high positions, were the main target of state-sponsored repressions. Of the 245 Bolshevik leaders whose biographies in 1927–1929 were included in the publication "The main figures of the USSR and the October Revolution," 38 percent were arrested and eventually executed or imprisoned in the Gulag, and 3 percent committed suicide (see *Komsomol'skaia pravda*, October 21, 1990).

5. As an interesting note, Stalin was never overly concerned about the number of party members among intellectuals. Indeed, Stalin may have had greater respect for scientists who were not party members. Without exception, during his rule, all of the presidents of the Academy of Sciences were nonmembers. Even the celebrity Trofim Lysenko was not a party member. The post-Stalin leadership, however, apparently rejected this policy. In their view, party membership demonstrated intellectuals' political loyalty and readiness to follow party directives.

6. See the report of the directorate of the cadres of the Soviet Academy of Sciences for 1979, in *Nezavisimaia gazeta-Nauka* 2 (February) 1997, p. 7.

7. One of my friends, who was known for his liberal leanings, was expelled from the party for his participation in the funeral of a dissident in 1968. His expulsion affected everything in his life, from his job to his housing conditions (he could not exchange his room in the Moscow region for a room in downtown Moscow). To rid himself of this stigma, he applied for the restoration of his membership to each Congress of the party between 1968 and 1986, but to no avail.

8. In 1990, 1.8 million people left the party (no more than 10 percent); that same year, 108,000 entered the party. Even in 1991 there was no panicked flight from the party. In the first three months of 1991, only 587,000 people left the party, while 46,000 people entered the party (*Nezavisimaia gazeta*, January 3, 1991).

9. Many Soviet literary works and movies give a realistic portrayal of the devotion of rank-and-file Communists to the tasks assigned by the Kremlin (see Ostrovsky 1979; see also the 1958 movie entitled *Communist* by Iulii Raizman and Evgenii Gabrilovich). Referring to my own family history, two of my aunts (Sara and Lidia Gurevich) were dedicated Communists since the civil war. Until the 1950s, they were proud of their Communist membership and were ready to perform literally any task for their leaders.

10. In 1952, while working at the Kiev regional statistical committee, I saw with my own eyes this decree signed by Stalin.

11. Even in these years, however, Trotsky had already noted a degeneration in the Communist bureaucracy (and not without grounds). He considered this the main cause of all Soviet problems (see Sirotkin 1990b, pp. 292–334).

12. Andrei Kolesnikov (a Russian author who was well acquainted with many apparatchiks) wrote, "It is a very specific mentality which in a most exotic way combines the cynicism of intellectuals, 'omniscient as a snake,' and Communist romanticism. It was the people who were not able to get rid of socialist illusions and who were forced to 'like the system' and the nomenklatura; in order to work well in the party apparatus, it was necessary to like it" (1993).

13. For more about the hardworking Soviet managers, see Alexander Bek's famous novel *Novoe naznachenie* (1987) and Vera Panova's *Kruzhilikha* (1948).

14. Russian journalists used the celebration of Efim Slavsky's 90th birthday (Slavsky had served as minister in charge of the nuclear industry) as a pretext for lamenting the low moral qualities of those who had inherited his job in post-Communist Russia (see Safronov 1998).

15. As a secretary of the Central Committee, Andrei Zhdanov positioned several people from Leningrad in the party and state apparatus (he had previously worked as the secretary of the party committee of Leningrad). Similarly, as chairman of the KGB, Lavrentii Beria brought in many of his former subordinates from Georgia.

16. Khrushchev brought with him many of his fellow countrymen from Ukraine: Fedor Kirichenko was installed as a secretary of the Central Committee; Andrei Grechko became minister of defense; Brezhnev was made a secretary of the Central Committee. Brezhnev, in turn, was dubbed the godfather of the "Dnepropetrovsk/Moldavian Mafia," because he had worked in both places and brought in many people from these areas.

17. Only a few important people from various sectors of society defected from the USSR. These included physicists (Georgii Gamov); KGB and GRU agents (Alexander Orlov, Walter Krivitsky, Georgii Agabekov, Ignatii Reiss, and G. Luzhkov in the late 1920s and 1930s; Igor Guzenko, Viktor Rezun-Suvorov, Yurii Nosenko, Vladimir Petrov, and Oleg Penkovsky in the 1940s–1960s, and a few others); a few politicians, such as Boris Bazhanov; trade specialists, such as Victor Kravchenko; diplomats (Grigorii Besedovsky, Arkadii Shevchenko); writers (Anatolii Kuznetsov and Arkadii Belinkov); sportsmen (Victor Korchnoi); journalists (Stanislav Levchenko); a few military officers (for instance, pilots Victor Belenko and Stanislav Lunev); and a few ballet dancers (Rudolf Nureyev and Mikhail Baryshnikov among them). For more about Soviet defectors, see Brook-Shepherd 1978, 1989; Krasnov 1985; Lunev 1998; Andrew and Mitrokhin 1999.

18. Olga Velikanova compared the bias of the political police's information with that of the party committees. Both bodies sent this information to the Kremlin in various reports. After extensive work in Soviet archives, Velikanova concluded that the political police's reports were much more objective about the mood of the population than the reports of the party apparatchiks, who were inclined to downgrade anti-Soviet attitudes among workers in the units for which they were responsible (Velikanova 1998).

19. Boasting about the achievements of the KGB, professor V. Demin, an analyst in the Russian Federal Service of Security (FSB; the KGB's successor), said that the KGB controlled the activity of 300 firms in three dozen countries (Demin 1997).

20. For more about the role of the KGB in stealing nuclear bomb technology, see

P. Sudoplatov 1994; Khariton and Smirnov 1994; see also Breindel 1994; Legvold 1994; Belokon 1994. For the debates about whose contribution to the development of the first Soviet nuclear bomb was greater, the KGB's or Soviet science's, see Moroz 1994.

21. Anatolii Sudoplatov, son of the notorious KGB general Pavel Sudoplatov, in an article he coauthored with Vladimir Malevannyi about the decimation of KGB personnel in 1936 and 1937, wrote: "Stalin delivered a blow against the second pillar of power of the regime (the first being the army) in order to demonstrate that this institution was ultimately only in his hands" (Sudoplatov and Malevannyi 1998).

22. Roi Medvedev insisted that the KGB's monitoring of party apparatchiks was limited (1993). For a similar position, see also the work of former KGB officer Mikhail Liubimov (1999). Victor Grishin maintained the opposite view, contending that the KGB could investigate and monitor anyone (1996). The positions of Victor Chebrikov, a former chairman of the KGB, was close to Grishin's opinion. He said that "the ban on monitoring party apparatchiks" was removed if "someone among the leading workers fell under suspicion" (Chebrikov 1998).

23. The published data (1990–1993) show that in the midst of mass terror, in 1937, the NKVD needed the Kremlin's advance approval for any action. For more on this issue, see Gevorkian 1992. Forty years later, when Andropov was the chairman of the KGB, he was as obedient to Leonid Brezhnev as Nikolai Yezhov had been to Stalin. Even in his last years, when Brezhnev was practically on his deathbed, Andropov did not act on his own initiative. Brezhnev, for instance, forbade Andropov to report the corrupt activities of the Ministry of Internal Affairs and its head, Nikolai Shchelokov, who was Brezhnev's pet (see *Komsomol'skaia pravda*, November 29, 1991).

24. Bukovsky saw the KGB as a crucial, independent institution which set the course of domestic and foreign policy. In his opinion, Yurii Andropov (its director from 1967 to 1982) was the sinister political genius of the Soviet establishment, who was responsible for all major developments in the country and for many political events outside it (including the attempt to murder the Pope). Bukovsky's theory about the origin of perestroika exaggerated the role of the KGB in Soviet society. According to the author, the whole project of perestroika was contrived by Andropov in the late 1970s and Gorbachev was chosen as the best candidate for its realization (1995, pp. 484, 487). In his eyes, perestroika was designed by the KGB in order to prevent Soviet Communism from crumbling under growing pressure from the discontented populace—to save the regime, and to superficially embellish the "Soviet concentration camp" à la Potemkin (1995, pp. 213, 262, 283, 489).

25. According to various public opinion surveys conducted after the fall of the USSR, Andropov was one of the most popular Russian leaders in Soviet history. In 1996, 1,600 Russians were asked to name the leaders of the past or present who insured the most order in society. Nineteen percent of the respondents chose Andropov; 12 percent, Stalin; 11 percent, Brezhnev; 6 percent, Lenin; 6 percent, Yeltsin; 3 percent, Khrushchev; and 2 percent, Gorbachev (*Moskovskie novosti*, April 27, 1997).

26. Another view was held by General William Odom, an American military expert, who was, in the opinion of the author, in error when he wrote: "Although Western scholars have too often denied or ignored it, Marxism-Leninism is indeed a significant factor in the explanation for why the Soviet Union built such a large military force and why they devised the kinds of war plans they did" (Odom 1998, p. 11). Odom believed that the Soviet leaders elaborated their military doctrine in order to achieve "the complete victory of socialism" (p. 11). Like several other scholars, Odom took the public declarations of Soviet leaders about the World Revolution at face value. However, in

Odom's analysis of the Soviet doctrine about the use of nuclear weapons, he found no room for "the ideological factor." He wrote that the Soviet military looked no less rational than their American adversaries who elaborated a strategy considered first of all the character of the weaponry at their disposal (pp. 65–87).

27. As British historian Geoffrey Hosking stated, "The unrivaled status of the military derived from the evident success of the armed forces in protecting the Soviet Union, underpinning its internal cohesion and guaranteeing its standing as one of the world's two superpowers" (Hosking 1999).

28. Nikita Mikhalkov's film *Kinfolk* (1982) depicts the farewell party for a young man going into the army as a great celebration. Between 1985 and 1991, 79 percent of the mothers of draftees reported that their sons had joined the army "with great aspirations" or "with a sense of duty" (see *Moskovskie novosti*, November 11, 1994). The situation changed drastically after 1991. By the end of the 1990s, the media were treating draft-dodgers like heroes. Avoiding army duty was seen as a form of civic protest. Army cadets had no prestige in society. According to a 1997 survey, only 18 percent of young Russians wanted to serve in the army (the survey was conducted by the Independent Institute of Social and National Issues, and published in *Moskovskii komsomolets* on February 2, 1998). Bribing recruiters and falsifying medical records were considered legitimate strategies for avoiding army service. Young people who were not able to skirt recruitment were viewed as misfits or failures because they did not have the resources (intellectual or financial) to avoid service. After 1991, one would be extremely hard pressed to find a rich Muscovite in the Russian armed forces. Russian families were no longer willing to sacrifice their children for any war, regardless of its official justification.

29. Vladimir Shubkin and David Konstantinovsky surveyed the prestige of various occupations in the Novosibirsk region in the early 1960s and at the end of the 1990s (see Shubkin 1970; see also Konstantinovsky 1999).

30. Draftees often escaped military duty by "convincing" doctors that they were sick with various physical or mental illnesses.

31. There are debates about the role that military commanders played as decision makers during the invasion of Afghanistan. As several sources show, the invasion in December 1979 went forward in spite of the strong reservations of the General Staff, its chief, Marshal Nikolai Ogarkov, and his deputy, Marshal Sergei Akhromeev. However, even if the General Staff was in favor of the invasion, there was no way it could pressure the political leadership either way. It could only give advice to the Politburo (Zabrodin 1991, p. 18).

32. Such a definition of the role of the army in Soviet society can be found in Garder 1966, p. 158.

33. Officials from the army and military industrial complex never gave any sort of ultimatum to the Soviet leadership (see Malei 1993). The myth about the KGB's influence on the leadership should also be dispelled. The heads of the army and KGB could influence leaders only with arguments. They attempted to demonstrate how valuable their advice would be if implemented, but there were no resignations made in protest of any official at any time.

34. For more about the role of "the imperial past" in the mentality of the Soviet officer corps, see Seaton and Seaton 1986, pp. 215–219.

35. Nikolai Ivnitsky based his deportation figures on a memo that Yagoda submitted to Stalin. The memo contained data on the numbers deported in 1930–1931. In this two-year period, roughly 241 thousand families were deported—a total of 1.2 million people (Ivnitsky 1990, 1996).

36. One of the revisionists who misunderstood the causes and character of collectivization was Sheila Fitzpatrick, who accepted Stalin's theory that kulak resistance was the cause of collectivization. She wrote, "Kulaks hid in the woods by day and returned to terrorize the village by night" (1982). Fitzpatrick suggested that "the regime reacted" by expropriating "kulaks and other trouble makers" (1982, p. 137). In her *Stalin's peasants* (1994b), Fitzpatrick changed the tone of her narration of Stalin's times but still presented the tragic transformation of Soviet peasants into serfs as simply unpleasant, "irksome," and an "annoyance and inconvenience to kolkhozniks." Fitzpatrick rejected her opponents' claims about the extremity of the famine, calling such claims an "almost pathological representation of the famine." She goes so far as to side with Stalin, suggesting that the peasants' "go slow strike" and "sabotage" were the real causes of the famine (1994b, p. 75). Her works after 1991 were much more balanced than before, particularly her book *Everyday Stalinism* (1999, pp. 122–125), but she remained a prisoner of many old, revisionist dogmas (on the evolution of her views, see Miner 1995, p. 30).

37. Revisionists also attacked the "totalitarianist" description of this gloomy chapter in Soviet history. Sheila Fitzpatrick and several of her supporters presented "the Soviet cultural revolution" in the 1920s and 1930s, with its persecution of the cream of the intelligentsia, as being sponsored by the masses and only reluctantly executed by Stalin. She also argued that the radicalism of Stalin's first five-year plan had been influenced by pressure "from below" (Fitzpatrick 1978, 1979). Echoing Fitzpatrick's analyses in the 1970s and 1980s, Siegelbaum accepted in 1997 the official version of the notorious Shakhty trial and the purges inside the party (Siegelbaum 1997, pp. 304–306).

38. First of all, revisionists tried to deny the scope of the repressions. Some scholars in the 1970s and 1980s estimated the number of victims of the "Great Purges" to be in the thousands, or at the very most, several hundred thousand. Jerry Hough wrote: "Western estimates of millions of deaths in the purge seem grossly inflated, but at a minimum tens of thousands died, and likely more" (1980, p. 38). For more about these estimates, see Hough and Fainsod 1979, pp. 176–177; Lewin 1974; Getty 1985; Thurston 1996. It is, however, also true that the totalitarianists went too far in the opposite direction, calculating the number of victims of Stalin's terror in the 1930s–1950s at up to 20 million. This estimate was not supported by the available data or even by elementary statistics taking into account the size of the population in 1930, which was about 108 million, including children (see Conquest 1990; Solzhenitsyn 1973; Shatunovskaia 1990). For more about the controversy concerning the number of Soviet victims, see Bacon 1994, pp. 101–122.

39. For more about these data, see the articles by KGB Deputy Chairman Viktor Pirozhkov (1990, p. 11); N. Katkov, vice chairman of the Committee of Party Control (1991); and Victor Luneev (1997, p. 180). See also the interview with KGB official Anatolii Grinenko in *Moskovskie novosti* (March 4, 1990). Other data were collected from the secret archives by Victor Zemskov, who worked for a special commission of the USSR's Academy of Sciences. These data do not conflict with the KGB numbers. By January 1, 1950, there were 579,000 political prisoners in the Gulag (see the Victor Zemskov interview in *Argumenty i fakty*, September 7, 1990; see also Zemskov, Getty, and Rittersporn 1993, p. 1022).

40. In the midst of famine, the USSR exported 1.8 million tons of grain to Western Europe; in 1933, 1 million tons were exported (Zavorotnyi and Polozhevez 1990).

41. In summarizing her feelings over four decades, and having named a chapter in her memoirs "Fear," Nadezhda Mandel'shtam wrote, "Akhmatova and I once con-

fessed to each other that the strongest feelings . . . stronger than love and jealousy, stronger than anything which is human, were fear and its derivations: the heinous awareness of shame, restrictions, and full helplessness" (Mandel'shtam 1990). The sentiments of Akhmatova and Mandel'shtam were echoed by filmmaker Evgenii Gabrilovich. Speaking rather philosophically about his life in the previous five decades, Gabrilovich commented, "As a close witness of those years, I can contend that the Academies of Sciences, Arts, and Marxism, in establishing the moving forces of history, have neglected a crucial, and perhaps even the most important, mainspring: fear. In order to understand so many of the puzzles, secrets, and absurdities of our complicated life, it is necessary to comprehend, most of all, the real significance of fear" (*Sovetskaia kul'tura*, June 17, 1989).

42. They took at face value the official Soviet materials on the people's participation in elections and other so-called "democratic institutions," such as trade unions and Communist youth leagues, and rebuked totalitarian theory primarily for its claim that the masses were "completely passive participants" in the state-society relationship (Lapidus 1975, pp. 115, 118; Hough 1977, p. 37; Hough 1980, p. 27; Fitzpatrick 1992, p. 126; Getty and Manning 1993, pp. 2–4; Friedgut 1977; Thurston 1986, pp. 213–34; Siegelbaum 1997, pp. 308, 310).

43. Attempting to portray Soviet society as politically similar to Western society, revisionists suggested that the masses played an active role not only in post-Stalin Russia but from the very beginning of the Soviet system. They described the October Revolution and the civil war as events during which the majority of the population actively supported the Bolsheviks; they usually disregarded developments in which the people were pitted against the Soviet leadership (see, for instance, Rosenberg 1988). Ronald Suny believed that Lenin's government was "potentially one of the most democratic in history" (1998). This view was derogated by Irina Pavlova's book (Pavlova 1993, pp. 44–65).

44. Dmitrii Volkogonov said that there were 11 million "seksots" (secret agents) in the Soviet Union by 1953. There was approximately 1 agent for every 15 citizens (Lanzman 1995). For comparison, according to various sources the proportion of informers to citizens in another totalitarian regime, the German Democratic Republic, was between 1:6 and 1:10. It is a well-established fact that in East Germany (with its population of 17 million people) the political police (Stasi) had 6 million individual files (Ash 1997; see also Koehler 1999; Cohen 1999, p. 3; for more about voluntary informers, see Sheila Fitzpatrick 1999, pp. 134–135).

45. A post-Soviet publication about Lev Landau, the famous physicist, suggests that his closest friends and colleagues studiously informed the KGB about every word he uttered (see a publication from the archive of the KGB about the monitoring of the scholar in *Komsomol'skaia pravda*, August 8, 1992).

Notes to Chapter 9: The Economy

1. See the description of the Soviet economic system as it functioned in the first year after the revolution, in Alexei Rykov's report to the presidium of the supreme economic council in September 1918 (Rykov 1990, pp. 55–67).

2. In 1921, the Russian economist Boris Bruzkus was certain that the Kremlin would build its economy on the basis of "natural socialism" and Marx's theory of value, and measure output only in labor units (Bruzkus 1995).

3. One sector of the economy worked exactly as these critics supposed. As they

suggested, the Gulag economy operated as a slave economy, with prisoners as the labor force. In Stalin's times it accounted for up to 10 percent of the GNP. The Gulag economy played an important role in the building industry. The prisoners of the Gulag were responsible for 13 percent of all work in this sector of the economy (Yemelin 1990). Forced labor was quite important also in several other sectors of the economy—for example, in the extraction of nonferrous metals (37 percent of the supply of gold in 1937), and in the timber industry (40 percent of timber in 1940) (Zemskov 1991a, p. 26; Ivanova 2000).

4. Political scientists and historians such as Seweryn Bialer (1986), Robert F. Byrnes (1983), Timothy Colton (1986), and David Lane (1985), and economists such as Paul Gregory and Robert Stuart (1974), underestimated how much the lack of consumer controls impacted the performance of the Soviet economy. Janos Kornai (1986) and to some degree Alec Nove (1980) paid special attention to this issue.

5. Manipulation of statistics became a "normal" feature of economic life. Eventually it dominated every facet of society (with the exception of the military).

6. This was particularly true for the so-called innovations in the organization of the economy. Many of these "innovations" (as was evident to the leadership and their subordinates) were fake. The main goal was to imitate dynamic activity. Among the fictitious innovations in the 1960s and 1970s were Nikita Khrushchev's various ideas about agriculture, and the "optimization of Soviet planning" with the help of mathematical methods (see Kontorovich and V. Shlapentokh 1986; see also V. Shlapentokh 1990).

7. According to VTsIOM data, 58 percent of the Soviet people in 1989 endorsed the statement "It is not important how you do your work, but how you report it"; only 20 percent did not share this view (Levada 1993, p. 72).

8. Comparing the Western-style economy to the command economy, clearly the market is superior from the perspective of mass consumption and technological progress. However, we should not disregard the fact that several spheres of Western society were similar to the Soviet society such as the army, sciences, and to some degree, bureaucracy and education.

9. For a discussion about the influence of ideology on the Soviet economy, see Nove 1979; Desai 1983.

10. In 1957, as an assistant professor of statistics at the Veterinary Institute, I was quite surprised when I discovered that the financial indicators (among them, the costs of milk and meat) for state farms were not at all affected by the attrition of cattle. I published an article on this issue in one official newspaper (V. Shlapentokh 1957).

11. The Bolsheviks believed in the almost magical potential of public property and the planning system. Interestingly, seventy years later their grandchildren maintained similar expectations regarding private property and the market in post-Communist Russia. Arkadii Gaidar, the grandfather of Yegor Gaidar (a major ideologue of liberal reforms), was one of the most fanatical Bolsheviks during the civil war; he later became a writer with deeply cemented beliefs in Marxist economic principles.

12. On the pluses and minuses of small private businesses in Soviet society, see Latsis 1987, pp. 40–41.

13. As a matter of fact, the Soviet leaders, from Stalin to Gorbachev, overestimated the readiness of the Russians to protest against the deterioration of their standard of living.

14. From 1990 to 1997, the intake of calories declined by 15 percent; protein, by 25 percent; fat, 25 percent; and carbohydrates, 8 percent. The consumption of meat declined 32 percent between 1990 and 1996 (Goskomstat 1998, p. 251). During the

same period, the consumption of milk and milk products dropped 38 percent; of eggs, 25 percent; fish, 40 percent; and sugar, 19 percent (Goskomstat 1997, p. 175).

15. Zara Witkin's memoir *An American engineer in Stalin's Russia* (1991) described his impressions of post-revolutionary Russia in the early 1930s. Witkin believed that the Soviet economy was plagued by the same bureaucratic inertia, incompetence, corruption, duplicity and inefficiency which would later be regarded as newly acquired features in the post-Stalin period. See also a book by another American engineer, who worked on the construction of the metallurgical complex in Magnitogorsk in the 1930s (Scott 1973). These and other books written by foreigners contrasted evidently with a series of ebullient "production novels" written by Il'ia Erenburg (1934) and Valentin Kataev (1933), who helped create a false picture of the Soviet economy in this period.

16. According to Khanin's computations, the annual rate of growth of the national income in 1951–1960 and the annual growth of capital goods were highest in the beginning of industrialization in 1928. Economic indicators such as the rate of growth of capital goods and labor productivity, as well as the use of raw material per units of production, were quite positive (Khanin 1991, pp. 174–196).

17. The meeting of the Central Committee in 1955 caused a sensation among Soviets because it contradicted Stalin's boasting about Soviet superiority in all domains of economic and social life. At this meeting, Khrushchev talked about the technological retardation of the economy in the areas of transportation and other branches. He continued to talk about this retardation for the next two years (Khrushchev 1957). Among other publications which influenced perceptions of the Soviet economy was the book by the vice minister of foreign trade, Nikolai Smeliakov (1970). His book offered a new perspective on the Western economy. The lectures and the book by Valerii Tereshchenko, an American business consultant and former Russian emigrant who returned to the motherland, also made an impression on the Soviet audience, with his description of the efficacy of the American economy (1963).

18. According to the CIA, the rate of growth of the Soviet GNP was 0.8 percent in 1979; in 1980, 1.2 percent; and in 1981, 1.8 percent (Central Intelligence Agency, *Handbook of economic statistics* 1982, p. 69).

19. The autonomy of directors was secured in several ways: First, the enterprise was declared "of all-union importance"; second, the director was given a high position in the state hierarchy (he might even combine the position of director with that of deputy minister, as did Ivan Likhachev, the director of the Moscow automobile factory); third, the party secretary of an enterprise was elevated to the rank of "special representative of the Central Committee" and was no longer under the command of the local party committee; fourth, he was "elected" (in fact, appointed) to the Central Committee of the party and to the Supreme Soviet; fifth, he had a special governmental telephone connection (the famous *vertushka*) which allowed him to call the general secretary, or other members of the Politburo directly (this was a symbol of great power in the USSR). These practices continued in post-Stalin times.

20. Stalin's speech in June 1931 was a hallmark of this type of change (Stalin 1952b, pp. 364–383). Another example of the new flexibility of the Kremlin during the 1930s was the creation of special stores that offered consumer goods in exchange for hard currency; later the Kremlin introduced so-called commercial stores, which sold consumer goods without coupons for high prices.

21. At the same time, the surplus of goods in low demand became a fixture of the Soviet economy in the last three decades of its existence. The surpluses were a direct

result of the mistakes made by the planning system and the refusal of consumers to purchase unwanted goods. In 1985, the stocks of unsold goods in retail and wholesale trades as well as in industry amounted to almost one third of the total value of the retail sales in the country. Roughly forty years earlier, in 1940, the same figure stood at 20 percent (TsSu SSSR 1986, p. 474).

22. My mother was a piano teacher in Stalin's times. On the eve of the war, she lived in Kiev, where she gave private piano lessons to numerous students. The revenue from this job allowed our family to live a decent life by the standards of the time. She never ran into any trouble with financial or state bodies. What is more, she also acted as a consumer in this type of economic activity: She hired a private tutor who taught me French and German.

23. During the war, I worked in Ufa, in a shop which belonged to an "industrial cooperation" that made buttons for army clothes. Even during the war the head of this small enterprise was permitted more freedom in various transactions than the director of a state company.

24. Considering the important role of the informal economy in Soviet society, it is hardly possible to accept the theories developed by Vitalii Naishul and Lev Timofeev, who described the Soviet economy as an almost totally "shadow" economy based on formally illegal private property owned by the nomenklatura (Naishul 1991; Timofeev 1992). These authors confused the means that managers applied with the goals of their economic activity. The motivation of this activity always remained closely related to the military targets of the Soviet command economy.

25. While many scholars, both Russian and Western, saw Stalin's rejection of the NEP as motivated only by his idealistic determination to develop a command economy, Grigorii Khanin, a prominent Russian economist, took the opposite view in 1989. He argued that in 1928 the NEP, in spite of the early advances made, was still far from achieving the economic performance of 1913 (labor productivity, for instance, was 23 percent lower). Khanin believed that the NEP had no future and had exhausted its potential by 1928. Without huge new investments, it could not go forward. To get these investments from internal resources, given the political structure, was impossible. This, according to Khanin, made a return to the planning system and coercive accumulation unavoidable for Soviet leaders, whose decisions were quite rational and not at all utopian (Khanin 1989b, 1993).

26. Some Russian and Western authors, in their anti-Stalin critiques, refused to recognize the necessity of rapid industrialization in the country. They dismissed the threat of war, even after 1933. Others discredited Soviet industrialization and its importance in the war with Hitler, pointing out that early in the war the Germans occupied territory where many Soviet industrial centers were located. However, they neglect the fact that the leadership was able to evacuate a considerable part of Soviet industry to the East (Burganov 1989, pp. 34–35).

27. Ten years after the collapse of the Soviet Union, former Soviet engineers and scholars still boasted about their development of a new, rocket-propelled torpedo in the late 1970s. This torpedo was able to travel at extremely high speed underwater. One American expert noted, "It was more advanced than ours in many respects." He added, "We were shocked when it appeared." In 2000, the updated version of this torpedo was seemingly beyond American achievements (Tyler 2000).

28. Soviet physics made fantastic progress and reached world standards in the 1930s, amidst the growing mass terror. This fact stands as a strong rebuttal to those who use only negatives in describing the Communist past (Gorelik 1992).

29. For instance, even during the 1970s and 1980s (when the country was completely calm), if the payment of salaries at the Kirov tractor factory in Leningrad had been postponed for even two days, it would have caused an emergency of national proportions. The general secretary would have been informed immediately. The director of the enterprise and the director of the local banks would have been fired the next day. The deputy minister and possibly the minister responsible for the tractor industry would have been strongly reprimanded, and the workers would have received their salaries as well as a formal apology.

30. "Wild vacationers" were people who, for various reasons, could not obtain a vacation package at a government-funded resort or rest home. Without lodging reservations or concrete plans, they ventured to resort cities and tried to rent rooms in private houses. Comfortable accommodations were limited and difficult to find.

31. It is possible to speak about the quick adjustment of the Soviet people to the conditions of their life during the prewar period, particularly after collectivization and the years of hunger. With the cancellation of rationing in December 1934, life improved significantly. This fact was reflected in the Harvard Project, which studied displaced persons in the 1950s. Seventy-seven percent of all professionals, 70 percent of semi-professionals, and 62 percent of skilled workers reported being "satisfied" with their jobs. The data on job satisfaction in the United States were quite similar. The same question brought the following U.S. response: 82 percent, 82 percent, and 84 percent respectively (the numbers for West Germany were 75 percent, 65 percent, and 47 percent respectively). Russian salary satisfaction was also quite high: 84–86 percent among professionals and managers; 77 percent among white-collar employees; and 73 percent among skilled workers (Inkeles and Bauer 1968, pp. 104, 114).

32. No more than 8 percent of men and 5 percent of women were inclined to use additional free time (if they had it) for moonlighting in attempts to earn extra money (Gordon and Klopov 1972).

33. According to various sources, 30 to 40 percent of workers had low labor discipline, yet only a few of them ran the risk of being fired during this period (V. Shlapentokh 1989, pp. 52–53).

34. From the author's personal archive.

35. In the 1980s, about half of all families complained about shortages of meat (Borodkin 1990, p. 75).

36. In 1990, only 3 percent of the population in Russia could afford products sold on the "free market" (Goskomstat 1991b, p. 282). These products were of much higher quality than what could be found in the state stores.

37. A few publications on this subject appeared in the late 1970s (see Timofeev 1982; see also V. Shlapentokh 1990).

38. In 1989, the existence of private property was supported by only 56 percent of Russians (Levada 1990, pp. 70, 83).

39. The same change of attitudes may have occurred even if the situation improved significantly. As Tocqueville explained, the discontent of people prior to the French Revolution grew exactly when life in the country was objectively improving (Tocqueville 1955).

40. According to calculations performed by the CIA, the growth of the Soviet GNP between 1981–1985 was 1.8 percent per year. This was a higher rate than between 1979–1981, when it was almost zero (data from the U.S. Congress, Joint Economic Committee, Measures of Soviet Gross National Product in 1982 prices, Washington, DC: GPO, 1990).

41. This phenomenon was repeated in the early 1990s. While most Russians bemoaned the crisis of their economy, they considered their individual economic status quite tolerable.

42. For a detailed analysis, see Ellman and Kontorovich 1998.

Notes to Chapter 10: Public Opinion

1. My view about the mass approval or neutrality of the Soviet citizenry conflicts with the views of several other researchers (see Figes 1996b; Miner 1997; Herzberg 1996). Also important to note here is that many conservative writers almost completely ignore public opinion in their analyses of the USSR. The books of two of the most prominent critics of Communism, Richard Pipes (1993) and Martin Malia (1994; 1999), mostly avoid the issue of public opinion and the Russian attitudes toward the Bolshevik regime.

2. This was the problem with Vladimir Brovkin's book *Russia after Lenin* (1998), which was based on numerous casual facts taken from party, Komsomol, and GPU archives. He ignored many other sources of information (for instance, memoirs, and other forms of media). The author offered no external validation for his images of the era, and did not devote one line in his book to an analysis of his sources. Brovkin said nothing about the validity of those historical sources. Meanwhile, he based major conclusions on the reports of inspectors of the party, Komsomol, and GPU bodies, who only looked for "negative facts" as dictated by their supervisors (Brovkin 1998). Sarah Davies's book on public opinion in Stalin's Russia, which was based on the study of the Leningrad archive, is very different. Appraising Soviet Russia with sober eyes (it is possible to place her in the totalitarian school of thought), she carefully evaluated the validity of her sources and compared them with each other, trying to come up with a clear idea about the representativeness of her data (S. Davies 1997, pp. 9–17). However, in some cases, Davies also forgot about the representativeness of her data; she wrote, for example, "The popular mood was summed up in a letter written in April 1938 by a foreman, who had been a worker since before 1917" (p. 38).

3. For more about the dual mentality of the Soviet people, see V. Shlapentokh 1985b; 1986. For a brilliant description of this mentality, see Yashin 1954.

4. This view is supported by several researchers of public opinion, including Detlev Peukert (1989 p. 65), who studied public opinion in Nazi Germany; Luisa Passerini (1987), who studied popular attitudes of Italian fascism; and Sarah Davies, who studied Soviet public opinion in Stalin's time (1997, p. 6).

5. The public mind is usually more eclectic in societies with political freedoms and pluralism in the media. In American society, a significant number of people consider themselves advocates of a certain ideology, though the number of "pure ideologists" is quite low (see the classic article on this subject in Converse 1964, pp. 206–261).

6. See the letters from the Soviet archives cited by Sarah Davies (1997, pp. 41–42). In the letters, the authors grumbled about the long lines for consumer goods and the rampant profiteering from scarce materials, but these comments cannot be treated as "anti-Soviet" in nature, even if the NKVD labeled them in this way at the time.

7. Sarah Davies cited data from Soviet archives about the number of anti-Soviet agitation cases that were recorded by the authorities. Before the mass terror in 1934, there were 16,900 such cases; in 1937, the number jumped to 234,300; in 1940, it declined to 18,300 cases. It would be ludicrous to interpret these data as showing a growth in resistance to the regime. Davies correctly noted that these data reflected mostly the changes in the severity of repressions (S. Davies 1997, p. 16).

8. The following story is a vignette from my life in the Soviet Union. In 1977, I complained to a representative from the Central Committee that my daughter was not admitted to the mathematical college of Moscow University because of flagrant discrimination during the admittance exams (Jewish applicants were given mathematical problems that were two or three times more difficult than non-Jewish applicants). When I explained that the university policy not only discriminated against my daughter but against all Jewish applicants, the representative interrupted me, saying in an angry tone, "Do not generalize, talk only about your daughter." I told him that "generalizations" were part of my profession. My daughter, Alexandra Shlapentokh, is currently a full professor of mathematics at an American university.

9. Vaclav Havel wrote that the Stalinist system "deliberately created a specific structure of values and models of behavior" which were "a perverted structure, one that went against all the natural tendencies of life." However, he conceded that "society nevertheless internalized it, or rather was forced to internalize it." This was also true of Czechoslovakia, a country with strong democratic traditions, which needed only two decades to internalize Communist values (Havel 1993, p. 8).

10. Galina Shtange, the wife of a Moscow non party member and professor at the Institute of Railroad Engineering, kept a diary. In her early fifties, Galina wrote on December 6, 1936, "Last night Stalin's new Constitution was adopted. I won't say anything about it; I feel as the rest of the country, i.e., absolute, infinite delight." She also told us how she and the members of her family were in haste to be the first at the election station during the first Soviet election in accordance with the new Constitution on December 12, 1937; this was a highly celebrated occasion in the Soviet media and deemed a gigantic progress in socialist democracy. Galina's family arrived at the station at 6 A.M. only to find a crowd of people who also wanted the honor of casting the first votes. After the voting, Galina wrote, "I felt a kind of excitement in my soul, I don't know why, and there was even a lump in my throat." Galina's sister Olga wrote her a letter explaining her own elation with the same election (Garros, Korenevskaya, and Lahusen 1995, pp. 181, 205–206). I myself also remember this day (I was then a thirteen-year-old boy and a member of a pioneer team in Kiev) and the general euphoria in favor of the regime. The diary of Russian engineer Leonid Potemkin is also pro-Soviet. The diary is full of examples of the author's vigorous support for every political campaign that took place in the country, including the show trials. He reports that he could not find words to express his joy at being appointed a political agitator. He enjoyed all of the ideologically loaded Soviet movies, including *Circus* (Garros, Korenevskaya, and Lahusen 1995, pp. 258, 260, 283, 288). Fedor Smirnov, a middle-level employee, ended his diary in 1938 with a glorification of Stalin (ibid., p. 95).

11. As editor of the liberal Russian magazine *Soiuz*, Lev Korneshov responded to a letter to the editor that ardently defended Stalin. Korneshov wrote, "Against all evidence, we were convinced that our life then (under Stalin) was indeed full of happiness, and nothing could shake this belief" (1990, p. 16).

12. The importance of these songs was indeed great. Dunaevsky, for instance, was twice awarded the Stalin Prize.

13. Five decades later, Oskar Kurganov wrote about the people's warm reaction to the safe return of the polar research team led by Papanin. Against those who claimed that the greeting was false and based only on fear, Kurganov insisted the people's celebration was genuine. He wrote, "It was Stalin who managed to carry these people away with his great, fantastic, utopian ideas about the happy future for all and not only the chosen few" (Kurganov 1996). In his turn, American author Michael Ignatieff

accepted this opinion. Having read the collection of the Russian diaries edited by Garros, Korenevskaya, and Lahusen (1995), he wrote, "For millions of ordinary people, the Stalinist slogan 'life has become better, comrades, life has become happier' felt profoundly true" (Ignatieff 1996, p. 6).

14. In most cases, if people were critical of the regime, they adopted a super-patriotic stance that advocated further efforts to sustain the country. In 1939, many people strongly disagreed with the official foreign policy toward Germany. They opposed the Soviet-German Pact in 1939, distrusted Hitler's intentions, and were quite skeptical about Stalin's evident compromise with Hitler (S. Davies 1997, p. 98).

15. Alexander Solzhenitsyn called this the "dear war of my generation." He continued, "And the amazing influence of this political ideology, of this heartless earthly religion of socialism, with what force it sweeps away young souls, with what spurious lucidity it shows them a seemingly simple solution to any problem!" (Solzhenitsyn 1991).

16. Solzhenitsyn wrote extensively about this phenomenon in The Gulag archipelago (1973). This "old Bolshevik phenomenon" is also discussed in Arthur Koestler's Darkness at noon (1941).

17. The people's real perceptions of Soviet reality were manifested quite clearly in the first hours, days, and weeks after their arrests. Most who were seized by the political police in the 1930s believed that they had been arrested by mistake. Later, having come to terms with their arrest, many continued to support the official picture of Soviet society. In his First circle (1968), Solzhenitsyn described the fiery debates about the nature of society among prisoners in the so-called Sharashki, a special-regime prison for privileged professionals involved in the construction of new weapons. Solzhenitsyn's hero Rubin, who was based on the real person Lev Kopelev, passionately defended the existing order against the committed enemies of the Soviet system (1968; see R. Medvedev 1974, p. 832).

18. Anyone who lived in Stalin's time (and even later) met many fanatics among their colleagues, neighbors, and acquaintances. I vividly remember Victor Shtein, my friend and fellow student at Kiev University in 1946–1948, who was fanatically devoted to the official ideology.

19. Leonid Potemkin, who finished his mining career in the Soviet Union as an official in the administration of the mining industry, recounted with joy in his diary the day he was inducted into the Komsomol (see Garros, Korenevskaya, and Lahusen 1995, pp. 254–255).

20. Parents with alternative social, moral, and religious views were vexed by their inability to transfer these values to their children. See, for instance, the diary of Andrei Arzhilovsky, a hater of the Soviet system, who described how he clenched his teeth when his daughter exclaimed her desire to join the pioneers (Garros, Korenevskaya, and Lahusen 1995, p. 113).

21. Dmitrii Volkogonov, former deputy chief of the directorate of political education of the Soviet army and former head of Soviet foreign intelligence, and Prime Minister Evgenii Primakov were among the many people with such family backgrounds.

22. One of Alexander Bek's novels, Novoe naznachenie (1987), describes a high-level Russian manager, Alexander Anisimov. As Bek's novel demonstrates, the major device for dealing with disharmony between official images and reality was to avoid all issues which were beyond everyday work; even the arrest and murder of his brother Ivan did not push Anisimov to reconsider the official picture of life in the country.

23. Some even gloated over the fate of party fanatics who implemented Stalin's mass terror and then became its victims (Radzinsky 1995).

24. Several movies of the 1930s, such as Fridrikh Ermler's *A great citizen* (1938–1939), as well as historical films such as Sergei Eisenstein's *Alexander Nevsky* (1938) and *Ivan the Terrible* (1945) and Petrov's *Peter the First* (1937–1939), substantiated the merciless extermination of "domestic enemies." Most people accepted these movies at face value (see D. Shlapentokh and V. Shlapentokh 1993, pp. 108–110).

25. Vladimir Putin asserted, in a book published on the eve of his election as the Russian president in March 2000, that when he volunteered to work in the KGB in the early 1970s he had no real knowledge of the terror in the 1930s (see Putin 2000, p. 19).

26. See the memoirs of Soviet dissidents Petr Grigorenko (1982), Raisa Orlova (1983), and Galina Vishnevskaia (1984).

27. Drawing from the empirical evidence of his careful study of life in Magnitogorsk in the 1930s, Stephen Kotkin was right when he wrote that the expressions of love for Stalin "were often deeply laden with affect and revealed a devout quality transcending reasonable arguments" (Kotkin 1995, p. 227).

28. According to his diary, Vladimir Stavsky, an official writer of the 1930s, was overwhelmed with his feelings toward a woman, apparently his mistress. He used the most passionate words, remembering with rapture their trysts. In the eulogy of his carnal love, he enmeshed the name of Stalin as a God who protected their love: "I want to love, together with the epoch, together with Stalin, together with you, my beloved, my darling" (Garros, Korenevskaya, and Lahusen 1995, p. 241).

29. As one Russian liberal recollected in 1990 during the ardent anti-Stalin campaign, "In a few churches that had been restored in the years of the war, people worshiped him, they addressed prayers to him as to Jesus Christ" (Korneshov 1990, p. 16).

30. For example, the media were flooded with proposals to rename Moscow "Stalin" (see "Pis'ma iz daleka").

31. The construction of the Magnitogorsk metallurgical plant was headed by the 26-year-old Ia. Guge, who coined the slogan "Build the blast furnace on time!" Two thousand workers endured incredibly harsh conditions to accomplish this goal, working around the clock. Many voluntarily worked weekends. Children and housewives also participated in the "storm" work (Borisov and Ivanov 1989, pp. 348–350). As Stephen Kotkin wrote, describing the labor enthusiasm during the construction of this plant, "The people of Magnitogorsk took pride in themselves for their accomplishments and rewards, and felt disappointment in their failures" (Kotkin 1995, p. 224).

32. For the debates on the Stakhanov movement, see V. Shlapentokh 1985a; Siegelbaum 1988; Kotkin 1995, pp. 207–215.

33. I remember vividly how proud I was to become a Pioneer on November 5, 1936, and a member of the Komsomol in 1942. These were important days in my Soviet life. However, in 1947–1948, my views and those of my closest friend, Isaak Kantorovich, changed radically while we were students at Kiev University. We became extremely critical of the regime, which we equated with Nazism.

34. Reviewing the various data in the Russian archives in St. Petersburg, Sarah Davies noted that the most acerbic statements against the system in the mid-1930s were made by the poorest workers whose "kids do not eat black bread" (S. Davies 1997, p. 28). Two Russian authors discovered compositions written by students in several rural high schools, during the winter of 1929. These compositions were full of apprehensions about hunger and also told of their parents' hatred of the regime (Bordiugov and Kozlov 1988).

35. In 1925, V. Izmozik calculated the number of "positive" and "negative" letters sent by soldiers in the Red Army to the countryside and from their relatives in the

countryside to the soldiers. While the soldiers sent 234 "positive" letters and 268 "negative" letters to the countryside, their relatives returned 77 "positive" and 257 "negative" letters (Izmozik 1995b, p. 34). In 1930, as Olga Velikanova discovered, the soldiers sent 447 "positive" letters and only 5 "negative" letters; their relatives sent the soldiers 338 "positive" and 1,077 "negative" letters (Olga Velikanova, "Svodki o politicheskikh nastroeniiakh v byvshikh partiinykh arkhivakh kak istoricheskii istochnik," unpublished).

36. According to Naum Jasny, in 1932–1933 the real wages of workers were only 49 percent of the 1928 wage level; by 1937, wages had risen to about 60 percent of the 1928 level (Jasny 1957, p. 41).

37. My grandfather, Yakov Izraelevich Gurevich, who before the revolution owned a few pharmacies, hated the Soviet regime (only the war with Germany somewhat reconciled him with the Bolsheviks). He used to say to my grandmother, "Pasha, we are on the eve of great events." What he meant was that the collapse of the Communist order was imminent. He died soon after the war, with a bitter understanding that his numerous prophecies were unlikely to be fulfilled.

38. Solzhenitsyn wrote about prisoners in the Gulag who harbored such desires, in *The Gulag archipelago* (1973).

39. The authors of the project were fully aware of the nature of their sample (Inkeles and Bauer 1968, pp. 25–40).

40. Three quarters of the respondents claimed (in some cases, probably in order to please their American interviewers) that they or some member of their family had been arrested (Inkeles and Bauer 1968, pp. 35–36).

41. According to the authors of the project, "The number of those who gave 'flattering' or 'distorted' answers (i.e., praise for subjects which they understood minimally) were generally low" (Inkeles and Bauer 1968, pp. 45, 47). The authors showed that the responses of people with "high flattery" and "low flattery" in most cases were not radically different.

42. The Russians assessed their lives as much worse in the 1990s than in the 1970s. According to the longitudinal studies of VTsIOM in 1992–1998, the number of respondents who were dissatisfied with their lives almost never fell below 50–60 percent (see VTsIOM, *Monitoring obshchestvennogo mneniia*, 1992–1998).

43. Brovkin used a large amount of data from the archives about the apolitical behavior of workers and peasants in the late 1920s; he wrote about their singular focus on everyday life and their disregard for party propaganda (Brovkin 1998).

44. This was the opinion of the prominent Russian Menshevik historian Boris Nikolaevsky, who even spoke of "mass defeatism" during the war (Nikolaevsky 1948a, 1948b, pp. 209–234; see also Volkogonov 1998b; Kalinin 1998).

45. When I was a teenager, my mother was approached during the war by the KGB and asked to cooperate as an informer. She was terribly upset by the proposition and even contemplated suicide.

46. The day that marks the victory of WWII was the most respected holiday in Soviet times. This holiday maintained its popularity in post-Soviet Russia (Levada 1993).

47. In the words of British historian Richard Overy, "Whether friend or foe of the regime, Russians were united over the ultimate wound the Germans inflicted on them" (Overy 1998a, p. 329).

48. Many Soviets criticized the regime for its ill-preparedness for the war with Germany (see Toman 1991, pp. 158–173). Stalin also recognized this failure and sought to bolster the people's loyalty to the regime. In a speech given on May 24, 1945, he

noted: "In other countries, after such defeats, people would say to their government, 'Go away, we will find some solution to our problems without you.' Russians, however, did not follow this pattern of behavior" (see Stalin's speech in *Zavtra* 18, 1995).

49. A Moscow historian asserted that some prisoners sincerely participated in patriotic campaigns inside the Gulag (i.e., the collection of warm clothes for the army, and the overfulfillment of production quotas). See Yemelin 1990.

50. According to Dmitrii Volkogonov, "Almost one million Soviet citizens did all they could to avoid returning to the motherland" (Volkogonov 1995, p. 200).

51. The most compelling fact is the size of Russian General Andrei Vlasov's army, which comprised thousands of Soviet soldiers who as prisoners of war joined the Germans to fight the Soviet army. While many authors contended that most of these soldiers changed sides only as a way to escape certain death in German prison camps, some writers saw these soldiers as committed enemies of Stalin's Russia (see Reitlinger 1960; Tepliakov 1990, pp. 8–9). While Russians made up the majority of German prisoners of war, they represented a minority in the military units assembled by the Germans to fight against the Soviet army. Non-Russians there greatly outnumbered Russians. By May 20, 1945, these military units comprised 43,000 Russians, 104,000 Latvians, 36,800 Lithuanians, 36,500 Azerbaijanis, 22,500 Tatars from Volga and Crimea; and 10,000 Estonians (Tepliakov 1990).

52. In *Doctor Zhivago*, Boris Pasternak wrote about the days in the aftermath of the war as having "the presentiment of freedom in the air."

53. The attitudes of the Russian masses toward the media therefore can be understood as an indirect sign of popular attitudes toward the system; the people identified the media with power. In general, attitudes toward the media were positive among most Russians. No less than two thirds of the Soviet people were satisfied with newspapers and TV before 1985 (see Grushin and Onikov 1980; see also V. Shlapentokh 1969a, 1969b).

54. Soviet journalists before the first surveys strongly overestimated (between 5 and 20 times) the number of readers with negative attitudes toward newspapers (see V. Shlapentokh 1969a, 1969b; Davydchenkov 1970).

55. In 1989, Levada found that 70 percent of Soviets under age 20, and 60 percent of those over 20, never even heard of the dissident movement. Even in 1988, only 1.5 percent of the respondents to a VTsIOM survey named the leading Soviet dissident Andrei Sakharov as "the man of the year" (Levada 1993, pp. 194–195, 258).

56. According to my own surveys of the readers of Russian newspapers *(Pravda, Izvestiia, Literaturnaia gazeta*, and *Trud)*, which encompassed practically the whole educated class in the country, 20 percent confessed straightforwardly that they listened to foreign radio (V. Shlapentokh 1969b, 1970).

57. In this latest book, Moscow pollster Boris Grushin characterized the Soviet people by classifying them into three groups, based on the empirical data that he collected during Khrushchev's period. The three groups included: Active supporters of the regime (mostly members of the party and state apparatus, people from the nontechnical intelligentsia, such as teachers and cultural workers, as well as "true believers" scattered throughout the general population); conformists (hardworking people in various industries who earned a decent living); and nonconformists (potential or actual political dissidents). According to Grushin, the majority of the Soviet people were "conformists" (Grushin 2001, pp. 534–537, see also pp. 252–253). Another Moscow pollster, Yurii Levada, submitted that no less than 70–80 percent of the Soviet population supported the regime during the post-Stalin period (Levada 2001, p. 14).

58. Vladimir Bukovsky's assertions that "Soviet society lived on a volcano," and that millions of Russians were ready to join the struggle against the Kremlin if they had been encouraged by the West and the Russian intelligentsia, is utterly "utopian" (Bukovsky 1995, pp. 133–134). Richard Pipes evidently shared this view, suggesting that Russians "pretended to conform while holding their private and often strong opinion to themselves." To say that they were dominated by official ideology "is grossly unfair" (Pipes 1999, p. 107). However, reflecting on the longevity of the Soviet system in the end of his big book on the Bolshevik regime, Pipes melancholically noted that the regime "had the support of its own people" (Pipes 1993a, p. 511). Two post-Soviet authors, belonging to the same school of thought as Pipes, simply avoided the discussion of popular attitudes toward the regime in their books on Soviet totalitarianism (see Pavlova 1993; and Kurskova 2000).

59. Forty-one percent of respondents to a VTsIOM survey supported "equality in income," against 38 percent who emphasized the necessity of differentiation in income as a stimulus to productivity (Levada 1993, p. 57).

60. See, for instance, the confession of Sergei Kirienko, a prominent Russian liberal and former prime minister (1998).

61. When asked in 1998 about the cause of the Soviet collapse, only 20 percent of respondents pointed to the "inefficacy of the socialist system" (in 1995, the figure was 23 percent); 63 percent blamed the Soviet leaders (VTsIOM, *Bulletin*, No. 6, 1998, p. 14). The November 1998 survey conducted by the Fund of Public Opinion found that 48 percent of Russians rejected capitalism as a good system for Russia and only 30 percent were in favor of it (*Bulletin*, Internet, November 27, 1998). In a survey of 2,000 people carried out by the Russian Institute for the Study of Social and National Issues in October 1998, 58 percent of respondents favored the nationalization of banks, 87 percent demanded the same for strategic branches of the economy (oil and gas industries, electricity, and others), and 70 percent were strongly against the buying and selling of land (Gorshkov 1998).

62. In the late 1960s, 28 percent of people in the Penza region and 22 percent in the Voronezh region declared themselves "believers." Among respondents under age 30, the proportion of believers was only 5 percent; among those older than 60, it was 40 percent. In rural areas the proportion of believers was two to three times greater than in the cities (Pivovarov 1974, p. 155; Yablokov 1979, pp. 139–140).

63. After the fall of the Soviet Union, Eduard Shevardnadze, who formerly had headed the Georgian KGB and had been a first secretary, became the president of the independent Georgian Republic. In this new capacity, he was baptized in the Orthodox church in 1992 (see Stanley 1999).

64. Among the intelligentsia in the Penza region, 4 percent were "believers"; the proportions among clerical workers, workers, and collective farmers were 4 percent, 8 percent, and 28 percent, respectively (Yablokov 1979, p. 140).

65. Various authors who were committed enemies of Stalin's regime have attested in their memoirs that Vladimir Vernadsky's diary entry in 1940, which stated that "the crowd supports Stalin," was true (Vernadsky 1992). The same views were conveyed by dissidents who published books in the West before glasnost (Orlova 1983; Kopelev 1975, 1978; Grigorenko 1982; Ulanovskaia and Ulanovskaia 1982) as well as in numerous publications in Russia after 1985.

66. Some fear lingered in the Russian mind, connected with the possibility of a new war. This fear was, however, relatively weak, since the official ideology promoted the idea of detente rather than confrontation with foreign powers. Even during

the Cuban missile crisis in October 1962, when the world was indeed on the verge of a nuclear catastrophe, the Soviet people remained calm. Only in the late 1960s, when Soviet-Chinese relations became quite tense, did the fear of war begin to spread somewhat in the country. It spread with low intensity, however, as the Kremlin sought to downplay catastrophic visions of the "yellow peril." Andrei Amalrik's famous book *Will the Soviet Union survive until 1984?* (1970), in which he predicted an outbreak of war between the USSR and China, only partially reflected the mood of the country.

67. Alexander Shpagin compared the mentality of Russian intellectuals of the 1970s and 1980s to their ancestors of the Silver Age (1890s to 1917), who were haunted by all kinds of apocalyptic fears. He wrote: "Then, in 'the period of stagnation' (Brezhnev's period) there was not a similar fear in the country. The apocalyptic presentiment and apprehensiveness which tore the personality into parts was not typical for the 1970s and 1980s" (Shpagin 1994). At worst, the heroes of movies and novels of the later era experienced only "little apocalypses," which meant only the destruction of their personal illusions about the Soviet world.

68. The leaflets of emigrant organization Russkoe Delo (March 1953) described "one insurrection after another," citing the "Altai rebellion" (1930–1934), Kubansk (1931), and Central Asia (1930–1931).

69. According to official data (evidently inflated by the NKVD), there were 2,200 different forms of discontent in the countryside in 1930. Some types were more serious than others, but none posed a real threat to the regime (Ivnitsky 1990). According to one Soviet historian, in January–March 1930, there were "two thousand anti–collective farm insurrections." This figure jarred with other data cited by the same author on the same page. These data reported that in January 1930 there were only "11 mass disturbances" (Kuleshov 1990, p. 259).

70. In 1946, a group of 15 to 20 "bandits, the descendants of kulak families," as reported in the minutes of the Cheliabinsk regional party committee, "attacked the managers and students of vocational schools who came for harvesting and the procurement of agricultural products." The regional committee ascribed this event to the chairman of a collective farm, who in the close circle of his relatives spoke very critically of peasants in Soviet society (*Slovo* 6, 1991). This event was very peculiar even for the postwar period. The full resignation of peasants to their fate during collectivization and the postwar period was described by Andrei Platonov in his novel *Chevengur* (1978) and by Boris Mozhaev in his novel *Zhizn' Fedora Kuz'kina* (1989).

71. The rebellion was headed by Mark Retiunin, who had been sentenced for banditism. He recruited 82 prisoners (12 others joined in later), who had been sent to the Gulag for "counterrevolutionary activity." In the beginning, the uprising was quite successful. The rebels seized Us-Usa, the district center, then fought with the military troops of the camp. During the struggle the troops sustained significant losses (33 were killed, 72 wounded). Forty-eight of the rebels were killed and 6 committed suicide. The authorities believed the goals of the rebels included the expansion of the revolt to the whole Komi republic, the release of all prisoners, the creation of their own army, the restoration of private property, and the establishment of contacts with Nazi Germany. Russian historians, however, supposed that the rebels only wanted to "leave the area and flee." See "Society memorial" ("Otriad Osobogo naznacheniia"), *Nezavisimaia gazeta*, January 23, 1992.

72. Individual protesters resorted mostly to the secret spreading of leaflets, like the hero in Hans Fallada's famous novel, *Jeder sterbt fur sich allein* (1964). A Russian edition of this antifascist novel was published in postwar Russia and was extremely

popular. It told the story of a German married couple who secretly disseminated anti-Nazi postcards in Berlin. The couple acted out their hatred of the Nazi regime in complete isolation from others. In the end, they were captured and put to death. Many of the book's readers perceived the developments in this novel as directly related to the Soviet Union. I and my close friend Isaak Kantorovich certainly took the story to heart in 1947–1948. We understood the feeling of isolation one experiences when hiding one's hatred of the system.

73. Gennadii Bordiugov and Vladimir Kozlov cited several letters that were very critical of Stalin during collectivization (1988, p. 11, 1992). Sarah Davies cited numerous archived letters addressed to the authorities or media which evidently looked like challenges to the system (S. Davies 1997, pp. 38–39, 41, 53, 94–95).

74. I knew from my experience working for *Literaturnaia gazeta* in the 1960s and 1970s that this newspaper's department of letters regularly sent a report to the KGB. The department highlighted any letter from its readership that contained "anti-Soviet" elements.

75. Torn between the necessity of expressing their feelings and the fear of doing so, some resorted to coding their diaries. Classical historian Solomon Lurie encoded his diary in 1947 using Latin and a Cypriot syllabary (R. Davies 1997, pp. 188–189).

76. The famous writer Mikhail Prishvin was among those who wrote diaries that were extremely critical of the Soviet regime. Andrei Arzhilovsky, a skilled farmer and community activist from the Tiumen region, was arrested by the Cheka in 1919. He was released in 1923 but imprisoned again in 1929. After his second release in 1936, he was arrested again in 1937 and executed the same year. During his imprisonment, he protested his treatment boldly, and kept a dangerously blunt diary at all times, even in the camps (Garros, Korenevskaya, and Lahusen 1995, pp. 111–165). Among other authors who kept diaries were Stepan Podlubny, the son of a deported kulak (ibid., pp. 293–332), Liubov Shaporina, the wife of the famous composer (ibid., pp. 333–382), and Maria Svanidze, the sister-in-law of Stalin's first wife (*Istochnik* 1, 1993, p. 26).

77. Roi Medvedev mentions two other anti-Stalinist manuscripts—one written in 1948–1949 by A. Spunde, a member of the first Soviet government, who after his expulsion from the party in 1938 worked as a bookkeeper in commerce; the other, by B. Griazny, a former party member in the Gulag, in 1940 (R. Medvedev 1974, pp. 976–977).

78. According to Vladlen Izmozik (1995b, p. 8), in one year (from October 1923 to October 1924), the workers of the department of political control of the GPU read 5 million letters and 8 million telegrams (see also Izmozik 1995a, 1995c).

79. A group of leading party members who were critical of Stalin's leadership (Alexander Smirnov, Nikolai Eismont and V. Tolmachev) also was detected by the GPU and later disappeared in the Gulag. A letter written by Moisei Frumkin (an old revolutionary and in the late 1920s a deputy minister of finance) was sent to the members of the Politburo in 1928. The prevailing sentiment in this letter was loyalty to Soviet ideology, but the content was a critique of Stalin's policy in the countryside. The letter was cited by historians of glasnost as a rare case of courage. Frumkin's life ended in the Gulag in 1938 (see Kossakovsky 1990). Beso Lominadze and Sergei Syrtsov, two prominent Communists, dared confess to each other their dissatisfaction with developments in the country in the autumn of 1929. An informer overheard their comments and the two men were expelled from the Central Committee and later perished in the Gulag (Service 1998, pp. 187–188).

80. One such article was published by the secretary of the Mordovian party committee in a local newspaper. The author bravely wrote, "Collective farmers have been

left with their problems." The Central Committee condemned this article as "noxious" (Aksenov 1991, pp. 198–199).

81. For instance, a student at the military political college, a war veteran, sent a letter to Georgii Malenkov, then the secretary of the party, in which he sharply criticized the situation on the collective farms, daring even to cite peasants who asked when the collective farms would be dismantled (Aksenov 1991, pp. 199–200).

82. Volkogonov offered a different story about Gordov. According to his source (*Izvestiia TsK KPSS* 8, 1991, pp. 197–221), Gordov was executed because he and his friend had listened to complaints from former Marshal Grigorii Kulikov about Stalin after the war (Volkogonov 1995, p. 216).

83. Japanese author Chiama Esiaki, in his book *The Japanese plans for a terrorist attempt on Stalin's life* (cited by Russian author Piotr Koroviakovsky), claims that Japanese agents, headed by Grigorii Liushkov (a leading NKVD officer in Khabarovsk who defected in 1938 to Manchuria), tried to blow up the Lenin mausoleum on May 1, 1939 (see Koroviakovsky 1990).

84. The insurrection of prisoners in the concentration camps in Norilsk continued for 100 days but was mercilessly crushed, like all the uprisings that had preceded it (Bukin 1998).

85. See Andropov's memo to the Central Committee in Bukovsky 1995, pp. 113, 129–130.

86. Some post-Soviet authors tried to enhance the scope of resistance to the Soviet system. Galina Kurskova contended that in the 1970s, "The resistance to the regime was accelerating." In fact, the resistance was on a sharp decline during this period. Kurskova simply cited the number of people who had been sentenced to prison by the courts in 1976 (976,000), and labeled them dissidents (Kurskova 2000, p. 192). The absolute majority of these people were ordinary criminals. In 1998, post-Soviet Russia had a much smaller population (147,000,000), compared to the USSR in 1979 (262,000,000), and yet the number of people in prison (none of whom were political prisoners) increased from 976,000 to 1,071,000 (Goskomstat 1999, p. 177).

87. A report to the Ministry of Internal Affairs on events surrounding the anniversary celebration of the October Revolution in November of 1956 mentioned 9 pamphlets with "counterrevolutionary contents" found in the outskirts of Barnaul; 5 pictures of Soviet leaders with "anti-Soviet captions," which were thrown during a demonstration in Batumi; and graffiti scribbled on buildings of the opera theater in Tallinn (*Izvestiia,* November 6, 1991).

88. In his book *Jugement à Moscou* (1995), Vladimir Bukovsky insisted that the dissident movement remained a powerful force opposing the regime until the USSR's demise. He went so far as to state, "We (dissidents) were the major obstacle to Soviet dominance of the world," and "The Soviet regime could not withstand any opposition, however symbolic" (1995, p. 187). Remarkably, all of the concrete episodes and incidents of resistance which the author cites in the substantiation of his thesis are relevant only to the 1960s and 1970s and not the first half of the 1980s—when the dissident movement was virtually obliterated (see pp. 126–142). Bukovsky himself recognized (in contradiction to many of his statements) that the dissident movement had been nearly defeated after the arrest of Natan Shcharansky and the rout of the Helsinki movement by the end of the 1970s (p. 231).

89. Only the demonstration in defense of Stalin after Khrushchev's famous public denunciation of him in 1956 in Tbilisi can be cited as a serious mass political action directed against Moscow. The demonstration was mercilessly crushed by the authorities.

90. See the study of public disturbances in the post-Stalin Soviet Union conducted by Vladimir Shevelev (1997).

91. One day after the strike started in Novocherkassk on June 1, 1962, almost half of the members of the Politburo (Frol Kozlov, Anastas Mikoyan, Kirilenko, Shelepin, Poliansky) as well as the head of the KGB, Vladimir Semichastny, arrived in the city in order to take the necessary measures (Trubin 1991; *Literaturnaia gazeta*, September 12, 1990; Deriabin and Bagley 1990).

92. For a negative assessment of Sablin's actions, see Ivanov 1997.

Notes to Chapter 11: The Regime and the Empire

1. For more about the role of the ethnic factor in Soviet policy, see Allworth 1971; Conquest 1986a and 1970; Gellner 1983; Khazanov 1988, pp.147–170; Pipes 1964; Nekrich 1978; Motyl 1987; Carrère d'Encausse 1979.

2. Among the 11 members of the Cheka who were endorsed by Lenin in 1918, at least 4 were non-Slavs. In 1920, Sovnarkom approved 13 members, at least 7 of whom were non-Slavs.

3. The Austro-Hungarian empire tried to accommodate its many different ethnic groups and provinces (only 23 percent of the population was German). The indigenous languages were maintained in Hungary, Galicia, and Croatia-Slavonia. The Habsburgs claimed to be patrons of all nations of the empire, and the polyglot Vienna court, where dozens of languages were spoken (almost all of which were also used by the empire's subjects, including Slavs), was truly cosmopolitan. Moreover, the ethnic heterogeneity of the central political elite in Vienna surpassed that of the Moscow nomenklatura in the last five decades of Soviet history (excepting the Kremlin when Lenin was leader). To the German ear, the names of the aristocratic families in Vienna (names such as Esterhazi, Razumovsky, and Palavicini) must have sounded as alien as the names of Soviet leaders in Moscow in 1918–1924 (names such as Dzerzhinsky, Trotsky, and Peters), some of whom hid their non-Russian names behind pseudonyms—Stalin for Dzhugashvili, Trotsky for Bronshtein, Zinoviev for Radomyslsky, Kamenev for Rosenfeld.

4. Interestingly, the Bolsheviks were considered foreigners by some Russians. The high number of non-Russians among them gave credence to this view. Later, in the 1970s, the theory about the original Bolsheviks and Marxists having been "small people" who came from abroad or from "internal exile" was rejuvenated by Russophiles (Shafarevich 1989).

5. Akbar, the founder of the empire, believed that "the various ethnic, national and religious groups in the nobility should be so balanced that the king did not become dependent on any one section and enjoyed the maximum freedom of action" (Chandra, Tripathi, and De 1972, p. XXX).

6. Debates on the nature of the pre-revolutionary Russian empire and Soviet empire raged among intellectuals in both the Soviet and post-Soviet periods. One group saw Russia as the dominant nation in both empires. They believed Russia's policies toward non-Russians had always been benevolent and fair (see Soloukhin 1995). Another group saw the Russian state since the sixteenth century as a geopolitical formation, a "third Rome," created by the Russian nation for pursuing its global, supranational goals (see Glushkova 1990). The third group, the advocates of the Eurasian ideology, insisted that tsarist Russia "never was a classic colonial empire" but was "home for people living on the territory of Russia" (S. Kortunov 1996; Kurginian 1992, pp. 78, 148–152, 177–193; Dugin 1996; Kara-Murza 1994b, p. 50).

7. The level of religious tolerance in the Russian empire also was rather high, and the conversion of people of other Christian denominations as well as of Jews and Muslims to the Orthodox church removed many obstacles to their careers. The situation changed drastically in Soviet times. The authorities recognized only ethnicity by blood and disregarded one's religious affiliation. In this way, religious conversions did nothing for one's status in society.

8. On one hand, the Roman authorities made a clear distinction between citizens and noncitizens of the empire. On the other hand, the highest positions in the Roman empire were open to people of any ethnic and cultural origin, and the Roman emperors came from several different provinces.

9. However, after the seventeenth century the Ottoman empire considered only Sunnites loyal citizens, rejecting Shiites and Christians as heretics. The conversion of newcomers and descendants of ethnic groups other than Inner Asian nomads in the last centuries was more difficult than it had been previously. However, the Ottomans harnessed the talents of many groups, including Slavs and Greeks, using them as high-level bureaucrats (see Goodvin 1999).

10. Hosking wrote, "One is driven to the conclusion that an internal community was not what Soviet leaders wished to create—at least not after Lenin—but rather an empire in which each nationality has its assigned place in the hierarchy dominated by Russians" (Hosking 1992).

11. In 1945, Stalin openly declared his chauvinistic policy. During a victory banquet in the Kremlin, he raised his famous toast to Russia and its people as "the most prominent nation among all nations in the Soviet Union" and as "the leading force of the Soviet Union among all people of our country" (*Zavtra* 18, 1995).

12. In a 1989 VTsIOM survey asking respondents to name the most popular historical figures, the Armenians and Azerbaijanis almost totally ignored Marx and Lenin (Levada 1993, p. 184).

13. After Stalin's death in May 1953, Lavrentii Beria replaced the Russian first secretaries in the republics with native people. This policy was perpetuated even after his execution a few months later.

14. However, before 1989, many non-Russians (particularly in Central Asia) tended to exaggerate their knowledge of the Russian language. The falsification of data by authorities who wished to demonstrate their loyalty to the empire should also be taken into account. These factors were probably significant in Uzbekistan, where the census of 1979 found a fantastic increase in the number of Uzbeks who had mastered Russian, in comparison with the previous census in 1969.

15. The yearning of non-Russians, particularly in "small republics," to have Russian as their main language was ignored by Anatolii Khazanov in his critique of Russification in the USSR (Khazanov 1995, pp. 12–14).

16. With the empire beginning to crumble in 1989–1991, the Russians fell into conflict with nationalist movements in various regions of the country. The Russian minorities became an important factor in the political struggle in the Soviet empire, particularly in the Baltic republics and Moldavia. Many Russians in these republics, though certainly not all (in the Baltic republic, a significant number of Russians supported the secessionist movement), were allies of the most conservative forces in Moscow.

17. The non-Russians' admiration for the Soviet Union was not an uncommon example of a minority showing devotion to the conqueror. For instance, many non-Roman authors, among them Flavius Josephus, expressed their delight in being citizens of the Roman empire.

18. This argument was voiced to me by a Lithuanian intellectual in a private discussion in 1973.

19. These data were influenced by the decline of Soviet ideology and the rise of fears during perestroika. Most likely, these events activated national feelings which had been inert before 1985 in many non-Russians (Levada 1993, pp. 132–133, 138, 140).

20. Increasing hostility of the dominant group toward its own empire shortly before imperial collapse is a familiar phenomenon in history. The liberal German party in the Habsburg empire, which professed Pan-Germanism, was not concerned about the survival of the empire but rather about the unification of Austria with Germany. Young Turks in the Ottoman empire, the advocates of Pan-Turkism, were also dissatisfied with the position of the dominant ethnic group in this empire and fought for its improvement during the revolution of 1908. Their nationalist aspirations were implemented only after the empire fell. During the Qing empire in the nineteenth century, even though the Chinese were the dominant ethnic and cultural group, a rabidly xenophobic, pro-Chinese movement emerged which was to some degree directed against the imperial court. The imperial dynasty was perceived by many Chinese as foreign, since it was of Manchu origin and maintained its native language, dress, and customs, which were distinct from Chinese ones.

21. According to an August 1990 VTsIOM survey, 35 percent of respondents endorsed a statement which suggested that "the changes in recent years" created the danger of "a spiritual degeneration" of the Russian nation; 42 percent selected an alternative which suggested that these changes led to "the loss of Russia's leading role" in the USSR (Levada 1993, p. 140).

22. Alexander Dugin suggested that the Russian Jews who lived during the Bolshevik Revolution fell into one of two categories: Eurasianist Jews (builders of the Soviet empire), or Atlanticist Jews (admirers of the West, and enemies of the empire). See Dugin 1997, p. 4.

23. Anti-Semitism was quite strong among discontented workers as well as peasants in the 1920s and 1930s (see S. Davies 1997, pp. 84–89; Fainsod 1958, pp. 43, 48). Brovkin found a document in Russian archives which shows that Anatolii Lunacharsky, who undertook an extensive trip across the country in 1928, was appalled by the intensity of anti-Semitism (Brovkin 1998, p. 186).

24. Sarah Davies found documents in the Leningrad archives that showed many pro-Soviet people had accused Jews of murdering Sergei Kirov in December 1934. In one of the letters received by a party official in the aftermath of this event, the author declared that "the sacred revolutionary Smolny is full of the Jewish nation" (1997, p. 86).

25. Between 1917 and 1929, 16 percent of those who held top positions in the Central Committee (i.e., members of the Politburo and the secretary of the Central Committee) were Jews; in the period between 1930 and 1989, this number declined to 2 percent (Vishnevsky 1997, p. 4).

26. See the reports of the Directorate of Cadres of the USSR Academy of Sciences in *Nezavisimaia gazeta-Nauka* 2, 1999, p. 15.

27. In a 1989 VTsIOM survey, the respondents were asked about the major features of Russians, Jews, Britons, and Uzbeks. All three of the most popular traits attributed to Russians, Britons, and Uzbeks were positive, while two of the three features attributed to Jews were negative; 74 percent considered Jews "hypocritical"; 26 percent, "stingy"; and 36 percent, "energetic" (Levada 1993, p. 141).

28. With its collapse, the Soviet Union and its ideology ceased to play a key civilizational role in many provinces, particularly in Central Asia, which chose the West as its model instead.

29. As an example of adaptation to the dominant political reality, we can cite the ethnic identification chosen by children of mixed marriages for inclusion in their internal passports. All Soviets were required to have official passports upon reaching sixteen years of age. As Victor Perevedentsev noted, in the 1960s, the choice of ethnicity depended on the hierarchy of the ethnic groups in the USSR. In almost all mixed marriages with a Russian male or female, the child would assume Russian ethnicity in his or her internal passport. In a mixed marriage in Uzbekistan, if one spouse was Uzbek and the other a non-Russian (Kirgiz or Tadzhik, for instance), the child would take the Uzbek ethnicity. In other words, mixed couples gave their children the dominant ethnic identity in the country or in the given region, whenever possible.

30. The case of Armenians and Azerbaijanis was remarkable. The number of mixed marriages between these groups was so high that it helped to save many Armenians during the pogroms in Baku in 1990.

31. According to sociological surveys conducted in the 1990s, more than two thirds of Russian respondents expressed negative attitudes toward these people (VTsIOM, *Monitoring obshchestvennogo mneniia*, No. 3, 1996).

32. In 1931, 88 percent of all children in Belorussia went to schools that used the Belorussian language; in 1988, this indicator was only 14 percent (Skvortsov 1996, pp. 39–40).

33. The differences between Americans' survey responses on ethnic and racial issues (most Americans in the 1970s–1990s expressed acceptance of equal rights and ethnic equalities) and their actual voting behavior (Americans often voted along racial lines) demonstrate that the suppression of racial and ethnic animosities is a universal fact (V. Shlapentokh 1985b).

34. Stephen White noted that the prospect of "complete unity" among the Soviet people before 1985 "might not be wholly unrealistic" (White 1993, p. 151).

35. These factors determined the scale of the exodus of Russians and other ethnic groups from the regions where they had lived for decades. The exodus of Russians from non-Slavic republics after 1989–1991 was enormous, particularly from Central Asia and Azerbaijan. The exodus was minimal from Ukraine, the Baltics, and Moldova (Shlapentokh, Sendich, and Payin 1994; Arutiunian 1994, pp. 125–132).

36. Prominent Russian intellectual Mikhail Chulaki went so far as to label most newly independent states such as Georgia, Azerbaijan, and Abkhazia "Nazist," in view of their genocidal policies toward other ethnic groups (Chulaki 1998).

Notes to Chapter 12: Reforms

1. Winston Churchill mused about what would have happened if the American civil war had ended differently (Churchill 1931). H.A. Fisher reflected on what might have happened to the world if Napoleon escaped Waterloo and went to America (Squire 1931). Geoffrey Parker, asked What if the Spanish Armada had triumphed? . . . Shakespeare would have mastered Español (Parker 1976, pp. 358–368). A book edited by Niall Ferguson, *Virtual history: Alternatives and counterfactuals* (1998), asked many of the same types of questions and aroused hot debates in the press (see Honan 1998; Carruthers 1997; Parker 1998).

2. Some revisionists in British historiography have gone so far as to assert, "The English civil war or Revolution was no more than a fortuitous accident, unrelated to fundamental political and social processes" (Kennedy 1991, p. 43; see also Kishlansky 1996).

3. Views that go against the deterministic interpretation of the French Revolution were reborn among the so-called revisionists in the 1970s and 1980s, with François Furet as their leader (see Furet and Ozouf 1989). See also Richard Cobb's *The French and their revolution* (1998), in which the author insisted that the course of events during the French revolution "had depended on accident, resentment, boredom and bullheaded folly."

4. Besides scholars, several novelists engulfed themselves in alternative scenarios of the American civil war (Moore 1976).

5. In the past decade, World War II has been discussed from "the alternative perspective" in Moscow, mostly in response to Victor Suvorov's book *Icebreaker* (1990), which suggested that Stalin could have attacked Hitler first. See also Abarinov 1992; Danilov 1990.

6. Those who studied Chinese history after 1949 identified many moments when, if even one factor had been different, events would have taken a radically different turn. For instance, Han Suyin, in his book on Zhou Enlai, stated that if Zhou, and not Mao, had been at the helm of the Chinese Communist party, "the Chinese Communist Party might have cut a deal with Chiang Kai-Shek in the 1930s or 1940s, and sat down with Franklin Delano Roosevelt in 1945" (Suyin 1994).

7. This view is shared by Timothy Garton Ash, an expert on postwar Eastern Europe. Ash wrote, "The closer we are to an event, both in time and place, the more likely we are to know about it" (Ash 1996).

8. Among the historians who have focused on the alternatives of history are several who sought to prove that each of the events which led to Stalinism was not predetermined. Stephen Cohen spoke about the alternatives to Stalinism in his *Bukharin and the Bolshevik Revolution: A political biography, 1888–1938* (1973). See Cohen's *Rethinking the Soviet experience: Politics and history since 1917* (1985); see also the book by Philip Zelikov and Condoleezza Rice, who contended that nothing could be more mistaken than to believe that German reunification and the cold war were inevitable (1995). Richard Pipes went so far as to say that "occurrence provides nine-tenths of historical justification," downgrading the role of objective, structural constraints (i.e., economic, social, psychological); see Pipes 1993a, p. 491.

9. Soviet liberals spoke openly about Russia's various alternatives in 1917 and berated conservatives who insisted that the October Revolution was predetermined by earlier developments (see the debates in Afanasiev 1987a, 1987b, 1988a; Butenko 1988, pp. 551–568; V. Kiselev 1988, pp. 354–369; Tsipko 1989a, pp. 46–56; Vasiliev 1990, pp. 9–59).

10. Yegor Gaidar, the architect of the economic reforms, often said that there were no alternatives to his "shock therapy."

11. For more about preventive and reactive reforms, see V. Shlapentokh 1988a, pp. 76–77.

12. It would be wrong to think that the Soviet leaders after Stalin did not have a more or less realistic picture of the Soviet economy and the standard of living in the country. As a leading Soviet statistician, Moisei Eidelman, has pointed out, the Soviet leaders regularly received dozens of secret bulletins with economic data from various agencies (1998, pp. 70–76). Other sources also have indicated that post-Stalin leaders were more or less aware of the economic problems of the country (see Mikoyan 1988).

13. For more about the Russian reforms, see Pipes 1974; Lincoln 1978; Wortman 1976. Several authors (e.g., Alexander Yanov) placed the conflict between reformers and counterreformers at the core of Russian history. Yanov depicted Russia after the fourteenth century as a country which failed on several occasions to break away from the despotic regime and catch up with the West (Yanov 1984, 1978; see also Lapkin and Pantin 1992).

14. Reforms were essential to the Habsburg empire after 1848–1849. During the next twenty years, Emperor Francis Joseph introduced several liberal reforms. By 1867, however, the reforms had ended (except for a few administrative changes) and the emperor resisted a new wave of reforms. Around the same time, other political figures (including crown princes Rudolf and Francis Ferdinand and social democrats Karl Brunner and Otto Bauer) elaborated their own programs. Their ideas primarily involved transforming the dual monarchy into a federation tentatively called the United States of Europe. None of these ideas were implemented by Vienna. Debates on the role of reforms in the history of the empire continue. One well-known expert on the Habsburg empire mused, "The Habsburg monarch might have survived if only this or that statesmen or people had been more sensible" (Taylor 1948; see also Crankshaw 1963).

15. One insider claimed that when Grigorii Romanov was the secretary of the Central Committee of the party (1983–1985), he locked horns with Dmitrii Ustinov, the powerful defense minister and Brezhnev's trusted man. According to this insider, Ustinov made Gorbachev the second-ranking state leader after Andropov's death so as to block Romanov from this position and ruin his chances to become general secretary (Legostaev 1998).

16. Gorbachev mused several years later about the circumstances under which he offered Yeltsin a job in Moscow. Nikolai Ryzhkov, who knew Yeltsin from Sverdlovsk, tried to dissuade Gorbachev from appointing Yeltsin. Ironically, Yegor Ligachev, who would become Yeltsin's worst adversary, convinced Gorbachev to go ahead (Gorbachev 1993). Yeltsin himself wrote that he "often wondered how Gorbachev chose" him for the job of Moscow party secretary (Yeltsin 1990, pp. 108–109).

17. Moscow journalist Vitalii Tretiakov, musing about the circumstances which could have prevented the fall of the Soviet empire, contended that if Yeltsin had been elected chairman of the Soviet parliament on May 25, and if a half year later Gorbachev had appointed him as his "political heir," the empire could have been saved. Tretiakov suggested that turning Yeltsin into a high official of the Soviet Union would have prevented him from becoming its major enemy (Tretiakov 1992; see Abalkin 1992, pp. 17–18).

18. Evgenii Chasov, who was head of the Kremlin hospital, watched Brezhnev and his illness very closely. He noted, "The pernicious influence of nurse N. (supposedly his mistress) on Brezhnev accelerated his degradation and in this way contributed more to the collapse of the country than dozens of actions of various dissident groups" (Chasov 1992).

19. Interestingly, Malenkov and Khrushchev got rid of Beria, then Khrushchev did the same to Malenkov. In each case, the defeated rival was accused of deviating from Marxist ideology.

20. See, for instance, the various textbooks on "Scientific Communism" (the official ideological and political doctrines) published in the late 1960s and 1970s (e.g., Afanasiev 1981a).

21. Andropov launched an attack against corruption in Moscow, Krasnodar, and

Uzbekistan. He removed Minister of Internal Affairs Nikolai Shchelokov, calling him a "seasoned crook." He fired Yurii Churbanov (Shchelokov's first deputy and Brezhnev's son-in-law) and the Uzbekistan Party leader Sharaf Rashidov, who suddenly died of a "heart attack." Andropov also removed S. Medunov, the party secretary of the Krasnodar region, and sent several members of the Moscow mafias connected with party secretary Victor Grishin to the gallows (see the account by Brezhnev's and Andropov's aide Andrei Alexandrov-Agentov 1994, pp. 278–280; see also Ligachev 1992, pp. 170–190).

Notes to Chapter 13: Reforming the System

1. Mancur Olson developed similar ideas when he spoke about the sclerotic processes in an "old" social system (1982). Another author, Joseph Tainter, who studied the same subject, focused on the transaction costs—that is, the cost of coordinating human activity in society (1990).

2. Gloomy predictions about the fall of empires were often unsubstantiated. The Habsburg, Russian, and Ottoman empires are cases in point, since lamentations regarding their demise preceded their true collapse by more than a century. In the case of the Soviet system, predictions regarding its collapse came at a time when it was actually gaining strength (from 1917 through the early 1940s). When the chronic diseases of the system worsened, such predictions actually disappeared. After the 1940s, observers both inside and outside the Soviet empire failed until 1991 to see a threat to the existence of the USSR, although they did acknowledge its economic and technological retardation (see, for instance, the collection of articles by leading American Sovietologists in Byrnes 1983; also see Bialer 1986; and Miller, Rigby, and Rigby 1987). The events after 1989, including the powerful separatist movements, stupefied contemporary observers.

3. See samizdat materials in the journal *Vol'noe slovo*, 1972–1978; see also Amalrik 1982; Grigorenko 1982; Kopelev 1978.

4. There were several advocates of this theory in Russia and in the West. Among Russian authors, see the accounts by Gorbachev's aide Georgii Shakhnazarov (1997) and Moscow political scientists Vladimir Filatov and Sergei Fateev (1997). Among Western authors see Basil Kerblay (1987, pp. 100–101), Anders Aslund (1995, pp. 27–28), Michael Dobbs (1997), John Dunlop (1993, p. 4), and Martin McCauley (1997, pp. 389–390). Some advocates of the "discontent theory" contended, "The Communist regime collapsed because of the fall of oil prices" (Kochetkov 1999).

5. The Russians remained calm through the economic disaster of 1992 when their savings were eliminated and the bottom dropped out of the standard of living. They also weathered the financial crisis of August 17, 1998 without any sign of public disturbance. The Russians tolerated the nonpayment of their salaries over several months and even years. What is more, millions of Russians suffered through record-setting cold winters with poor heating systems and a lack of electricity (see V. Shlapentokh 1995, pp. 247–280).

6. "The permission for private property to exist" was supported by only 56 percent of Russians (Levada 1990, pp. 70, 83).

7. It is noteworthy that several prominent politicians and business people (for instance, Vladlen Kirienko, the liberal prime minister in 1998, and two leading Russian oligarchs Boris Khodorkovsky and Vladimir Potanin) in post-Communist Russia started their public life in the early 1980s by entering the Komsomol. In the 1990s, on the eve of perestroika, they still professed their sincere belief in Communism.

8. The most detailed version of this concept was elaborated by Steven L. Solnick (1998, pp. 24–42). Solnick, however, could not even remotely explain what pushed Gorbachev to start the reforms. Robert Daniels also supported this theory (2000). Among partial advocates of this theory, see Kotz 1997. Among Russian advocates of the "nomenklatura" theory, see Gennadii Burbulis, adviser to Yeltsin in 1991–1992 (1993) and Yurii Yaremenko, a prominent Soviet economist and the director of the Institute of Scientific and Technological Progress of the Soviet Academy of Sciences (on Yaremenko's views, see Belanovsky 1996).

9. By 1985, a significant number of apparatchicks had doctorates (up to 10 percent among the party apparatchiks at the regional and central levels). To a very great extent, however, the educational changes in the party and state apparatus were fictitious. Many people from the nomenklatura graduated from low-quality, evening colleges. Several apparatchiks, particularly in the non-Russian republics, were awarded honorary diplomas on the sole basis of their positions in bureaucracy; these degrees were purely symbolic and nominal. Being unaware of these facts, several Sovietologists (among them Seweryn Bialer and Jerry Hough in the late 1970s and 1980s) overestimated the real rise of the apparatchiks' educational level as well as their impact on the modernization of Soviet society.

10. In my 1968 survey of *Pravda*'s readers, one third of the respondents answered the "general comments" question with a harsh critique of bureaucracy. Perestroika opened the gate for anti-bureaucratic feelings (see Kozhanov 1997).

11. Some authors defended the Yeltsin regime, with its all-pervasive corruption, by contending that it was no more corrupt than Soviet Russia and that the totalitarian regime was also unable to fight corruption (see Kliamkin and Timofeev 1999; Summers 1999). This was patently untrue. Corruption was much less pervasive not only in Stalin's time but even in the "period of stagnation." Discussing the period of Brezhnev's rule, Russian historian Petr Rodionov noted that corruption in the 1970s and early 1980s "was a childish prank in comparison with what is going on in Russia now" (Rodionov 1996).

12. In 1988, Evgenii Nosov wrote: "Russian bureaucrats tried to create a favorable environment for enriching themselves by arousing the most primitive instincts in people. They attempted to replace spiritual values with money as their main idols" (Nosov 1988).

13. See the memoir's of Alexander Anipkin (1991), who was the last first party secretary of the Volgograd region (he abandoned this post after the August coup in 1991). In this seemingly honest book apparatchiks are described as devoted to "the cause" in the late 1980s.

14. The famous "Cotton Case" (the investigation of mass corruption in Uzbekistan related to the falsification of cotton production data), in which many Uzbek apparatchiks in the early 1980s were implicated, did not extend to the Moscow ruling elite, although Vadim Churbanov, Brezhnev's son-in-law, was partially involved in the scandal (on corruption in non-Russian republics in the 1970s and early 1980s, see S. Pavlenko 1989, pp. 190–202; Raig 1989, pp. 203–216; Simis 1982; Vaksberg 1987, p. 13).

15. For more about the advocates of this theory, see Gaidar 1997; Popov 1999; Radzikhovsky 1995; Vodolazov 1997; Kurginian 1997; Strakhov 1997, p. 30; A. Kortunov 1997.

16. After 1991, Gorbachev reminisced about "what a noisy reaction there was in the country when we uttered for the first time the words 'individual property' and 'private property'" (Gorbachev 1997b, p. 8). There is no empirical evidence of the existence of a "pro-capitalist coalition" (the term of Kotz and Weir) inside the

nomenklatura before 1985. As noted by Peter Rutland, the advocates of this theory tried to prove their case by identifying the beneficiaries of the transition, implying that they generated perestroika in their best material interest (Rutland 1998).

17. For more detailed critiques of the dissident theory, see Gelman 1997, p. 10; E. Kliamkin 1995.

18. See the debates about the role of the liberal intelligentsia of the 1960s in the development of perestroika in Bershin and Vinogradov 1996; Burtin 1997. Bershin and Vinogradov denied that the intelligentsia played a significant role, while Burtin held the opposite view. For more about "the intellectual roots of the Soviet bloc's collapse," see Taras 1992, pp. 8, 10.

19. Proclaiming Gorbachev as the designer of Russian democratic society before 1985, in 2000 Alexander Tsipko contended, without any empirical data, that Gorbachev's major focus from the very beginning had been freedom and democracy. He pointed out that Gorbachev was a "humanitarian, a graduate of the law school at Moscow University, a person of the 1960s, and ultimately . . . a typical Russian, for whom the humanistic issues are always the most important" (Tsipko 2000). However, contrary to this position, only a few years earlier, in 1996, Tsipko had written: "Starting perestroika, Gorbachev did not want to destroy Marxist socialism and break with Marxist ideology. He only wanted, as all reformers—Czech, Hungarian, and Polish —to rejuvenate socialism" (Tsipko 1996).

20. Gorbachev wrote in his memoirs that in April 1985, at the beginning of perestroika, during his first meeting with the Central Committee, the issue of democracy was reduced to the standard Soviet clichés: "Of course we could not free our minds from previous shackles and blinkers in a single stroke" (Gorbachev 1995, p. 174). However, five years later, as a participant at a conference on the origin of perestroika, he asserted that "the quest for freedom" was his major initial motivation for reforms (*New Perspectives Quarterly*, Winter 1996). In 2000, during the commemoration of the 15th anniversary of perestroika, Gorbachev also presented his choice in 1985 as having been between democracy and "a terrible political system" (Gorbachev 2000a). In another article, Gorbachev, against evident facts, implied that he had planned to start perestroika with political reforms (Gorbachev 2000b). We find the same contradictions in Yakovlev's statements. Talking about his meeting with Gorbachev in Canada in 1983 (Yakovlev served there as Soviet ambassador), he recognized in 1989 that their conversation was very general and that Gorbachev did not talk specifically about the necessity that "society has to change," dispelling the rumors that both future leaders had at that time elaborated a program for the democratic transformation of the country. Yakovlev acknowledged that he returned from Canada to Moscow in 1984 as a believer in the "socialist mode of life," even if it was based on "non-Stalinist principles" (Yakovlev 1991, pp. 32–33). However, his other texts alluded to the existence of a program for the democratic transformation of society (Yakovlev 1991, pp. 41–42).

21. There have been other instances in history of a decaying empire being propped up by other countries. In the fourteenth century, various Western countries and the Papacy tried to prolong the existence of the Byzantine empire. The Habsburg empire was evidently backed by Russia and even by Prussia during the stormy years of 1848– 1849. And the Western powers tried to save (though cautiously and without resolve) the Russian empire after the October Revolution. The Chinese empire in the last decades of its existence was protected by foreign powers that wanted to reverse its dissolution, even if these powers extricated various concessions from China in the process. Arguing against those who described Britain, Germany, Russia, and America

as enemies which yearned for a chunk of Chinese territory, Arthur Waldron writes, "The truth is quite different, for the last thing the Powers wanted was an actual disintegration and partition of China." For this reason, they supported the existing regime, regardless of how poorly it operated (Waldron 1990, pp. 29–30, 38).

22. When Bush visited Kiev in August 1991, only a few weeks before the fall of the USSR, he appealed to the Ukrainian parliament to reject "suicidal nationalism" and be loyal to Gorbachev's Moscow (see Gates 1996).

23. In the late 1970s and early 1980s, Western experts believed that the Soviet empire would live a long life. None of them predicted the revolution or the collapse of the empire (Nove 1975; Bialer 1980; Laqueur 1977, pp. 39–44; Highland 1979, pp. 51–66; Ford 1984, pp. 1132–1144). Even Russian experts in 1988 did not see a threat to the Soviet Union (Y. Afanasiev 1988b).

24. While sitting in jail after the August coup, Vladimir Kriuchkov hatched a theory about Western plans "to reduce the population of the Soviet Union and to transfer Soviet natural resources to other parts of the world" (see *Den'*, April 18, 1992).

25. Gennadii Ziuganov, the leader of the Russian Communist Party, in speaking about the Western strategy against the Soviet Union, wrote, "The core of their strategy was the scenarios of defeat and the elimination of the Soviet Union from the world arena and the subsequent demolition of the existing geopolitical balance of forces" (Ziuganov 1993). Another leader of the same party, Victor Zorkaltsev, insisted that the growing deficit of "raw materials" in the world explained why America designed perestroika (1995).

26. Sergei Kara-Murza wrote, "The team which came to power openly and conscientiously moved to the side of the adversary and blocked all possibilities which could restore stability in the Soviet Union" (Kara-Murza 1996a; see Yakovlev 1996).

27. One of these was Gleb Pavlovsky, who contended, "Reagan and the chief of the CIA Casey ultimately destroyed the USSR" (1996).

28. Zinoviev wrote: "The organizers and executors of 'the cold war' have to atomize Soviet society psychologically, morally and politically. They must shatter the social and political structures, deprive the masses of the ability to resist, and destroy the psychological immunity of the population from the adversary. They used as the means for the achievement of their goals powerful propaganda, which diverts people from social issues toward sex, the intimate life of movie stars and gangsters, toward criminality and perverted forms of pleasures. . . Dozens or even hundreds of thousands of experts and volunteers, including the agents of the secret service, professors, journalists and tourists were involved in this work. This work was done on the basis of the experience of the past, particularly Goebbels's propaganda machine, as well as through the achievements of psychology and medicine, particularly psychoanalysis" (Zinoviev 1993).

29. There were several different conspiracy theories that explained the Soviet collapse. Gorbachev prevailed as the main actor in most of them. Other theories blamed Yakovlev as the leading person. He was accused of being a Freemason and a puppet of Zionists in an article written by an anonymous author (see "Strategicheskaia izmena," *Den'*, September 4 and 11, 1993).

30. Many times in history, the mere perception of a military threat (regardless of its validity) has generated major policy changes. For instance, in the 1960s, Washington took at face value Khrushchev's false declaration about the vastness of the Soviet missile arsenal. This so-called missile gap between the USSR and the USA greatly impacted American foreign and military policy (see Bottome 1971).

31. Military experts were divided on the level of the potential threat to the USSR.

Those who did not see the SDI as a serious threat included I. Belousov, the head of the military-industrial committee in 1988–1991, and to some degree General V. Lobov, the chief of the General Staff. The opposite view was held by Makhmut Gareev, the general deputy chief of the General Staff (for more about the debates on the SDI among Russian generals, see Ellman and Kontorovich 1998, pp. 55–59). Among non-military authors, the polarization was also quite pronounced. On one hand, the famous physicist Vitalii Goldansky firmly insisted that in 1983 the Soviet Union "over-strained itself after Reagan announced his SDI" (1998). On the other, Anatolii Dobrynin, Soviet ambassador to the United States, recognized that the spiraling arms race jeopardized "our social and economic development," but refused to agree that "the problem of keeping up militarily with the United States, especially with 'the Star Wars,' was the last straw that produced the Soviet crash" (1995).

32. See the materials on this memorable discussion in *New Perspectives Quarterly*, Winter, 1996. See also the authors who supported the SDI theory for the origins of perestroika, in Power 1996, p. 24; and Kotz 1997, p. 55. For more about the various views about the SDI, see Mandelbaum and Talbott 1984; Gates 1996; Nitze 1986; Blank 1990.

33. Anatolii Alexandrov, then president of the Soviet Academy of Sciences, complained to the 27th Party Congress about "stagnation in certain branches of science and technology," that Soviet managers did not trust Soviet scholars, and that all new equipment and technology was being ordered from abroad. At the 19th Party Conference in 1988, Yurii Marchuk, the new president of the Academy of Sciences, continued to lament "the drastic decrease of the role of science in social life" and "the growing gap" between Soviet and Western science. He was seconded by Anatolii Logunov, president of Moscow University, who warned that if Soviet scientists failed to reorganize science, "we will simply not understand what is going on in Western science" (July 1, 1988). Similar sentiments regarding the retardation of Soviet science were expressed by many prominent scholars in 1987–1988 (see Frank-Kamenetski 1988; Sagdeiev 1988a, and 1988b; see also the debates on this subject in *Literaturnaia gazeta*, June 22, 1988).

34. News of Gorbachev's election by the Politburo was received with a long and evidently sincere ovation by the members of the Central Committee at its meeting on March 11, 1985 (see Boldin 1995, p. 89).

35. After 1987 there was a strong belief inside the party bureaucracy that Gorbachev had deceived them all (see Ligachev 1992, Ryzhkov 1995; V. Pavlov 1995; Grishin 1996).

36. See the memoirs of Gorbachev's aides in Boldin 1995, pp. 97–107; Vadim Medvedev 1994, pp. 26–41; and Alexandrov-Agentov 1994, pp. 278–280; see also Mozhin 1998a, p. 165.

37. For an interesting characterization of the last Soviet leader, see Novikov 1995.

38. As Eduard Shevardnadze exclaimed in 1991, "We all were the victims of political illiteracy" (1991, p. 316). Gavriil Popov, a prominent activist of perestroika, lamented that "The people who ran the country during perestroika had only vague ideas about it" (1999, p. 3).

39. Gorbachev, for instance, falsely believed that the Baltic countries would perish economically if they left the Soviet Union (for more on Gorbachev's views on national issues, see Cherniaev 1993, pp. 242–253).

40. For more about the Kremlin's naive perceptions of the West during perestroika, see the account by Gorbachev's economic adviser Leonid Abalkin (1992, p. 103).

41. Like the initial conduct of many of his predecessors, in the beginning of his tenure Gorbachev's conduct toward the Politburo was democratic in nature. Soon after, however, he began to behave as a normal totalitarian leader. He did not listen to his interlocutors, he ignored many members of the Politburo, he ousted some of them on a whim, and he fomented his own "cult of personality" (see Ryzhkov 1995, p. 354; Vorotnikov 1995, p. 63; see also Popov 1994, p. 47).

42. Alexander Gelman, a well-known Russian intellectual and fervent supporter of perestroika, wrote: "Who started in 1985 the real perestroika in the USSR: the militant, radical opposition, the open adversaries of the dictatorship of the CPSU? It was nothing like this. It was a quite cautious opposition inside the CPSU" (Gelman 1997).

43. In December 1985, Yevgenii Yevtushenko became the first of the Moscow intellectuals to call upon his colleagues to honestly address the past and the present. Just days before the Congress of Soviet Writers which opened in June 1986, Gorbachev met with a group of prominent authors and encouraged them to take an aggressive stand against official lies.

44. As a result, references to direct links between "glasnost and the 1960s" became a fixture in the Soviet mass media in 1987 and 1988 (see, for instance, *Znanie i sila*, June 1988, pp. 18–25).

45. Valentin Alexandrov, an aide to Vadim Medvedev (the ideological secretary of the Central Committee during perestroika), found that even in 1988 neither his boss nor Gorbachev had read Solzhenitsyn's works, which had been circulating widely in samizdat since the early 1960s. What is more, in the same year, Gorbachev was hostile toward the intentions of the famous literary magazine *Novyi mir* to publish Solzhenitsyn's samizdat novels (Alexandrov 1999).

46. Cherniaev wrote that it was not until 1987 that Gorbachev (after reading Stephen Cohen's *Bukharin)* reconsidered the official verdict on Bukharin, from a "Leninist" point of view. Gorbachev's conclusion was still far from unbiased, but at least he did not assess Bukharin as a wrecker and a spy. Such accusations were groundless, as almost everyone else had concluded by the 1960s (Cherniaev 1993, p. 183).

47. Glasnost and the change in attitudes toward the intelligentsia stemmed from Andropov's heritage. From his first days in office, Andropov underscored his rejection of the anti-intellectual policies of his predecessors and emphasized his plans to actively employ the nation's intellectual resources (Andropov 1983a).

48. The intelligentsia and intellectuals played many roles for Gorbachev. For example, they delegitimized Brezhnev's regime in general and the Stalinist model of society in particular, which Gorbachev intended to at least partially demolish. Also of crucial importance was their support and elaboration of reforms throughout all spheres of Soviet life. In addition, Gorbachev was certain that the intellectuals and the mass intelligentsia would be his most faithful allies because these groups would most appreciate the dramatic reactivation of political and cultural life which would be engendered by his liberalization efforts. And, in fact, the intelligentsia was the stratum which profited most from glasnost, while the masses, who had, at best, a trifling interest in intellectual activities and political freedoms, gained little.

49. The decree against "nonlabor income" adopted in May 1985 attacked elements of the private economy in the USSR. It led to soaring prices, and spread panic throughout the country. Millions of peasants were barred from shopping in neighboring cities and villages, tenants were evicted by landlords, car owners were afraid to drive people to hospitals even in emergencies, and scholars could not find typists for their manuscripts.

50. Party bureaucrats were the first victims of Gorbachev's innovation. The anti-

alcohol campaign spoiled their lives much more than it did the lives of ordinary people whose jobs were not at stake. Apparatchiks had to forget about their long binges and "hunting parties" which were organized by their subordinates. During a trip I made to Moldova in 1977 as the head of a sociological team working for *Pravda*, I was invited by local party bosses to one of their hunting lodges and saw how they rested and entertained themselves. Gorbachev's campaign put an end to this life, at least temporarily.

51. In the early years under Gorbachev, even the call for limited autonomy in enterprises was considered a sign of liberalism. Yet, Stalin had raised this issue in 1933.

52. The failure of the Acceleration project was fully recognized by the Kremlin in January 1987 (see Vadim Medvedev 1998).

53. On Gorbachev's shift from economic to political reforms, see Popov 1994, p. 52.

54. Mikhail Gorbachev straightforwardly said that "the artistic intelligentsia . . . had an indispensable role to play in mobilizing people for perestroika" (1996, p. 213).

55. Anatolii Rybakov's novel *Children of the Arbat* (1987) made a special contribution to the collapse of the official ideology, along with works by Anatolii Pristavkin (1988) and Vladimir Dudintsev (1988).

56. Nikolai Shmelev (1987), Gavriil Popov (1987), Vasilii Seliunin, and Grigorii Khanin (1987) were the most active among economists in fighting the official dogmas.

57. Yurii Kariakin, Yurii Afanasiev, and Natan Eidelman were best known for their participation in the demolition of Soviet ideology.

58. The most famous among them were Anatolii Streliany (1988) and Vasilii Seliunin (1988).

59. The publication of Andrei Platonov's novels, particularly *Chevengur* (1978) and *The foundation pit* (1996), and Vladimir Korolenko's letters to Anatolii Lunacharsky about the atrocities of the Bolsheviks during the civil war (see *Novyi mir*, October 1988) dealt serious blows to the once inviolable icons of Soviet ideology.

60. Alexander Tsipko was the initial proponent of this new concept. In a series of articles in *Nauka i zhizn'*, he discussed "the main truth" about the direct connection between the Stalinist system and "the Marxist project of society," which was based on unrealistic assumptions such as "a non commodity and non money economy, social property, the exaggeration of the role of theory in social development, the disregard for democratic principles, and so on" (Tsipko 1989a). Tsipko was joined by Igor Kliamkin, who openly declared that socialism, as conceived by Marxists, could not guarantee an efficient and humane society (Kliamkin 1989).

61. Increased openness in society had serious consequences for several different empires. The Ottoman empire in the eighteenth and nineteenth centuries was one example. Following a relatively closed period, the sultans gradually granted various privileges to foreign merchants and artisans. Having borrowed money from European banks, the Porta became so economically dependent on foreign countries that the Europeans created the Office of Public Debt Administration, which had broad economic powers and significantly weakened the empire. Developments in China differed from those in the Ottoman and Soviet empires. Chinese openness was imposed by force, and the Chinese emperor, under fire from British cannons, was compelled to sign a series of unequal treaties that inaugurated an era of Western control over China. Thereafter, Western influences tended to destabilize Chinese politics. The Taiping rebellion, for example, was directly influenced by Christianity. In China, as in other empires, increased foreign contact proved quite detrimental and contributed significantly to the gradual disintegration of the imperial structures.

62. It is difficult to overestimate the role of such apologists of privatization in the destruction of the old ideology (see Piasheva 1990a, 1990b, 1990c; Seliunin 1990a, 1990b; Shatalin and Petrakov 1990; Shatalin, Petrakov, and Yavlinsky 1990a, 1990b; Bunich 1990, 1991a, 1991b; Chernichenko 1991).

63. With the support of Stanislav Shatalin, Grigorii Yavlinsky almost persuaded Gorbachev to accept his program "500 days," promising to make the decaying Soviet economy prosperous in less than two years (for more about this program, see Shatalin, Petrakov, and Yavlinsky 1990a; Yavlinsky and Shatalin 1991; and Yasin 1988, pp. 234–237).

64. The participants in an economic seminar organized by *Izvestiia* were almost unanimous on this issue. Timur Kadyrov suggested that an owner is one "who, possessing the means of production, works as a free individual and is free in disposing of the fruits of his labor." Vladimir Bashmachnikov, in his turn, suggested that workers should be "the real owners of the means of production" (*Izvestiia,* December 20, 1988). Pavel Bunich stated that "the individual is not interested in a market without property because otherwise he is a seasonal worker who does not think about the future" (Bunich 1991a). Vladislav Inozemtsev suggested that in a capitalist society "economic coercion" has been replaced by "social coercion." In other words, he said that in a liberal capitalist society people work for the prestige of their job or for creative activity, instead of simply to survive. This allows the society to overcome to some extent "the alienation of work" (Inozemtsev 1991, p. 39; see also Zamoshkin 1991).

65. Nikolai Ryzhkov, then Gorbachev's prime minister, wrote that in 1990 during the debates on Yavlinsky's program "500 days," they "forgot a small detail in it—the state" (Ryzhkov 1995, p. 377).

66. The prominent Soviet economist Alexander Matlin expressed the dominant view among his colleagues when he wrote: "The state cannot be trusted with the management of the economy because the combination of political and economic power leads unavoidably toward monopoly and the war of the state against its own people" (*Izvestiia,* September 21, 1991).

67. Summarizing the views of the Russian contributors to their book on Gorbachev's economic reforms, Ellman and Kontorovich wrote, "There was a certain consistency about the first crop of Gorbachev's policy initiatives—they were all command in nature, as opposed to those which would emerge only a few years later" (Ellman and Kontorovich 1998, p. 17).

68. The Kremlin's economic experiment with the expansion of enterprise autonomy in 1986–1988 was a good example. Soon it became clear that the experiment was being carried out in ways that clearly invalidated its results. Several enterprises which participated in the experiment received special priority in the allocation of raw materials; this was hardly a good way to find out how new processes and procedures would fare under real-market circumstances (see V. Shlapentokh 1993b, p. 4).

69. For more about "show" innovations in Gorbachev's Russia, see Yun 1998; Prostiakov 1998a, 1998b.

70. Among the evidently adventurous innovations was the introduction of the principle of self-sufficiency or self-financing (*khozraschet*) for the regions. The principle supposed that each Soviet republic and region should be economically autonomous.

71. See the minutes from the 27th Congress of the CPSU (Moscow: Politizdat, 1986, pp. 140–145).

72. Before he became president, Yeltsin's refusals of various privileges were his most famous demonstrations against the party apparatus (see Yeltsin 1994, p. 35). No

one could have predicted that Yeltsin would later lead an extraordinarily lavish lifestyle as the Russian president.

73. Yeltsin's campaign for social justice and his struggle against party privileges were never taken seriously by Gorbachev, who, in the most demagogic way, simply denied the evident facts about the existence of special perks for apparatchiks (see Vadim Medvedev 1994; see also Cherniaev 1993, p. 187).

74. The storm did not strike entirely without warning. The outcome of the 1989 election only confirmed the results of a survey conducted on the eve of the election by Yurii Levada and his colleagues at the Center for Public Opinion in Moscow. Their survey revealed that if there was a consensus on anything in Soviet society, it was the people's hatred of bureaucracy. When asked to identify the origins of the current crisis in the country, 63 percent of the respondents named the party and state apparatus, 60 percent blamed corruption, 44 percent pointed to the mistakes of the previous leadership, and 39 percent blamed the incompetence of superiors (Levada 1990, pp. 280–291). Apparatchiks across the country dismissed the warnings of the sociologists. They were convinced that through various rude and cynical tricks they could either prevent their opponents from being included on the ballot or at least discredit them in some nasty fashion.

75. For the details of Yeltsin's unprecedented show of courage at the October meeting of the Central Committee, see Cherniaev 1993, p. 176.

76. Only a few days before the election, Vadim Medvedev, Gorbachev's main ideologist, announced (with Gorbachev's implicit endorsement, if not at his urging) that the Central Committee had created a special committee to investigate the loyalty of the former Moscow secretary.

77. It would be wrong to say that Gorbachev did not use various tricks in order to undermine Yeltsin's position in 1990–1991. Gorbachev attempted to block a televised speech by Yeltsin in May 1990. In February 1991, he tried to arrange for Yeltsin's impeachment in the Russian parliament, using Yeltsin's deputies for this purpose. If Gorbachev had dealt with Yeltsin with the same determination as his predecessors, however, he could have ended Yeltsin's career even in 1990–1991 (see Yeltsin 1990, pp. 241–257; Pikhoia 1996; V. Shlapentokh 1993a, pp. 141–144, 182–184).

78. The peak of Gorbachev's confrontation with Yeltsin and the democratic forces which supported the latter occurred on March 27, 1991. Downtown Moscow was occupied by tanks meant to scare the Russian parliament and force it to remove its chairman, who had openly demanded Gorbachev's resignation on March 9, 1991. However, Gorbachev yielded to the mass demonstration of Muscovites and withdrew the troops (for a description of these events, see Anipkin 1991, pp. 69–76; see also Popov 1994).

79. Gorbachev used various means to obstruct Yeltsin's election as president of the Russian Federation (including the use of the KGB). Among other things, he supported Yeltsin's rival Nikolai Ryzhkov (Yeltsin 1994, pp. 43–44; Chebarshin 1992, p. 270).

80. Unlike Yeltsin, Gorbachev never took serious political risks. Gorbachev avoided his own direct election to the first All-Union Congress of People's Deputies in March 1989 and invented a special election procedure which permitted him to be "elected" by secret votes of the Central Committee, which had to "choose" 100 deputies from among as many candidates (Vadim Medvedev 1994, p. 88). Likewise, during the elections for the chairmanship of the Soviet Supreme in June 1989 and for the presidency in March 1990, Gorbachev brazenly declared himself free of opposition. He never even contemplated being elected by a popular vote in 1990. However, had he been elected by the people (and this was quite possible), he would have deprived Yeltsin of his power and influence as the first Russian president to be elected by the population.

Gorbachev also tried to skirt any responsibility for the bloody events during his tenure: the shootings during the demonstration in Tbilisi in 1989, and the carnage in Baku in January 1990, and in Vilnius in January 1991 (see Sobchak 1991; Cherniaev 1993, pp. 405–419).

81. For more about this group, see the account by one of its founders: Popov 1994, pp. 69–82.

Notes to Chapter 14: Consequences

1. While the Moscow media energetically advanced the idea of private property, only 29 percent of respondents in a 1990 all-Union survey agreed with the statement "Big factories should belong to private Soviet citizens." Sixty percent of all respondents had a positive outlook on "the development of state industry" (*Obshchestvennoe mnenie v tsifrakh*, Vol. 9, part 2, 1991, pp. 6, 11, 12). Only a minority (30 percent) were ready to give farmers complete property rights on their land, including the rights to sell it and bequeath it to their children (ibid., pp. 8–9).

2. In 1992, Yeltsin attempted to make June 12 (this was the same day he was elected as president of the Russian Federation in 1991) the "day of Russia's sovereignty." His attempt failed because very soon it became evident, even to the Kremlin, that such a holiday was absurd. In 1997, this day was proclaimed "the day of Russia" without any hint about its "independence." It is amusing that in 1995 the textbook *Istoriia sovremennoi Rossii, 1985–1994* straightforwardly and without even a tinge of irony featured a lengthy chapter entitled, "Russia in the USSR: The formation of an independent state" (Volobuev 1995, pp. 49–110).

3. In the 1980s, up to one third of the adult population in many Soviet cities in Siberia and the northern part of the country were ex-convicts.

4. For instance, the state cooperative ANT (Aircraft Scientific Technological Association) was given the right to engage in foreign trade and to barter without a license. The corporation could skirt the Soviet rules, thereby generating unknown amounts of revenue. Attempts to punish the organizers of shady deals failed (see Sobchak 1991, pp. 55–59).

5. As Vladimir Mozhin pointed out, "The economy was hit hard by the consequences of the political reforms. Party organs were dislodged from the reins of economic control at a time when the economic reform was making its first steps and the economic levers of coordination were lacking" (Mozhin 1998a, p. 165).

6. The decisive role of the economic factor in determining the nature of perestroika, and the instrumental character of democratic reforms, was noted by a number of Soviet authors. One of them, Vladislav Lektorsky, complained in *Pravda*, "We reduce even the problem of democracy to its role as a factor which helps society to be economically more efficient" (*Pravda*, January 22, 1990).

7. There is no question that Gorbachev's liberal innovations damaged the Soviet economy; but his policies before 1988, which did not contradict the essence of the command economy, were, in fact, quite successful (for instance, the extension of individual initiative and the critique of bureaucracy). Indeed, several indicators of the Soviet economy (the productivity of labor, the level of investment, agricultural production, and personal consumption) looked quite impressive between 1985 and 1988 (Goskomstat 1990, pp. 7–8).

8. The alarming decline in labor ethics was recognized by all authoritative Soviet experts. Among them was Leonid Abalkin, who in a number of interviews and articles in

1988–1989 underscored the catastrophic consequence of this fact (see, for instance, *Komsomol'skaia pravda,* February 8, 1989). Similar views were advanced by Vadim Kirichenko, head of the Central Statistical Committee, who noted "the drastic fall of labor discipline" as a major cause of economic decline (*Argumenty i fakty,* February 2, 1990).

9. Remarkably, agriculture, and particularly husbandry, was the single sector of the economy which profited from perestroika. While the growth of the national income declined from 3.2 percent to 1.3 percent between the periods 1981 to 1985 and 1986 to 1990 respectively, the production of agriculture rose in the latter period by 1.9 percent, against 1.1 percent in the former period.

10. According to calculations by Alexander Zaichenko, who refuted the official Soviet data on the 1989 GNP, the national income, along with industrial and agricultural production, greatly declined in 1989 as compared with the previous year (*Moskovskie novosti,* January 28, 1990).

11. In the past, the party, with its network of committees, always guaranteed the success of major economic and political campaigns, including the harvest. Party committees wielded unrestrained power over everyone in their territories, regardless of rank. With a single phone call, a committee could mobilize an entire territory for a harvest, appropriate every truck, close institutions and offices, and send workers to the fields. Once there, unskilled manual laborers would work side by side with professors, doctors, and engineers, picking potatoes by hand. No single accomplishment affected a party secretary's career as much as fulfilling the state's plan for grain or vegetable procurement. By the summer of 1990, however, party committees had lost their hold over the people and institutions in their regions. They could not have carried out their traditional role as organizers and guarantors of the harvest even if they had wanted to; and it is possible that, given their frustration at having been stripped of some of their powers, some party committees may have chosen to sabotage, rather than facilitate, the harvest.

12. In the beginning of 1990, *Pravda* begged the leaders of the lumber industry to increase the supply of paper; the newspaper even threatened to stop its publication (*Pravda,* January 25, 1990). The shortage of meat by the beginning of 1990 was also quite serious.

13. In September 1990, during a visit to Moscow, I stayed at one of the best hotels, the Sputnik. For breakfast I had only pastries. The restaurant's standard breakfast fare (eggs, sausages, and toast) was simply unavailable. One morning, my schedule dictated that my breakfast of pastries be followed by a meeting with a prominent scholar, who was both the director of a leading research institution and a deputy of the Soviet parliament. After the meeting, my hostess invited me to lunch; but she could only offer pastries, explaining that even if she had had bread, she had nothing to spread on it. For more about food shortages in the country in these years, see *Nedelia,* August 6, 1989; *Komsomol'skaia pravda,* March 3, 1989.

14. For more about the bread and tobacco crises in Moscow in 1990, see Popov 1994, pp. 102–113.

15. Facing the growing shortage of goods, the Soviet authorities invented exotic schemes of distribution. For instance, they used lotteries to determine who among the workers of a given institution would be entitled to "buy," for example, one of ten pairs of Italian shoes, or one of five jackets made in France, that had been allotted to their institution. Winners of these lotteries rarely refused items that did not fit them or their family members (for more about everyday life in the Soviet Union in 1989–1991, see V. Shlapentokh 1993a, pp. 93–171).

16. By 1989, taxi drivers in Moscow were going to great lengths to avoid passen-

gers who paid the official rate. They were persuaded only by double fares in hard currency. People in restaurants and other enterprises behaved similarly, refusing to provide services at the official rate.

17. As a Moscow author wrote, several people were sure that "the Karabakh conflict was a detonator which blasted the unity of the Soviet Union" (Tumanov 1995).

18. Vytautas Landsbergis, the leader of the Lithuanian national front (which was the most active of the national organizations in the Baltic in the late 1980s), mentioned in *Daily Mail* (April 7, 1990): "Gorbachev watched our movement for independence for two years. He could have stopped it at any moment . . . But he did not."

19. Under the spell of liberal propaganda, many Russians in 1989 and 1991 took an anti-imperial stance, although they were often ambivalent. A nationwide poll conducted in early 1990 by VTsIOM, the All-Russian Center of Public Opinion, revealed not only that nearly three fourths of all ethnic Russians denied in one way or another that they had a right to interfere in the business of other peoples but that nearly the same proportion regarded the secession of the national republics as inevitable. When Gorbachev asked the population to support the Soviet Union in the referendum on March 17, 1991, 76 percent of those who took part in the referendum voted for the preservation of the Soviet Union. However, no more than 57 percent of the potential voters participated in the referendum. The majority of the population in several republics boycotted the referendum, and in Moscow, Leningrad, and several other cities only half of the participants of the referendum supported Gorbachev. The results of the referendum were ambiguous. It could be treated as a victory for Gorbachev, but also for Yeltsin, who had called on people not to vote (see Pikhoia 1996; Yeltsin 1994). However, in 1992–1994, Russians almost unanimously bemoaned the collapse of the Soviet Union. A survey by the Institute of Sociology of Parliamentarism discovered in July 1992 that 67 percent of Muscovites—the most liberal people in the country—felt nostalgia for the USSR (*Izvestiia,* July 27, 1992). Five years later the same polling firm (surveying the whole population of Russia this time) found that 71 percent in one or another form regretted the collapse of the Soviet Union (*Argumenty i fakty* 34, August 1997).

20. The ferocity of interethnic conflicts in the Habsburg empire forced several minorities to make a difficult choice regarding their maximal autonomy: Should they support the empire in its fight against the other, more powerful minorities, and hope to someday gain autonomy from the empire? Or should they join the other ethnic groups with similar backgrounds? Or should they demand their own state? This dilemma faced the Croats, for example, who had to choose between creating their own state, or joining the United States of Southern Slavs, as well as the Ukrainians, who had to decide whether to remain within the empire, create their own state, or seek autonomy within the Polish state. Thus, interethnic conflicts weakened the Habsburg monarchy instead of helping it to retain its power.

21. Vladimir Kriuchkov has described the motivation of participants in the "State Emergency Committee" (GKChP, in Russian transliteration). See Kriuchkov 1996, pp. 134–138.

22. According to the data of the Center of Public Opinion Studies, 42 percent of Soviets in 1990 believed in telepathy; 57 percent believed in "TV curing"; 42 percent in astrology; and 35 percent in sorcery (*Obshchestvennoe mnenie v tsifrakh,* Vol. 10, 1990, p. 7).

23. According to the Center of Public Opinion Studies, no more than 10 percent of the Soviet adult population in 1990 could be considered true believers, although as

many as 50 percent declared themselves "religious people" (*Obshchestvennoe mnenie v tsifrakh*, Vol. 2, 1990, p. 12).

24. In 1988, for instance, high officials maligned the cooperative movement launched by Gorbachev. They hoped to defeat this reform by riding a wave of popular hatred for individuals who enriched themselves with speculation and fraud. However, not one word was said against the general secretary himself (see the interview with Finance Minister Gostev in *Ogonek*, July 1988).

25. Nina Andreeva's article entitled "I cannot forsake my principles" was the first frontal attack on perestroika. The publication was supported by Yegor Ligachev, the leader of the conservative forces in the Central Committee in 1987–1991, in a rather pusillanimous way (Andreeva 1988; see the different versions of this "dramatic" story in Gorbachev 1996, pp. 252–253; see also Ligachev 1992, pp. 126–128).

26. Without understanding the logic of democratization, the delegates accepted Gorbachev's proposal to combine the positions of first party secretary and chairman of the soviets at all levels. The party secretaries saw this as an enhancement of their public role. These apparatchiks did not foresee any difficulties in getting elected as chairmen of the soviets by popular vote on the territory which was until now under their full control. The election in March of the next year, when many party secretaries were shamefully defeated, showed how poorly the party officials understood the developments around them. Gavriil Popov even suggested that Gorbachev intentionally duped party officials whom he hated (Popov 1994, p. 53). As his aide Anatolii Cherniaev recalled, Gorbachev gloated over the electoral defeat of the complacent party bosses (Cherniaev 1993, p. 284).

27. In May 1990, only 14 percent of Soviets said that they trusted the Soviet leadership completely. By June, that already low figure had fallen to 6 percent.

28. For more about the influence of the Moscow public on the conservatives, see Anipkin 1991, pp. 72–73.

29. At the congress of the Russian Communist Party, General Albert Makashov's thinly veiled threat of a military coup was not only greeted with thunderous applause from the delegates but was swallowed by Gorbachev, who, looking rather confused, dared not react to the abrasive and arrogant speech. Attacks on Gorbachev abounded at the congress, with conservative Yegor Ligachev pledging "a coming feast on our street," and Ivan Polozkov, the newly elected first secretary, promising a crusade for the restoration of Communist ideals (Ligachev 1992). The conservatives' success at this congress was so overwhelming that Soviet liberals such as Fedor Burlatsky began to talk of "the specter of Stalin that again hangs over the country" and of the prospect of returning to "the worst days of the Gulag."

30. The speakers at the April 1991 meeting of the Central Committee were almost unanimous in either directly or indirectly condemning almost all elements of Gorbachev's domestic policy, especially in regard to the national republics and glasnost. Dmitrii Yazov, the minister of defense, recited a long litany of evils inflicted on the army through recent developments sponsored by the general secretary (although Yazov stopped short of mentioning Gorbachev by name). The outrages described by Yazov ranged from ethnic conflicts in the army to the denigration of officers and soldiers occupying several republics. Another official, Mikhail Nenashev, the head of Soviet TV and Radio, complained (along with many others at the Central Committee meeting) that glasnost had deprived the party of its authority. Several speakers, such as Yurii Karabasov, the Moscow party secretary, and Yurii Yelchenko, the Ukrainian party secretary, foretold the imminent collapse of the Soviet Union, socialism, and the

Communist Party, should the existing policy of tolerance toward national aspirations and popular movements continue unabated. The criticisms leveled at Gorbachev were particularly clear in the speech by Semen Grossu, the Moldavian first party secretary. However, for all this criticism, the Central Committee did not dare dismiss Gorbachev.

31. For more about the defeatist feelings of the party apparatus and the KGB after the June meeting of the Central Committee, see Chebarshin 1992, pp. 273–274.

32. One triggering event occurred during the secret meeting of Gorbachev, Yeltsin, and Nursultan Nazarbaev, the head of Kazakhstan, on July 29–30, 1991, in Novo-Ogarevo. During this meeting, which was recorded by the KGB, they made decisions about the new, so-called Novo-Ogarevo treaty among republics, the creation of a new federal state, and the removal from power of practically all leading Soviet figures. The still-secret text of the treaty, which clearly showed the transformation of the Soviet Union into a relatively loose (in the opinion of Gorbachev's enemies) confederation, was published by *Moskovskie novosti* (without Gorbachev's permission) on August 15 (see Popov 1994, pp. 195–196; Kriuchkov 1996, pp. 132–138; Pavlov 1995, p. 11).

33. See Daniil Granin's portrait of an apparatchik, entitled "Nash dorogoi Roman Avdeevich," as well as Vladlen Sirotkin's "Nomenklatura v istoricheskom razreze," both in Protashchik 1990, pp. 106–131 and pp. 292–334, respectively.

34. The putschists could have easily won, had they been determined to fight. The Soviet apparatchiks did not try to exploit the coup. On the first day of the putsch, when its outcome was unknown, the party apparatus as a whole was afraid to support those who represented their interests. Even in a few regions (Novgorod, Krasnodar, Altai, Lipetsk, Tambov, Saratov, Samara, Ulianovsk) where local leaders revealed their sympathy for the coup, they did not make any efforts to defend the leaders of the State Emergency Committee. By the third day, they had vowed their loyalty to Yeltsin.

35. There is a dispute over which branch of the Soviet dominant class was the most active in resisting the reforms and the collapse of the empire: the party bureaucracy, the army elite, or the KGB leadership. To some degree, this problem was reduced to the question of who was the main instigator of the August coup: Kriuchkov, the head of the KGB; Yazov, the head of the army; or Baklanov, the highest party official among the conspirators. See Yurii Shchekochikhin's article, which develops a theory ascribing the key role to Baklanov, as the representative of the military-industrial complex (1991).

36. See, for instance, the discussion of the social democratic future for Russia by Burlatsky, Sergei Alexeev, and Shatalin, in *Literaturnaia gazeta*, January 30, 1991; see also Burlatsky 1991.

37. Gorbachev sent tanks into Moscow's streets on March 27, 1991; he reacted passively to speeches by Pavlov, Yazov, and Kriuchkov, with their almost direct call for a state of emergency, during the meeting of the Supreme Soviet on June 17, 1991; he dismissed as nonsense the information about the coup which was being prepared by these people (Matlock 1996). Had Gorbachev been seriously opposed to the speakers at this meeting—all of them future members of the junta—he could have easily fired them after their anti-perestroika speeches; see the analysis of these developments in the book by former Moscow Mayor Gavriil Popov (1994, pp. 203–219); see also Cherniaev 1993, pp. 450–452. Among other major developments in the Kremlin, where the leader oscillated between the liberal and the authoritative course, were the events surrounding the resignation of Soviet foreign minister Eduard Shevardnadze on December 20, including Shevardnadze's speech at the 4th Congress of People's Deputies about the imminent coup; and the bloodshed in Vilnius in January, which was perpetrated by Soviet special units.

BIBLIOGRAPHY

Abalkin, Leonid. 1989. Interview. *Komsomol'skaia pravda*. 8 February.
——. 1992. *K tseli cherez krizis: Spustia god*. Moscow: Luch.
Abarinov, Vlad. 1992. "'Barbarossa': Vozhdelennoe krovoprolitie." *Nezavisimaia gazeta*. 19 June.
Abbott, John. 1882. *The empire of Russia: Its rise and present power*. New York: Dodd, Mead, and Company.
Abel, Lionel. 1984. *The intellectual follies: A memoir of the literary venture in New York and Paris*. New York: Norton.
Afanasiev, Victor. 1981a. *Nauchnyi kommunizm*. Moscow: Progress.
——. 1981b. *Osnovy filosofskikh znanii*. Moscow: Mysl'.
Afanasiev, Yurii. 1987a. "Nelepo boiat'sia samikh sebia." *Moskovskie novosti*. 13 September.
——. 1987b. "Sotsial'naia pamiat' chelovechestva." *Nauka i zhizn'*. 9:56–60.
——. 1988a. "Otvet istorika." *Pravda*. 26 July.
Afanasiev, Yurii (ed.). 1988b. *Inogo ne dano*. Moscow: Progress.
——. 1995. *Golod 1932–1933 godov*. Moscow: Rossiiskii gosudarstvennyi gumanitarnyi universitet.
Afanasiev, Yurii. 1998. "My tak i ne vyrvalis' iz sotsializma." *Moskovskie novosti*. 20 December.
Agursky, Mikhail. 1980. *Ideologiia natsional-bol'shevizma*. Paris: YMCA Press.
——. 1987. *The third Rome: National bolshevism in the USSR*. Boulder, Colo.: Westview Press.
Aitmatov, Chingiz. 1988. "Podryvaiutsia li osnovy." *Izvestiia*. 4 May.
Akhiezer, Alexander. 1991. *Rossiia: Kritika istoricheskogo opyta*. Vol. 2. Mocow: Izd. Filosofskogo obshchestva.
Aksenov, Yurii. 1991. "Stalinizm: Poslevoennye utopii i realii." In Vitalii Zhuravlev (ed.), *Trudnye voprosy istorii*. Moscow: Gospolitizdat.
Aksiutin, Yurii (ed.). 1992. *L. I. Brezhnev: Materialy dlia biografii*. Moscow: Politizdat.
Alexander, Jeffrey C. (ed.). 1985. *Neofunctionalism*. Beverly Hills, Calif.: Sage.
Alexandrov, Aleksandr (ed.). 1971. *Finansy SSSR*. Moscow: Finansy.

Alexandrov, Valentin. 1999. "Trupu nanimaet direktor." *Nezavisimaia gazeta-Kulisy.* 11 December.

Alexandrov-Agentov, Andrei. 1994. *Ot Kollontai do Gorbacheva.* Moscow: Mezhdunarodnye otnosheniia.

Alexeev, Sergei. 1995. "Miatezh na 'Storozhevom.'" *Moskovskie novosti.* 31 December.

Alexeeva, Ludmila. 1984. *Istoriia inakomysliia v SSSR: Noveishii period.* Benson, Vt.: Khronika Press.

Alexeeva, Ludmila, and Valerii Chalidze. 1985. *Mass rioting in the USSR.* Silver Springs, Md.: Foundation for Soviet Studies.

Alford, Robert R. 1963. *Party and Society: The Anglo-American democracies.* Chicago: Rand McNally.

Allworth, Edward (ed.). 1971. *Soviet nationality problems.* New York: Columbia University Press.

Alpatov, Vladimir. 1998. "Khrushchev protiv Stalina." *Nezavisimaia gazeta.* 2 February.

Amalrik, Andrei. 1970. *Will the Soviet Union survive until 1984?* New York: Harper and Row.

———. 1982. *Notes of a revolutionary.* New York: Knopf.

Amvrosov, Anatolii. 1982. *Aktual'nye problemy nauchnogo kommunizma.* Moscow: Mysl'.

Analiticheskii Tsentr Izvestiia. 1994. "Neizvestnaia voina s korruptsiei." *Izvestiia.* 22 October.

Andreev, Sergei. 1989. "Nashe proshloe, nastoiashchee i budushchee." In Fridrikh Borodkin, Leonid Kosals, and Rozalina Ryvkina (eds.), *Postizhenie.* Moscow: Progress.

Andreeva, Nina. 1988. "Ne mogu postupit'sia printsipami." *Sovetskaia Rossiia.* 13 March.

Andrew, Christopher, and Oleg Gordievsky. 1990. *KGB: The inside story of its foreign operations from Lenin to Gorbachev.* New York: HarperCollins.

Andrew, Christopher, and Vasilii Mitrokhin. 1999. *The sword and the shield: The Mitrokhin archive and the secret history of the KGB.* New York: Basic Books.

Andropov, Igor. 1994. "Otets ne sobiralsia tak rano ukhodit'." *Komsomol'skaia pravda.* 10/17 June.

Andropov, Yurii. 1983a. *Izbrannye stat'i i rechi.* Moscow: Politizdat.

———. 1983b. "Rech' na soveshchanie veteranov partii." *Kommunist* 13.

Anfilov, Victor. 1999. "Novaia versiia i real'nost'." *Nezavisimaia gazeta.* 7 April.

Anipkin, Alexander. 1991. *Ia byl poslednim pervym.* Volgograd: Vedo.

Antonov, Sergei. 1987. "Vas'ka." *Iunost'* 3:4.

Antosenkov, Evgenii, and Valentina Kalmyk (eds.). 1970. *Otnoshenie k trudu i tekuchest' kadrov.* Novosibirsk: Nauka.

Anweiler, Oskar. 1974. *The Soviets: The Russian workers, soldiers and peasants councils, 1905–1921.* New York: Pantheon.

Arbatov, Georgii. 1992. *The system: An insiders' life in Soviet politics.* New York: Times Books.

Arendt, Hannah. 1951. *The origins of totalitarianism.* New York: Harcourt, Brace.

Arkadievich, Genrikh. 1990. "Ukradennaia pobeda." *Komsomol'skaia pravda.* 5 May.

Aronson, Grigorii. 1960. *K istorii pravogo techeniia sredi men'shevikov.* New York.

Artemov, Victor. 1990. "Dinamika obraza zhizni sel'skogo naseleniia." *Sotsiologicheskie issledovaniia* 4.

Arutiunian, Yurii. 1994. "Russkie i rol' natsional'nogo men'shinstva v stranakh

blizhnego zarubezh'ia." In Andrei Zdravomyslov (ed.), *Vzaimodeistvie politicheskikh i natsional'no-etnicheskikh konfliktov.* Vol. 2. Moscow: Rossiiskii institut sotsial'nykh i natsional'nykh problem.
————. 1995. *Rossiiane: Zhiteli goroda i derevni.* Moscow: Institut etnologii i antropologii.
Arzhilovsky, Andrei. 1995. In Veronique Garros, Natalia Korenevskaya, and Thomas Lahusen (eds.), *Intimacy and terror: Soviet diaries of the 1930s.* New York: New Press.
Ascher, Abraham (ed.). 1976. *The Mensheviks in the Russian revolution.* Ithaca, N.Y.: Cornell University Press.
Ascher, Abraham. 1988. *The revolution of 1905: Russia in disarray.* Stanford: Stanford University Press.
Ash, Timothy Garton. 1996. "Hungary's revolution: Forty years on." *New York Review of Books.* 14 November.
————. 1997. *The file: A personal history.* New York: Random House.
Ashkenazy, Vladimir. 1985. *Beyond frontiers.* London: Collins.
Aslund, Anders. 1989. *Gorbachev's struggle for economic reform: The Soviet reform process, 1985–1988.* Ithaca, N.Y.: Cornell University Press.
————. 1994. "Economic reforms: A liberal perspective." In Anders Aslund (ed.), *Economic transformation in Russia.* New York: St. Martin's Press.
————. 1995. *How Russia became a market economy.* Washington, D.C.: Brookings Institution.
Auchincloss, Louis. 2000. *Woodrow Wilson: A Penguin life.* New York: Viking Penguin.
Avidar, Joseph. 1983. *The party and the army in the Soviet Union.* University Park: Pennsylvania State University Press.
Avzeger, V. 1993. "Ia vskryval vashi pis'ma." *Rodina* 10:56.
Babosov, Evgenii. 1990. *Chelovek i perestroika: sotsiologicheskii analiz.* Minsk: Nauka i tekhnika.
Babosov, Evgenii, (ed.). 1985. *Nravstvennyi oblik Sovetskoi molodezhi.* Minsk: Nauka i tekhnika.
Bacon, Edwin. 1994. *The Gulag at war.* London: Macmillan.
Bakatin, Vadim. 1995. Interview. *Moskovskii komsomolets.* 19 April.
Barnouin, Barabara, and Yurii Changgen. 1993. *Ten years of turbulence: The Chinese cultural revolution.* London and New York: Kegan Paul International.
Barrett, William. 1982. *The truants: Adventures among the intellectuals.* Garden City, N.Y.: Anchor Press/Doubleday.
Barron, John. 1974. *KGB: The secret work of the Soviet secret agents.* London: Hodder.
————. 1980. *MIG pilot: The final escape of Lieutenant Belenko.* New York: Reader's Digest Press.
Bartlett, Lee. 1984. *Red scare.* Elmwood, Conn.: Poets Press.
Batalov, Eduard. 1989. "Kul't lichnosti i obshchestvennoe soznanie." In Yurii Senokosov (ed.), *Surovaia drama naroda.* Moscow: Politizdat.
Batkin, Leonid. 1988. "Vozobnovlenie istorii." In Yurii Afanasiev (ed.), *Inogo ne dano.* Moscow: Progress.
Baturin, Yurii. 1994. "Shakhmatnaia diplomatiia v Novo-Ogarevo." *Demokratizatsia.* Vol. 2. Spring: 212–221.
Bauman, Zygmunt. 1976. *Socialism: The active utopia.* New York: Holmes & Meier.
Beatty, Bessie. 1918. *The red heart of Russia.* New York: Century Co.

Beer, Max. 1957. *The general history of socialism and social struggles.* New York: Russell & Russell.

Bek, Aleksandr. 1987. *Novoe naznachenie.* Moscow: Knizhnaia palata.

Belanovsky, Sergei. 1996. "Yurii Yaremenko dumal, chto sovetskaia ekonomika ne budet spasena rynochnymi reformami." *Segodnia.* 20 September.

Belikova, Galina, and Alexander Shokhin. 1987. "Chernyi rynok: liudi, veshchi, fakty." *Ogonek* 36.

Belokon, Valentin. 1994. "Sovetskaia A-bomba: Sobstvennoe izobretenie ili plagiat?" *Literaturnaia gazeta.* 29 June.

Berberova, Nina. 1983. *Kursiv moi: Avtobiografiia.* Vols. 1 and 2. New York: Russica.

Berdiaev, Nikolai. 1948, 1937. *The origin of Russian communism.* London: G. Bles.

Berdiaev, Nikolai, S. Bulgakov, M. Gershenzon, A. Izgoiev, B. Kistiakovsky, P. Struve, and S. Frank. 1967. *Vekhi: Sbornik statei o russkoi intelligentsii.* Frankfurt: Posev.

Berg, Mikhail. 1995. "Kompleks Ksantipy." *Literaturnaia gazeta.* 16 August.

Berg, Raisa. 1983. *Sukhovei: Vospominaniia genetika.* New York: Chalidze.

Bergson, Abram, and Herbert S. Levine (eds.). 1983. *The Soviet economy: Toward the year 2000.* Boston and London: G. Allen & Unwin.

Bergson, Henri. 1960. *Time and free will: An essay on the immediate data of consciousness.* New York: Harper.

Bershin, Yefim, and Igor Vinogradov. 1996. "Shestidesiatniki–iavlenie mifologicheskoe." *Literaturnaia gazeta.* 13 November.

Besançon, Alain. 1986. "Nationalism and Bolshevism in the USSR." In Robert Conquest (ed.), *The last empire: Nationality and the Soviet future.* Stanford, Calif.: Hoover Institution Press.

Bezirgani, Georgii. 1999. "Lavrentii Beria: Sto let i sto dnei." *Nezavisimaia gazeta.* 3 April.

Bialer, Seweryn. 1980. *Stalin's successors: Leadership, stability, and change in the Soviet Union.* Cambridge: Cambridge University Press.

———. 1983. *The U.S.S.R. after Brezhnev.* New York: Foreign Policy Association.

———. 1986. *The Soviet paradox: External expansion, internal decline.* New York: Knopf.

Birman, Igor. 1978. "From the achieved level." *Soviet Studies* 30:2, p. 153.

———. 1983. *Ekonomika nedostach.* New York: Chalidze Publications.

———. 1989. *Personal consumption in the USSR and USA.* New York: St. Martin's Press.

———. 1991. *Velichina sovetskikh voennykh raskhodov: Metodicheskii aspekt.* Stockholm: Stockholm School of Economics, Stockholm Institute of Soviet and East European Economics.

Blanchard, William H. 1984. *Revolutionary morality: A psychosexual analysis of twelve revolutionists.* Santa Barbara, Calif.: ABC-CLIO Information.

Blank, Stephen. 1990. *SDI and defensive doctrine: The evolving Soviet debate.* Washington, D.C.: Wilson Center, Kennan Institute for Advanced Russian Studies.

Bliakhman, Leonid, and Ovsei Shkaratan. 1973. *Nauchnaia revolutsiia, rabochii klass i intelligentsiia.* Moscow: Politizdat.

Blinkova, Mira. 1983. "Volkhonka 14–Dmitria Ul'ianova 19." *Kontinent* 38:221–256.

Blinov, Nikolai, and Mikk Titma. 1985. "Nravstvennye orientatsii sovetskoi molodezhi." *Sotsiologicheskie issledovaniia* 1:9–17.

Blium, Arlen. 1994. *Za kulisami "Ministerstva pravdy": Tainaia istoriia sovetskoi tsenzury, 1917–1929.* St. Petersburg.

Blondel, Jean. 1990. *Introduction to comparative government.* New York: Harper.
Boffa, Giuseppe. 1984. *Istoriia Sovetskogo soiuza.* Vol. 1. Moscow: Mezhdunarodnye otnosheniia.
Boguslavsky, Sergei. 1991. "Zagovor akademikov." *Literaturnaia gazeta.* 28 August.
Boldin, Valerii. 1995. *Krushenie pedestala.* Moscow: Respublika.
Bordiugov, Gennadii, and Vladimir Kozlov. 1988. "'Revoliutsiia 'sverkhu' i tragediia 'chrezvychaishchiny.'" *Literaturnaia gazeta.* 12 October.
———. 1992. *Istoriia i kon'iunktura: Sub"ektivnye zametki ob istorii sovetskogo obshchestva.* Moscow: Politizdat.
Borev, Yurii Borisovich. 1978. *Metodologiia sovremennogo literaturovedeniia: Problemy istorizma.* Moscow: Nauka.
Borisov, Yurii, and Vladislav Ivanov. 1989. *Perepiska na istoricheskie temy.* Moscow: Politizdat.
Borodin, Leonid. 1998. "Dissidenty o dissidentskom dvizhenii." *Znamia* 96:172.
Borodkin, Fridrikh (ed). 1990. *Blagosostoianie gorodskogo naseleniia Sibiri.* Novosibirsk: Nauka.
Borodkin, Fridrikh, Leonid Kosals, and Rozalina Ryvkina (eds.). 1989. *Postizhenie.* Moscow: Progress.
Borshchagovsky, Alexander. 1990a. "V chetyre nochi prishli iz GPU." *Komsomol'skaia pravda.* 1 March, 25 September.
———. 1990b. "Prislushaemsia k golosu Riutina." *Moskovskie novosti.* 27 May.
Bottome, Edgar. 1971. *The missile gap: A study of the formulation of military and political policy.* Madison, N.J.: Fairleigh Dickinson University Press.
Bovin, Alexander. 1997. "Velikaia revoliutsiia." *Izvestiia.* 5 November.
Bozhkov, Oleg, and Vladimir Golofast. 1985. "Otsenka naseleniem uslovii zhizni v krupnykh gorodakh." *Sotsiologicheskie issledovaniia* 3.
Breindel, Eric. 1994. "A case of book burning." *National Review.* 29 August.
Breslauer, George (ed). 1990. *Can Gorbachev's reforms succeed?* Berkeley: Berkeley-Stanford Program in Soviet Studies, Center for Slavic and East European Studies, University of California at Berkeley.
———. 1992. *Soviet policy in Africa. From the old to the new thinking.* Berkeley: University of California Press.
Brezhnev, Leonid. 1972. *Otchetnyi doklad tsentral'nogo komiteta KPSS XXIV s"ezdu Kommunisticheskoi partii Sovetskogo soiuza.* Moscow: Politizdat.
———. 1976. *Otchet Tsentral'nogo Komiteta KPSS I ocherednye zadachi partii v oblasti vnutrennei i vneshnei politiki.* Moscow: Politizdat.
———. 1981. *Otchetnyi doklad tsentral'nogo komiteta KPSS XXVI s"ezdu Kommunisticheskoi partii Sovetskogo soiuza i ocherednye zadachi partii v oblasti vnutrennei i vneshnei politiki.* Moscow: Politizdat.
Brook-Shepherd, Gordon. 1978. *Storm petrels: The flight of the first Soviet defectors.* New York: Harcourt Brace Jovanovich.
———. 1989. *The storm birds: Soviet post-war defectors.* New York: Weidenfeld and Nicolson.
Brooks, Jeffrey. 1999. *Thank you, Comrade Stalin! Soviet public culture from revolution to cold war.* Princeton: Princeton University Press.
Broué, Pierre. 1997. *Histoire de l'Internationale communiste: 1919–1943.* Paris: Fayard.
Brovkin, Vladimir (ed.). 1991. *Dear comrades: Menshevik reports on the Bolshevik Revolution and the Civil War.* Stanford: Hoover Institution Press.

Brovkin, Vladimir. 1994. *Behind the front lines of the Civil War.* Princeton: Princeton University Press.

Brovkin, Vladimir (ed). 1997. *The Bolsheviks in Russian society: The Revolution and the Civil War.* New Haven, Conn.: Yale University Press.

Brovkin, Vladimir. 1998. *Russia after Lenin: Politics, culture and society, 1921–1929.* London and New York: Routledge.

Brown, Archie. 1996. *The Gorbachev factor.* London: Oxford University Press.

Brumberg, Abraham. 1998. "In the year of mass murder." *Times Literary Supplement.* 11 December.

Bruzkus, Boris. 1995. *Sovetskaia Rossiia i sotsializm.* St. Petersburg: Zvezda.

Brzezinski, Zbigniew. 1967. *Ideology and power in Soviet politics.* New York: Praeger.

———. 1989. *The grand failure.* New York: Macmillan.

Brzezinski, Zbigniew, and Samuel Huntington. 1964. *Political power: USA/USSR.* New York: Viking Press.

Buchanan, Merial. 1918. *The city in trouble.* New York: Charles Scribner.

Bukharin, Nikolai. 1920. *Problemy teorii i praktiki sotsializma.* Moscow.

———. 1924. *Ataka: sbornik teoreticheskikh statei.* Moscow: Gos. izd-vo.

———. 1966. *The ABC of communism: A popular explanation of the program of the Communist Party of Russia.* Ann Arbor: University of Michigan Press.

———. 1971. *Economics of the transformation period.* New York: Bergman.

———. 1990. *Izbrannye proizvedeniia: Put' k sotsializmu.* Novosibirsk: Nauka.

Bukin, Sergei. 1998. "Chernye flagi nad zonoi." *Obshchaia gazeta.* 15 April.

Bukovsky, Vladimir. 1979. *I vozvrashchaetsia veter.* New York: Khronika Press.

———. 1995. *Jugement à Moscou.* Paris: Robert Laffont.

Bullock, Allan. 1991. *Hitler and Stalin.* London: HarperCollins.

Bunich, Pavel. 1990. "Chto mozhet pravitel'stvo? Chto khochet narod?" *Ogonek* 18.

———. 1991a. "Est' li vykhod?" *Ogonek* 17.

———. 1991b. "Poidet li strana s molotka." *Komsomol'skaia pravda.* 22 February.

Burbank, Jane. 1986. *Intelligentsia and revolution: Russian views of Bolshevism: 1917–1922.* Oxford: Oxford University Press.

Burbulis, Gennadii. 1993. "Agoniia nomenklatury chrevata potriaseniami." *Izvestiia.* 15 October.

Burganov, Agdas. 1989. "Istoriia–mamasha surovaia." In Yurii Senokosov (ed.), *Surovaia drama naroda.* Moscow: Politizdat.

Burlatsky, Fedor. 1970. *Lenin, gosudarstvo, politika.* Moscow: Nauka.

———. 1987. "Politicheskoe zaveshchanie." *Literaturnaia gazeta.* 22 July.

———. 1991. "Kommunizm ili sotsial'naia demokratiia." *Literaturnaia gazeta.* 6 March.

Burtin, Yurii. 1997. "'Shestidesiatniki' pered sudom sovremennogo konformizma." *Literaturnaia gazeta.* 22 January.

———. 1998a. "Rossiia i konvergentsiia." *Oktiabr'* 1.

———. 1998b. "Konvergentsia." *Nezavisimaia gazeta.* 4 April.

———. 1999. "Tri Lenina." *Nezavisimaia gazeta.* 21 January.

Bushnell, Timothy, Vladimir Shlapentokh, Christopher K. Vanderpool, and Jeyaratnam Sundram (eds.). 1991. *State organized terror: The case of violent internal repressions.* Boulder, Colo.: Westview Press.

Butenko, Anatolii. 1988. "O revoliutsionnoi perestroike gosudarstvenno-administrativnogo sotsializma." In Yurii Afanasiev (ed.), *Inogo ne dano,* Moscow: Progress.

Byrnes, Robert F. (ed.). 1983. *After Brezhnev: Sources of Soviet conduct in the 1980s.* Bloomington: Indiana University Press.

Carr, Edward Hallett. 1964. *Socialism in one country, 1924–1926.* London: Macmillan.

Carrère d'Encausse, Hélène. 1979. *Decline of an empire: The Soviet socialist republics in revolt.* New York: Newsweek.

————. 1993. *The end of the Soviet Empire: The triumph of the nations.* New York: BasicBooks.

Carruthers, Susan L. 1997. "Alternatives and counterfactuals." *International Affairs.* October.

Central Intelligence Agency. 1982. *Handbook of economic statistics.*

Chalidze, Valerii (ed). 1981. *Otvetstvennost' pokolenii.* New York: Chalidze.

Chandra, Bipan, Amales Tripathi, and Barun De. 1972. *Freedom struggle.* New Delhi: National Book Trust.

Changli, Irina. 1978. *Sotsialisticheskoe sorevnovanie: Voprosy teorii i praktiki organizatsii.* Moscow: Nauka.

Charles, Milene. 1980. *The Soviet Union and Africa: The history of the involvement.* Lanham, Md.: University Press of America.

Chasov, Evgenii. 1991. "Na ego rukakh skonchalas' tselaia epokha." *Komsomol'skaia pravda.* 27 September.

————. 1992. "V Politbiuro TsK KPSS: Diagnoz vracha." *Komsomol'skaia pravda.* 18 January.

Chebarshin, Leonid. 1992. *Ruki Moskvy.* Moscow: Tsentr-100.

Chebrikov, Victor. 1998. Interview. *Moskovskii komsomolets.* 23 December.

Cherkashin, Nikolai. 1990. "Poslednii parad." *Komsomol'skaia pravda.* 1 and 3 March.

Cherniaev, Anatolii. 1993. *Shest' let s Gorbachevym: Po dnevnikovym zapisiam.* Moscow: Progress.

Chernichenko, Yurii. 1988. "Dve tainy." *Literaturnaia gazeta.* 13 April.

————. 1991. "Pchely v podzemel'ie, ili chego khochet krest'ianskaia partiia Rossii." *Demokraticheskaia gazeta* 6.

Chuiko, Liubov'. 1974. "Opyt analiza mezhnatsional'nykh brakov v SSSR." In Dmitrii Valentei (ed.), *Razvitie naseleniia.* Moscow: Statistika.

Chukovskaia, Lidiia. 1998. *Sofia Petrovna.* London: Bristol Classic Press.

Chulaki, Mikhail. 1998. "Svastika i natsionalizm." *Izvestiia.* 11 August.

Churchill, Winston. 1931. "If Lee had won the Battle of Gettysburg." In John Collings Squire, *History rewritten.* New York: Viking Press.

Churbanov, Yurii. 1992. *Ia rasskazhu vse, kak bylo.* Moscow: Nezavisimaia gazeta.

Clements, Douglas H. 1989. *Computers in elementary mathematics education.* Englewood Cliffs, N.J.: Prentice Hall.

Cobb, Richard. 1998. *The French and their revolution.* London: John Murray.

Coghill, Jeffrey J. 1970. *The red scare and radical labor, 1919–1920.* A report from an Independent Study. Dissertation: Thesis (Undergraduate)—Maryville College, 1970. By Jeffrey J. Coghill for the Department of History.

Cohen, Roger. 1999. "For the wall's fall, East Germans are given their due." *New York Times.* 10 November.

Cohen, Stephen. 1973. *Bukharin and the Bolshevik Revolution: A political biography, 1888–1938.* New York: A.A. Knopf.

————. 1985. *Rethinking the Soviet experience: Politics and history since 1917.* New York: Oxford University Press.

————. 1992. "What's really happening in Russia?" *Nation* 254:8 (2 March).

————. 1994. "America's failed crusade in Russia." *Nation* 258:8 (28 February).

————. 1996. "'Transition' of tragedy?" *Nation* 263:22 (30 December).

Colton, Timothy. 1986. *The dilemma of reform in the Soviet Union.* New York: Council on Foreign Relations.

Comaroff, John L., and Paul C. Stern (eds.). 1995. *Perspectives on nationalism and war.* Australia: Gordon and Breach Publishing Group.

Conquest, Robert. 1970. *The national killers: The Soviet deportation of nationalities.* London: Macmillan.

Conquest, Robert (ed.). 1986a. *The last empire: Nationality and the Soviet Empire.* Stanford: Hoover Institution Press.

Conquest, Robert. 1986b. *The harvest of sorrow: Soviet collectivization and the terror-famine.* London: Hutchinson.

————. 1990. *The great terror: A reassessment.* New York: Oxford University Press.

————. 1992. "The party in the dock." *Times Literary Supplement.* 6 November.

————. 1993. "Red to go." *Times Literary Supplement.* 9 July.

————. 1994. "Reds." *New York Review of Books.* 14 July.

Converse, Phillip. 1964. "The nature of the belief system of mass publics." In David Apter (ed.), *Ideology and discontent.* London: Free Press of Glencoe.

Corson, William R., and Robert T. Crowley. 1985. *The new KGB, engine of Soviet power.* New York: Morrow.

Courtois, Stephan (ed.). 1997. *Le livre noir du communisme: Crimes, terreures et repression.* Paris: R. Laffont.

Crankshaw, Edward. 1963. *The fall of the house of Habsburg.* New York: Viking Press.

————. 1966. *Khrushchev: A career.* New York: Viking Press.

Crozier, Brian, and Arthur Seldon. 1986. *Socialism: The grand delusion.* New York: Universe Books.

Curtis, Michael (ed.). 1990. *Introduction to comparative government.* New York: Harper.

Cust, Richard. 1991. "Revising the high politics of English Stuart England." *Journal of British Studies* 30:325.

Dahl, Robert. 1972. *Poliarchy: Participation and opposition.* New Haven, Conn.: Yale University Press.

Dallin, David. 1922. *Posle voin i revoliutsii.* Berlin: Grani.

Dallin, David, and Boris Nikolaevsky. 1947. *Forced labor in Soviet Russia.* New Haven, Conn.: Yale University Press.

Dallin, Alexander. 1973. "Biases and blunders in the American studies on the USSR." *Slavic Review* 32:3, pp. 560–576.

————. 1988. *U.S.-Soviet security cooperation: Achievements, failures, lessons.* New York: Oxford University Press.

Dan, Lidia. 1959. *Martov i ego blizkie: Sbornik.* New York: Rausen Bros.

Daniels, Robert. 2000. "Was communism reformable?" *Nation.* 3 January.

Danilov, Victor, et al. 1990. *Central problems of Russian and Soviet history: New research and aproaches.* Moscow: "Social Sciences Today" Editorial board, Nauka.

Danilov, Viktor, and Teodor Shanin. 1994. *Krest'ianskoe vosstanie v Tambovskoi gubernii v 1919–1921. "Antonovshchina": dokumenty i materialy.* Tambov: Redaktsionno-izdatel'skii sovet.

Davies, Robert. 1997. *Soviet history in the Yeltsin era.* London: Macmillan.

Davies, Sarah. 1997. *Public opinion in Stalin's Russia: Terror, propaganda, and dissent, 1934–1941.* Cambridge: Cambridge University Press.

Davydchenkov, Vasilii. 1970. "Organizatsiia sotsiologicheskogo obsledovaniia i vnedrenie poluchennykh rezul'tatov v tsentral'noi gazete." In Vladimir Shlapentokh (ed.), *Sotsiologiia pechati.* Vol. 2. Novosibirsk: Nauka.

Dementiev, Alexander. 1969. "O traditsii i narodnosti." *Novy mir* 4.

Demin, V. 1997. "Sopernichestvo s nicheinym schetom." *Sovetskaia Rossiia.* 20 December.

Deriabin, Peter, and Tennent Bagley. 1990. *KGB: Masters of the Soviet Union.* New York: Hippocrene Books.

Desai, Padma (ed.). 1983. *Marxism, central planning, and the Soviet economy: Economic essays in honor of Alexander Erlich.* Cambridge, Mass.: MIT Press.

Deviatyi s"ezd RKP (b) Protokoly. 1960. Moscow: Politizdat.

Dick, Philip. 1988. *The man in the high castle.* Harmondsworth, England: Penguin Books.

DiMaggio, Thomas. 2000. "Russian perceptions of the West." *Times Literary Supplement.* 15 September.

Dmytryshyn, Basil. 1974. *Modernization of Russia under Peter I and Catherine II.* New York: Wiley.

Dobbs, Michael. 1997. *Down with Big Brother: The fall of the Soviet empire.* New York: Knopf.

Dobrovolsky, Alexander. 1999. "Vosstavshii Gulag." *Moskovskii komsomolets.* 15 November.

Dobrynin, Anatolii. 1995. *In confidence: Moscow ambassador to America's six Cold War presidents.* New York: Random House.

Doder, Dusko. 1986. *Shadows and whispers.* New York: Random House.

———. 1990. *Gorbachev: Heretic in the Kremlin.* New York: Viking.

Dolgorukov, Pavel. 1964. *Velikaia razrukha.* Madrid (no publishing house).

Dontsov, Alexander. 1984. *Psikhologiia kollektiva: Metodologicheskie problemy issledovaniia.* Moscow: Izd. Moskovskogo universiteta.

Dorr, Retha Childe. 1917. *Inside the Russian Revolution.* New York: Macmillan.

Draper, Theodore. 1957. *The roots of American communism.* New York: Viking Press.

———. 1960. *American communism and Soviet Russia: The formative period.* New York: Viking Press.

Drobizheva, Leokadia. 1978. "Tendentsii izmeneniia mezhetnicheskikh ustanovok." In T.V. Riabushkin (ed.), *Sotsiologiia i problemy sotsial'nogo razvitiia.* Moscow: Nauka.

Druzhnikov, Yurii. 1997. *Voznesenie Pavlika Morozova.* New Brunswick, N.J.: Transaction Publishers.

Dubnow, Simon. 1916. *History of the Jews in Russia and Poland, from the earliest times until the present day.* Philadelphia: Jewish Publication Society of America.

Dudintsev, Vladimir. 1957. *Ne khlebom edinym: Roman v chetyrekh chastiakh.* Munich: TsOPE.

———. 1988. *Belye odezhdy.* Moscow: Knizhnaia palata.

Dugin, Alexander. 1996. *Misterii Evrazii.* Moscow: Artogeia.

———. 1997. "Evrei i Evrazia." *Zavtra* 47.

———. 1998. "Al'ternativa." *Zavtra* 8.

Dunlop, John. 1993. *The rise of Russia and the fall of the Soviet empire.* Princeton: Princeton University Press.

Durkheim, Emile. 1938. *The rules of sociological methods.* Chicago: University of Chicago Press.

Eidelman, Moisei. 1998. "Monopolized statistics under a totalitarian regime." In Michael Ellman and Vladimir Kontorovich (eds.), *The destruction of the Soviet economic system: An insiders' history.* Armonk, N.Y.: M.E. Sharpe.

Eklof, Ben, John Bushnell, and Larissa Zakharova (eds.). 1994. *Russia's great reforms, 1855–1881.* Bloomington: Indiana University Press.

Eley, Geoff. 1986. "History with the politics left out—again." *Russian Review* 45.

Ellman, Michael, and Vladimir Kontorovich (eds.). 1998. *The destruction of the Soviet economic system: An insiders' history.* Armonk, N.Y.: M.E. Sharpe.

Elster, Jon. 1979. *Ulysses and the sirens: Studies in rationality and irrationality.* New York: Cambridge University Press.

Erenburg, Il'ia. 1934. *Den' vtoroi.* Moscow: Khudozhestvennaia literatura.

Eysenk, Hans Jürgen. 1954. *The psychology of politics.* London: Routledge and Kegan Paul.

Fainsod, Merle. 1958. *Smolensk under Soviet rule.* Cambridge: Harvard University Press.

———. 1963. *How Russia is ruled.* Cambridge: Harvard University Press.

Fairbanks, Charles. 1993. "The nature of the beast." *National Interest.* Spring.

Fallada, Hans. 1964. *Jeder stirbt für sich allein.* Hamburg: Rowohlt.

Fedoseev, Petr (ed.). 1985. *Nauchnyi kommunizm: Uchebnik.* Moscow: Politizdat.

Fedotoff White, Dimitrii. 1944. *The growth of the Red Army.* Princeton: Princeton University Press.

Fedotova, Valentina. 2001. "Rossia v globalnom i vnutrennem mire." *Nezavisimaia gazeta.* 21 February.

Felshtinksy, Yurii (ed.). 1995. *VchK-GPU.* Moscow: Dokumenty i materialy.

Ferguson, Niall (ed.). 1998. *Virtual history: Alternatives and counterfactuals.* Trans-Atlantic Publications.

Fetisov, Tom. 1997. *Prem'er izvestnyi i neizvestnyi: Vospominaniia o A.N. Kosygine.* Moscow: Respublika.

Field, Mark. 1991. "Health problems." In Anthony Jones, Walter Connor, and David Powell (eds.), *Soviet social problems.* Boulder, Colo.: Westview Press.

Figes, Orlando. 1996a. "Sheep or wolf?" *Times Literary Supplement.* 31 May.

———. 1996b. *A people's tragedy: The Russian Revolution, 1917–1924.* New York: Penguin.

———. 1997. "Peasant armies." In Edward Acton, Vladimir Cherniaev, and William Rosenberg (eds.), *Critical companion to the Russian Revolution, 1914–1921.* Bloomington: Indiana University Press.

Filatov, Vladimir, and Sergei Fateev. 1997. "Mify liberal'noi ekonomiki." *Nezavisimaia gazeta-Stsenarii.* 17 January.

Firsov, Boris. 1977. *Puti razvitiia sredstv massovoi kommunikatsii.* Leningrad: Nauka.

Fisher, Wesley. 1980. *The Soviet marriage market: Mate-Selection in Russia and the USSR.* New York: Praeger.

Fitzpatrick, Sheila (ed). 1978. *Cultural revolution in Russia, 1928–1931.* Bloomington: Indiana University Press.

Fitzpatrick, Sheila. 1979. *Education and social mobility in the Soviet Union, 1921–1934.* Cambridge and New York: Cambridge University Press.

———. 1982. *The Russian Revolution.* New York: Oxford University Press.

———. 1986. "New perspectives on Stalinism." *Russian Review* 45:357–373.

———. 1992. *The cultural front: Power and culture in Revolutionary Russia.* Ithaca: Cornell University Press.

————. 1994a. *The Russian Revolution*. New York and Oxford: Oxford University Press.

————. 1994b. *Stalin's peasants: Resistance and survival in the Russian village after collectivization*. New York and Oxford: Oxford University Press.

————. 1999. *Everyday Stalinism: Ordinary life in extraordinary times: Soviet Russia in the 1930s*. New York: Oxford University Press.

Ford, Robert. 1984. "The Soviet Union: The next decade." *Foreign Affairs*. (Summer):1132–1144.

Frank-Kamenetski, Maxim. 1988. "Pochemu molchat uchenyie." *Literaturnaia gazeta*. 16.

Freemantel, Brian. 1984. *KGB: Inside the world's largest intelligence network*. New York: Holt.

Freinkman, Lev. 1998. "Politics and enterprise behavior." In Michael Ellman and Vladimir Kontorovich (eds.), *The destruction of the Soviet economic system: An insiders' history*. Armonk, N.Y.: M.E. Sharpe.

Friedgut, Theodore. 1977. *Political participation in the USSR*. Princeton: Princeton University Press.

Friedrich, Carl J., and Zbigniew Brzezinski. 1956. *Totalitarian dictatorship and autocracy*. Cambridge: Harvard University Press.

Frisby, David, and Derek Sayer. 1986. *Societies*. New York: Tavistock Publications.

Frumkin, Jacob, Gregor Aronson, and A. Gol'denveizer (eds.). 1968. *Kniga o russkom evreistve, 1917–1967*. New York: Soiuz russkikh evreev.

Fukuyama, Francis. 1992. *The end of history and the last man*. New York: Free Press; Toronto: Maxwell Macmillan Canada.

Furet, François, and Mona Ozouf (eds.). 1989. *A critical dictionary of the French Revolution*. Cambridge, Mass.: Belknap Press of Harvard University Press.

Gachev, Georgii. 1994. "Ia sovetskii chelovek." *Nezavisimaia gazeta*. 29 January.

Gaddis, John. 1997. *We know now: Rethinking Cold War history*. New York: Oxford University Press.

Gaddy, Clifford. 1996. *The price of the past: Russia's struggle with the legacy of a militarized economy*. Washington, D.C.: Brookings Institution.

Gaidar, Yegor. 1997. *Gosudarstvo i evoliutsiia: Kak otdelit' sobstvennost' ot vlasti i povysit' blagosostoianie rossian*. St. Petersburg: Norma.

Gal'tseva, Renata. 1988. "Uchastie v diskussii 'Istoria-protsess, istoria-drama.'" *Znanie-Sila*. 23 July.

Garder, Michel. 1966. *A history of the Soviet army*. London: Pall Mall Press.

Garros, Veronique, Natalia Korenevskaya, and Thomas Lahusen (eds.). 1995. *Intimacy and terror: Soviet diaries of the 1930s*. New York: New Press.

Garvy, George. 1977. *Money, financial flows, and credit in the Soviet Union*. New York: National Bureau of Economic Research.

Gates, Robert. 1996. *From the shadows: The ultimate insider's story of five presidents and how they won the Cold War*. New York: Simon & Schuster.

Gatovsky, Lev, and Leonid Abalkin. 1984. *Ispol'zovanie ekonomicheskikh zakonov v planovom upravlenii khoziaistvom*. Moscow: "Ekonomika."

Gay, Peter. 1998. "The elusiveness of the bourgeoisie." *Times Literary Supplement*. 28 August.

Gefter, Mikhail. 1988. "Stalin umer vchera." In Yurii Afanasiev (ed.), *Inogo ne dano*. Moscow: Progress.

Gellner, Ernest. 1983. *Nations and nationalism*. Ithaca: Cornell University Press.

Gelman, Alexander. 1997. "'Iabloko,' kuda ty katish'sia." *Moskovskie novosti.* 25 June.

Getty, John Arch. 1985. *Origins of the great purges: The Soviet Communist Party reconsidered, 1933–1938.* New York: Cambridge University Press.

Getty, John Arch, and Roberta Manning. 1993. "Introduction." In John Arch Getty and Roberta Manning (eds.). *Stalinist terror: New perspectives.* New York: Cambridge University Press.

Getty, John Arch, and Oleg Naumov. 1999. *The road to terror: Stalin and the self-destruction of the Bolsheviks, 1932–1939.* New Haven, Conn.: Yale University Press.

Gevorkian, Natalia. 1992. "Vstrechnye plany po unichtozheniiu sobstvennogo naroda." *Moskovskie novosti.* 21 June.

———. 1995. "Organy silny sviaz'iu s narodom." *Moskovskie novosti.* 10 September.

Giddens, Anthony. 1998. *The third way: The renewal of social democracy.* Cambridge, Eng.: Polity Press.

Gidoni, Alexander. 1980. *Solntse idet s zapada: Kniga vospominanii.* Toronto: Sovremennik.

Gimpelson, Efim. 1995. *Formirovanie sovetskoi politicheskoi sistemy.* Moscow: Nauka.

Gingrich, Newt, and William R. Forstchen. 1995. *1945.* Riverdale, NY: Baen Publishing Enterprises.

Ginzburg, Evgenia. 1967. *Into the whirlwind.* London: Collins.

———. 1985. *Krutoi marshrut.* Vol. 1. New York: Posev.

Ginzberg, Lev. 1993. "Neobkhodimye utochneniia." *Nezavisimaia gazeta.* 2 October.

———. 1999. "Gosudarstvennyi antisemitizm: 70-ti letniaia traditsiia." *Izvestiia.* 16 January.

Glantz, David. 1998. *Stumbling colossus: The red army on the eve of world war.* Lawrence, Kans.: University Press of Kansas.

Glavatsky, Mikhail (ed.). 1995. *Rossiia, kotoruiu my ne znaem.* Cheliabinsk: Iuzhno-Uralskoe knizhnoe izdatel'stvo.

Glazer, Nathan. 1984. "New York intellectuals: Up from revolution." *New York Times Review of Books.* 26 February.

Gleason, Abbott. 1995a. "Totalitarianism and cold war: A personal view." *Newsnet, the News Letter of the AAASS.* 35:4 (September).

———. 1995b. *Totalitarianism: The inner history of the Cold War.* New York: Oxford University Press.

Glezerman, Grigorii, Mikhail Rutkevish, and S. Vishnevsky (eds.). 1980. *Sotsialisticheskii obraz zhizni.* Moscow: Politizdat.

Glushkova, Tatiana. 1990. "Na ruinakh imperskogo soznaniia." *Zavtra* 32.

Gnedin, Evgenii. 1982. *Vykhod iz labirinta.* New York: Chalidze.

Goebbels, Joseph. 1982. *The Goebbels diaries, 1939–1941.* London: H. Hamilton.

Goldansky, Vitalii. 1998. "Epitafiia XX veku." *Nezavisimaia gazeta.* 11 November.

Goodin, Robert E. 1976. *The politics of rational man.* London and New York: Wiley.

Goodvin, Jason. 1999. *Lords of horizons: A history of the Ottoman empire.* London: Vintage.

Gorbachev, Mikhail. 1985. *Izbrannye rechi i stat'i.* Moscow: Gospolitizdat.

———. 1986. *Izbrannye rechi i stat'i.* Moscow: Politizdat.

———. 1987a. *Izbrannye rechi i stat'i.* Vol. 2. Moscow: Gospolitizdat.

———. 1987b. *Izbrannye rechi i stat'i.* Vol. 3. Moscow: Gospolitizdat.

———. 1990. *Izbrannye rechi i stat'i.* Vol. 7. Moscow: Politizdat.

————. 1993. "Esli nado budet spasat' stranu, ia vernus'." *Komsomol'skaia pravda.* 9 October.

————. 1995. *Zhizn' i reformy.* Moscow: Novosti.

————. 1996. *Memoirs.* New York: Doubleday.

————. 1997a. "Istoriia ne fatal'na." *Moskovskie novosti.* 2 November.

————. 1997b. Interview. *Argumenty i fakty* 36.

————. 1997c. Interview. *Nezavisimaia gazeta.* 6 November.

————. 1998. *Razmyshleniia o proshlom i budushchem.* Moscow: Terra.

————. 2000a. "Istoria—eto priniatie reshenii." *Nezavisimaia gazeta.* 12 April.

————. 2000b. Interview. *Nezavisimaia gazeta.* 29 April.

Gordon, Leonid, Eduard Klopov. 1972. *Chelovek posle raboty.* Moscow: Nauka.

————. 1989. *Chto eto bylo.* Moscow: Politizdat.

Gorelik, Gennadii. 1992. "Za chto sidel Lev Landau." *Izvestiia.* 8 January.

————. 1995. "Lev Landau, pro-socialist prisoner of the Soviet state." *Physics Today.* May.

Gorshkov, Mikhail. 1998. "Strana posle ocherednogo krizisa." *Nezavisimaia gazeta.* 25 November.

Goskomstat. 1987. *Narodnoe khoziaistvo SSSR za 70 let.* Moscow: Finansy i statistika.

————. 1988. *Narodnoe khoziaistvo SSSR v 1987 godu.* Moscow: Finansy i statistika.

————. 1990. *Narodnoe khoziaistvo SSSR v 1989 godu.* Moscow: Financy i statistika.

————. 1991a. *Narodnoe khoziaistvo SSSR v 1990 godu.* Moscow: Finansy i statistika.

————. 1991b. *Mneniia naseleniia o tsenakh na tovary i uslugi.* Moscow: Goskomizdat.

————. 1997. *Rossiiskii statisticheskii ezhegodnik.* Moscow: Goskomstat.

————. 1998. *Rossiiskii statisticheskii ezhegodnik.* Moscow: Goskomizdat.

————. 1999. *Rossiiskii statisticheskii ezhegodnik.* Moscow: Goskomizdat.

Grachev, Andrei. 1994. *Kremlevskaia 'Khronika.'* Moscow: "EKSMO."

Granin, Daniil. 1990. "Nash dorogoi Roman Avdeevich." In Andrei Protashchik (ed.), *Cherez ternii.* Moscow: Progress.

Gray, John. 1998. "Hollow triumph." *Times Literary Supplement.* 8 May.

Grechin, A. 1983. "Opyt sotsiologicheskogo issledovaniia pravosoznaniia." *Sotsiologicheskie issledovaniia* 2.

Gregory, Paul, and Robert Stuart. 1974. *Soviet economic structure and performance.* New York: Harper & Row.

Grigorenko, Piotr. 1982. *Memoirs.* New York: Norton.

Grinenko, Anatolii. 1990. Interview. *Moskovskie novosti.* 4 March.

Grishin, Victor. 1996. *Ot Khrushcheva do Gorbacheva.* Moscow: Aspol.

Grossman, Gregory. 1977. "'The second economy of the Soviet Union." *Problems of Communism* 26:5.

Grossman, Vasilii. 1970. *Vse techet.* Frankfurt: Posev.

————. 1980. *Zhizn' i sud'ba.* Lausanne: L'Age d'homme.

Grushin, Boris. 1967. *Mir mnenii i mneniia o mire.* Moscow: Politizdat.

————. 2001. *Chetyre zhizni Rossii v zerkale oprosov obshchestvennogo mnenia.* Moscow: Progress Traditsia.

Grushin, Boris, and Lev Onikov (eds.). 1980. *Massovaia informatsiia v sovetskom promyshlennom gorode.* Moscow: Politizdat.

Gulbinsky, Nikolai, and Marina Shakina. 1994. *Epizody politicheskoi biografii Aleksandra Rutskogo.* Moscow: Lada-M.

Gulyga, Arsenii. 1988. "Stat' zerkalom dushi naroda." *Voprosy filosofii* 9.

Gurov, Alexander. 1995. *Krasnaia mafia.* Moscow: Samotsvet.

Gustafson, Thane, and M. Mann. 1986. "Gorbachev's first year building power and authority." *Problems of Communism.* May–June:1–2.

Gvozdev, Nikolai. 1985. *Stimuly sotsialisticheskoi ekonomiki.* Moscow: Ekonomika.

Gwertzman, Bernard, and Michael T. Kaufman (eds.). 1992. *The decline and fall of the Soviet empire.* New York: Times Books.

Hajda, Lubomyr, and Mark Beissinger (eds). 1990. *The Nationalities factor in Soviet politics and society.* Boulder, Colo.: Westview Press.

Hanson, Philip. 1968. *The consumer in the Soviet economy.* Evanston, Ill.: Northwestern University Press.

Harries, Merion, and Susie Harris. 1997. *Last days of innocence: America at war, 1917–1918.* New York: Random House.

Harris, Robert. 1992. *Fatherland.* New York: Random House.

Harrison, Mark. 1998. "Soviet Union: The defeated victor." In Harrison (ed.), *The economics of World War II: Six great powers in international comparison.* Cambridge: Cambridge University Press.

Harvey, John H., William John Ickes, and Robert F. Kidd (eds.). 1976. *New directions in attribution research.* Hillsdale, N.J.: Lawrence Erlbaum Associates.

Haslam, Jonathan. 1983. *Soviet foreign policy, 1930–1933: The impact of depression.* New York: St. Martin's Press.

Havel, Vaclav. 1993. "The post-Communist nightmare." *New York Review of Books.* 27 May.

Hayek, Friedrich von (ed.). 1935. *Collectivist economic planning: Critical studies on the possibilities of socialism.* London: G. Routledge.

Hayek, Friedrich von. 1944. *The road to serfdom.* Chicago: University of Chicago Press.

Haynes, John, and Harvey Klehr. 1999. *Venona: Decoding Soviet espionage in America.* New Haven, Conn.: Yale University Press.

Heilbrunn, Jacob. 1998. *The New Republic.* 12 October.

Heilbrunn, Otto. 1956. *The Soviet secret service.* New York: Praeger.

Heller, Mikhail, and Alexander Nekrich. 1982. *Utopiia u vlasti: Istoriia Sovetskogo soiuza s 1917 goda do nashikh dnei.* London: Overseas Publications Interchange.

Hellman, Lillian. 1976. *Scoundrel time.* Boston: Little, Brown.

Herzberg, James. 1996. "Litany of misery." *New York Times Book Review.* 1 December.

Hessler, Julie. 1998. "A postwar perestroika? Toward a history of private enterprise in the USSR." *Slavic Review* 57:3 (Fall).

Highland, William. 1979. "Brezhnev and beyond." *Foreign Affairs.* Fall:51–66.

Hoch, Steven. 1986. *Serfdom and social control in Russia: Petrovskoe, a village in Tambov.* Chicago: University of Chicago Press.

Hollander, Paul. 1998. *Political pilgrims: Western intellectuals in search of the good society.* New Brunswick, N.J.: Transaction Publishers.

Honan, William H. 1998. "Historians warming to games of 'what if.'" *New York Times.* 7 January.

Hosking, Geoffrey. 1991. *The awakening of the Soviet Union.* London: Mandarin.

———. 1992. "Heirs of the tsarist empire." *Times Literary Supplement.* 6 November.

———. 1999. "War by other means." *Times Literary Supplement.* 16 April.

Hough, Jerry. 1977. *The Soviet Union and social science theory.* Cambridge: Harvard University Press.

————. 1980. *Soviet leadership in transition.* Washington, D.C.: Brookings Institution.

————. 1987. "Gorbachev consolidating power." *Problems of Communism.* July–August: 21–43.

Hough, Jerry, and Merle Fainsod. 1979. *How the Soviet Union is governed.* Cambridge: Harvard University Press.

Houghteling, James Lawrence. 1918. *A diary of the Russian revolution.* New York: Dodd, Mead and Company.

Howe, Irving. 1982. *A margin of hope: An intellectual autobiography.* San Diego: Harcourt Brace.

Howe, Irving, and Lewis Coser. 1957. *The American Communist Party: A critical history, 1919–1957.* Boston: Beacon Press.

Howson, Gerald. 1999. *Arms for Spain: The untold story of the Spanish civil war.* New York: St. Martin's Press.

Huntington, Samuel. 1996. *The clash of civilizations and the remaking of world order.* New York: Simon & Schuster.

Ignatieff, Michael. 1996. "Whispers from the abyss." *New York Review of Books.* 23 September.

Inkeles, Alex, and Raymond Bauer. 1968. *The Soviet citizen: Daily life in a totalitarian society.* New York: Atheneum.

Ioffe, Genrikh, and Yurii Korablev (eds.). 1989. *Rossiia, 1917: Vybor istoricheskogo puti.* Moscow: Nauka.

Ionescu, Ghita. 1965. *The break-up of the Soviet empire in Eastern Europe.* Baltimore: Penguin Books.

Isserman, Maurice. 1999. "They led two lives." *New York Times Book Review.* 9 May.

Ivanov, Sergei. 1997. "Povernuv shtyk." *Sovetskaia Rossiia.* 30 January.

Ivanova, Galina. 2000. *Labor camp socialism: The Gulag in the Soviet totalitarian system.* Armonk, N.Y.: M.E. Sharpe.

Ivnitsky, Nikolai. 1990. "Raskulachivanie." *Soiuz* 3.

————. 1995. *Golod 1932–1933 godov.* Moscow: Rossiiskii gosudarstvennyi gumanitarnyi universitet.

————. 1996. *Kollektivizatsiia i raskulachivanie: Nachalo 30–kh godov.* Moscow: Magistr.

Izmozik, Vladlen. 1995a. "Perlustratsia." *Voprosy istorii* 8:34.

————. 1995b. "Pishite pis'ma, ikh prochtut." *Argumenty i fakty* 38.

————. 1995c. *Glaza i ushi rezhima: Gosudarstvennyi politicheskii kontrol' za naseleniem sovetskoi Rossii v 1918–1928 godakh.* St. Petersburg: Izd. Sankt-Peterburgskogo universiteta ekonomiki i finansov.

James, Lawrence. 1994. *The rise and fall of the British empire.* London: Little, Brown.

Jasny, Naum. 1957. *The Soviet 1956 statistical yearbook: Commentary.* East Lansing, Mich.: Michigan State University Press.

Jones, Ellen. 1985. *Red Army and society: A sociology of the Soviet military.* Boston: Allen & Unwin.

Jones, Ellen, and K. Davis. 1964. "From acts to disposition: The attribution process in person perception." In Leonard Berkovitz (ed.), *Advances in experimental social psychology.* Vol. 2. New York: Academic Press.

Joseph, William A., Christine P.W. Wong, and David Zweig (eds.). 1991. *New perspectives on the cultural revolution.* Cambridge, Mass.: Council on East Asian Studies, Harvard University.

Josephson, Paul. 1997. *New Atlantis revisited: Akademgorodok, the Siberian city of science*. Princeton: Princeton University Press.

Judt, Tony. 1997. "Why the cold war worked." *New York Review of Books*. 9 October.

———. 1998. "The 'third way' is no route to paradise." *New York Times*. 27 September.

Kalinin, Nikolai. 1998. "Nasil'no patriotom ne stanesh." *Izvestiia*. 7 July.

Kalugin, Oleg. 1994. *The First Directorate: My 32 years in intelligence and espionage against the West*. New York: St. Martin's Press.

Kapustin, Evgenii (ed.). 1984. *Ekonomicheskii stroi sotsializma*. Vol. 3. Moscow: Ekonomika.

Kara-Murza, Sergei. 1994a. "Prostye voprosy nashim vozhdiam." *Pravda*. 12 October.

———. 1994b. "'Imperiia' i 'natsiia.'" In Andrei Zdravomyslov (ed.), *Vzaimodeistvie politicheskikh i natsional'no-etnicheskikh konfliktov*. Vol. 2. Moscow: Rossiiskii institut sotsial'nykh i natsional'nykh problem.

———. 1995a. "Kto my, i otkuda vyshli." *Pravda*. 7 February.

———. 1995b. "Komu nuzhno razdelenie naroda." *Pravda*. 10 March.

———. 1996a. "Kak zaveli nas v tupik." *Sovetskaia Rossiia*. 10 September.

———. 1996b. "Effekt babochki." *Sovetskaia Rossiia*. 19 October.

———. 1997a. "Strela iskrivleniia." *Sovetskaia Rossiia*. 6 January.

———. 1997b. "Zhestkii demontazh." *Sovetskaia Rossiia*. 9 January.

Karagedov, Raimond. 1970. "Reforma glazami direktora." *Eko* 1.

Karpinsky, Len. 1972. "Novaia rabochaia arena." *Novy mir* 5.

———. 1987. "Ne vredno posmotret' na sebia so storony." *Moskovskie novosti*. 11 October.

Kataev, Valentin. 1933. *Time, forward!* New York: Farrar & Rinehart.

Katkov, N. 1991. "Dolg pamiati i spravedlivosti." *Pravda*. 13 April.

Katsenelinboigen, Aron. 1976. "Color markets in the Soviet Union." *Soviet Studies* XXIX:1, pp. 62–85.

———. 1978. *Studies in Soviet economic planning*. White Plains, N.Y.: M.E. Sharpe.

———. 1980. *Soviet economic thought and political power in the USSR*. Elmsford, N.Y.: Pergamon.

———. 1990. *The Soviet Union: Empire, nation, and system*. New Brunswick, N.J.: Transaction Publishers.

Kazakov, Victor (ed.). 1989a. *Perestroika*. Moscow: Progress.

———. 1989b. *Sovetskii pisatel'*. Moscow: Progress.

Kennan, George. 1961. *Russia and the West under Lenin and Stalin*. Boston: Little, Brown.

Kennedy, Mark E. 1991. "Legislation, foreign policy, and the 'proper business' of the parliament of 1624." *Albion* 23:1.

Kenzer, Peter. 1986. "Stalinism as humdrum politics." *Russian Review* 45:375–384.

Kerblay, Basil. 1987. *Gorbachev's Russia*. New York: Pantheon Books.

Khanin, Grigorii. 1989a. "Pochemu i kogda pogib NEP." *Eko* 10:73.

———. 1989b. "Ob otsenke ob"ema i dinamiki osnovnykh proizvodstvennykh fondov." *Ekonomicheskie nauki* 6.

———. 1991. *Dinamika ekonomicheskogo razvitiia SSSR*. Novosibirsk: Nauka.

———. 1993. *Sovetskii ekonomicheskii rost: Analiz zapadnykh otsenok*. Novosibirsk: EKOR.

———. 1998. "Attempts to inform the leaders." In Michael Ellman and Vladimir

Kontorovich (eds.), *The destruction of the Soviet economic system: An insiders' history*. Armonk, N.Y.: M.E. Sharpe.

Kharchev, Anatolii (ed.). 1976. *Moral' razvitogo sotsializma (Aktual'nye problemy teorii)*. Moscow: Mysl'

Khariton, Yulii, and Yurii Smirnov. 1994. "Otkuda vzialos' i bylo li nam neobkhodimo iadernoe oruzhie." *Izvestiia*, 21 July.

Khazanov, Anatolii. 1988. "The current ethnic situation in the USSR." *Nationalities Papers* 2:147–170.

———. 1995. *After the USSR*. Madison: University of Wisconsin Press.

Khinshtein, Alexander. 1994. "Dobryi kapitan gosbezopasnosti." *Moskovskii komsomolets*. 15 October.

Khrushchev, Nikita. 1957. *On the further improvement of management in industry and construction in the U.S.S.R.: Report and reply to discussion at the seventh session of the Supreme Soviet, 7–10 May 1957*. London: Soviet News.

———. 1961. *O programme Kommunisticheskoi partii Sovetskogo soiuza: doklad na XXII s" ezde Kommunisticheskoi partii Sovetskogo soiuza, 18 oktiabria 1961 goda*. Moscow: Gospolitizdat.

———. 1970. *Khrushchev remembers*. Vol. 1. New York: Random House.

Khrushchev, Sergei. 1990. *Khrushchev on Khrushchev: An inside account of the man and his era*. Boston: Little, Brown.

———. 2000. *Rozhdenie sverkhderzhavy: Kniga ob ottse*. Moscow: Vremia.

Kim, Maksim. 1983. *Problemy teorii i istorii real'nogo sotsializma*. Moscow: Nauka.

Kirienko, Sergei. 1998. "Ne nado teshit' sebia illiuziami, chto krizis zakonchilsia." *Nezavisimaia gazeta*. 11 May.

Kiselev, Grigorii. 1992. *Tragediia obshchestva i cheloveka: Popytka osmysleniia opyta sovetskoi istorii*. Moscow: Nauka.

Kiselev, V. 1988. "Skol'ko modelei sotsializma bylo v SSSR?" In Yurii Afanasiev (ed.), *Inogo ne dano*. Moscow: Progress.

Kishlansky, Marc. 1996. *A monarchy transformed: Britain, 1603–1714*. London: Penguin.

Kissinger, Henry. 1979. *The White House years*. Boston: Little, Brown.

———. 1994. *Diplomacy*. New York: Simon & Schuster.

Klehr, Harvey, John Haynes, and Kyrill Anderson. 1998. *The Soviet World of American Communism*. New Haven, Conn.: Yale University Press.

Klementev, Dmitrii. 1984. *Lichnost' razvitogo sotsialisticheskogo obshchestva*. Moscow: Moskovskii universitet.

Kliamkin, Eduard. 1995. "Blesk i nishcheta dissidentov." *Literaturnaia gazeta*. 11 October.

Kliamkin, Igor. 1987. "Kakaia ulitsa idet k khramu?" *Novy mir* 9:150.

———. 1989. "Pochemu trudno govorit' pravdu." *Novy mir* 2.

Kliamkin, Igor, and Lev Timofeev. 1999. "Tenevaia Rossiia nakanune vybora." *Nezavisimaia gazeta–Stsenarii*. 8 December.

Knight, Amy. 1993. *Beria: Stalin's first lieutenant*. Princeton: Princeton University Press.

Kochergin, Al'bert, and Vladimir Kogan. 1980. *Problemy informatsionnogo vzaimodeistviia v obshchestve: Filosofsko-sotsiologicheskii analiz*. Novosibirsk: Nauka.

Kochetkov, Andrei. 1999. "Kommunisticheskii rezhim rukhnul, potomu chto upali tseny na neft.'" *Literaturnaia gazeta*. 31 March.

Koehler, John O. 1999. *Stasi: The untold story of the East German secret police*. Boulder, Colo.: Westview Press.

Koenker, Diane, and William Rosenberg. 1989. *Strikes and revolution in Russia, 1917.* Princeton, N.J.: Princeton University Press.

Koestler, Arthur. 1941. *Darkness at noon.* New York: Modern Library.

Kogan, Leonid (ed.). 1983. *Sotsial'no-kul'turnye predposylki samorealizatsii lichnosti v sotsialisticheskom obshchestve.* Sverdlovsk: Ural'skii nauchnyi tsentr.

Kolakowski, Lezsek. 1978. *Main currents of Marxism.* Oxford: Clarendon Press.

Kolesnikov, Andrei. 1993. "Angazhement dlia intellektuala." *Nezavisimaia gazeta.* 22 June.

Kolodnitsky, Mark. 1993. "Ia noshu poztret Stalina." *Rossiiskaia gazeta.* 27 April.

Kon, Igor. 1980. *Druzhba.* Moscow: Politizdat.

———. 1983. *Slovar' po etike.* Moscow: Politizdat.

———. 1997. "Moral culture." In Dmitrii Shalin (ed.), *Russian culture at the crossroads.* Boulder, Colo.: Westview Press.

Konstantinovsky, David. 1999. "Musorshchiku platiat kak professoru." *Argumenty i fakty* 51.

Kontorovich, Vladimir, and Vladimir Shlapentokh. 1986. *Organizational innovation, the Carl Beck papers.* Pittsburgh, Pa.: University of Pittsburgh.

Kopelev, Lev. 1975. *Khranit' vechno.* Ann Arbor, Mich.: Ardis.

———. 1978. *Sotvorim sebe kumira.* Ann Arbor, Mich.: Ardis.

———. 1982a. *O pravde i terpimosti.* New York: Khronika Press.

———. 1982b. *Derzhava i narod.* Ann Arbor, Mich.: Ardis.

Kornai, Janos. 1980. *Economics of shortage.* New York: North-Holland Pub. Co.

———. 1986. *Contradictions and dilemmas: Studies on the socialist economy and society.* Cambridge, Mass.: MIT Press.

Korneshov, Lev. 1990. "Kak prazdnovali 70 letie 'vozhdia narodov.'" *Soiuz* 27:16.

Korolev, Sergei. 1999. "Strakh pered mirom." *Nezavisimaia gazeta.* 3 December.

Koroviakovsky, Piotr. 1990. "Nerazgadannaia taina." *Argumenty i fakty.* 16 February.

Kortunov, Andrei. 1997. "Amerikanskii vzgliad na rossiiskuiu vneshniuiu politiku: Strakhi i fantazii." In Marina Pavlova-Silvanskaia (ed.), *V izmenivshemsia mire.* Moscow: Fond Karnegi za mezhdunarodnyi mir.

Kortunov, Sergei. 1996. "Kaiat'sia Rossii ne v chem." *Nezavisimaia gazeta.* 31 January.

———. 1998. "Sud'ba russkogo kommunizma." *Nezavisimaia gazeta-Stsenarii.* 11 November.

Korzhakov, Alexander. 1997. *Ot zakata do rassveta.* Moscow: Interbuk.

Kossakovsky, Igor. 1990. "Opponent Stalina." *Literaturnaia gazeta.* 26 December.

Kostyrchenko, Gennadii. 1995. *Out of the red shadow: Anti-Semitism in Stalin's Russia.* Amherst, N.Y.: Prometheus Books.

Kotkin, Stephen. 1973. "Preface." In John Scott, *Behind the Urals: An American worker in Russia's city of steel.* Bloomington: Indiana University Press.

———. 1995. *Magnetic Mountain: Stalinism as a civilization.* Berkeley: University of California Press.

Kotz, David M. (with Fred Weir). 1997. *Revolution from above: The demise of the Soviet System.* London: Routledge.

Kozhanov, Nikolai. 1997. "Demokratiia i biurokratiia." *Pravda.* 12 October.

Kozhinov, Vadim. 1998. "Zagadka kosmopolitov." *Sovetskaia Rossiia.* 14 November.

KPSS v rezoliutsiiakh i resheniiakh s"ezdov, konferentsii i plenumov TsK. 1953. Moscow: Politizdat.

KPSS v rezoliutsiiakh i resheniiakh s"ezdov, konferentsii i plenumov TsK. 1954. Vol. 2. Moscow: Politizdat.

KPSS v rezoliutsiiakh i resheniiakh s" ezdov, konferentsii i plenumov TsK. 1986. Vol. 11. Moscow: Gospolitizdat.

KPSS v rezoliutsiiakh. Vol. 2, 1953. Moscow: Politizdat.

Krasnov, Vladislav. 1985. *Soviet defectors: The KGB wanted list.* Stanford, Calif.: Hoover Institution Press.

Kriuchkov, Vladimir. 1996. *Lichnoe delo.* Moscow: Olimp.

Krutova, Ol'ga. 1985. *Chelovek kak tvorets morali.* Moscow: Znanie.

Kuleshov, Sergei (ed.). 1990. *Nashe otechestvo.* Moscow: Terra.

Kurchatkin, Anatolii. 1993. "Oboitis' bez samoubiistva." *Literaturnaia gazeta.* 20 October.

Kurganov, Oskar. 1996. "Zhdite." *Izvestiia.* 24 August.

Kurginian, Sergei. 1992. *Sed'moi stsenarii.* Vol. 3. Moscow: Eksperimental'nyi tvorcheskii tsentr.

———. 1997. "Vystuplenie na discussii o 5 letnei s godovshchiny Gaidarovskikh reform." *Nezavisimaia gazeta–Stsenarii.* 13 February.

Kurskova, Galina. 2000. *Totalitarianaia sistema v SSSR: istoki i puti preodolenia.* Moscow: Monolit.

Kuschpèta, O. 1978. *The banking and credit system of the USSR.* Boston: Nijhoff Social Sciences Division.

Kuznetsov, Yurii. 1998. "Local party organs and the economy during perestroika." In Michael Ellman and Vladimir Kontorovich (eds.), *The destruction of the Soviet economic system: An insiders' history.* Armonk, N.Y.: M.E. Sharpe.

Kuznetsov, Valentin. 1990. *Novye formy kooperatsii v SSSR.* Moscow: Mysl'.

Lacis, Vilis. 1958 (1948.) *Towards new shores.* Moscow: Foreign Languages Publishing House.

Laidler, Harry Wellington. 1968. *History of socialism: A comparative survey of socialism, communism, trade unionism, cooperation, utopianism, and other systems of reform and reconstruction.* New York: Crowell.

Lakshin, Vladimir. 1977. *La réponse à Soljenitsyne.* Paris: Albin Michel.

———. 1980. *Solzhenitsyn, Tvardovsky, and Lakshin.* Cambridge, Mass.: MIT Press.

Lane, David. 1985. *Soviet economy and society.* Oxford: Blackwell.

Lanzman, Mikhail. 1995. "Tol'ko pravda i nichego krome pravdy." *Segodnia.* 13 August.

Lapidus, Gail. 1975. "Political mobilization, participation, and leadership." *Comparative Politics.* October.

Lapkin, Vladimir, and Vladimir Pantin. 1992. "Strannye tsikly rossiiskikh reform." *Nezavisimaia gazeta.* 4 June.

Laqueur, Walter. 1977. "Russia: Beyond Brezhnev." *Commentary.* August: 39–44.

———. 1994. *The dream that failed: Reflections on the Soviet Union.* New York: Oxford University Press.

Latsis, Otto. 1987. *Ekonomicheskaia tsentralizatsiia i tsentralizatsiia upravleniia: Problemy vzaimosviazi.* Moscow: Nauka.

———. 1988. "Perelom." *Znamia* 6:155, 170.

———. 1989a. "Stalin protiv Lenina." In X. Kabo (ed.), *Kul't Stalina.* Moscow: Progress.

———. 1989b. "Perelom." In Yurii Senokosov (ed.), *Surovaia drama naroda.* Moscow: Politizdat.

———. 1990. "The deep roots of our problems." In Abraham Brumberg (ed.), *Chronicle of a revolution.* New York: Pantheon Books.

————. 1993. "Neuslyshannoe preduprezhdenie." *Izvestiia*. 28 August.
————. 1995. "Novye ideologi–starye idei." *Izvestiia*. 31 May.
Laue, Theodore von. 1974. *Sergei Witte and the industrialization of Russia.* New York: Atheneum.
Leeman, Wayne A. 1977. *Centralized and decentralized economic systems: The Soviet-type economy, market socialism, and capitalism.* Chicago: Rand McNally.
Legostaev, Valerii. 1998. "Tenevik demokratii." *Zavtra* 48 (December).
Legvold, Robert. 1994. "Eastern Europe and the former Soviet republics." *Foreign Affairs* 73 (July/August).
Lenin, Vladimir. 1947–1951. *Sochinenia Chetvertoie iz danie.* Moscow: Politizdat.
————. 1960–1965. *Polnoe sobranie sochinenii.* Moscow: Gos. izd-vo polit. lit-ry.
Leontiev, Yaroslav. 1998. "Odinokii meshchanin Yagoda." *Obshchaia gazeta.* 12 March.
Lerner, Warren. 1982. *A history of socialism and communism in modern times: Theorists, activists, and humanists.* Englewood Cliffs, N.J.: Prentice-Hall.
Levada, Yurii (ed.). 1990. *Est' mnenie.* Moscow: Progress.
————. 1993. *Sovetskii prostoi chelovek.* Moscow: Intertsentr.
Levada, Yurii. 1998. "Sovetskii chelovek: Fiktsiia ili real'nost'?" *VTsIOM, Monitoring obshchestvennogo mneniia: Ekonomicheskie i sotsial'nye peremeny* 2.
————. 2001. "Chelovek Sovetskii: Problema rekonstruktsii iskhodnykh form." *VTsIOM, Monitoring obshchestvennogo mneniia: Ekonomicheskie i sotsial'nye peremeny* 2.
Levchenko, Stanislav. 1988. *On the wrong side: My life in the KGB.* Washington, D.C.: Pergamon-Brassey's.
Levy, Marion J. 1996. *Modernization & the structure of societies.* New Brunswick, N.J.: Transaction Publishers.
Levykin, Ivan. 1984. "K voprosu ob integralnykh pokazateliakh sotsialisticheskogo obraza zhizni." *Sotsiologicheskie issledovania* 2.
Levykin, Ivan (ed.). 1987. *Obshchee i osobennoe v obraze zhizni sotsial'nykh grupp sovetskogo obshchestva.* Moscow: Nauka.
Lewin, Moshe. 1968. *Lenin's last struggle.* New York: Pantheon Books.
————. 1974. *Political undercurrents in Soviet economic debates: From Bukharin to the modern reformers.* Princeton: Princeton University Press.
————. 1988. *The Gorbachev phenomenon: A historical interpretation.* Berkeley: University of California Press.
Lichtheim, George. 1969. *The origins of socialism.* New York: Praeger.
————. 1970. *A short history of socialism.* New York: Praeger.
Ligachev, Yegor. 1992. *Zagadka Gorbacheva.* Novosibirsk: Interbuk.
Lincoln, Bruce. 1978. *Nicholas I: Emperor and autocrat of all the Russias.* Bloomington: Indiana University Press.
————. 1986. *Passage through Armageddon: The Russians in war and revolution, 1914–1918.* New York: Simon & Schuster.
————. 1990. *The great reforms: Autocracy, bureaucracy, and the politics of change in imperial Russia.* DeKalb, Ill.: Northern Illinois University Press.
Lipset, Seymour, and Stein Rokkan (eds.). 1967. *Party systems and voter alignments: Cross-national perspectives.* New York: Free Press.
Lisenkov, Mikhail. 1977. *Kul'turnaia revoliutsiia v SSSR i armiia.* Moscow: Voenizdat.
Lisichkin, Gennadii. 1989. *Mify i real'nost'.* Moscow: Znanie.
————. 2000. "Rossiiu istoshchaiet imperskii virus." *Literaturnaia gazeta.* 31 December.

Lisov, Yevgenii. 1992. "Rassledovanie: Zelenen'kie dlia krasnykh." *Ogonek.* 9 February.
Liubimov, Mikhail. 1999. "O bednom chekiste zamolvite slovechko." *Nezavisimaia gazeta.* 23 February.
Lobanov, Nikolai, and Georgii Cherkasov. 1981. *Sotsial'nye faktory povysheniia effektivnosti truda.* Leningrad: Nauka.
Lobanov-Rostovsky, Andrei. 1935. *The grinding mill: Reminiscences of war and revolution in Russia, 1913–1920.* New York: Macmillan.
Lopatin, Leonid (ed.). 1993. *Rabochee dvizhenie Kuzbassa.* Kemerovo: Sovremennaia otechestvennaia kniga.
Lukin, Alexander. 1996. "Vybory i nashi politicheskie predstavleniia." *Nezavisimaia gazeta.* 15 March.
Luneev, Victor. 1997. *Prestupnost' XX veka.* Moscow: Nauka.
Lunev, Stanislav. 1998. *Through the eyes of the enemy: Russia's highest ranking military defector reveals why Russia is more dangerous than ever.* Washington, D.C.: Regnery Pub.; Lanham, Md: National Book Network.
Macksey, Kenneth (ed.). 1995. *The Hitler options: Alternate decisions of World War II.* London: Greenhill Books.
Macridis, Roy. 1986. *Modern political regimes.* Boston: Little, Brown.
Malei, Mikhail. 1993. "The reform of the military industrial complex." *Nezavisimaia gazeta.* 27 August.
Malenkov, Andrei. 1992. *O moem ottse Georgii Malenkove.* Moscow: NTTS "Tekhnoekos."
Malia, Martin. 1992. "Why Amalrik was right." *Times Literary Supplement.* 2 November.
———. 1993. "A Fatal Logic." *National Interest.* Spring: 80–90.
———. 1994. *The Soviet tragedy: A history of socialism in Russia, 1917–1991.* New York: Free Press.
———. 1999. *Russia under western eyes.* Cambridge: Harvard University Press.
Malle, Sylvana. 1997. "War Communism." In Edward Acton, Vladimir Cherniaev, and William Rosenberg (eds.), *Critical companion to the Russian Revolution, 1914–1921.* Bloomington: Indiana University Press.
Mandelbaum, Michael, and Strobe Talbott. 1984. *Russians and Reagan.* New York: Vintage Press.
Mandel'shtam, Nadezhda. 1990. *Vtoraia kniga.* Moscow: Moskovskii rabochii.
Mannheim, Carl. 1929. *Ideology and utopia.* New York: Harcourt and Brace.
Marples, David. 1992. *Stalinism in Ukraine in the 1940s.* New York: St. Martin's Press.
Martin Du Gard, Roger. 1993. *Les Thibault (Sixieme Partie, La Mort Du Père).* Paris: Gallimard.
Marx, Karl. 1935. *The eighteenth Brumaire of Louis Bonaparte.* New York: International Publishers.
———. 1940. *The civil war in France.* With an introduction by Frederick Engles. New York: International publishers.
Matlock, Jack. 1995. *Autopsy on an empire: Observing the collapse of the Soviet Union.* New York: Random House.
———. 1996. "Gorbachev's lingering mysteries." *New York Review of Books.* 19 October.
Matthews, Mervyn. 1989. *Patterns of deprivation in the Soviet Union under Brezhnev and Gorbachev.* Stanford, Calif.: Hoover Institution Press.
Maximova, Ella. 1992. "Podslushali i rasstreliali." *Izvestiia.* 16 July.

Mazover, Mark. 1999. *Dark continent: Europe's twentieth century.* New York: A.A. Knopf.

McCagg, William. 1978. *Stalin embattled, 1943–1948.* Detroit Wayne State University Press.

McCauley, Martin. 1976. *Khrushchev and the development of Soviet agriculture: the virgin land program, 1953–1964.* New York: Holmes & Meier.

———. 1997. "From perestroika towards new order, 1985–1995." In Gregory Freeze (ed.), *Russia: A history.* Oxford: Oxford University.

———. 1998a. *Gorbachev.* London and New York: Longman.

———. 1998b. *Russia, America and the cold war, 1949–1991.* London: Longman.

McCleland, J.S. 1996. *A history of Western political thought.* London: Routledge.

McCormick, Charles H. 1997. *Seeing reds: Federal surveillance of radicals in the Pittsburgh mill district, 1917–1921.* Pittsburgh, Pa.: University of Pittsburgh Press.

McDermott, Kevin, and Jeremy Agnew. 1997. *The Comintern: A history of international communism from Lenin to Stalin.* New York: St. Martin's Press.

Medvedev, Roi. 1974. *K sudu istorii: Genezis i posledstviia stalinizma.* New York: A.A. Knopf.

———. 1990a. *O Staline i stalinizme.* Moscow: Progress.

———. 1990b. "A.N. Kosygin." *24 Chasa.* 5 (June): 3.

———. 1991. "Vo glave KGB." *Sovetskaia Rossiia.* 5 December.

———. 1993. *Gensek s Liubianki.* Moscow: "LETA."

Medvedev, Vadim. 1994. *V komande Gorbacheva: Vzgliad iznutri.* Moscow: Bylina.

———. 1998. "Under Andropov and Gorbachev." In Michael Ellman and Vladimir Kontorovich (eds.), *The destruction of the Soviet economic system: An insiders' history.* Armonk, N.Y.: M.E. Sharpe.

Medvedev, Vladimir. 1994. *Chelovek za spinoi.* Moscow: Russlit.

Medvedev, Zhores. 1983. *Andropov.* Oxford: Blackwell.

———. 1987. *Gorbachev.* Oxford: Basil Blackwell.

———. 1997. "Ot Sovetskogo soiuza k sovetskoi Rossii: Stalin kak russkii natsionalist." *Nezavisimaia gazeta.* 18 December.

Mikhailov, Nikolai. 1991a. "Tainoe golosovanie." *Dialog* 1.

———. 1991b. "V iiule 53–go." *Izvestiia.* 3 and 4 January.

Mikoyan, Anastas. 1975. *Vnachale dvadtsatykh.* Moscow: Politizdat.

———. 1988. *Memoirs of Anastas Mikoyan.* Madison, Conn.: Sphinx Press.

Miliukov, Pavel. 1921–1924. *Istoriia vtoroi russkoi revoliutsii. Tom I, vyp. 1–3.* Sofia: Rossiisko-bolgarskoe izd-vo.

———. 1955. *Vospominaniia, 1859–1917.* 2 vols., New York: Izd-vo im. Chekhova.

Millar, James R. (ed.). 1987. *Politics, work, and daily life in the USSR: A survey of former Soviet citizens.* Cambridge and New York: Cambridge University Press.

Miller, Robert F., John H. Rigby, and Thomas H. Rigby. 1987. *Gorbachev at the helm.* London: Croom Helm.

Milosz, Czeslaw. 1953. *The captive mind.* New York: Knopf.

Miner, Steven. 1995. "Revelations, secrets, gossip and lies: Sifting warily through the Soviet archives." *New York Times Book Review.* 4 May.

———. 1997. "A revolution doomed from the start." *New York Times Book Review.* 9 March.

Minkin, Alexander. 1998. "Proshchaii umytaia Rossia." *Novaia gazeta.* 2 November.

Mises, Ludwig von. 1951. *Socialism: An economic and sociological analysis.* New Haven, Conn.: Yale University Press.

Mitev, Peter-Emil, Veronika Ivanova, and Vladimir Shubkin. 1998. "Katastroficheskoe soznanie v Bolgarii i Rossii." *Sotsiologicheskie issledovaniia* 10.

Mlynar, Zdenek. 1980. *Nightfrost in Prague: The end of humane socialism.* New York: Karz Publishers.

Mogilevkin, Il'ia. 1999. "Geopolitika v SSSR." *Nezavisimaia gazeta.* 5 March.

Mondich, Mikhail. 1950. *Smersh.* New York: Holt.

Moor, Wilbert. 1979. *World modernization: The limits of convergence.* New York: Elsevier.

Moore, Ward. 1976. *Bring the jubilee.* New York: Avon Books.

Moroz, Oleg. 1994. "Pervaia sovetskaia A-bomba byla deistvitel'no plagiatom, no v ostal'nom P. Sudoplatov i V. Belokon kleveshchut." *Literaturnaia gazeta.* 27 July.

Morris, William E., and Belfort Bax. 1893. *Socialism, its growth & outcome.* London and New York: Scribner.

Morton, Henri. 1987. "Housing quality and housing classes in the Soviet Union." In Horst Herlemann (ed.), *Quality of life in the Soviet Union.* Boulder, Colo.: Westview Press.

Motyl, Alexander. 1987. *Will the non-Russians rebel?* Ithaca, N.Y.: Cornell University Press.

Moynihan, Bryan. 1989. *Claws of the bear: The history of the Red Army from the revolution to the present.* Boston: Houghton Mifflin.

Moynihan, Daniel. 1998. *Secrecy: The American experience.* New Haven, Conn.: Yale University Press.

Mozhaev, Boris. 1988. *Muzhiki i baby: Roman.* Moscow: Sovremennik.

———. 1989. *Zhizn' Fedora Kuz'kina.* In B. Mozhaev, *Sobranie sochinenii v chetyrekh tomakh.* Moscow: Khudozhestvennaia lit-ra.

Mozhin, Vladimir. 1998a. "The party and the economic reform." In Michael Ellman and Vladimir Kontorovich (eds.), *The destruction of the Soviet economic system: An insiders' history.* Armonk, N.Y.: M.E. Sharpe.

———. 1998b. "Rulers did not know what to do." In Michael Ellman and Vladimir Kontorovich (eds.), *The destruction of the Soviet economic system: An insiders' history.* Armonk, N.Y.: M.E. Sharpe.

———. 1998c. "It was about the enterprise economy." In Michael Ellman and Vladimir Kontorovich (eds.), *The destruction of the Soviet economic system: An Insiders' history.* Armonk, N.Y.: M.E. Sharpe.

Myslovsky, Ye. 1991. "Labirinty tenevoi ekonomiki." *Molodaia gvardiia* 7:10–18.

Nagle, John. 1985. *Introduction to comparative politics.* Chicago: Nelson-Hall.

Naishul, Vitalii. 1991. *The supreme and last stage of socialism: An essay.* London: Center for Research into Communist Economies.

Narinsky, Mikhail. 1996. "Stalin i Torez." *Novaia i noveishaia istoriia* 1.

Naumov, Vladimir, and Alexander Korotkov. 1994. "Lavrentii Beria–laskovyi palach." *Moskovskie novosti.* 11 September.

Nekrich, Alexander. 1978. *The punished people.* New York: Norton.

Nikolaevsky, Boris. 1948a. "O novoi i staroi emigratsii." *Sotsialisticheskii vestnik.* 28 January.

———. 1948b. "Porazhenchestvo 1941–1945 godov i general Vlasov." *Novyi zhurnal* 18.

Nitze, Paul. 1986. *The impact of SDI on U.S.-Soviet relations.* Washington, D.C.: U.S. Dept. of State, Bureau of Public Affairs, Office of Public Communication, Editorial Division.

Nollau, Günther. 1961. *International communism and world revolution: History and methods.* New York: Praeger.

Nosov, Evgenii. 1988. "Chto my perestraivaem." *Literaturnaia gazeta.* 20 April.

Nove, Alec. 1961. *The Soviet economy: An introduction.* New York: F. A. Praeger.

———. 1975. *Stalinism and after.* London: Allen & Unwin.

———. 1979. *Political economy and Soviet socialism.* London and Boston: G. Allen & Unwin.

———. 1980. *The Soviet economic system.* London and Boston: Allen & Unwin.

———. 1989. *An economic history of the USSR.* London: Penguin Books.

Novikov, Andrei. 1995. "Shag vlevo, shag vpravo." *Literaturnaia gazeta.* 5 April.

Novikov, Andrei, and Leonid Shinkarev. 1992. "Kogo boialas' Staraia Ploshchad." *Izvestiia.* 17 August.

Nozick, Robert. 1974. *Anarchy, state and utopia.* New York: Basic Books.

Odom, William. 1998. *The collapse of the Soviet military.* New Haven, Conn.: Yale University Press.

Ogarkov, Nikolai. 1981. "Na strazhe." *Kommunist* 10.

———. 1982. *Vsegda v gotovnosti k zashchite otechestva.* Moscow: Voenizdat.

———. 1985. *Istoriia uchit bditel'nosti.* Moscow: Voenizdat.

Olson, Mancur. 1982. *The rise and decline of nations.* New Haven, Conn.: Yale University Press.

O'Neill, William. 1982. *A better world. The great schism: Stalinism and the American intellectuals.* New York: Simon and Schuster.

Openkin, L. 1991. *Ottepel': kak eto bylo.* Moscow: Izd-vo "Znanie."

Orlova, Raisa. 1982. "Frida Vigdorova." *Vnutrennie protivorechiia* 3.

———. 1983. *Memoirs.* New York: Random House.

Osipova, Taisia. 1997. "Peasant rebellions: Origin, scope, dynamics and consequences." In Vladimir Brovkin (ed.), *The Bolsheviks in Russian society: The Revolution and the Civil War.* New Haven, Conn.: Yale University Press.

Ostapenko, A., and N. Subbotina. 1993. "Nekotorye problemy russkikh v Blizhnem Zarubezh'e." *Rossiiskii etnograf* 2:286.

Ostrovsky, Nikolai. 1979. *How the steel was tempered.* Moscow: Progress.

Ostrovsky, Vladimir (ed.). 1988. *Lichnoe podsobnoe khoziaistvo.* Moscow: Nauka.

Overy, Richard. 1998a. *Russia's war.* New York: Penguin Books.

———. 1998b. "Who really won the arms race." *Times Literary Supplement.* 13 November.

Ovrutsky, Lev. 1988. "Istoriia v uslovnom naklonenii." *Sovetskaia kul'tura.* 4 February.

———. 1992. "Zagadka L.I." *Moskovskie novosti.* 24 May.

Panova, Vera. 1948. *Kruzhilikha.* Moscow: Sovetskii pisatel'.

Paramonov, Boris. 1996. "Historical culture." In Dmitrii Shalin (ed.), *Russian culture at the crossroads.* Boulder, Colo.: Westview Press.

Parker, Geoffrey. 1976. "If the Armada had landed." *History* 61.

———. 1998. *The grand strategy of Philip II.* New Haven: Yale University Press.

Parsons, Talcott. 1954. *Social system.* Glencoe, Ill.: Free Press.

Parsons, Talcott, and Neil Smelser. 1956. *Economy and society.* Glencoe, Ill.: Free Press.

Paschal, Donald. 1958. *Russia under Malenkov: Internal developments in the Soviet Union from the death of Stalin to the resignation of Malenkov.* Charlottesville, Va.: Master's thesis for the University of Virginia.

Pasmanik, Daniil. 1923. *Russkaia revoliutsiia i evreistvo: Bol'shevizm i iudaizm.* Paris: Izd. Franko-russkaia pechat'.

Passerini, Luisa. 1987. *Fascism in popular memory: The cultural experience of the Turin working class.* Cambridge: Cambridge University Press.

Pasternak, Boris. 1958. *Doctor Zhivago.* New York: H. Wolff.

Pavlenko, Petr. 1950. *Happiness.* Moscow: Foreign Languages Pub. House.

Pavlenko, Sergei. 1989. "Neformal'nye upravlencheskie vozdeistviia." In Fridrikh Borodkin, Leonid Kosals, and Rozalina Ryvkina (eds.), *Postizhenie.* Moscow: Progress.

Pavliuchenko, Sergei. 1997. "Workers protest movement against War Communism." In Vladimir Brovkin (ed.), *The Bolsheviks in Russian society: The Revolution and the Civil War.* New Haven, Conn.: Yale University Press.

Pavlov, Anton. 2000. "Skromnye sekrety narodnykh slug." *Moskovskie novosti.* 6 November.

Pavlova, Irina. 1993. *Stanovlenie mechanizma vlasti.* Novosibirsk, Russia: Sibirskii Khronograf.

Pavlov, Valentin. 1993. *Avgust iznutri: Gorbachev-putch.* Moscow: Delovoi mir.

———. 1995. *Upushchen li shans.* Moscow: Terra.

———. 1996. "Esli khotite, sam Mikhail Sergeevich byl . . . chlen GKChP." *Pravda.* 5:12–19 (April).

Pavlovsky, Gleb. 1996. "Kak oni unichtozhili Sovetskii soiuz." *Nezavisimaia gazeta.* 14 November.

Payin, Emil. 1999. "Russkii vopros." *Literaturnaia gazeta.* 27 January.

Pazenok, Victor (ed.). 1983. *Razvitoi sotsializm i lichnost'.* Kiev: Kievskii universitet.

Pechenev, Vadim (ed.). 1990. *Neformaly: Kto oni? Kuda zovut?* Moscow: Politizdat.

Pells, Richard. 1985. *The liberal mind in a conservative age: American intellectuals in the 1940s and 1950s.* New York: Harper and Row.

"Peregovory v Kremle, 23 and 26 August 1968." 1998. *Nezavisimaia gazeta.* 19 August.

Perry, Lewis. 1984. *Intellectual life in America: A history.* New York: F. Watts.

Peukert, Detlev. 1989. *Inside Nazi Germany: Conformity, opposition, and racism in everyday life.* London: Penguin.

Phillips, William. 1983. *A partisan view: Five decades of the literary life.* New York: Stein and Day.

Piasheva, Larisa. 1989. "Kontury radikal'noi sotsial'noi reformy." In Fridrikh Borodkin et al. (eds.), *Postizhenie.* Moscow: Progress.

———. 1990a. "Umom poniat' Rossiiu." *Ogonek* 44 (October).

———. 1990b. "V korzinke i koshelke." *Literaturnaia gazeta.* 5 September.

———. 1990c. "Kak v Parizhe." *Literaturnaia gazeta.* 26 December.

———. 1990d. "Kak budem zhit' v usloviiakh rynka." *Literaturnaia gazeta.* 30 May.

———. 1991. "Son o trekh ukazakh." *Literaturnaia gazeta.* 13 March.

Pikhoia, Rudolf. 1996. "Plan deistvii-28." *Moskovskie novosti.* 24 March.

———. 1999. "Stalin: Ot smerti do pokhoron." *Moskovskie novosti.* 29 January.

Pipes, Richard. 1964. *The formation of the Soviet Union: Communism and nationalism, 1917–1923.* Cambridge: Harvard University Press.

———. 1974. *Russia under the old regime.* New York: Scribner.

———. 1984. *Survival is not enough.* New York: Simon & Schuster.

———. 1989. *Collected essays on Russian and Soviet history.* Boulder, Colo.: Westview Press.

———. 1990. *The Russian Revolution.* New York: Knopf.

———. 1992a. *Russia under the old regime.* New York: Collier Books.

————. 1992b. "Seventy five years on. The great October Revolution as a clandestine coup d'etat." *Times Literary Supplement.* 6 November.

————. 1992c. "Russia's chance." *Commentary* 93:3 (March).

————. 1993a. *Russia under the Bolshevik regime.* New York: Knopf.

————. 1993b. "Yeltsin's move: The struggle to achieve stable and effective government in Russia." *Times Literary Supplement.* 8 October.

————. 1994. *Communism, the vanished specter.* Oslo: Scandinavian University Press; New York: Oxford University Press.

————. 1995. "The national prospect: A symposium." *Commentary* 100:5 (November).

Pipes, Richard (ed.). 1996. *The unknown Lenin: From the secret archive.* Translation of Russian documents by Catherine A. Fitzpatrick. New Haven, Conn.: Yale University Press.

Pipes, Richard. 1998. "Without the people." *Times Literary Supplement.* 13 February.

————. 1999. "East is east." *New Republic.* 26 April.

————. 2000a. "Banging the shoe, not the gun." *Times Literary Supplement.* 1 September.

————. 2000b. "Russia's wars with the West." *Times Literary Supplement.* 6 October.

Pirozhkov, Viktor. 1987. *V.I. Lenin and VChK.* Moscow: Politizdat.

————. 1990. "I eshche o reabilitatsii." *Nedelia* 20:11.

"Pis'ma iz daleka." 1998. *Moskovskii komsomolets.* 8 December.

Pittman, Thane S. 1998. "Motivation." In Daniel Gilbert, Susan Fiske, and Gardner Lindzey, *The handbook of social psychology.* New York: Random House.

Pivovarov, Vladimir. 1974. *Na etapakh sotsiologicheskogo issledovaniia.* Grozny: Checheno-Ingushskoe izdatel'stvo.

Plaksy, Sergei. 1982. *Tvoi molodoi sovremennik.* Moscow: Molodaia gvardia.

Platonov, Andrei. 1978. *Chevengur.* Ann Arbor, Mich.: Ardis.

————. 1996. *Kotlovan.* London: Harvill Press.

Podhoretz, Norman. 1979. *Breaking ranks: A political memoir.* New York: Harper & Row.

Poliakov, Yurii. 1993. "Pochemu ia vdrug zatoskoval po sovetskoi literature." *Komsomol'skaia pravda.* 20 July.

Polianovsky, Eduard. 1999. "Ubiistvo Kirova." *Izvestiia.* 1 December.

Polikanov, Sergei. 1983. *Razryv: Zapiski atomnogo fizika.* Frankfurt: Posev.

Poole, Ernest. 1918. *"The dark people," Russia's crisis.* New York: Macmillan.

Popov, Gavriil. 1987. "Tochka zreniia ekonomista." *Nauka i zhizn'* 4.

————. 1990. *Blesk i nishcheta administrativnoi sistemy.* Moscow: Pik.

————. 1994. *Snova v oppozitsii.* Moscow: Galaktika.

————. 1998a. "Mesiats skorpiona, god krasnoi zmei." *Izvestiia.* 6 November.

————. 1998b. "Rodoslovnaia Lenina." *Izvestiia.* 18 April.

————. 1999. "Istoriia blizkaia, no neizvestnaia." *Argumenty i fakty* 27.

Porter, Andrew. 1996. "Conquerors and colonists." *New York Times Book Review.* 14 January.

Potresov, Alexander. 1927. *V plenu u illiuzii.* Paris (no publishing house).

Powell, David. 1991. "Aging and the elderly." In Anthony Jones, Walter Connor, and David Powell (eds.), *Soviet social problems.* Boulder, Colo.: Westview Press.

Power, Thomas. 1996. "Who won the cold war." *New York Review of Books.* 20 June.

Powers, Richard Gid. 1995. *Not without honor: The history of American anticommunism.* New York: Free Press.

Prazauskas, Algis. 1993. "GKChP and the collapse of the Union of Soviet Socialist Republics." *Nezavisimaia gazeta*. 22 April.
Pristavkin, Anatolii. 1988. *Nochevala tuchka zolotaia: Povesti*. Moscow: Sovetskii pisatel´.
Prokhorov, Alexander (ed.). 1973. *Great Soviet encyclopedia*. New York: Macmillan.
Prostiakov, Igor. 1998a. "Bad design and fraudulent implementation." In Michael Ellman and Vladimir Kontorovich (eds.), *The destruction of the Soviet economic system: An insiders' history*. Armonk, N.Y.: M.E. Sharpe.
———. 1998b. "Economic reforms in the interregnum." In Michael Ellman and Vladimir Kontorovich (eds.), *The destruction of the Soviet economic system: An insiders' history*. Armonk, N.Y.: M.E. Sharpe.
Protashchik, A. (ed.). 1990. *Cherez ternii*. Moscow: Progress.
Pumpiansky, Alexander. 1995. "Tak nuzhno li povtoriat´ Tiananmen na Krasnoi Ploshchadi." *Novoe vremia* 28:25.
Putin, Vladimir. 2000. "Ot pervogo litsa." *Ogonek* 9.
Radosh, Ronald, and Milton Joyce. 1997. *The Rosenberg file*. New Haven, Conn.: Yale University Press.
Radzikhovsky, Leonid. 1995. "Nomenklatura meniaet 'Kapital' na kapital." *Izvestiia*. 7 March.
Radzinsky, Edward. 1995. "Iz-pod stalinskoi shineli vylupilas´ vsia strana." *Segodnia*. 11 May.
———. 1996. *Stalin: The first in-depth biography based on explosive new documents from Russia's secret archives*. New York: Doubleday.
———. 1997. "Rossiia na puti ot Stalina k Khristu." *Izvestiia*. 16 June.
Raig, Ivar. 1989. "Nelegal´naia ekonomicheskaia deiatel´nost´." In Fridrikh Borodkin, Leonid Kosals, and Rozalina Ryvkina (eds.), *Postizhenie*. Moscow: Progress.
Ratnikov, Valentin. 1978. *Kollektiv kak sotsial´naia obshchnost´*. Moscow: Izd. Moskovskogo universiteta.
Rees, E. A. (ed.). 1997. *Decision-making in the Stalinist command economy, 1932–37*. New York: St. Martin's Press.
Reitlinger, Gerald. 1960. *The house built on sand: The conflicts of German policy in Russia, 1939–1945*. New York: Viking Press.
Remnick, David. 1993a. *Lenin's tomb*. New York: Random House.
———. 1993b. "The counterrevolutionary." *New York Review of Books*. 25 March.
———. 1994. "Getting Russia right." *New York Review of Books*. 22 September.
Renouvier, Charles. 1901. *Uchronie: L'Utopie en histoire*. Paris: Felix Alcan.
Reshin, L.E. and Vladimir Naumov (eds.). 1998. *1941 god*. Moscow: Mezhdunarodnyi fond "Demokratiia."
Revoliutsiia v materialakh i dokumentakh. Khrestomatiia, 1901–1905. 1924. Moscow: Gos. izd-vo.
Reznikov, M. 1984. *Vospominaniia starogo muzykanta*. London: Overseas Publications.
Riabushkin, Timon, and Georgii Osipov. 1982. *Sovetskaia sotsiologiia*. Moscow: Izd-vo. "Nauka."
Riabushkin, Timon (ed.). 1978. *Problemy sotsial´nogo razvitiia*. Moscow: Institut sotsiologicheskikh issledovanii.
Richelson, Jeffrey. 1986. *Sword and shield: The Soviet intelligence and security apparatus*. Cambridge, Mass.: Ballinger.
Rigby, Thomas H. 1990. *Political elites in the USSR*. Aldershot, Eng.: Edward Elgar.
———. 1992. "The reconceptualising of the Soviet system." In Stephen White, Alex

Pravda, and Zvi. Gitelman (eds.), *Developments in Soviet and post-Soviet politics.* Durham, N.C.: Duke University Press.

Robinson, John P., Vladimir G. Andreyenkov, and Vasily D. Patrushev. 1989. *The rhythm of everyday life: How Soviet and American citizens use time.* Boulder, Colo.: Westview Press.

Rodionov, Petr. 1996. "Proshchennyi Brezhnev." *Pravda.* 12 December.

Rogovin, Vadim. 1984. *Obshchestvo zrelogo sotsializma: Sotsial'nye problemy.* Moscow: Mysl'.

———. 1991. *Dialektika sotsial'nogo ravenstva i sovremennyi period razvitiia sovetskogo obshchestva.* Moscow: Institut sotsiologii Akademii nauk.

———. 1992. *Sotsial'naia spravedlivost' i perekhod k rynochnoi ekonomike.* Moscow: Institut sotsiologii Akademii nauk.

———. 1993. *Iz istorii sotsial'noi politiki i sotsiopoliticheskoi mysli v SSSR.* Moscow: Institut sotsiologii Akademii nauk.

Ro'i, Yaacov (ed.). 1995. *Jews and Jewish life in Russia and the Soviet Union.* Portland, Ore.: F. Cass.

Rosenberg, William. 1988. "Identities, power and interaction in revolutionary Russia." *Slavic Review* 47:1.

———. 1997. "Problems of social welfare and everyday life." In Edward Acton, Vladimir Chernieav, and William Rosenberg (eds.). *Critical companion to the Russian Revolution, 1914–1921.* Bloomington: Indiana University Press.

Rositzke, Harry. 1981. *The KGB: The eyes of Russia.* Garden City, N.Y.: Doubleday.

Ross, Edward. 1918. *Russia in upheaval.* New York: Century.

Ross, Mikhail, and Garth Fletcher. 1985. "Attribution and social perception." In Gardner Lindzey and Elliot Aronson, *The handbook of social psychology.* New York: Random House.

Rotter, Seymour. 1954. *Soviet and Comintern policy toward Germany, 1919–1923: A case study of strategy and tactics.* New York: Thesis for Columbia University.

Rozman, Gilbert. 1987. *The Chinese debate about Soviet socialism, 1978–1985.* Princeton, N.J.: Princeton University Press.

Rumer-Zaraev, Mikhail. 1996. "Do ottepeli piat' let." *Nezavisimaia gazeta.* 28 June.

Rumiantsev, Alexei. 1965. "Narod i intelligentsiia." *Pravda.* 21 February.

———. 1970. "V.I. Lenin i sotsiologiia." In *Lenin i sovremennaia nauka.* Vol. 1. Moscow: Nauka.

Rumiantsev, Alexei (ed.). 1983. *Nauchnyi kommunizm: Slovar'.* Moscow: Politizdat.

———. 1985. *Politicheskaia ekonomiia: Uchebnik dlia neekonomicheskikh vuzov.* Moscow: Gospolitizdat.

Rush, Myron. 1993. "Fortune and fate." *National Interest.* Spring:19–25.

Rutland, Peter. 1993. "Sovietology: Notes for a Post-Mortem." *National Interest.* Spring: 109–122.

———. 1998. "Explaining the Soviet collapse." *Transition.* February.

Rybakov, Anatolii. 1988. *Children of the Arbat.* Boston: Little, Brown.

Rykov, Alexei. 1990. *Izbrannye proizvedeniia.* Moscow: Ekonomika.

Ryzhkov, Nikolai. 1986. "Ob osnovnykh napravleniiakh ekonomicheskogo i sotsial'nogo razvitiia SSSR na 1986–1990 gody i na period do 2000 goda." *Pravda.* 4 March.

———. 1995. *Desiat' let velikikh potriasenii.* Moscow: Kniga. Prosveshchenie. Miloserdie.

Safronov, Alexander. 1998. "Slavsky." *Kommersant Daily.* 28 October.

Sagdeiev, Roald. 1988a. "Gde my poteriali temp." *Izvestiia.* 28 April.

———. 1988b. "Adademia nauk na perelome." *Moskovskie novosti.* 3 January.

Sakharov, Andrei D. 1970. *Progress, coexistence, and intellectual freedom.* New York: Norton.

Sakharov, Andrei N. 1996. *Reformy i reformatory v istorii Rossii: Sbornik statei.* Moskva: Institut istorii.

Sakwa, Richard. 1993. *Russian politics and society.* London: Routledge.

Sapir, Boris, et al. 1988. *Men'sheviki.* Benson, Vt.: Chalidze.

Schrank, Robert. 1998. *Wasn't that a time? Growing up radical and red in America.* Cambridge, Mass.: MIT Press.

Schwarz, Solomon. 1951. *The Jews in the Soviet Union.* Syracuse, N.Y.: Syracuse University Press.

Scott, James. 1985. *Weapons of the weak: Everyday forms of peasant resistance.* New Haven, Conn.: Yale University Press.

Scott, John. 1973. *Behind the Urals: An American worker in Russia's city of steel.* Bloomington: Indiana University Press.

Seaton, Albert, and Joan Seaton. 1986. *Soviet army: 1918 to the present.* London: Bodley Head.

Sedaitis, Judith B., and Jim Butterfield (eds.). 1991. *Perestroika from below: Social movements in the Soviet Union.* Boulder, Colo.: Westview Press.

Sédillot, René. 1977. *Histoire des socialismes.* Paris: Fayard.

Segal, Boris. 1990. *The drunken society.* New York: Hippocrene Books.

Seliunin, Vasilii. 1988. "Istoki." *Novy mir* 5.

———. 1990a. "Rynok: Khimery i real'nost'." In Andrei Protashchik (ed.), *Cherez ternii.* Moscow: Progress.

———. 1990b. "U nas poluchitsia." *Ogonek* 8 (February).

Seliunin, Vasilii, and Grigorii Khanin. 1987. "Lukavaia tsifra." *Novy mir* 2:181–192.

Selvern, Susan J. 1968. "Red scare in New York State, 1919–1920." Senior honors thesis, Brandeis University, Waltham, Mass.

Semanov, Sergei Nikolaevich. 1995. *Yurii Vladimirovich: Zarisovki iz teni.* Moscow: Stolitsa.

Service, Robert. 1998. *History of twentieth-century Russia.* Cambridge: Harvard University Press.

Seth, Ronald. 1967. *The executioners: The story of Smersh.* London: Cassell.

Shafarevich, Igor. 1989. "O rusofobii." *Vremia i my* 104:145–172.

Shakhnazarov, Georgii. 1997. "Kto kogo predal." *Nezavisimaia gazeta.* 25 January.

Shalin, Dmitrii N. (ed.). 1996. *Russian culture at the crossroads: Paradoxes of post-Communist consciousness.* Boulder, Colo.: Westview Press.

Shatalin, Stanislav, Nikolai Petrakov. 1990. "Shag k svobode." *Komsomol'skaia pravda.* 26 April.

Shatalin, Stanislav, and Nikolai Petrakov, and Grigorii Yavlinsky. 1990a. *Perekhod k rynku.* Moscow (no publishing house).

———. 1990b. "Chelovek, svoboda i rynok." *Komsomol'skaia pravda.* 4 September.

Shatrov, Mikhail. 1988. Interview. *Ogonek* 45:16.

Shatunovskaia, Ol'ga. 1990. "Fal'sifikatsiia." *Argumenty i fakty* 22.

Shchekochikhin, Yurii. 1991. "VPK (bol'shevikov)." *Literaturnaia gazeta.* 2 October.

Sheinis, Victor. 1995. Interview. *Moskovskii komsomolets.* 19 April.

Shevardnadze, Eduard. 1991. *Moi vybor.* Moscow: Novosti.

Shevelev, Vladimir. 1997. "Temirtau." *Moskovskie novosti.* 13 December.

Shevtsova, Lilia. 1997. "Was the collapse of the Soviet Union inevitable?" In Anne de Tingy (ed.), *The fall of the Soviet empire.* New York: Columbia University Press.

Shidlovsky, Sergei. 1923. *Vospominaniia.* Berlin: Otto Kirchner.

Shimshilevich, Lev. 1969. *Kolkhoznoe proizvodstvo i ego sblizhenie s obshchenarodnym na sovremennom etape.* Irkutsk: Vostochno-Sibirskoe knizhnoe izdatel'stvo.

Shishkin, Oleg. 2000. "Diktatura brilliantov." *Nezavisimaia gazeta.* 11 March.

Shlapentokh, Dmitrii. 1991a. "Popular support for the Soviet political trials of the late 1920s and the origin of the great purge." In T. Bushnell et al., *State organized terror.* Boulder, Colo.: Westview Press.

———. 1991b. "Drunkenness and anarchy in Russia." *Russian History* 4:465–467.

———. 1994. "Drunkenness in the context of political culture: The case of the Russian Revolution." *International Journal of Sociology and Social Policy* 14:8 (special issue).

———. 1998. " 'Red-to-brown' Jews and Russian liberal reform." *Washington Quarterly* 21:4, p. 107.

———. 1999. *The counter-revolution in revolution: Images of Thermidor and Napoleon at the time of Russian Revolution and civil war.* New York: St. Martin's Press.

Shlapentokh, Dmitrii, and Vladimir Shlapentokh. 1990. "Letters to the editor on the ideologies in the USSR during the 1980s." In Anthony Jones (ed.), *Research on the Soviet Union and Eastern Europe.* Greenwich, Conn.: Jay Press.

———. 1993. *Soviet cinematography, 1918–1991.* New York: Aldine De Gruyter.

Shlapentokh, Vladimir (ed.). 1969a. *Chitatel' i gazeta: Chitatel'i 'Truda.'* Moscow: Institut konkretnykh sotsial'nykh issledovanii.

———. 1969b. *Sotsiologiia pechati.* Vols. 1 and 2. Novosibirsk: Nauka.

Shlapentokh, Vladimir. 1957. "Ob ischislenii seleestoimosti produkyii zhivotnovodstva." *Sel'skaya gazeta.* 12 July.

———. 1970. *Sotsiologiia dlia vsekh.* Moscow: Sovetskaia Rossiia.

———. 1975. *Kak segodnia izuchaiut zavtra.* Moscow: Sovetskaia Rossiia.

———. 1984a. *Love, marriage and friendship in the Soviet Union: Ideals and practices.* New York: Praeger.

———. 1984b. "Moscow's war: Propaganda and Soviet public opinion." *Problems of Communism.* September–October.

———. 1985a. *Evolution of the Soviet sociology of work: From ideology to pragmatism, the Carl Beck papers.* Pittsburgh, Pa.: Pittsburgh University Press.

———. 1985b. "Two levels of public opinion: The Soviet case." *Public Opinion Quarterly* 49:443–459.

———. 1986. *Soviet public opinion and ideology.* New York: Praeger.

———. 1987. *The politics of sociology in the Soviet Union.* Boulder, Colo.: Westview Press.

———. 1988a. *Soviet ideologies in the period of glasnost.* New York: Praeger.

———. 1988b. "The Stakhanovite movement: Changing perceptions over fifty years." *Journal of Contemporary History* 23:2 (April).

———. 1989. *Public and private life of the Soviet people.* Oxford: Oxford University Press.

———. 1990. *Soviet intellectuals and political power.* Princeton: Princeton University Press.

———. 1993a. *The last years of the empire: Snapshots from 1985–1991.* Westport, Conn.: Praeger.

—————. 1993b. "Privatization debates in Russia: 1989–1922." *Comparative Economic Studies* 35:2 (Summer).

—————. 1995. "Russian patience: A reasonable behavior and a social strategy." *Archives européenenes de sociologie* 2.

—————. 1996. "Early feudalism: The best parallel for contemporary Russia." *Europe-Asia Studies* 3:48 (Spring).

—————. 1997a. "Bonjour stagnation: Russia's next years." *Europe-Asia Studies* 49:5.

—————. 1998a. "Sotsial'noe ravenstvo i spravedlivost' v Rossii i Amerike." *Sotsiologicheskii zhurnal* 3/4.

—————. 1998b. "'Old,' 'new' and 'post' liberal attitudes toward the West: From love to hate." *Communist and Post-Communist Studies* 31:3.

—————. 1998c. "The changing Russian view of the West: From admiration in the early 1990s to hostility in the late 1990s." In Tom Casier and Katlijn Malfliet (eds.), *Is Russia a European Power? The position of Russia in a new Europe.* Louvain, Belgium: Leuven University Press.

—————. 1998d. "Four Russias." *Tocqueville Review* XIX:1.

—————. 1998e. "Fear of the future in the modern world: A Russian case." *International Journal of Comparative Sociology* 1.

—————. 1999a. "Social inequality in post-Communist Russia: The attitudes of the political elite and the masses (1991–1998)". *Europe-Asia Studies* 51:7.

—————. 1999b. "The Soviet Union: A normal totalitarian society." *Journal of Communist Studies and Transition Politics* 15:4.

—————. 2000. "A normal society? False and true explanations for the collapse of the USSR." *Times Literary Supplement.* 15 December.

Shlapentokh, Vladimir, Roman Levita, and Mikhail Loiberg. 1998. *From submission to rebellion.* Boulder, Colo.: Westview Press.

Shlapentokh, Vladimir, Munir Sendich, and Emil Payin (eds.). 1994. *The new Russian diaspora: Russian minorities in the former Soviet republics.* Armonk, N.Y.: M.E. Sharpe.

Shlapentokh, Vladimir, Christopher Vanderpool, and Boris Doktorov (eds.). 1999. *The new elite in post-Communist Eastern Europe.* College Station: Texas A&M University Press.

Shlykov, Vitalii. 1991. "Dekabr'skii variant." *Soiuz.* 6 February.

Shmelev, Nikolai. 1987. "Avansy i dolgi." *Novy mir* 3.

—————. 1989. "Pered povorotom." In Yurii Senokosov (ed.), *Surovaia drama naroda.* Moscow: Politizdat.

Shokhina, Victoria. 1995. "O sovetskikh poetakh." *Nezavisimaia gazeta.* 17 May.

Shpagin, Alexander. 1994. "Rekviem v stile roka." *Literaturnaia gazeta.* 31 August.

Shpakov, Yurii. 1990. "Komanda brat'iam po lageriu." *Moskovskie novosti.* 15 July.

Shubkin, Vladimir. 1970. *Sotsiologicheskie opyty.* Moscow: Mysl'.

—————. 1997. "Strakhi v Rossii." *Sotsiologicheskii zhurnal* 3.

Shubkin, Vladimir, and Veronika Ivanova. 1999. "Strakhi v post-sovetskom prostranstve." *VTsIOM Monitoring obshchestvennogo mneniia: Ekonomicheskie i sotsial'nye peremeny* 3:31–37.

Shulgin, Vasilii. 1990. *Gody; Dni; 1920.* Moscow: Novosti.

Sica, Alan. 1988. *Weber, irrationality and social order.* Berkeley: University of California Press.

Siegelbaum, Lewis. 1988. *Stakhanovism and the politics of productivity in the USSR, 1935–1941.* Cambridge: Cambridge University Press.

————. 1997. "Building Stalinism, 1929–1941." In Gregory Freeze (ed.), *Russia: A history.* Oxford: Oxford University Press.

Simis, Konstantin. 1982. *USSR: The corrupt society.* New York: Simon and Schuster.

Sirotkin, Vladlen. 1990a. "Kak my okazalis´ v osazhdennoi kreposti." *Izvestiia.* 5 September.

————. 1990b. "Nomenklatura v istoricheskom razreze." In Andrei Protashchik (ed.), *Cherez ternii.* Moscow: Progress.

————. 1992. "Osvobozhdenie ot khimery." *Nezavisimaia gazeta.* 23 October.

Skilling, Gordon, and Franklyn Griffiths (eds.). 1971. *Interest groups in Soviet politics.* Princeton: Princeton University Press.

Skoczylas, Elehie. 1965. *The realities of Soviet anti-Semitism.* Philadelphia: University of Pennsylvania, Foreign Policy Research Institute.

Skvortsov, N. 1996. "Etnichnost´ v protsesse sotsial´nykh izmenenii." *Sotsial´no-politicheskii zhurnal* 1:39–40.

Smeliakov, Nikolai. 1970. *Delovaia Amerika. (Zapiski inzhenera).* Moscow: Politizdat.

Smelser, Neil. 1988. "Social structure." In Neil Smelser (ed.), *Handbook of Sociology.* Newbury Park, Calif.: Sage.

Smirnov, Georgii. 1971. *Sovetskii chelovek. Formirovanie Sovetskogo. Tipa lichnosti.* Moscow: Politizdat.

Smith, Hedrick. 1976. *The Russians.* New York: Quadrangle/New York Times Book Co.

————. 1991. *The new Russians.* New York: Random House.

Smith, Robert, and David Christian. 1984. *Social and economic history of food and drink in Russia.* Cambridge: Cambridge University Press.

Sobchak, Anatolii. 1991. *Khozhdenie vo vlast´.* Moscow: Novosti.

————. 1995. *Zhila-byla kommunisticheskaia partiia.* St. Petersburg: Lenizdat.

Sokolov, Vladimir. 1981. *Nravstvennyi mir sovetskogo cheloveka.* Moscow: Politizdat.

Solnick, Steven L. 1998. *Stealing the state: Control and collapse in Soviet institutions.* Cambridge: Harvard University Press.

Solomon, Susan (ed.). 1983. *Pluralism in the Soviet Union.* London: Macmillan.

Soloukhin, Vladimir. 1995. "Opiraias´ na korennoe naselenie." *Zavtra* 32: p. 6.

Solzhenitsyn, Alexander. 1968. *The first circle.* New York: Harper & Row.

————. 1973. *The Gulag archipelago, 1918–1956: An experiment in literary investigation.* New York: Harper & Row.

————. 1975. *Bodalsia telenok s dubom.* Paris: YMCA Press.

————. 1991. "Razmyshleniia po povodu dvukh grazhdanskikh voin." *Komsomol´skaia pravda.* 4 June.

Sontag, Raymond, and James Beddie (eds.). 1948. *Nazi-Soviet relations, 1939–1941.* (Documents from the archives of the German Foreign Office). Washington, D.C.: U.S. Dept. of State.

Sorel, Georges. 1908/1925. *Reflections on violence.* London: Allen & Unwin.

Sorokin, Pitirim. 1950. *Leaves from Russian diary and thirty years after.* Boston: Beacon Press.

Soviet Union. 1925. *Konstitutsiia (osnovnoi zakon) Soiuza Sovetskikh Sotsialisticheskikh Respublik: S prilozheniem vazhneishikh deistvuiushchikh uzakonenii ob organizatsii i deiatel´nosti tsentral´nykh organov Soiuza SSR* (Soviet Constitution of 1924). Moscow: Iuridicheskoe izdatel´stvo Narkomiusta RSFSR.

Soviet Union. 1987. *Konstitutsiia (osnovnoi zakon) Soiuza Sovetskikh Sotsialisticheskikh Respublik: Priniata na vneocherednoi sed'moi sessii Verkhovnogo soveta SSSR deviatogo sozyva 7 oktiabria 1977 g. s dopolneniem, vnesennym Zakonom SSSR ot 24 iiunia 1981 g.* (Soviet Constitution of 1977). Moscow: Iurid. lit-ra.

Spechler, Dina. 1982. *Permitted dissent in the USSR: Novy mir and the Soviet regime.* New York: Praeger.

Spengler, Oswald. 1962. *The decline of the West.* New York: Modern Library.

Spiridovich, Alexander. 1960–1962. *Velikaia voina i fevral'skaia revoliutsiia.* 3 vols. New York: Vseslavianskoe izdatel'stovo.

Squire, John Collings (ed.). 1931. *History rewritten.* New York: Viking Press.

———. 1932. *If it happened otherwise.* London: Longmans, Green and Co.

Stalin, Joseph. 1946–1951. *Sobranie sochienii.* Moscow: Politizdat.

———. 1952a. *Ekonomicheskie problemy sotsializma v SSSR.* Moscow: Politizdat.

———. 1952b. *Voprosy Leninizma.* Eleventh edition. Moscow: Gospolitizdat.

Stanley, Alessandra. 1999. "Pope meets Georgian Orthodox at a religious distance." *New York Times.* 9 November.

Starikov, E. 1989. "Marginaly." In Anatolii Vishnevsky (ed.), *V chelovecheskom izmerenii.* Moscow: Progress.

Starkov, Boris. 1993. "Koe-chto novenkoe o Berii." *Argumenty i fakty.* November (p. 6).

Starostin, Vladimir. 1999. "Voennoe velikoderzhavie Rossii: Beda ili blago naroda?" *Znamia* 1.

Steel, Ronald. 2000. "Mister Fix-it." *New York Review of Books.* 5 October.

Stenograficheskii otchet VI kongressa Kominterna. 1929. Vol. 3. Moscow (no publisher).

Stepankov, Valentin, and Evgenii Lisov. 1992. *Kremlevskii zagovor: Versiia sledstviia.* Moscow: Ogonek.

Strakhov, Vladimir. 1997. Interview. *Zavtra* 17 (April).

Streliany, Anatolii. 1988. "Strel'ba na vzlet." *Druzhba narodov* 6.

———. 1992. "Skif." *Literaturnaia gazeta.* 8 January.

Strom, Carl Gustaf. 1996. "Die Strategie von Stalin für Krieg und Frieden." *Die Welt.* 16 July.

Sudoplatov, Anatolii, and Vladimir Malevannyi. 1998. "Proshchanie s epokhoi perevorotov." *Nezavisimaia gazeta.* 28 August.

Sudoplatov, Pavel. 1994. *Special tasks: The memoirs of an unwanted witness, a Soviet spymaster.* Boston: Little, Brown.

Summers, Larry. 1999. Speech. *New York Times.* 22 September.

Suny, Ronald Grigor. 1998. *The Soviet experiment: Russia, the USSR, and the successor states.* New York: Oxford University Press.

Suvorov, Victor. 1984. *Inside Soviet military intelligence.* New York: Macmillan.

———. 1990. *Icebreaker.* London: Hamish Hamilton.

Suyin, Han. 1994. *Eldest son: Zhou Enlai and the making of modern China, 1898–1976.* New York: Hill and Wang.

Tainter, Joseph. 1990. *The collapse of complex societies.* Cambridge: Cambridge University Press.

Tannenhouse, Sam. 1999. "The red scare." *New York Review of Books.* 14 January.

Taras, Raymond. 1992. "Introduction." In Raymond Taras (ed.), *The road to disillusion: From critical Marxism to post-communism in Eastern Europe.* Armonk, N.Y.: M.E. Sharpe.

Tarasenkov, Anatolii. 1966. *Russkie poety dvadtsatogo veka, 1900–1955.* Moscow: Sovetskii pisatel'.

Tarasov, Anatolii. 1974. "Professional'naia orientatsiia molodezhi sel'skikh shkol." In *Opyt sotsial'nogo izucheniia professional'noi orientatsii sel'skoi molodezhi.* (No editor). Rostov on Don: Gospedinstitut.

Taylor, Alan. 1948. *The Habsburg monarchy, 1809–1918: A history of the Austrian empire and Austria-Hungary.* London: H. Hamilton.

Telitsyn, Vadim. 1999. "My vmeste i porozn." *Obshchaia gazeta.* 19 August.

Tepliakov, Yurii. 1990. "Po tu storonu fronta." *Moskovskie novosti.* 13 May.

Tereshchenko, Valerii. 1963. *Amerika, v kotoroi ia zhil.* Kiev: Politizdat.

Thornton, Richard. 1972. *The bear and the dragon: Sino-Soviet relations and the political evolution of the Chinese People's Republic, 1949–1971.* New York: American-Asian Educational Exchange.

Thurston, Robert. 1986. "Fear and beliefs in the USSR's 'Great Terror.'" *Slavic Review* 2.

———. 1996. *Life and terror in Stalin's Russia, 1934–1941.* New Haven, Conn.: Yale University Press.

Timofeev, Lev. 1982. *Tekhnologiia chernogo rynka i krest'ianskii sposob golodaniia.* Bayville, N.J.: Izd. Zarubezhnykh pisatelei.

———. 1985. *Posledniaia nadezhda vyzhit'.* Tenafly, N.J.: Ermitazh.

———. 1992. *Russia's secret rulers.* New York: Knopf.

Tocqueville, Alexis de. 1955. *The old regime and the French Revolution.* Garden City, N.Y.: Doubleday.

Tökés, Rudolf L. (ed.). 1975. *Dissent in the USSR: Politics, ideology, and people.* Baltimore: Johns Hopkins University Press.

Tolz, Vera. 1990. *The USSR's emerging multiparty system.* Washington, D.C.: Center for Strategic and International Studies; New York: Praeger.

Toman, Tamilla. 1991. "1941–1942: Dva velikikh bedstviia v soznanii sovremennikov." In Vitalii Zhuravlev (ed.), *Trudnye voprosy istorii: Poiski, razmyshleniia, novyi vzgliad na sobytiia i fakty.* Moscow: Politizdat.

Toshchenko, Zhan. 1994. "Regional'nye osobennosti etnosotsial'nykh konfliktov." In Andrei Zdravomyslov (ed.), *Vzaimodeistvie politicheskikh i natsional'no-etnicheskikh konfliktov.* Vol. 2. Moscow: Rossiiskii institut sotsial'nykh i natsional'nykh problem.

Treml, Vladimir. 1987. "Alcohol abuse and the quality of life in the Soviet Union." In Horst Herlemann (ed.), *Quality of life in the Soviet Union.* Boulder, Colo.: Westview Press.

———. 1991. "Drinking and alcohol abuse in the USSR in the 1980s." In Anthony Jones, Walter D. Connor, and David E. Powell (eds.), *Soviet social problems.* Boulder, Colo.: Westview Press.

Tretiakov, Vitalii. 1992. "Pervyi god prezidenta Yeltsina." *Nezavisimia gazeta.* 11 June.

———. 1998. "Razvalitsia li Rossiia." *Nezavisimaia gazeta.* 12 December.

Trotsky, Leon. 1906. *Istoriia Soveta rabochikh deputatov goroda S. Peterburga.* St. Petersburg: Kn-vo N. Glagoleva.

———. 1917. *Perspektivy russkoi revoliutsii.* Berlin: Izd. T-va I. P. Ladyzhnikova.

———. 1923. *Novaia ekonomicheskaia politika i perspektivy mirovoi revoliutsii.* Moscow: Moskovskii rabochii.

———. 1960. *The history of the Russian Revolution.* Ann Arbor: University of Michigan Press.

————. 1991. *Moia zhizn'*. Moscow: Kniga.

————. 1993a. "Chto dal'she? (VI kongressu Kominterna)." In Leon Trotsky, *Kommunisticheskii Internatsional posle Lenina*. New York and Moscow: Spartakovets.

————. 1993b. *Predannaia revoliutsiia: Chto takoe SSSR, i kuda on idet?* Cambridge, Mass.: Iskra Research.

Trubin, Nikolai. 1991. "Kak eto bylo." *Pravda*. 3 June.

Tsipko, Alexander. 1989a. "Egoizm mechtatelei." *Nauka i zhizn'* 1:46–56.

————. 1989b. "O zonakh zakrytykh dlia mysli." In Yurii Senokosov (ed.), *Surovaia drama naroda*. Moscow: Politizdat.

————. 1990. "Spor o Rossii." *Novoe vremia* 50:7.

————. 1996. "Gorbachev postavil na 'sotsialisticheskii vybor' i proigral." *Nezavisimaia gazeta*. 21 November.

————. 2000. "On ne mog skazat' rasstreliat." *Literaturnaia gazeta*. 26 December.

Tsoi, B. 1994. "Sotsial'nye i ekonomicheskie aspekty reabilitatsii narodov i grazhdan, repressirovannykh v SSSR po politicheskim motivam." *Gosudarstvo i pravo* 12:12.

TsSU SSSR. 1956. *Narodnoe khoziaistvo SSSR: Statisticheskii sbornik*. Moscow: Gosstatizdat.

————. 1982. *Narodnoe khoziaistvo SSSR, 1822–1982*. 1982. Moscow: Finansy i statistika.

————. 1984. *Narodnoe khoziaistvo SSSR v 1983 godu*. Moscow: Finansy i statistika.

————. 1986. *Narodnoe khoziaistvo SSSR v 1985*. Moscow: Finansy i statistika.

Tucker, Aviezer. 1999. "Historiographical counterfactuals and historical contingency." *History and Theory*. May.

Tucker, Robert. 1963. *The Soviet political mind*. New York: Praeger.

————. 1987. *Political culture and leadership in Soviet Russia: From Lenin to Gorbachev*. New York: Norton.

————. 1990. *Stalin in power: The revolution from above, 1928–1941*. New York: Norton.

Tumanov, Boris. 1995. "Ostalos' ugovorit' nevestu." *Literaturnaia gazeta*. 31 May.

Tvardovsky, Alexander. 1974. *O samom glavnom*. Moscow: Sovetskii pisatel'.

————. 1985. *Pis'ma o literature*. Moscow: Sovetskii pisatel'.

Tvardovsky, Ivan. 1988. "Stranitsy perezhitogo." *Iunost'* 3.

Tyler, Patrick. 2000. "Behind spy trial in Mocow: A super fast torpedo." *New York Times*. 1 December.

Ulam, Adam. 1965. *Bolsheviks*. London: Secker & Warburg.

————. 1992a. "The myth of Leninism." *Times Literary Supplement*. 6 November.

————. 1992b. "Looking at the past: The unraveling of the Soviet Union." *Current History* 91:567, p. 344.

————. 1992c. *The communists: The story of power and lost illusions, 1948–1991*. New York: Scribner's.

————. 1997. "Bolshevism's grim saga." *New Leader*. 13 January.

————. 1998. *The Bolsheviks: The intellectual and political history of the triumph of communism in Russia*. Cambridge: Harvard University Press.

Ulanovskaia, Maria, and Nadezhda Ulanovskaia. 1982. *Istoriia odnoi sem'*. New York: Chalidze.

United States Congress. 1981. *Consumption in the USSR: An international comparison. A study prepared for the use of the Joint Economic Committee, Congress of the United States*. Washington, D.C.: U.S. G.P.O.

Jrusov, Mikhail. 1995. "Miatezh na bortu." *Moskovskie novosti* 82.

Jtkin, Anatolii. 1997. "Nasha i 'eta' strana." *Nezavisimaia gazeta-Stsenarii.* 9 December.

Vaksberg, Arkadii. 1987. "Sud'a prokurora." *Literaturnaia gazeta.* 28 October.

———. 1991. "Priglashenie k sporu." *Literaturnaia gazeta.* 15 May.

Vandervelde, Emile. 1918. *Three aspects of the Russian Revolution.* London: George Allen and Unwin.

Varennikov, Valentin. 1994. "Protivodeistvie razvalu strany bylo neizbezhno." *Pravda.* 13 July.

Vasiliev, Leonid. 1990. "Krizis sotsializma." In Andrei Protashchik (ed.), *Cherez ternii.* Moscow: Progress.

Veber, Alexander, et al. (eds.). 1985. *Soiuz mozhno bylo sokhranit': Belaia kniga.* Moscow (no publishing house).

Velidov, Alexei. 1991. "Rossiia posle eksperimentov." *Moskovskie novosti.* 3 March.

Velikhov, Evgenii. 1999. "Sovetskaia A-bomba: I ad, i pervaia liubov'." *Izvestiia.* 28 August.

Verkhovskaia, Alla. 1972. *Pis'ma v redaktsiiu i chitateli.* Moscow: Izdatel'stvo Moskovskogo universiteta.

Vernadsky, Vladimir. 1992. "Ia ochen' redko vizhu ideinykh kommunistov." *Nezavisimaia gazeta.* 9 June.

Vincent, David. 1998. *The culture of secrecy: Britain, 1832–1998.* Oxford: Oxford University Press.

Viola, Lynne. 1996. *Peasant rebels under Stalin: Collectivization and the culture of peasant resistance.* New York: Oxford University Press.

Vishnevskaia, Galina. 1984. *Galina.* New York: Random House.

Vishnevsky, Anatolii (ed.). 1989. *V chelovecheskom izmerenii.* Moscow: Progress.

Vishnevsky, Anatolii. 1997. "Vysshaia elita RKP (b), VKP (b) i KPSS (1917–1989)." *Naselenie i obshchestvo: Informatsionnyi biulleten' Tsentra demografii i ekologii Instituta narodnokhoziaistvennogo prognozirovaniia RAN.* 21: September.

———. 1998. *Serp i rubl'.* Moscow: OGI.

Vlasov, Viacheslav. 1996. "Privilegii krasnykh baronov." *Argumenty i fakty* 20.

Vodolazov, Grigorii. 1997. "Nomenklaturnyi kapitalizm." *Nezavisimaia gazeta.* 14 June.

Volkogonov, Dmitrii. 1988. *Kontrpropaganda: Teoriia i praktika.* Moscow: Voen. Izd-vo.

———. 1990. "Deviatyi val Vandei." *Literaturnaia gazeta.* 30 May.

———. 1991. "S voinoi pokonchili my schety?" *Komsomol'skaia pravda.* 22 June.

———. 1995. *Sem' vozhdei.* Moscow: Novosti.

———. 1998a. *Etiudy o vremeni: Iz zabytogo, nezamechennogo, nenapechatannogo.* Moscow: Novosti.

———. 1998b. *The rise and fall of the Soviet Empire: Political leaders from Lenin to Gorbachev.* London: HarperCollins.

Volobuev, Oleg (ed.). 1995. *Istoriia sovremennoi Rossii.* Moscow: Terra.

Vorotnikov, Vitalii. 1995. *A bylo eto tak.* Moscow: Sovet veteranov knigoizdaniia.

Voshchanov, Pavel. 1995. "Peremen trebuiut nashi serdtsa." *Komsomol'skaia pravda.* 20 April.

Voslensky, Mikhail. 1984. *Nomenklatura: The Soviet ruling class.* Garden City, N.Y.: Doubleday.

Waldron, Arthur. 1990. *The Great Wall of China: From history to myth.* Cambridge, Eng. and New York: Cambridge University Press.

Waller, Philip. 1998. "Virtual history: Alternatives and counterfactuals." *English Historical Review* (Harlow). June.

Ward, Geoffrey. 1995. Review of David Donald, *Lincoln* (New York: Simon and Schuster, 1995). *New York Times Book Review.* 22 October.

Weber, Max. 1978. *Economy and society.* Vol. 1. Berkeley: University of California Press.

Weinstein, Allen, and Alexander Vasiliev. 1999. *The haunted wood: Soviet espionage in America–the Stalin era.* New York: Random House.

Welch, William. 1970. *American images of Soviet foreign policy: An inquiry into recent appraisals from the academic community.* New Haven, Conn.: Yale University Press.

Westad, Odd Arne (ed.). 1998. *Brothers in arms: The rise and fall of the Sino-Soviet alliance, 1945–1963.* Washington, D.C.: Woodrow Wilson Center Press.

White, Stephen. 1993. *After Gorbachev.* New York: Cambridge University Press.

———. 1996. *Russia goes dry: Alcohol, state and society.* New York: Cambridge University Press.

William, Albert Ryss. 1967. *Through the Russian Revolution.* New York: Monthly Review Press.

Witkin, Zara. 1991. *An American engineer in Stalin's Russia.* Berkeley: University of California Press.

Woytinsky, Vladimir S. 1924. *Gody pobed i porazhenii.* Berlin: Izd. Z. I. Grzhebina.

Wolf, Charles. 1986. *The costs and benefits of the Soviet empire, 1981–1983.* Santa Monica, Calif.: Rand.

Wolfe, Tom. 1979. *The right stuff.* New York: Farrar, Straus, and Giroux.

Wortman, Richard. 1976. *The development of a Russian legal consciousness.* Chicago: University of Chicago Press.

XIX vseso uznaia konferentsiia Kommunisticheskoi partii Sovetskogo soiuza, 28 iiunia–1 iiulia 1988: Stenograficheskii otchet. 1988. Vol. 2. Moscow: Politizdat.

XIV s"ezd vsesiouznoi Kommunisticheskoi partii: Stenograficheskii otchet. 1925. Moscow: Politizdat.

XXIII s"ezd Kommunisticheskoi partii Sovetskogo soiuza: Stenograficheskii otchet. 1966. Moscow: Politizdat.

XXVII s"ezd Kommunisticheskoi partii Sovetskogo soiuza: Stenograficheskii otchet. 1986. Vol. 1. Moscow: Politizdat.

Yablokov, Igor. 1979. *Sotsiologiia religii.* Moscow: Mysl'.

Yadov, Vladimir (ed.). 1979. *Sotsial'no-psikhologicheskii portret inzhenera.* Moscow: Nauka.

——— (ed.). 1984. *Samoreguliatsiia i prognozirovanie povedeniia lichnosti.* Leningrad: Nauka.

Yadov, Vladimir, Andrei Zdravomyslov, and Vasilii Rozhin (eds.). 1967. *Chelovek i ego rabota.* Moscow: Mysl'.

Yakovlev, Alexander. 1991. *Muki prochteniia bytiia.* Moscow: Novosti.

———. 1994. *The bitter cup.* Yaroslavl': Verkhne-Volzhskoe izdatel'stvo.

Yakovlev, Alexander (ed.). 1998. *Molotov, Malenkov, Kaganovich.* Moscow: Mezhdunarodnyi fond 'Demokratiia.'

Yakovlev, Alexander. 2000. "Malenkie tainy velikogo vremeni." *Argumenty i fakty* 18.

Yakovlev, Nikolai. 1996. "Pochemu raspalsia Sovetskii soiuz." *Zavtra* 20 and 21.

Yanaev, Gennadii. 1999. "Ot Lebedinnogo ozera pakhlo pokhoronami svobody." *Literaturnaia gazeta.* 17 August.

Yanov, Alexander. 1978. *The Russian new right: Right-wing ideologies in the contemporary USSR.* Berkeley: University of California, Institute of International Studies.

———. 1984. *The drama of the Soviet 1960's: A lost reform.* Berkeley: University of California, Institute of International Studies.

———. 1988. *Russkaia ideia i 2000 god.* New York: Liberty Publishing House.

Yaroshinskaia, Alla. 1994. *Chernobyl: The forbidden truth.* Oxford, Eng.: J. Carpenter.

Yarov, Sergei. 1997. "Workers." In Edward Acton, Vladimir Cherniaev, and William Rosenberg (eds.), *Critical companion to the Russian Revolution, 1914–1921.* Bloomington: Indiana University Press.

Yashin, Alexander. 1954. "Rychagi." *Literaturnaia Moskva.* Vol. 2. Moscow: Sovetskii pisatel'.

Yasin, Yevgenii. 1998. "The parade of market transformation programs." In Michael Ellman and Vladimir Kontorovich (eds.), *The destruction of the Soviet economic system: An insiders' history.* Armonk, N.Y.: M.E. Sharpe.

———. 1999. "Porazhenie ili otstuplenie." *Nezavisimaia gazeta.* 2 March.

Yavlinsky, Grigorii, and Stanislav Shatalin. 1991. *500 days: Transition to the market.* New York: St. Martin's Press.

Yazov, Dmitrii. 1994. "My obnadezhili narod." *Pravda.* 19 August.

Yeltsin, Boris. 1990. *Against the grain.* New York: Summit Books.

———. 1994. *Zapiski prezidenta.* Moscow: Ogonek.

Yemelin, A. 1990. "'Zeki' na altare pobedy." *Soiuz* 38.

Yergin, Daniel, and Hjesophe Stanislav. 1998. *The commanding heights: The battle between government and marketplace that is remaking the modern world.* New York: Simon & Schuster.

Yevladov, Boris, Anatolii Pokrovsky, and Vladimir Shlapentokh. 1969. "4001 Interviews." *Zhurnalist* 10:34–37.

Yun, Oleg. 1998. "A promising departure." In Michael Ellman and Vladimir Kontorovich (eds.), *The destruction of the Soviet economic system: An insiders' history.* Armonk, N.Y.: M.E. Sharpe.

Zabrodin, V. 1991. "Novogodnie rozygryshi." *Literaturnaia Rossiia.* 11 January.

Zaltsman, Isaak, and G. Edelhaus. 1984. "Uroki tankograda." *Kommunist* 16.

Zaslavskaia, Tatiana. 1984. "Paper to Moscow seminar." *Russia* 9:27.

Zavorotnyi, Sergei, and Petr Polozhevez. 1990. "Operatsiia 'Golod.'" *Komsomol'skaia pravda.* 3 February.

Zdravomyslov, Andrei. 1994. *Sotsiologiia konflikta.* Moscow: Aspekt.

Zelikov, Philip, and Condoleezza Rice. 1995. *Germany unified and Europe transformed.* Cambridge: Harvard University Press.

Zemskov, Victor. 1990a. Interview. *Argumenty i fakty.* 7 September.

———. 1990b. "Spetsposelentsy." *Sotsiologicheskie issledovaniia* 11:11 and 6:75.

———. 1991a. "Gulag (istoriko-sotsiologicheskie aspekt)." *Sotsiologicheskie issledovania.* 6:26.

———. 1991b. Article in *Voenno–istoricheskii zhurnal* 7:69.

Zemskov, Victor, John Arch Getty, and Gabor Rittersporn. 1993. "Victims of the Soviet penal system in the pre-war years: A first approach on the basis of archival evidence." *American Historical Review* 4.

Zemtsov, Il'ia. 1985. *The private life of the Soviet elite.* New York: Crane Russak.

Zhigulin, Anatolii. 1988. "Chernye kamni: Avtobiograficheskaia povest'." *Znamia* 7 and 8.

Zhiromskaia, Valentina. 1998. "Tainy perepisi naseleniia 1937 goda." *Nezavisimaia gazeta.* 18 July.

Zhukov, Arkadii. 1992. "'Delo' marshala Zhukova: Nerazorvavshaiasia bomba." *Literaturnaia gazeta.* 5 August.

Zhukov, Georgii. 1989. "Korotko o Staline." *Pravda.* 20 January.

Zhuravlev, Vitalii (ed.). 1990. *Bukharin: Chelovek, politik, uchenyi.* Moscow: Politizdat.

Zimbardo, Philip G., and Michael R. Leippe. 1991. *The psychology of attitude change and social influence.* Philadelphia: Temple University Press.

Zimin, A. (pseudonym). 1981. *Sotsializm i neostalinizm.* New York: Chalidze.

Zinoviev, Alexander. 1979. *The yawning heights.* New York: Random House.

————. 1992. *Katastroika: Perestroika in Partygrad.* London: Peter Owen.

————. 1993. "Kolonial'naia demokratiia." *Den'.* 24 July.

————. 1994. "Zavershenie russkoi kontrrevoliutsii." *Pravda.* 1 October.

Ziuganov, Gennadii. 1993. "Vozrozhdenie Rossii i mezhdunarodnoe polozhenie." *Pravda.* 10 December.

————. 1999. "Dusha i stiag." *Sovetskaia Rossiia.* 28 October.

Zolotusky, Igor. 1998. "Zhizn' ne po lzhi." *Nezavisimaia gazeta.* 11 December.

Zorkaltsev, Victor. 1995. Interview. *Moskovskii komsomolets.* 19 April.

Zotov, Victor. 1989. "Natsional'nyi vopros: Deformatsiia proshlogo." In Yurii Senokosov (ed.), *Surovaia drama naroda.* Moscow: Politizdat.

Zubok, Vladislav, and Konstantin Pleshakov. 1996. *Inside the Kremlin's cold war: From Stalin to Khrushchev.* Cambridge: Harvard University Press.

Zuyev, Alexander, and Malcolm McConnell. 1992. *Fulcrum: A Top Gun pilot's escape from the Soviet Empire.* New York: Warner Books.

Name Index

Subject Index

Afghanistan, 22, 50, 60, 76, 95, 141, 163, 181, 249
Albania, 157, 217, 236
alcoholism: 96, 122, 124, 182; Gorbachev's anti-alcohol campaign, 80, 191, 277–8
Andropov: anti-corruption campaign of, 178, 191, 197, 271–2; attitude toward intellectuals, 277; attitude toward the masses, 35; and economy, 112, 171, 191; high popularity of, 248; ideology of, 38, 60, 156, 188, 237; and the KGB, 94, 150–1, 248; treatment of dissidents, 183; and the World Revolution, 47
anti-Communism, 9, 22, 55, 230; revolution of, 18, 206, 227, 337
anti-Semitism. *See* Jews
apparatchiks. *See* nomenklatura
Armenia, 144, 154–5, 159, 163–5, 184, 209–10, 269
arms race, 118, 126, 186–8, 276
army: 24–26, 31, 49, 52, 118, 131, 139–40, 149, 152, 175, 261; corruption of, 96, 200; ethnic groups in, 97, 154; prestige of, 95, 200, 249; privileges of, 37; quality of, 94–96,

army, quality of *(continued)*
182; Red Army, 9, 23, 32, 43–44, 49, 72, 79, 132, 231, 234–5, 259

"backwardness" of Russia and USSR, 17–19, 223
Baltic Republics, 136, 144, 158, 165, 184, 209, 267
Brezhnev: attitude toward masses, 138, 171; attitude toward party rank and file, 35; attitude toward workers, 65, 239; and the Communist Party, 86–87; and covert propaganda, 60; and economy, 112, 117; high style of life of, 74; ideology of, 60; illness of, 271; importance of the standard of living, 76; and invasion of Czechoslovakia, 77; and Marxism, 74; and the Politburo, 82–83; reforms of, 171, 177; utopian ideas of, 77–78; and the World Revolution, 47

Central Asia (in the USSR), 43, 155, 157, 164, 166, 172, 205, 209, 220, 225, 263, 267, 269
Central Intelligence Agency, 185–6, 253, 255

About the Author

Vladimir Shlapentokh, a former Senior Fellow of the Moscow Sociological Institute, is a sociology professor at Michigan State University. He is the author of 22 books, including *The Center Versus the Province: From Submission to Rebellion* (1997), and of numerous professional articles on Soviet and Russian issues, including, on the subject of the present volume, "A Normal System? False and True Explanations for the Collapse of the USSR" (*Times Literary Supplement*, December 15, 2000). His opinion pieces have appeared in the *New York Times*, the *Los Angeles Times*, the *Washington Post*, and the *Christian Science Monitor*.

DATE DUE

GAYLORD			PRINTED IN U.S.A.